Betty Dunkins
Joy Gray

◆

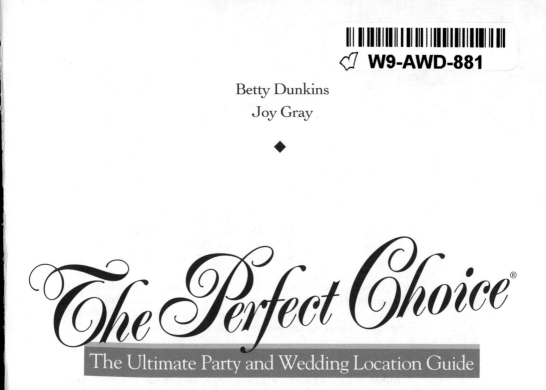

The Perfect Choice®

The Ultimate Party and Wedding Location Guide

Second Edition, Completely Revised

◆

Gray McPherson Publishing Co., Silver Spring, Maryland 20916

Published by
Gray McPherson Publishing Co.
Post Office Box 6080
Silver Spring, MD 20916

Front Cover Photos: Top Row: Oxon Hill Manor, photo courtesy Vince Cowan, Photographer; Historic Car Barn, photo courtesy John Drew, Professional Image Photography. Center Row: Renaissance Mayflower Hotel, photo courtesy John Drew, Professional Image Photography; Raspberry Plain, photo courtesy Raspberry Plain. Bottom Row: Willard Hotel, photo courtesy Jim Johnson Photography; *Odyssey*, photo courtesy Odyssey Cruises.

Divider Photos: Washington, D.C., photo courtesy Bob Blanken Photography Studio and Gallery; Maryland, George Peabody Library, photo courtesy George Peabody Library; Virginia, The Longbarn, photo courtesy The Longbarn; Surrounding States, Hackwood, photo courtesy Encore Special Events, Inc.

Back Cover: Center Café, courtesy Ark Restaurants.

Production, Graphic Design & Typography: Tripplaar & Associates, Inc.

Second Edition
10 9 8 7 6 5 4 3

Library of Congress No. 97-094688
ISBN: 0-9641379-1-7

Printed in the United States of America

TABLE OF CONTENTS

Washington, D.C.
L O C A T I O N S

Maryland

Virginia

Surrounding Areas
L O C A T I O N S

Questionnaire & Index

ACKNOWLEDGEMENTS

To all the people connected with Tripplaar & Associates, Inc. especially to David Orcutt, for his hard work and endless enthusiasm for this project, and to Frans Tripplaar, for his creative approach to the design of this book.

To Nancy Parker, for her tireless editorial assistance and endless patience.

To Bob Blanken, Vince Cowan, John Drew, and Jim Johnson for their wonderful photographs and their generosity in letting us use their work.

To Kevin Bedell for his advice, words of encouragement, and constant support.

Special thanks to Mark Austrian, whose patience and support contributed enormously to the success of this project.

What is the perfect site? While the ultimate answer varies with each person, location is a key component in planning a wedding, corporate celebration, reunion, fund raiser, or other special event.

Where you decide to have your event will largely determine what type of affair it will be, so it is important to start the planning process early and give yourself time to investigate your options. Popular sites tend to book early, with most planners advising that you reserve your site at least one year in advance.

Choosing Wedding and other Social Event Sites

The Perfect Choice® will help you find your dream location - whether's that's something old, something new, something borrowed straight out of a fairy tale, or something blue as the waters of the Chesapeake. This guide will suggest ideas you may not have considered, and with it you will discover sites that will make your wedding uniquely yours.

As you browse through the pages of this guide, remember that the choice of the location will affect all other details of the wedding, from the style of the wedding gown to the size of the band. Let this guide spark your imagination.

Planning an anniversary celebration, birthday party, bat/bar mitzvah, or other special occasion is easy when you start with a great location. Match the location with the theme, mood or personality of the event. Holding your function in a unique space that has an atmosphere compatible with your theme will save you lots of work. By not having to dress up/dress down, add or remove furniture or equipment, customize or disguise your space…you'll save time and money.

If your ideal party theme is one of romance and nostalgia, an anniversary celebration held at a Bed and Breakfast or country inn can create a weekend of splendor, not only for the happy couple, but for the guests, as well. Guests can take in the local attractions, such as winery tours, historical sites, garden tours, golf outings, bike trips, or they can pamper themselves at an elegant afternoon tea.

How about celebrating your 50th birthday in a fifties-style club? Or, holding a celebration with a western or country theme in a barn or farmhouse? All of these and hundreds more "dream locations" are possible in many of the unusual places around the metropolitan area.

Choosing Corporate Event Sites

Whether you're a meeting planner with years of experience, or someone whose job description doesn't include event planning, but you're expected to do it anyway, *The Perfect Choice*® can help. Use it to conveniently locate the right site, and then spend your time on other critical details.

Look for a location that fits the type of event. Will it be casual? Formal? Geared to learning and work or to play and relaxation? Bear in mind these questions: what image do you want to present? What is the purpose of the event? How many guests are you going to invite? Is the site a desirable place and is it situated in a location that your guests can reach easily?

Our unusual settings often provide whimsical touches, unique features, and an opportunity for guests to do more than dine and dance. Consider also coveted city sites, which include leading cultural and historical institutions, museums and mansions that once housed distinguished citizens.

Using *The Perfect Choice*®

The right site for you will be the one that gives you the atmosphere you want at a price you can afford. This book will save you time-consuming research by giving you instant access to over 200 locations in the metropolitan area and nearby states.

We have arranged the book in an easy-to-use, easy-to-read format. The main body of this guide is divided into regional sections: Washington, DC, Maryland, Virginia and Surrounding States. Each regional section is divided categorically (e.g., Atriums, Ballrooms, Banquet Rooms, etc.). In each category, sites are listed alphabetically.

First, skim through a few sections to familiarize yourself with the book: understanding its structure will help you make the most of the wealth of information it offers. Next, select the state where you would like to hold your reception and then locate the category that best suits your ideal setting. If, for example, you want your reception held on or near the water, look under the following categories: Water Locations, Boats, Schooners & Yachts, Views. If you are planning a corporate retreat, you might look under Conference Centers, Inns, Resorts. A reception checklist, which will answer many of your questions as you start your search for the perfect site, is also included.

Once you have selected several sites that appeal to you, call the locations for more information and to arrange a visit. Please tell them your were referred by *The Perfect Choice*®.

Give us a call at our toll free number (1-800-350-2028) or e-mail us at GMAssoc@ix.netcom.com and let us know which site you selected and why. We will also be happy to send you any updates we have of information which may have changed. We welcome your comments and feedback!

We fully believe that between these covers lies your ideal site. Be open-minded to the possibilities, let your imagination run free, and enjoy planning your special celebration!

BETTY DUNKINS
JOY GRAY
Authors

Washington, D.C.

TABLE OF CONTENTS

ANA Hotel   202-429-2400

2401 M Street, N.W. • Washington, DC 20037

One of Washington's most fashionable addresses, this hotel has been described as having the gracious ambience of the French Embassy. Whether it's a reception in the Colonnade's enchanting garden courtyard, or a candlelight dinner in the ballroom, your wedding day will be unforgettable.

Capacity: 450 seated in the ballroom; 200 seated in the Colonnade; 700 standing in the ballroom; 350 standing in the Colonnade.

Catering: In-house. Wedding packages from $100 to $160 per person.

Parking: On the premises. Valet parking available.

Note: Wedding ceremonies are permitted. Facility is handicap accessible.

The Galleria at Lafayette Centre   202-835-0093

1155 21st Street, N.W. • Washington DC 20036

This distinctive and elegant facility in downtown Washington features Italian marble floors, a dramatic split staircase and a 50-foot glass atrium ceiling.

Capacity: 300 seated; 750 standing.

Catering: Approved caterers list or your own caterer if caterer has proper insurance. Using an outside caterer requires the approval of the facility manager and there is an additional fee of $600.

Rental Fee: $3,500 Monday to Thursday; $4,500 Friday to Sunday. Rental fee includes use of facility for 10 hours. There is a separate fee of $500 for wedding ceremonies.

Parking: On the premises. Valet parking is available.

Restrictions: Monday to Friday events must start after 5:00 p.m. No events past 1:30 a.m. — last call for bar at 1:00 a.m. No smoking.

Note: Wedding ceremonies are permitted. No helium balloons. No rice, confetti throwing or fog machines. No flower petals thrown during ceremony.

The Mexican Cultural Institute   202-728-1670

2829 16th Street, N.W. • Washington, DC 20009

On the first floor, the entrance hall boasts an 18th-century baroque altar piece. Positioned under a magnificent staircase is an antique marble table and beautiful Talavera jar. The José Clemente Orozco Gallery, with 600 feet of exhibition space, and the Auditorio

Juarez have proven to be excellent spaces for art exhibits, conferences, slide shows, theatrical and dance performances, musical events and receptions. On the second floor, the restored Music Room, a replica of a salon at the Fontainebleau castle in France, has outstanding acoustics and is ideal for chamber music. The Golden Room, decorated in the French Renaissance style, is distinguished by a Federal convex mirror hanging over its marble fireplace and beautiful seascapes of Venice by the American artist Lucien Powell. In the elegant Dining Room, a Bacarat crystal chandelier, hand-carved furniture, and a painting by Benjamin Dominguez adds grace and charm. Muralist Roberto Cueva del Rio decorated the Atrium, using fine tiles produced in his native Puebla. The colorful tiles are geared acoustically for concerts and background music.

Capacity:	200 seated; 300 standing.
Catering:	You must provide your own caterer.
Rental Fee:	$3,000 and up.
Parking:	On the premises.
Restrictions:	No smoking.
Note:	Wedding ceremonies are permitted.

Old Ebbitt Grill   202-347-4800

675 15th Street, N.W. • Washington, DC 20005

Old Ebbitt Grill has been a landmark gathering spot for this city's professionals, politicians, theatergoers and shoppers since 1856. Two private spaces are available. The Cabinet Room, which is fully enclosed, shares the ambience of the handsome main dining room. The Atrium is lovely, with a glass-enclosed ceiling, marble floor, and marble and gold fountain. The Atrium may be fully private or semi-private depending on group size. Old Ebbitt Grill is just around the corner from the White House, and a convenient walk to museums, monuments, cultural attractions, and shopping. Join the crowd assembled at the bar and in the high-backed booths of the handsome dining room for a fun-filled evening.

Capacity:	350 seated; 600 standing; 50 seated in Cabinet Room; 70 standing in Cabinet Room.
Catering:	In-house. Entrees range from $25 to $60 per person.
Rental Fee:	$50 daytime, $75 night time, $250 for entire Atrium after 6 p.m. Monday- Saturday, after 12 p.m. Sunday.
Parking:	Street parking and nearby garages. Complimentary valet parking available.

Washington Court Hotel   202-628-2100

525 New Jersey Avenue, N.W. • Washington, DC 20001

The Washington Court Hotel has the perfect solution to your worries about an outdoor reception — Washington's finest skylit ballroom. Capitol Hill's only atrium ballroom is the perfect setting for your special day. The Washington Court also offers a newly renovated, elegant formal ballroom for large events, such as fund raisers and corporate galas.

Capacity: 320 seated with dance floor in ballroom; 500 standing in ballroom; 150 seated with dance floor in atrium.

Catering: In-house. Packages start at $60 per person.

Rental Fee: If minimum food and beverage not met, room rental fee is charged.

Parking: On the premises. Valet parking available.

Note: Wedding ceremonies are permitted. Guest rooms are available at special rates.

ANA Hotel   202-429-2400

2401 M Street, N.W. • Washington, DC 20037

One of Washington's most fashionable addresses, this hotel has been described as having the gracious ambience of the French Embassy. Whether it's a reception in the Colonnade's enchanting garden courtyard, or a candlelight dinner in the ballroom, your wedding day will be unforgettable.

Capacity: 450 seated in the ballroom; 200 seated in the Colonnade; 700 standing in the ballroom; 350 standing in the Colonnade.
Catering: In-house. Wedding packages from $100 to $160 per person.
Parking: On the premises. Valet parking available.
Note: Wedding ceremonies are permitted. Facility is handicap accessible.

The Arbor Ballroom   202-636-8919

3600 New York Avenue, N.E. • Washington, DC 20002

An elegant Washington location without the downtown hassle! Conveniently located off the Baltimore-Washington Parkway and Route 50, next to the National Arboretum, this exquisite facility offers luxurious surroundings, superior service and ample parking.

Capacity: 400 seated; 700 standing.
Catering: In-house or your own caterer. Entrees range from $22 to $50 per person when using in-house caterer.
Rental Fee: $2,000 to $4,000.
Parking: On the premises. Valet parking available.
Note: Wedding ceremonies are permitted.

Columbus Club of Union Station
East Hall of Union Station   202-289-8300

c/o Special Events at Union Station
50 Massachusetts Avenue, N.E. • Washington, DC 20002

This site offers two magnificent areas to choose from: The East Hall and Columbus Club. The Columbus Club, built in 1903 with its once "fancy soda fountain," arched portals and classic skylights is a dramatic setting for any occasion. The East Hall of Union Station, known for its skylights which produce glorious natural lighting, is a wonderful setting for receptions and social events. Guests will pass through the magnificent Main Hall with its 100-foot vaulted coffered ceilings and polished Italian floors.

Capacity: 240 seated in Columbus Club; 500 seated in East Hall; 450 standing in Columbus Club; 900 standing in East Hall.

Catering: In-house. Entrees range from $40 to $120 per person.
Rental Fee: $1,500 Columbus Club; $6,000 East Hall.
Parking: Parking on the premises and nearby parking lot. Valet
                parking can be arranged.

The Galleria at Lafayette Centre   202-835-0093

1155 21st Street, N.W. • Washington DC 20036

This distinctive and elegant facility in downtown Washington features Italian marble floors, a dramatic split staircase and a 50-foot glass atrium ceiling.

Capacity: 300 seated; 750 standing.
Catering: Approved caterers list or your own caterer if caterer
                has proper insurance. Using an outside caterer re-
                quires the approval of the facility manager and there
                is an additional fee of $600.
Rental Fee: $3,500 Monday to Thursday; $4,500 Friday to Sun-
                day. Rental fee includes use of facility for 10 hours.
                There is a separate fee of $500 for wedding ceremo-
                nies.
Parking: On the premises. Valet parking is available.
Restrictions: Monday to Friday events must start after 5:00 p.m.
                No events past 1:30 a.m. — last call for bar at 1:00 a.m.
                No smoking.
Note: Wedding ceremonies are permitted. No helium bal-
                loons. No rice, confetti throwing or fog machines. No
                flower petals thrown during ceremony.

Georgetown University
Conference Center & Guest House   202-687-7642

3800 Reservoir Road, N.W. • Washington, DC 20057

This marvelous ballroom, decked with Tiffany-style lamps, exquisite English carpets, and intricate handcrafted woodwork, is just right for conferences, private parties, and wedding receptions. The Center is surrounded by the 104 dogwood-covered acres of the Georgetown University campus, and its 200-year-old Gothic architecture.

Capacity: 850 seated in grand ballroom; 1,200 standing in grand
                ballroom; 3,000 on terrace; 3,000 with tent.
Catering: In-house. Wedding packages range from $55 to $80
                per person.
Parking: On the premises.
Note: Wedding ceremonies are permitted. Guest rooms are
                available. Wedding package includes bridal suite.

Historic Car Barn   202-333-6784

3600 M Street, N.W. • Washington, DC 20007

The Historic Car Barn is a brick structure built into a hill in Georgetown. In 1761, it was the site of a tobacco warehouse. Eventually, the barn was used to quarter horses and trolley cars, hence its name—Car Barn. Today, the penthouse offers two large rooms and a grand expanse of terrace. It features 12-foot high ceilings with grand brass chandeliers, hardwood floors, 8-foot high windows with breathtaking views of Washington and the Potomac River, working fireplace, marble foyer separating the two suites, and outside terraces with flower gardens overlooking the river.

Capacity: 250 seated; 550 standing; 400 in garden; 350 with tent.
Catering: Approved caterers list.
Rental Fee: $1,000 to $4,500.
Parking: On the premises. Valet parking. Parking garages nearby.
Note: Wedding ceremonies are permitted.

Kennedy Warren Ballroom   202-483-2058

3133 Connecticut Avenue, N.W. • Washington, DC 20008

Steeped in the romance of yesterday with its 1920s art deco architecture and elegant atmosphere, this site provides a perfect location for your reception and ceremony. The Warren Room has large windows overlooking the courtyard, wall-to-wall carpeting, large chandeliers and decorative moldings. The deco design flourishes in the design of the columns that mark off an alcove in the room. The art deco theme continues in the Kennedy Room with stenciled ceiling beams, decorated columns and gold and silver accents. There is a large built-in bandstand and a balcony that embraces the room on one side. This ideal setting is in tranquil historic Cleveland Park, next to the National Zoo.

Capacity: 200 seated, 400 standing in the Warren Room; 300 seated, 600 standing in the Kennedy Room.
Catering: In-house. Entrees range from $65 to $85 per person.
Rental Fee: Varies. Call for more information.
Parking: Parking lot nearby.
Note: Wedding ceremonies are permitted.

McLean Gardens Ballroom   202-966-9781

3811 Porter Street, N.W. • Washington, DC 20016

McLean Gardens Ballroom is a historic special-event facility in northwest Washington, D.C., central to Georgetown, Washington Cathedral and Embassy Row. The Ballroom boasts a 40-foot ceiling, is furnished in Williamsburg antiques, and has the appearance of a large intimate living room. It has two working fireplaces, five grand chandeliers, six 20-foot windows with a view and tremendous architectural details.

Capacity: 150 seated; 350 standing.
Catering: You must provide your own caterer.
Rental Fee: $2,250 for 8 hours, includes round tables.
Parking: Residential parking. Valet parking can be arranged.
Note: Wedding ceremonies are permitted.

The Mexican Cultural Institute   202-728-1670

2829 16th Street, N.W. • Washington, DC 20009

On the first floor, the entrance hall boasts an 18th-century baroque altar piece. Positioned under a magnificent staircase is an antique marble table and beautiful Talavera jar. The José Clemente Orozco Gallery, with 600 feet of exhibition space, and the Auditorio Juarez have proven to be excellent spaces for art exhibits, conferences, slide shows, theatrical and dance performances, musical events and receptions. On the second floor, the restored Music Room, a replica of a salon at the Fontainebleau castle in France, has outstanding acoustics and is ideal for chamber music. The Golden Room, decorated in the French Renaissance style, is distinguished by a Federal convex mirror hanging over its marble fireplace and beautiful seascapes of Venice by the American artist Lucien Powell. In the elegant Dining Room, a Bacarat crystal chandelier, hand-carved furniture, and a painting by Benjamin Dominguez adds grace and charm. Muralist Roberto Cueva del Rio decorated the Atrium, using fine tiles produced in his native Puebla. The colorful tiles are geared acoustically for concerts and background music.

Capacity: 200 seated; 300 standing.
Catering: You must provide your own caterer.
Rental Fee: $3,000 and up.
Parking: On the premises.
Restrictions: No smoking.
Note: Wedding ceremonies are permitted.

National Museum of
Women in the Arts   202-783-5000

1250 New York Avenue, N.W. • Washington, DC 20005

A beautiful and well-equipped space is available for corporate and private events of all kinds. Conveniently located at New York Avenue and 13th Street, N.W., the museum is close to downtown hotels, Metro Center, the White House, Convention Center and other attractions in the heart of the nation's capital. The ground floor of the facility offers an ample reception area and exquisite

ballroom. Sweeping double staircases and balustrades lead upward to a mezzanine, where guests may promenade or gaze upon
the festivities below. Several galleries are also available for smaller
groups, as well as the newest addition, the Reception Room in the
Elisabeth A. Kasser Wing. These rooms offer the surroundings of
outstanding works of art, making the event truly special. The
museum's 200-seat theater/auditorium is comfortable, beautiful
and functional. Outfitted with state-of-the-art Dolby sound and
professional motion picture and slide capabilities, it is ideal for
meetings, seminars and small performances of all kinds. Fees for
the use of the museum include a donation to the museum, which
is tax deductible to the extent permissible by law.

Capacity: 550 seated; 1,100 standing; 80 seated, 100 standing in
                 Reception Room; 200 seated in Auditorium.
Catering: Approved caterers list or your own caterer. Entrees
                 range from $18 and up.
Rental Fee: Great Hall $8,000 to $12,000. Third Floor $2,000 to
                 $3,500. Reception Room $1,250 to $2,500. Audito-
                 rium $800 to $1,250.
Parking: Parking lot nearby. Valet parking available.
Note: Wedding ceremonies are permitted.

National Press Club   202-662-7597

529 14th Street, N.W. • Washington, DC 20045

The National Press Club, with its historic atmosphere, stately
decor, and prestigious location two blocks from the White House,
will lend a note of distinction to your special event. The Club's two
lounges are well suited for wedding ceremonies and cocktail
receptions. The traditional Holeman Lounge features a working
gas fireplace, built-in bar, and hardwood floors, while the First
Amendment Lounge boasts a picturesque view from windows
that span floor to ceiling. Adjacent to the lounges is a large
ballroom with two balconies and a rolling mahogany ceiling. The
staff will tailor the menu to your satisfaction, and will assist in
planning every detail of your event. The Club provides all equipment including tables, chairs, linens, china, glassware, and silverware.

Capacity: 360 seated with dance floor; 500 standing.
Catering: In-house. Entree prices vary. Minimum requirement
                 of $5,000 food and beverage purchases on weekends
                 and holidays.
Rental Fee: Varies. Call for more information.
Parking: Parking garages are nearby. Valet parking can be
                 arranged.
Note: Wedding ceremonies are permitted.

Old Cafritz House   202-829-1388

5001 16th Street, N.W. • Washington, DC 20011

Built in the roaring 20s on Washington's "Avenue of the Presidents," the Old Cafritz House is a Mediterranean-style home of grand character. The showcase of the house is the 1,000 square-foot Grand Salon, which has been brought back to its original splendor with 14-foot beamed ceilings, wrought iron chandeliers, Mexican tile floor, and beautiful period artwork. Nineteen windows provide the room with spectacular light by day and romantic charm at night. The dining room is spacious with a beautiful beamed ceiling, a large crystal chandelier, and French doors leading to a beautifully manicured garden, landscaped with annuals and perennials ranging from hydrangeas and crepe myrtle trees, to hibiscus and palms. In addition there is a beautiful sunroom and sitting room inside.

Capacity: 100 seated; 125 standing; 120 seated or standing in garden.
Catering: Approved caterers list only.
Rental Fee: $1,600 to $2,200.
Restrictions: No smoking inside mansion.
Note: Residential parking only, but very plentiful.

University Club International
Center of Washington   202-862-1400

1800 K Street, N.W. • Washington, DC 20006

This contemporary city club provides the perfect atmosphere for any special occasion. Floor-to-ceiling windows line the elegant Embassy Dining Room. This lovely location is fully staffed and every care is taken for the comfort of its guests. Events are for members or must be member-sponsored.

Capacity: 150–200 seated; 400 standing.
Catering: In-house. Entrees range from $25 to $100 per person.
Parking: Pay lots. Metro nearby.
Note: Wedding ceremonies are permitted.

Washington Court Hotel   202-628-2100

525 New Jersey Avenue, N.W. • Washington, DC 20001

The Washington Court Hotel has the perfect solution to your worries about an outdoor reception—Washington's finest skylit ballroom. Capitol Hill's only atrium ballroom is the perfect setting for your special day. The Washington Court also offers a newly renovated, elegant formal ballroom for large events, such as fund raisers and corporate galas.

Capacity: 320 seated with dance floor in ballroom; 500 standing in ballroom; 150 seated with dance floor in atrium.

Catering: In-house. Packages start at $60 per person.

Rental Fee: If minimum food and beverage not met, room rental fee is charged.

Parking: On the premises. Valet parking available.

Note: Wedding ceremonies are permitted. Guest rooms are available at special wedding rates.

Woman's National Democratic Club 202-232-7363

**1526 New Hampshire Avenue, N.W.
Washington, DC 20036**

Built in 1892 as a private home, the Woman's National Democratic Club is one of Washington's most historic and elegant establishments. The mansion, beautifully appointed with crystal chandeliers, oriental rugs and period furniture, is an inviting setting for your wedding, reception or celebration. You may hold your ceremony in the Post/Hamlin Rooms, and then dance the night away in the Stevenson Ballroom. For striking wedding photos, pose in the entrance foyer with its graceful staircase, or on the club's lovely patio. There are six additional rooms upstairs, and a balcony that overlooks the patio. The club's professional staff will assist you in planning your menu and will ensure your event is truly memorable.

Capacity: 150 seated; 300 standing; 50 in garden; 100 seated in Post/Hamlin Rooms.

Catering: In-house. Entrees range from $35 for lunch and $45 for dinner.

Rental Fee: $1,500 for members, $3,000 for non-members.

Parking: Parking garages are nearby. Valet parking may be arranged.

Restrictions: No smoking. No rice, birdseed or confetti.

Note: Wedding ceremonies are permitted.

The Arbor Ballroom   202-636-8919

3600 New York Avenue, N.E. • Washington, DC 20002

An elegant Washington location without the downtown hassle! Conveniently located off the Baltimore-Washington Parkway and Route 50, next to the National Arboretum, this exquisite facility offers luxurious surroundings, superior service and ample parking.

Capacity: 400 seated; 700 standing.
Catering: In-house or your own caterer. Entrees range from $22 to $50 per person when using in-house caterer.
Rental Fee: $2,000 to $4,000.
Parking: On the premises. Valet parking available.
Note: Wedding ceremonies are permitted.

Columbus Club of Union Station
East Hall of Union Station   202-289-8300

c/o Special Events at Union Station
50 Massachusetts Avenue, N.E. • Washington, DC 20002

This site offers two magnificent areas to choose from: The East Hall and Columbus Club. The Columbus Club, built in 1903 with its once "fancy soda fountain," arched portals and classic skylights is a dramatic setting for any occasion. The East Hall of Union Station, known for its skylights which produce glorious natural lighting, is a wonderful setting for receptions and social events. Guests will pass through the magnificent Main Hall with its 100-foot vaulted coffered ceilings and polished Italian floors.

Capacity: 240 seated in Columbus Club; 500 seated in East Hall; 450 standing in Columbus Club; 900 standing in East Hall.
Catering: In-house. Entrees range from $40 to $120 per person.
Rental Fee: $1,500 Columbus Club; $6,000 East Hall.
Parking: Parking on the premises and nearby parking lot. Valet parking can be arranged.

H.H. Leonards Mansion on "O" Street   202-659-8787

2020 O Street, N.W. • Washington, DC 20036

Built in 1891, this elegant five-story Victorian mansion combines elegant ambience with the best of modern technology. Beautifully decorated with fine art, antiques, crystal chandeliers and fireplaces, the mansion is an enchanting and magical place. Amenities include elevator access, gorgeous bathrooms, fully equipped kitchens, and overnight accommodations. The mansion is a popular site for weddings, corporate meetings, and other events.

Capacity: 200.
Catering: In-house. Entrees range from $35 to $600 per guest.
Rental Fee: Private membership fee of $300/year.
Parking: Parking lot nearby, residential parking, and valet parking available.
Restrictions: Bus, valet and limo controls. No photographs outside.
Note: Guest rooms are available. Wedding ceremonies are permitted.

Kennedy Warren Ballroom   202-483-2058

3133 Connecticut Avenue, N.W. • Washington, DC 20008

Steeped in the romance of yesterday with its 1920s art deco architecture and elegant atmosphere, this site provides a perfect location for your reception and ceremony. The Warren Room has large windows overlooking the courtyard, wall-to-wall carpeting, large chandeliers and decorative moldings. The deco design flourishes in the design of the columns that mark off an alcove in the room. The art deco theme continues in the Kennedy Room with stenciled ceiling beams, decorated columns and gold and silver accents. There is a large built-in bandstand and a balcony that embraces the room on one side. This ideal setting is in tranquil historic Cleveland Park, next to the National Zoo.

Capacity: 200 seated, 400 standing in the Warren Room; 300 seated, 600 standing in the Kennedy Room.
Catering: In-house. Entrees range from $65 to $85 per person.
Rental Fee: Varies. Call for more information.
Parking: Parking lot nearby.
Note: Wedding ceremonies are permitted.

La Colline Restaurant   202-737-0400

400 N. Capitol Street, N.W. • Washington, DC 20001

Conveniently located across from Union Station, this wonderful space offers a magnificent view of the U.S. Capitol. This spectacular banquet room, with its contemporary decor, California redwood, beautiful hanging plants and floor-to-ceiling windows is a most unusual setting for your special day. The spacious terrace is perfect for wedding ceremonies and receptions during pleasant weather.

Capacity: 150 seated; 200 standing; 200 on the terrace.
Catering: In-house. Entrees range from $20 and up.
Parking: On the premises.
Note: Wedding ceremonies are permitted indoors or outdoors.

Mount Vernon College — Post Hall   202-625-4538

2100 Foxhall Road, N.W. • Washington, D.C. 20007

Post Hall is a gift from one of the College's most distinguished alumnae, Mrs. Marjorie Merriweather Post. The Hall is handsomely furnished with Georgian-style furniture, crystal chandeliers and a fireplace with a carved marble mantelpiece. This elegant room opens onto a stone patio overlooking the lovely campus.

Capacity: 100 seated; 150 standing; 50 on the patio.
Catering: In-house. Approved caterers list or your own caterer with prior approval from college.
Rental Fee: $700.
Parking: On the premises and parking lot nearby.
Note: Wedding ceremonies are permitted.

Occidental Grill   202-737-4147

1475 Pennsylvania Avenue, N.W. • Washington, DC 20004

Occidental Grill provides elegant private dining facilities for small or large wedding receptions, rehearsal dinners, brunches, and other parties. Just steps from the White House, the restaurant specializes in regional American cuisine — intriguing appetizers, grilled meats, seafood, and rich desserts. The Occidental Grill, with more than 2500 autographed photographs of this century's powerful and famous, creates an atmosphere which is quintessentially Washington, D.C. Since 1906, Occidental Grill has maintained a reputation for innovative food and friendly, attentive service.

Capacity: 150 seated; 300 standing.
Catering: In-house. Entrees vary from $20 to $35 per person. Cake cutting fee if you provide your own cake.
Rental Fee: Varies.
Parking: Parking garage nearby. Valet parking available. Complimentary after 6:00 p.m.
Note: Wedding ceremonies are permitted.

Old Ebbitt Grill   202-347-4800

675 15th Street, N.W. • Washington, DC 20005

Old Ebbitt Grill has been a landmark gathering spot for this city's professionals, politicians, theatergoers and shoppers since 1856. Two private spaces are available. The Cabinet Room, which is fully enclosed, shares the ambience of the handsome main dining room. The Atrium is lovely, with a glass-enclosed ceiling, marble floor, and marble and gold fountain. The Atrium may be fully private or semi-private depending on group size. Old Ebbitt Grill is just around the corner from the White House, and a convenient walk to museums, monuments, cultural attractions, and shopping. Join the crowd assembled at the bar and in the high-backed booths of the handsome dining room for a fun-filled evening.

Capacity: 350 seated; 600 standing; 50 seated in Cabinet Room; 70 standing in Cabinet Room.

Catering: In-house. Entrees range from $25 to $60 per person.

Rental Fee: $50 daytime, $75 night time, $250 for entire Atrium after 6 p.m. Monday- Saturday, after 12 p.m. Sunday.

Parking: Street parking and nearby garages. Complimentary valet parking available.

Phillips Flagship 202-488-8515

900 Water Street, S.W. • Washington, DC 20024

Celebrate your wedding in the romantic splendor of Phillips Flagship. Situated on the Washington waterfront and just minutes from downtown, Phillips offers distinctive facilities for up to 2,000 guests. Choose the first-floor Marble Room with its rose-hued tones, fireplace, antique accents and adjoining Parkside Patio, an enclosed room that allows direct access to the outside patio and waterfront. Or, sweep up the grand staircase to the River Room and Upper Deck and enjoy breathtaking views of the Washington Channel, Capital Yacht Club and Hains Point Park. Choose from a wide selection of seafood, chicken, beef or vegetarian meals, or let its chefs create a delicious menu especially for your wedding or special event.

Capacity: 25 to 1,400 seated; 25 to 2,000 standing. The Marble Room seats up to 220 and an additional 100 in the enclosed Parkside Patio. The Presidential Room and Executive Room seat up to 120 people together or 60 people separately.

Catering: In-house. Entrees range from $26 to $50 per person.

Parking: On the premises, and nearby parking lot.

Sequoia Restaurant 202-333-3011

3050 K Street, N.W. • Washington, DC 20007

Located at Washington Harbour on the Potomac River, this site is the premier space for private and corporate events in the nation's capital. The atmosphere is elegant, with spacious proportions complementing the unsurpassed views of the Monuments, The Kennedy Center, Watergate and historic Virginia. The interior space is gracefully defined with walls of mahogany, floors of terrazzo & cherry, and a panoramic two-story wall of windows overlooking a terrace that descends to the water's edge.

Capacity: 500 seated; 1,500 standing; 2,500 with tent.

Catering: In-house. Menus range from $25 to $90 per person.

Parking: On the premises and nearby parking lots.
Note: Wedding ceremonies are permitted.

University Club International
Center of Washington   202-862-1400

1800 K Street, N.W. • Washington, DC 20006

This contemporary city club provides the perfect atmosphere for any special occasion. Floor-to-ceiling windows line the elegant Embassy Dining Room. This lovely location is fully staffed and every care is taken for the comfort of its guests. Events are for members or must be member-sponsored.

Capacity: 150–250 seated; 400 standing.
Catering: In-house. Entrees range from $25 to $100 per person.
Parking: Pay lots. Metro nearby.
Note: Wedding ceremonies are permitted.

Walsh-Reckord Hall of States   202-789-0031

c/o National Guard Association of the United States
One Massachusetts Avenue, N.W. • Washington, DC 20001

Located in Washington's Capitol Hill area, one block from the magnificent Union Station, the National Guard Memorial is ideal for meetings, fund raisers, luncheons, seminars or dinners. The striking Walsh-Reckord Hall of States, symbolic of the National Guard's state-federal partnership, provides a dramatic backdrop for any function. The Memorial, home of the National Guard Association of the United States, was designed by an award-winning architect and maintains the true Federalist architecture of its neighboring buildings. From the rare Tennessee pink marble that graces the foyer and building interior to the Constitutional green of the Hall of States, the National Guard Memorial offers the perfect ambiance for a media function, reception, dinner or other special event.

Capacity: 200 seated; 500 standing.
Catering: You must provide your own caterer. A fee is required for use of kitchen facilities, and tables and chairs.
Rental Fee: $600 to $2,100.
Parking: Paid parking on premises and nearby parking lots.
Note: Wedding ceremonies are permitted.

Odyssey Cruises   202-488-6010

600 Water Street, S.W. • Washington, DC 20024

Imagine exchanging vows on board the romantic *Odyssey* as it cruises the Potomac. Designed in the style of European canal ships and completely enclosed in glass, *Odyssey* provides a breathtaking view of the Capitol from the sparkling waters of the Potomac. From a ceremony against a stunning sunset to a fabulous four-course dinner, a cruise on *Odyssey* will be unforgettable. After dinner, enjoy *Odyssey's* inviting dance floors and professional entertainment. The experienced consulting and service staff will help you plan the perfect engagement party, bridal shower, rehearsal dinner, or other festivity. Party options include brunch, lunch, or dinner cruises.

Capacity:	600 seated/standing.
Catering:	In-house.
Parking:	Parking on premises and nearby parking lots.
Note:	Wedding ceremonies are permitted.

Spirit Cruises   202-554-8013 ext. 626

Pier 4 • 6th & Water Streets, S.W. • Washington, DC 20024

Consider the wonder of a wedding on the water with Spirit Cruises. Celebrate your festivities on a beautiful, yacht-like ship with your choice of enclosed, climate-controlled decks banked by windows. On the outdoor promenade decks, guests can catch a fresh breeze under the open sky and enjoy a view of the Potomac's historic skyline.

Capacity:	20 to 575 seated; 120 to 600 standing.
Catering:	In-house. Entrees range from $55.85 to $134 per person.
Rental Fee:	Call for rates. Rates are based on a 4-hour rental.
Parking:	On the premises and there is a parking lot nearby.
Note:	Wedding ceremonies are permitted.

Church of the Holy City –
The Wedding Chapel   202-462-6734

1611 Sixteenth Street, N.W. • Washington, DC 20009

The main sanctuary is majestic, its nave filled with soft color from lovely stained glass. Its spacious chancel is adaptable for various wedding arrangements. The more intimate chapel upstairs is strikingly simple. Reached by a winding staircase, the chapel has a gabled, medieval-beamed ceiling of rich dark wood that contrasts with the simple white walls. Casement windows let in natural light for a quiet, spiritual atmosphere. The straw fabric-covered wooden chairs and brown wall-to-wall carpet heighten the sense of charming simplicity.

Capacity: 300 in main sanctuary; 50 in chapel.
Rental Fee: $175 to $650 in main sanctuary; $150 to $450 in chapel. Fee is based on type of ceremony performed.

Institute for Spiritual Development   301-897-5440

5419 Sherrier Place, N.W. • Washington, DC 20016

Reception hall with kitchen facilities available for wedding reception.

Capacity: 100.
Rental Fee: Price begins at $150, additional fees are based upon the type of ceremony performed.

Mount Vernon College –
Hand Chapel   202-625-4538

2100 Foxhall Road, N.W. • Washington, DC 20007

The Florence Hollis Hand Chapel won the 1971 Honor Award from the American Institute of Architects, the nation's highest award for architectural excellence. The Chapel is located in a wooded ravine in a picturesque corner of the campus. Skylights on the dramatically sloped ceiling provide natural light throughout the space. Acoustically, the Chapel is among the finest facilities in the Washington, D.C., area.

Capacity: 250 seated.
Rental Fee: $700.

Peoples Congregational
United Church of Christ   202-829-5511

4704 13th Street, N.W. • Washington, DC 20011

This newly renovated facility is conveniently located in northwest Washington, D.C. The motif of the sanctuary expresses the African-American religious experience. The narthex, a large vestibule, features carved wooden doors and a skylight at its highest point.

Capacity: 850 seated in sanctuary.
Rental Fee: Call for more information.

The Way of the Cross
Church of Christ   202-543-0500

9th & D Streets, N.E. • Washington, DC 20002

Capacity: 1,300.
Rental Fee: $600.

Washington Ethical Society   202-882-6650

7750 Sixteenth Street, N.W. • Washington, DC 20012

This facility is available for wedding receptions and bar/bat mitzvahs, provided that the ceremony is also held there. The ivy-covered meetinghouse includes a foyer and main hall on the upper level and a kitchen and two classrooms on the lower level. The main hall is large, with high ceilings, burgundy carpeting and flexible seating. Floor-to-ceiling windows on two walls flood the hall with natural light, and there's a 20-foot by 15-foot stage with a baby grand piano. A lovely small garden is also available for quiet events.

Capacity: 250 for ceremony; 175 for reception.
Rental Fee: $450 for 4 hours.

Peoples Congregational
United Church of Christ   202-829-5511

4704 13th Street, N.W. • Washington, DC 20011

This newly renovated facility is conveniently located in northwest Washington, D.C. The fellowship hall has a stage and an adjacent kitchen. Small and large conference rooms are available for meetings. An enclosed courtyard makes a great setting for pictures. Amenities include central air conditioning, an elevator, access for the disabled, dressing rooms, and a 60-car parking lot.

Capacity: 300 seated in fellowship hall.
Catering: Approved caterers list or your own caterer.
Rental Fee: $1,000.
Parking: Parking on premises.
Note: Wedding ceremonies are permitted.

Washington Ethical Society   202-882-6650

7750 Sixteenth Street, N.W. • Washington, DC 20012

This facility is available for wedding receptions and bar/bat mitzvahs, provided that the ceremony is also held there. The ivy-covered meetinghouse includes a foyer and main hall on the upper level and a kitchen and two classrooms on the lower level. The main hall is large, with high ceilings, burgundy carpeting and flexible seating. Floor-to-ceiling windows on two walls flood the hall with natural light, and there's a 20-foot by 15-foot stage with a baby grand piano. A lovely small garden is also available for quiet events.

Capacity: 175 seated; 250 standing; 100 in garden.
Catering: You must supply your own caterer.
Rental Fee: $450 for 4 hours.
Parking: Limited parking on premises and street parking.
Restrictions: You must supply dance floor; no smoking.

Georgetown University
Conference Center & Guest House   202-687-7642

3800 Reservoir Road, N.W. • Washington, DC 20057

This marvelous ballroom, decked with Tiffany-style lamps, exquisite English carpets, and intricate handcrafted woodwork, is just right for conferences, private parties, and wedding receptions. The Center is surrounded by the 104 dogwood-covered acres of the Georgetown University campus, and its 200-year-old Gothic architecture.

Capacity: 850 seated in grand ballroom; 1,200 standing in grand ballroom; 3,000 on terrace; 3,000 with tent.

Catering: In-house. Wedding packages range from $55 to $80 per person.

Parking: On the premises.

Note: Wedding ceremonies are permitted. Guest rooms are available. Wedding package includes bridal suite.

American News Women's Club   202-332-6770

1607 22nd Street, N.W. • Washington, DC 20008

The Club serves as headquarters to the 60-year-old professional organization of women writers, editors, journalists and publicists. This beautifully renovated turn-of-the-century, four-story brick townhouse is perfect for meetings, small private dinners, and wedding receptions. It has an elevator, Steinway grand piano, and speaker system. Some party and meeting equipment is available with the rental. The Club is conveniently located near Dupont Circle and is two blocks from the metro.

Capacity: 36 seated in formal dining room; 110 standing.
Catering: You may use your own caterer or one of the caterers that are familiar with the club. Caterers must be insured.
Rental Fee: $500 an event or by the hour. Monthly and weekly rates are available for meetings and other corporate events.
Parking: Parking lot nearby and residential parking.
Restrictions: Dancing and music are allowed, but must be kept at a reasonable volume.
Note: Wedding ceremonies are permitted. Facility is handicap accessible.

National Press Club   202-662-7597

529 14th Street, N.W. • Washington, DC 20045

The National Press Club, with its historic atmosphere, stately decor, and prestigious location two blocks from the White House, will lend a note of distinction to your special event. The Club's two lounges are well suited for wedding ceremonies and cocktail receptions. The traditional Holeman Lounge features a working gas fireplace, built-in bar, and hardwood floors, while the First Amendment Lounge boasts a picturesque view from windows that span floor to ceiling. Adjacent to the lounges is a large ballroom with two balconies and a rolling mahogany ceiling. The staff will tailor the menu to your satisfaction, and will assist in planning every detail of your event. The Club provides all equipment including tables, chairs, linens, china, glassware, and silverware.

Capacity: 360 seated with dance floor; 500 standing.
Catering: In-house. Entree prices vary. Minimum requirement of $5,000 food and beverage purchases on weekends and holidays.
Rental Fee: Varies. Call for more information.
Parking: Parking garages are nearby. Valet parking can be arranged.
Note: Wedding ceremonies are permitted.

University Club International
Center of Washington   202-862-1400

1800 K Street, N.W. • Washington, DC 20006

This contemporary city club provides the perfect atmosphere for any special occasion. Floor-to-ceiling windows line the elegant Embassy Dining Room. This lovely location is fully staffed and every care is taken for the comfort of its guests. Events are for members or must be member-sponsored. Facility is handicap accessible.

Capacity: 150–250 seated; 400 standing.
Catering: In-house. Entrees range from $25 to $100 per person.
Parking: Pay lots. Metro nearby.
Note: Wedding ceremonies are permitted.

Woman's National Democratic Club 202-232-7363

1526 New Hampshire Avenue, N.W.
Washington, DC 20036

Built in 1892 as a private home, the Woman's National Democratic Club is one of Washington's most historic and elegant establishments. The mansion, beautifully appointed with crystal chandeliers, oriental rugs and period furniture, is an inviting setting for your wedding, reception or celebration. You may hold your ceremony in the Post/Hamlin Rooms, and then dance the night away in the Stevenson Ballroom. For striking wedding photos, pose in the entrance foyer with its graceful staircase, or on the club's lovely patio. There are six additional rooms upstairs, and a balcony that overlooks the patio. The club's professional staff will assist you in planning your menu and will ensure your event is truly memorable.

Capacity: 150 seated; 300 standing; 50 in garden; 100 seated in Post/Hamlin Rooms.
Catering: In-house. Entrees range from $35 for lunch and $45 for dinner.
Rental Fee: $1,500 for members, $3,000 for non-members.
Parking: Parking garages are nearby. Valet parking may be arranged.
Restrictions: No smoking. No rice, birdseed or confetti.
Note: Wedding ceremonies are permitted.

Galleria at Lafayette Centre   202-835-0093

1155 21st Street, N.W. • Washington DC 20036

This distinctive and elegant facility in downtown Washington features Italian marble floors, a dramatic split staircase and a 50-foot glass atrium ceiling.

Capacity: 300 seated; 750 standing.
Catering: Approved caterers list or your own caterer if caterer has proper insurance. Using an outside caterer requires the approval of the facility manager and there is an additional fee of $600.
Rental Fee: $3,500 Monday to Thursday; $4,500 Friday to Sunday. Rental fee includes use of facility for 10 hours. There is a separate fee of $500 for wedding ceremonies.
Parking: On the premises. Valet parking is available.
Restrictions: Monday to Friday events must start after 5:00 p.m. No events past 1:30 a.m. — last call for bar at 1:00 a.m. No smoking.
Note: Wedding ceremonies are permitted. No helium balloons. No rice, confetti throwing or fog machines. No flower petals thrown during ceremony.

The Mexican Cultural Institute   202-728-1670

2829 16th Street, N.W. • Washington, DC 20009

On the first floor, the entrance hall boasts an 18th-century baroque altar piece. Positioned under a magnificent staircase is an antique marble table and beautiful Talavera jar. The José Clemente Orozco Gallery, with 600 feet of exhibition space, and the Auditorio Juarez have proven to be excellent spaces for art exhibits, conferences, slide shows, theatrical and dance performances, musical events and receptions. On the second floor, the restored Music Room, a replica of a salon at the Fontainebleau castle in France, has outstanding acoustics and is ideal for chamber music. The Golden Room, decorated in the French Renaissance style, is distinguished by a Federal convex mirror hanging over its marble fireplace and beautiful seascapes of Venice by the American artist Lucien Powell. In the elegant Dining Room, a Bacarat crystal chandelier, hand-carved furniture, and a painting by Benjamin Dominguez adds grace and charm. Muralist Roberto Cueva del Rio decorated the Atrium, using fine tiles produced in his native Puebla. The colorful tiles are geared acoustically for concerts and background music.

Capacity: 200 seated; 300 standing.
Catering: You must provide your own caterer.
Rental Fee: $3,000 and up.
Parking: On the premises.
Restrictions: No smoking.
Note: Wedding ceremonies are permitted.

The National Aquarium   202-482-2826

U.S. Department of Commerce Bldg., Room B-075
14th Street and Constitution Ave., N.W.
Washington, DC 20230

History and underwater adventures give atmosphere to the intimate spaces of the National Aquarium. This country's first public
aquarium, originally founded in 1873, hides in the basement of the
Department of Commerce Building. Utilizing its limited space,
caterers can wonderfully transform this daytime aquarium into a
setting for a memorable evening. Use the creative backdrop of 70
tanks of curious fish for your next social, literary or political
gathering.

Capacity: 150 seated; 300 standing.
Catering: Approved caterers list or your own caterer. No kitchen
               facilities.
Rental Fee: $1,500.
Parking: On-street parking, parking lots and access to metro.
Restrictions: Available only between 5:30 p.m.-11:30 p.m.
Note: Wedding ceremonies are permitted.

National Museum
of Women in the Arts   202-783-5000

1250 New York Avenue, N.W. • Washington, DC 20005

A beautiful and well-equipped space is available for corporate and
private events of all kinds. Conveniently located at New York
Avenue and 13th Street, N.W., the museum is close to downtown
hotels, Metro Center, the White House, Convention Center and
other attractions in the heart of the nation's capital. The ground
floor of the facility offers an ample reception area and exquisite
ballroom. Sweeping double staircases and balustrades lead upward to a mezzanine, where guests may promenade or gaze upon
the festivities below. Several galleries are also available for smaller
groups, as well as the newest addition, the Reception Room in the
Elisabeth A. Kasser Wing. These rooms offer the surroundings of
outstanding works of art, making the event truly special. The
museum's 200-seat theater/auditorium is comfortable, beautiful
and functional. Outfitted with state-of-the-art Dolby sound and
professional motion picture and slide capabilities, it is ideal for
meetings, seminars and small performances of all kinds. Fees for
the use of the museum include a donation to the museum, which
is tax deductible to the extent permissible by law.

Capacity: 550 seated; 1,100 standing; 80 seated, 100 standing in
               Reception Room; 200 seated in Auditorium.
Catering: Approved caterers list or your own caterer. Entrees
               range from $18 and up.

Rental Fee: Great Hall $8,000 to $12,000. Third Floor $2,000 to $3,500. Reception Room $1,250 to $2,500. Auditorium $800 to $1,250.

Parking: Parking lot nearby. Valet parking available.

Note: Wedding ceremonies are permitted.

ANA Hotel   202-429-2400

2401 M Street, N.W. • Washington, DC 20037

One of Washington's most fashionable addresses, this hotel has been described as having the gracious ambience of the French Embassy. Whether it's a reception in the Colonnade's enchanting garden courtyard, or a candlelight dinner in the ballroom, your wedding day will be unforgettable.

Capacity: 450 seated in the ballroom; 200 seated in the Colonnade; 700 standing in the ballroom; 350 standing in the Colonnade.
Catering: In-house. Wedding packages from $100 to $160 per person.
Parking: On the premises. Valet parking available.
Note: Wedding ceremonies are permitted. Facility is handicap accessible.

Decatur House Museum   202-842-0917

748 Jackson Place, N.W. • Washington, DC 20006

Right in the heart of the District, the Decatur House Museum and Carriage House provides an elegant wedding environment. With its vaulted ceilings and floor-to-ceiling French windows opening onto a spacious courtyard, the Decatur House has carried on a 175-year tradition as a premier locale for wedding ceremonies. The first celebration was the marriage of President Monroe's daughter. This functional multi-faceted site includes a courtyard and a contemporary 2,100 square-foot Carriage House.

Capacity: Carriage House interior holds 120 seated; 250 standing; Courtyard with tent holds 220 seated; and standing combined space can accommodate 500.
Catering: Approved caterers list.
Rental Fee: $3,000 for reception; $3,500 for ceremony and reception.
Parking: Parking garage nearby.
Restrictions: No music after 11:30 p.m. Parties must end at midnight.
Note: You pay for the time guests are on site, not for caterer's set-up and take-down.

Dumbarton House   202-337-2288

2715 Que Street, N.W. • Washington, DC 20007

Dating back to the first years of the American Republic, Dumbarton House has stood on the heights of Georgetown for almost two centuries. From the library to the dining room, through the music room to the parlor to the bedrooms upstairs, this stately brick home is filled with furniture, paintings, textiles, silver, ceramics and other period treasures. To celebrate its centennial in 1991, The National Society renovated Dumbarton House, adding a park and a large Palladian-inspired room which opens onto a terraced courtyard. Enjoy cocktails in the upper garden and dinner in the Belle Vue Room. The Belle Vue Room, with its 15-foot ceiling, hosts Society programs, educational presentations and period concerts, and is available for a variety of individual and corporate events. When docents are present, the museum is open for tour.

Capacity: 150 seated; 170 standing.
Catering: Approved caterers list.
Rental Fee: $4,000 for 4 hours.
Parking: Street parking normally available.
Restrictions: Band acceptable; no DJs. Tent mandatory.

Ella Smith House   703-739-1030

c/o Capitol Catering
3rd and Maryland Avenue, N.E. • Washington, DC 20002

Two blocks from the Capitol Building on the Senate side is this handsome Victorian mansion, built in 1889. Even as you approach the townhouse, you'll notice several distinctive features: the capacious front courtyard, its beautiful rose garden and the house's charming turret. Inside is an unusually wide center hall with a spectacular 40-foot curving staircase, complete with the original cherrywood railing. In addition to the hall, the first floor holds three rooms, each with its original fireplace, plaster cornices and woodwork. On the turret side of the house is the salon, where plush banquettes fit snugly against the bay window. Across the hall is the dining room, with paneled wainscoting and brass chandelier. Beyond the dining room is the kitchen, where a grill rests upon the century-old brick of what was once the fireplace. The second and third floor rooms are available to guests who want to view the Capitol from the turret windows.

Capacity: 40 seated; 75 standing; 25 in garden.
Catering: In-house. Entrees range from $30 to $100 per person.
Rental Fee: $500.
Restrictions: No smoking.
Note: Wedding ceremonies are permitted.

Historic Car Barn   202-333-6784

3600 M Street, N.W. • Washington, DC 20007

The Historic Car Barn is a brick structure built into a hill in Georgetown. In 1761, it was the site of a tobacco warehouse. Eventually, the barn was used to quarter horses and trolley cars, hence its name — Car Barn. Today, the penthouse offers two large rooms and a grand expanse of terrace. It features 12-foot high ceilings with grand brass chandeliers, hardwood floors, 8-foot high windows with breathtaking views of Washington and the Potomac River, working fireplace, marble foyer separating the two suites, and outside terraces with flower gardens overlooking the river.

Capacity: 250 seated; 550 standing; 400 in garden; 350 with tent.
Catering: Approved caterers list.
Rental Fee: $1,000 to $4,500.
Parking: On the premises. Valet parking. Parking garages nearby.
Note: Wedding ceremonies are permitted.

La Colline Restaurant   202-737-0400

400 N. Capitol Street, N.W. • Washington, DC 20001

Conveniently located across from Union Station, this wonderful space offers a magnificent view of the U.S. Capitol. This spectacular banquet room, with its contemporary decor, California redwood, beautiful hanging plants and floor-to-ceiling windows is a most unusual setting for your special day. The spacious terrace is perfect for wedding ceremonies and receptions during pleasant weather.

Capacity: 150 seated; 200 standing; 200 on the terrace.
Catering: In-house. Entrees range from $50 and up.
Parking: On the premises.
Note: Wedding ceremonies are permitted indoors or outdoors.

Meridian House   202-939-5592

1630 Crescent Place, N.W. • Washington, DC 20009

Considered by many to be the best example of French urban architecture in the United States, Meridian House was built in 1921 as the retirement home for American Ambassador Irwin Laughlen. Meridian's entrance features an impressive limestone facade with solid oak doors, while the style of Louis XVI is reflected throughout the home's interior. Meridian House, renowned for its formal pebbled terrace shaded by linden trees, has a spacious lawn and gardens which make a perfect setting for outdoor events.

Capacity: 200 seated with dance floor; 350 standing.
Catering: You must provide your own caterer.
Rental Fee: $5,500.
Parking: Parking on premises. Valet parking can be arranged.
Restrictions: No red food or beverages. No cash bars. No throwing confetti, etc. No smoking.
Note: Wedding ceremonies are permitted indoors or outdoors.

Morrison-Clark Inn   1-800-332-7898/202-898-1200

**Massachusetts Avenue and Eleventh Street, N.W.
Washington, DC 20001**

The Morrison-Clark Historic Inn and Restaurant is a Victorian
mansion located in the heart of Washington, D.C. It is the only inn
to be listed on the National Register of Historic Places in the
nation's capital. Built in 1864, this elegant Victorian inn offers
modern comforts amidst Old-World grandeur and historic charm.
Nationally ranked in *Gourmet* magazine, the restaurant features
New American cuisine with southern and regional influences. The
restaurant is also consistently featured in the *Washington Post's*
annual "50 Favorite Restaurants." Each dining room is individually decorated and appointed with period furnishings. During
pleasant weather, guests can enjoy the enclosed garden courtyard.

Capacity:	84 seated; 100 standing; 130 with tent.
Catering:	In-house. Entrees range from $37 and up per person. Cake cutting fee if you provide own cake.
Parking:	Parking on premises and nearby lots. Valet parking available.
Note:	Wedding ceremonies are permitted.

Old Cafritz House   202-829-1388

5001 16th Street, N.W. • Washington, DC 20011

Built in the roaring 20s on Washington's "Avenue of the Presidents," the Old Cafritz House is a Mediterranean-style home of
grand character. The showcase of the house is the 1,000 square-
foot Grand Salon, which has been brought back to its original
splendor with 14-foot beamed ceilings, wrought iron chandeliers,
Mexican tile floor, and beautiful period artwork. Nineteen windows provide the room with spectacular light by day and romantic
charm at night. The dining room is spacious with a beautiful
beamed ceiling, a large crystal chandelier, and French doors
leading to a beautifully manicured garden, landscaped with annuals and perennials ranging from hydrangeas and crepe myrtle
trees, to hibiscus and palms. In addition there is a beautiful
sunroom and sitting room inside.

Capacity:	100 seated; 125 standing; 120 seated or standing in garden.
Catering:	Approved caterers list only.
Rental Fee:	$1,600 to $2,200.
Restrictions:	No smoking inside mansion.
Note:	Residential parking only, but very plentiful.

Swann House   202-265-4414

1808 New Hampshire Avenue • Washington, DC 20009

Swann House was designed and built in 1883 in grand Richardson Romanesque style by Walter Paris, an architect in service to the British Crown and famous Washington watercolorist. Enter through an expansive arched front porch and feel the ambiance created by 12-foot ceilings outlined in 18-inch crown moldings. Fluted woodwork, inlaid wood floors, crystal chandeliers, and elaborate mantels enhance the elegance of this fine mansion. Open, airy spaces invite entertaining. Through three sets of French doors, a sunroom with a wet bar overlooks the lush private garden and pool. The mansion offers a wonderful assortment of decks, porches, patios and gardens in which to linger. Located on a prominent corner in the Dupont Circle historic district, it is located just a few blocks from the Dupont Circle Metro Station. You will find it is just a 15-minute walk to the White House and many of Washington's most famous landmarks. The Swann House is available for rent by individuals and groups for business meetings and social functions. It is an ideal venue for wedding receptions, cocktail parties, and rehearsal dinners as well as board meetings, corporate retreats, small conferences and luncheons. The Swann House offers six charmingly decorated bedrooms and suites, each with a private bath and several with working fireplaces. Other amenities include oversized showers, antique pedestal sinks, and a Jacuzzi tub.

Capacity: 60 seated; 125 standing; 25 in garden.
Catering: Approved caterers list.
Rental Fee: $1,800.
Parking: Parking lot nearby. Valet parking may be arranged.
Restrictions: No amplified music.
Note: Wedding ceremonies are permitted.

White-Meyer House   202-939-5592

1624 Crescent Place, N.W. • Washington, DC 20009

This classic brick mansion was built in 1911 by American Ambassador Henry White and later purchased by *Washington Post* owner Eugene Meyer. The Georgian mansion features formal wrought iron gates and a circular driveway leading visitors up to a pillared entrance into the home's stately, grand interior. Rich walnut paneled double doors from the reception hall open into the sitting room, library and dining room. Beyond is a paved terrace overlooking the city, which provides a particularly lovely view at night. Traveling art exhibits are also regularly on display in the home.

Capacity: 175 seated with dance floor; 250 standing.
Catering: You must supply your own caterer.

Rental Fee: $5,500.
Parking: Parking on premises and in nearby lot. Valet parking
               possible.
Restrictions: No red food or beverages. No cash bars. No throwing
               confetti, etc. No smoking.
Note: Wedding ceremonies are permitted.

Woodrow Wilson House   202-387-4062

2340 S Street, N.W. • Washington, DC 20008

The Woodrow Wilson House, Washington's only presidential
museum, is located in the historic Embassy Row neighborhood.
The 1915 Georgian Revival townhouse offers the use of five
historically furnished rooms, a terrace and garden. Groups under
40 may dine in the presidential dining room and stroll through the
library and drawing room with their cocktails. Many of the
Wilsons' own wedding gifts and gifts of State from around the
world are on display. Larger groups may be accommodated for
wedding ceremonies in the garden or on the terrace with a tent.
The Woodrow Wilson House is a National Trust Historic Site.

Capacity: 40 seated; 200 standing; 125 in garden; 150 with tent.
Catering: Approved caterers list.
Rental Fee: $2,500.
Parking: On-street parking available for small groups. Valet
               parking available.
Restrictions: No red liquids. No smoking. No lit tapers or sterno in
               house. No amplified music or dancing in house. Mu-
               sic is allowed in garden, but must cease at 10:00 p.m.
Note: Wedding ceremonies are permitted.

Columbus Club of Union Station
East Hall of Union Station   202-289-8300

c/o Special Events at Union Station
50 Massachusetts Avenue, N.E. • Washington, DC 20002

This site offers two magnificent areas to choose from: The East Hall and Columbus Club. The Columbus Club, built in 1903 with its once "fancy soda fountain," arched portals and classic skylights is a dramatic setting for any occasion. The East Hall of Union Station, known for its skylights which produce glorious natural lighting, is a wonderful setting for receptions and social events. Guests will pass through the magnificent Main Hall with its 100-foot vaulted coffered ceilings and polished Italian floors.

Capacity: 240 seated in Columbus Club; 500 seated in East Hall; 450 standing in Columbus Club; 900 standing in East Hall.
Catering: In-house. Entrees range from $40 to $120 per person.
Rental Fee: $1,500 Columbus Club; $6,000 East Hall.
Parking: Parking on the premises and nearby parking lot. Valet parking can be arranged.

The Folger Shakespeare Library   202-675-0324

201 East Capitol Street, S.E. • Washington, DC 20003

The Folger Shakespeare Library, opened in 1932, is listed on the National Register of Historic Places. The following spaces are available for private special events. The Folger's Great Hall is styled after the royal reception rooms of Elizabethan England. Capacity is 250 for a reception, and 180 for dinner. Modeled on the royal and collegial Tudor style halls of Shakespeare's day, the Old Reading Room is used for research by scholars from around the world. Capacity is 250 for a reception, and 180 for dinner. The Board Room, decorated in an English Regency style, has a large retractable screen for slide and film presentations. Capacity is 50 for a reception or dinner. The Founder's Room evokes a Tudor-like atmosphere. Capacity is 40 for a reception or dinner. The Elizabethan Garden is also available for special events and features a garden with herbs and flowers popular in Shakespeare's time. The Office of Special Events provides liaison assistance with caterers, decorators, florists, valet parking, musicians, actors, Museum Shop services, and docents.

Capacity: 40-180 seated; 60-500 standing; 150 in garden; 150 with tent.
Catering: Approved caterers list.
Rental Fee: $2,500 to $25,000.
Parking: Valet parking available.
Restrictions: No smoking. Foods that leave stains, such as berries,

are discouraged. The Library reserves the right of
final approval of caterers and vendors for an event.

Note: Wedding ceremonies are permitted.

Mount Vernon College—Post Hall   202-625-4538

2100 Foxhall Road, N.W. • Washington, D.C. 20007

Post Hall is a gift from one of the College's most distinguished
alumnae, Mrs. Marjorie Merriweather Post. The Hall is handsomely furnished with Georgian-style furniture, crystal chandeliers and a fireplace with a carved marble mantelpiece. This
elegant room opens onto a stone patio overlooking the lovely
campus.

Capacity: 100 seated; 150 standing; 50 on the patio.
Catering: In-house. Approved caterers list or your own caterer
with prior approval from college.
Rental Fee: $700.
Parking: On the premises and nearby parking lot.
Note: Wedding ceremonies are permitted.

Peoples Congregational
United Church of Christ   202-829-5511

4704 13th Street, N.W. • Washington, DC 20011

This newly renovated facility is conveniently located in northwest
Washington, D.C. The fellowship hall has a stage and an adjacent
kitchen. Small and large conference rooms are available for
meetings. An enclosed courtyard makes a great setting for pictures. Amenities include central air conditioning, an elevator,
access for the disabled, dressing rooms, and a 60-car parking lot.

Capacity: 300 seated in fellowship hall; 850 seated in sanctuary.
Catering: Approved caterers list or your own caterer.
Rental Fee: $1,000.
Parking: Parking on premises.
Note: Wedding ceremonies are permitted.

Walsh-Reckord Hall of States   202-789-0031

**c/o National Guard Association of the United States
One Massachusetts Avenue, N.W. • Washington, DC 20001**

Located in Washington's Capitol Hill area, one block from the
magnificent Union Station, the National Guard Memorial is ideal
for meetings, fund raisers, luncheons, seminars or dinners. The
striking Walsh-Reckord Hall of States, symbolic of the National
Guard's state-federal partnership, provides a dramatic backdrop
for any function. The Memorial, home of the National Guard
Association of the United States, was designed by an award-

winning architect and maintains the true Federalist architecture of its neighboring buildings. From the rare Tennessee pink marble that graces the foyer and building interior to the Constitutional green of the Hall of States, the National Guard Memorial offers the perfect ambiance for a media function, reception, dinner or other special event.

Capacity: 200 seated; 500 standing.
Catering: You must provide your own caterer. A fee is required for use of kitchen facilities, and tables and chairs.
Rental Fee: $600 to $2,100.
Parking: Paid parking on premises and nearby parking lots.
Note: Wedding ceremonies are permitted.

1789 Restaurant   202-965-1789

1226 36th Street, N.W. • Washington, DC 20007

Located in a Federal-style townhouse, this fine dining establishment serves contemporary American cuisine in a formal atmosphere. The Middleburg Room, seats 56 people, has a charming
bay window. The more casual F. Scott Fitzgerald next door is
available for evening and daytime rentals. Decorated with original art from the 1920s and 1930s, F. Scott's has a dance floor, DJ
booth and full bar.

Capacity: 60 seated; 75 standing.
Catering: In-house. Entrees range from $50 to $75 per person.
               Cake cutting fee if you provide your own cake.
Parking: Parking lot nearby. Complimentary valet parking is
               available.
Note: Wedding ceremonies are permitted.

American News Women's Club   202-332-6770

1607 22nd Street, N.W. • Washington, DC 20008

The Club serves as headquarters to the 60-year-old professional
organization of women writers, editors, journalists and publicists.
This beautifully renovated turn-of-the-century, four-story brick
townhouse is perfect for meetings, small private dinners, and
wedding receptions. It has an elevator, Steinway grand piano, and
speaker system. Some party and meeting equipment is available
with the rental. The Club is conveniently located near Dupont
Circle and is two blocks from the metro.

Capacity: 36 seated in formal dining room; 110 standing.
Catering: You may use your own caterer or one of the caterers that
                  are familiar with the club. Caterers must be insured.
Rental Fee: $500 an event or by the hour. Monthly and weekly
                  rates are available for meetings and other corporate
                  events.
Parking: Parking lot nearby and residential parking.
Restrictions: Dancing and music are allowed, but must be kept at
                  a reasonable volume.
Note: Wedding ceremonies are permitted. Facility is handi-
                  cap accessible.

Columbus Club of Union Station
East Hall of Union Station   202-289-8300

c/o Special Events at Union Station
50 Massachusetts Avenue, N.E. • Washington, DC 20002

This site offers two magnificent areas to choose from: The East
Hall and Columbus Club. The Columbus Club, built in 1903 with

its once "fancy soda fountain," arched portals and classic skylights is a dramatic setting for any occasion. The East Hall of Union Station, known for its skylights which produce glorious natural lighting, is a wonderful setting for receptions and social events. Guests will pass through the magnificent Main Hall with its 100-foot vaulted coffered ceilings and polished Italian floors.

Capacity: 240 seated in Columbus Club; 500 seated in East Hall; 450 standing in Columbus Club; 900 standing in East Hall.
Catering: In-house. Entrees range from $40 to $120 per person.
Rental Fee: $1,500 Columbus Club; $6,000 East Hall.
Parking: Parking on the premises and nearby parking lot. Valet parking can be arranged.

Decatur House Museum   202-842-0917

748 Jackson Place, N.W. • Washington, DC 20006

Right in the heart of the District, the Decatur House Museum and Carriage House provides an elegant wedding environment. With its vaulted ceilings and floor-to-ceiling French windows opening onto a spacious courtyard, the Decatur House has carried on a 175-year tradition as a premier locale for wedding ceremonies. The first celebration was the marriage of President Monroe's daughter. This functional multi-faceted site includes a courtyard and a contemporary 2,100 square-foot Carriage House.

Capacity: Carriage House interior holds 120 seated, 250 standing; Courtyard with tent holds 220 seated, and standing combined space can accommodate 500.
Catering: Approved caterers list.
Rental Fee: $3,000 for reception; $3,500 for ceremony and reception
Parking: Parking garages nearby.
Restrictions: No music after 11:30 p.m. Parties must end at midnight.
Note: You pay for the time guests are on site, not for caterer's set-up and take-down.

Dumbarton House   202-337-2288

2715 Que Street, N.W. • Washington, DC 20007

Dating back to the first years of the American Republic, Dumbarton House has stood on the heights of Georgetown for almost two centuries. From the library to the dining room, through the music room to the parlor to the bedrooms upstairs, this stately brick home is filled with furniture, paintings, textiles, silver, ceramics and other period treasures. To celebrate its centennial in 1991, The National Society renovated Dumbarton House, adding a park and a large Palladian-inspired room which opens onto a terraced courtyard. Enjoy cocktails in the upper garden and dinner in the Belle Vue Room. The Belle Vue Room, with its 15-

foot ceiling, hosts Society programs, educational presentations and period concerts, and is available for a variety of individual and corporate events. When docents are present, the museum is open for tour.

Capacity: 150 seated; 170 standing.
Catering: Approved caterers list.
Rental Fee: $4,000 for 4 hours.
Parking: Street parking normally available.
Restrictions: Band acceptable; no DJs. Tent mandatory.

Ella Smith House   703-739-1030

c/o Capitol Catering
3rd and Maryland Avenue, N.E. • Washington, DC 20002

Two blocks from the Capitol Building on the Senate side is this handsome Victorian mansion, built in 1889. Even as you approach the townhouse, you'll notice several distinctive features: the capacious front courtyard, its beautiful rose garden and the house's charming turret. Inside is an unusually wide center hall with a spectacular 40-foot curving staircase, complete with the original cherrywood railing. In addition to the hall, the first floor holds three rooms, each with its original fireplace, plaster cornices and woodwork. On the turret side of the house is the salon, where plush banquettes fit snugly against the bay window. Across the hall is the dining room, with paneled wainscoting and brass chandelier. Beyond the dining room is the kitchen, where a grill rests upon the century-old brick of what was once the fireplace. The second and third floor rooms are available to guests who want to view the Capitol from the turret windows.

Capacity: 40 seated; 75 standing; 25 in garden.
Catering: In-house. Entrees range from $30 to $100 per person.
Rental Fee: $500.
Restrictions: No smoking.
Note: Wedding ceremonies are permitted.

Erickson House   703-739-1030

c/o Capitol Catering
437 New Jersey Avenue, S.E. • Washington, DC 20003

Four blocks from the U.S. Capitol on the House side is this private home of a retired naval officer. Erickson House is a century-old painted brick townhouse filled with an astonishing array of oriental art and furniture acquired by the owner during his travels — Vietnamese vases, Japanese woodblock prints and Peruvian mirrors. Your event will take place in the living room, spacious hall and dining room. A large bay window, a working fireplace and sliding paneled doors that can close for privacy add to the living room's charm. Foreign art treasures rest on the oak floor of the generously sized hall. Past the staircase leading to the second floor is the dining room, which has an expandable teak table and a large harp from Paraguay. When the weather is pleasant, your party can spill out into the fenced-in front yard. From here, you can look up the street and get a tremendous view of the Capitol.

Capacity: 20 seated; 75 standing; 10 in garden.
Catering: In-house. Entree range from $30 to $100 per person.
Rental Fee: $500.
Restrictions: No smoking.
Note: Wedding ceremonies are permitted.

The Folger Shakespeare Library   202-675-0324

201 East Capitol Street, S.E. • Washington, DC 20003

The Folger Shakespeare Library, opened in 1932, is listed on the National Register of Historic Places. The following spaces are available for private special events. The Folger's Great Hall is styled after the royal reception rooms of Elizabethan England. Capacity is 250 for a reception, and 180 for dinner. Modeled on the royal and collegial Tudor style halls of Shakespeare's day, the Old Reading Room is used for research by scholars from around the world. Capacity is 250 for a reception, and 180 for dinner. The Board Room, decorated in an English Regency style has a large retractable screen for slide and film presentations. Capacity is 50 for a reception or dinner. The Founder's Room evokes a Tudor-like atmosphere. Capacity is 40 for a reception or dinner. The Elizabethan Garden is also available for special events and features a garden with herbs and flowers popular in Shakespeare's time. The Office of Special Events provides liaison assistance with caterers, decorators, florists, valet parking, musicians, actors, Museum Shop services, and docents.

Capacity: 40-180 seated; 60-500 standing; 150 in garden; 150 with tent.
Catering: Approved caterers list.
Rental Fee: $2,500 to $25,000.
Parking: Valet parking available.
Restrictions: No smoking. Foods that leave stains, such as berries, are discouraged. The Library reserves the right of final approval of caterers and vendors for an event.
Note: Wedding ceremonies are permitted.

H.H. Leonards Mansion
on "O" Street   202-659-8787

2020 O Street, N.W. • Washington, DC 20036

Built in 1891, this elegant five-story Victorian mansion combines elegant ambience with the best of modern technology. Beautifully decorated with fine art, antiques, crystal chandeliers and fireplaces, the mansion is an enchanting and magical place. Amenities include elevator access, gorgeous bathrooms, fully equipped kitchens, and overnight accommodations. The mansion is a popular site for weddings, corporate meetings, and other events.

Capacity: 200.
Catering: In-house. Entrees range from $35 to $600 per guest.
Rental Fee: Private membership fee of $300/year.
Parking: Parking lot nearby, residential parking, and valet parking available.
Restrictions: Bus, valet and limo controls. No photographs outside.
Note: Guest rooms are available. Wedding ceremonies are permitted.

Historic Car Barn   202-333-6784

3600 M Street, N.W. • Washington, DC 20007

The Historic Car Barn is a brick structure built into a hill in Georgetown. In 1761, it was the site of a tobacco warehouse. Eventually, the barn was used to quarter horses and trolley cars, hence its name—Car Barn. Today, the penthouse offers two large rooms and a grand expanse of terrace. It features 12-foot high ceilings with grand brass chandeliers, hardwood floors, 8-foot high windows with breathtaking views of Washington and the Potomac River, working fireplace, marble foyer separating the two suites, and outside terraces with flower gardens overlooking the river.

Capacity: 250 seated; 550 standing; 400 in garden; 350 with tent.
Catering: Approved caterers list.
Rental Fee: $1,000 to $4,500.
Parking: On the premises. Valet parking is available. Parking garages nearby.
Note: Wedding ceremonies are permitted.

Kennedy Warren Ballroom   202-483-2058

3133 Connecticut Avenue, N.W. • Washington, DC 20008

Steeped in the romance of yesterday with its 1920s art deco architecture and elegant atmosphere, this site provides a perfect location for your reception and ceremony. The Warren Room has large windows overlooking the courtyard, wall-to-wall carpeting, large chandeliers and decorative moldings. The deco design flourishes in the design of the columns that mark off an alcove in the room. The art deco theme continues in the Kennedy Room with stenciled ceiling beams, decorated columns and gold and silver accents. There is a large built-in bandstand and a balcony that embraces the room on one side. This ideal setting is in tranquil historic Cleveland Park, next to the National Zoo.

Capacity: 200 seated, 400 standing in the Warren Room; 300 seated, 600 standing in the Kennedy Room.

Catering: In-house. Entrees range from $65 to $85 per person.
Rental Fee: Varies. Call for more information.
Parking: Parking lot nearby.
Note: Wedding ceremonies are permitted.

McLean Gardens Ballroom   202-966-9781

3811 Porter Street, N.W. • Washington, DC 20016

McLean Gardens Ballroom is a historic special-event facility in northwest Washington, D.C., central to Georgetown, Washington Cathedral and Embassy Row. The Ballroom boasts a 40-foot ceiling, is furnished in Williamsburg antiques, and has the appearance of a large intimate living room. It has two working fireplaces, five grand chandeliers, six 20-foot windows with a view and tremendous architectural details.

Capacity: 150 seated; 350 standing.
Catering: You must provide your own caterer.
Rental Fee: $2,250 for 8 hours, includes round tables.
Parking: Residential parking. Valet parking can be arranged.
Note: Wedding ceremonies are permitted.

Meridian House   202-939-5592

1630 Crescent Place, N.W. • Washington, DC 20009

Considered by many to be the best example of French urban architecture in the United States, Meridian House was built in 1921 as the retirement home for American Ambassador Irwin Laughlen. Meridian's entrance features an impressive limestone facade with solid oak doors, while the style of Louis XVI is reflected throughout the home's interior. Meridian House, renowned for its formal pebbled terrace shaded by linden trees, has a spacious lawn and gardens which make a perfect setting for outdoor events.

Capacity: 200 seated with dance floor; 350 standing.
Catering: You must provide your own caterer.
Rental Fee: $5,500.
Parking: Parking on premises. Valet parking can be arranged.
Restrictions: No red food or beverages. No cash bars. No throwing confetti, etc. No smoking.
Note: Wedding ceremonies are permitted indoors or outdoors.

The Mexican Cultural Institute   202-728-1670

2829 16th Street, N.W. • Washington, DC 20009

On the first floor, the entrance hall boasts an 18th-century baroque altar piece. Positioned under a magnificent staircase is an antique marble table and beautiful Talavera jar. The José Clemente

Orozco Gallery, with 600 feet of exhibition space, and the Auditorio Juarez have proven to be excellent spaces for art exhibits, conferences, slide shows, theatrical and dance performances, musical events and receptions. On the second floor, the restored Music Room, a replica of a salon at the Fontainebleau castle in France, has outstanding acoustics and is ideal for chamber music. The Golden Room, decorated in the French Renaissance style, is distinguished by a Federal convex mirror hanging over its marble fireplace and beautiful seascapes of Venice by the American artist Lucien Powell. In the elegant Dining Room, a Bacarat crystal chandelier, hand-carved furniture, and a painting by Benjamin Dominguez adds grace and charm. Muralist Roberto Cueva del Rio decorated the Atrium, using fine tiles produced in his native Puebla. The colorful tiles are geared acoustically for concerts and background music.

Capacity: 200 seated; 300 standing.
Catering: You must provide your own caterer.
Rental Fee: $3,000 and up.
Parking: On the premises.
Restrictions: No smoking.
Note: Wedding ceremonies are permitted.

Morrison-Clark Inn 1-800-332-7898/202-898-1200

**Massachusetts Avenue and Eleventh Street, N.W.
Washington, DC 20001**

The Morrison-Clark Historic Inn and Restaurant is a Victorian mansion located in the heart of Washington, D.C. It is the only inn to be listed on the National Register of Historic Places in the nation's capital. Built in 1864, this elegant Victorian inn offers modern comforts amidst Old-World grandeur and historic charm. Nationally ranked in *Gourmet* magazine, the restaurant features New American cuisine with southern and regional influences. The restaurant is also consistently featured in the *Washington Post's* annual "50 Favorite Restaurants." Each dining room is individually decorated and appointed with period furnishings. During pleasant weather, guests can enjoy the enclosed garden courtyard.

Capacity: 84 seated; 100 standing; 130 with tent.
Catering: In-house. Entrees range from $37 and up per person. Cake cutting fee if you provide own cake.
Parking: Parking on premises and nearby lots. Valet parking available.
Note: Wedding ceremonies are permitted.

National Museum
of Women in the Arts   202-783-5000

1250 New York Avenue, N.W. • Washington, DC 20005

A beautiful and well-equipped space is available for corporate and private events of all kinds. Conveniently located at New York Avenue and 13th Street, N.W., the museum is close to downtown hotels, Metro Center, the White House, Convention Center and other attractions in the heart of the nation's capital. The ground floor of the facility offers an ample reception area and exquisite ballroom. Sweeping double staircases and balustrades lead upward to a mezzanine, where guests may promenade or gaze upon the festivities below. Several galleries are also available for smaller groups, as well as the newest addition, the Reception Room in the Elisabeth A. Kasser Wing. These rooms offer the surroundings of outstanding works of art, making the event truly special. The museum's 200-seat theater/auditorium is comfortable, beautiful and functional. Outfitted with state-of-the-art Dolby sound and professional motion picture and slide capabilities, it is ideal for meetings, seminars and small performances of all kinds. Fees for the use of the museum include a donation to the museum, which is tax deductible to the extent permissible by law.

Capacity: 550 seated; 1,100 standing; 80 seated, 100 standing in Reception Room; 200 seated in Auditorium.

Catering: Approved caterers list or your own caterer. Entrees range from $18 and up.

Rental Fee: Great Hall $8,000 to $12,000. Third Floor $2,000 to $3,500. Reception Room $1,250 to $2,500. Auditorium $800 to $1,250.

Parking: Parking lot nearby. Valet parking available.

Note: Wedding ceremonies are permitted.

National Press Club   202-662-7597

529 14th Street, N.W. • Washington, DC 20045

The National Press Club, with its historic atmosphere, stately decor, and prestigious location two blocks from the White House, will lend a note of distinction to your special event. The Club's two lounges are well suited for wedding ceremonies and cocktail receptions. The traditional Holeman Lounge features a working gas fireplace, built-in bar, and hardwood floors, while the First Amendment Lounge boasts a picturesque view from windows that span floor to ceiling. Adjacent to the lounges is a large ballroom with two balconies and a rolling mahogany ceiling. The staff will tailor the menu to your satisfaction, and will assist in planning every detail of your event. The Club provides all equipment including tables, chairs, linens, china, glassware, and silverware.

Capacity:	360 seated with dance floor; 500 standing.
Catering:	In-house. Entree prices vary. Minimum requirement of $5,000 food and beverage purchases on weekends and holidays.
Rental Fee:	Varies. Call for more information.
Parking:	Parking garages are nearby. Valet parking can be arranged.
Note:	Wedding ceremonies are permitted.

Occidental Grill   202-737-4147

1475 Pennsylvania Avenue, N.W. • Washington, DC 20004

Occidental Grill provides elegant private dining facilities for small or large wedding receptions, rehearsal dinners, brunches, and other parties. Just steps from the White House, the restaurant specializes in regional American cuisine — intriguing appetizers, grilled meats, seafood, and rich desserts. The Occidental Grill, with more than 2500 autographed photographs of this century's powerful and famous, creates an atmosphere which is quintessentially Washington, D.C. Since 1906, Occidental Grill has maintained a reputation for innovative food and friendly, attentive service.

Capacity:	150 seated; 300 standing.
Catering:	In-house. Entrees vary from $20 to $35 per person. Cake cutting fee if you provide your own cake.
Rental Fee:	Varies.
Parking:	Parking garage nearby. Valet parking available. Complimentary after 6:00 p.m.
Note:	Wedding ceremonies are permitted.

Old Cafritz House   202-829-1388

5001 16th Street, N.W. • Washington, DC 20011

Built in the roaring 20s on Washington's "Avenue of the Presidents," the Old Cafritz House is a Mediterranean-style home of grand character. The showcase of the house is the 1,000 square-foot Grand Salon, which has been brought back to its original splendor with 14-foot beamed ceilings, wrought iron chandeliers, Mexican tile floor, and beautiful period artwork. Nineteen windows provide the room with spectacular light by day and romantic charm at night. The dining room is spacious with a beautiful beamed ceiling, a large crystal chandelier, and French doors leading to a beautifully manicured garden, landscaped with annuals and perennials ranging from hydrangeas and crepe myrtle trees to hibiscus and palms. In addition there is a beautiful sunroom and sitting room inside.

Capacity:	100 seated; 125 standing; 120 seated or standing in garden.

Catering: Approved caterers list only.
Rental Fee: $1,600 to $2,200.
Restrictions: No smoking inside mansion.
Note: Residential parking only, but very plentiful.

Robert Todd Lincoln House   202-739-1030

c/o Capitol Catering
1300 17th Street, N.W. • Washington, DC 20036

The Robert Todd Lincoln House, within walking distance of fashionable Connecticut Avenue and not too far from the White House itself, is the scene of gracious Pen Women receptions and executive board meetings. The twenty-room mansion was built in 1895 and gained special note when it was leased for several months in the winter of 1920 by Robert Todd Lincoln, eldest son of the former president. The spacious entrance hall, glittering chandeliers in drawing room and dining room, the sweeping staircase and the nine fireplaces each with its original mantel provide an air of dignity. The beauty of the house has been enhanced by handsome furnishings received from estates or donated by individuals from all parts of the United States.

Capacity: 50 seated; 150 standing.
Catering: In-house. Entrees range from $30 to $100 per person.
               Cake cutting fee if provide own cake.
Rental Fee: $500 to $1,000.
Parking: Parking lot nearby.
Restrictions: No smoking.
Note: Wedding ceremonies are permitted.

Swann House   202-265-4414

1808 New Hampshire Avenue • Washington, DC 20009

Swann House was designed and built in 1883 in grand Richardson Romanesque style by Walter Paris, an architect in service to the British Crown and famous Washington watercolorist. Enter through an expansive arched front porch and feel the ambiance created by 12-foot ceilings outlined in 18-inch crown moldings. Fluted woodwork, inlaid wood floors, crystal chandeliers, and elaborate mantels enhance the elegance of this fine mansion. Open, airy spaces invite entertaining. Through three sets of French doors, a sunroom with a wet bar overlooks the lush private garden and pool. The mansion offers a wonderful assortment of decks, porches, patios and gardens in which to linger. Located on a prominent corner in the Dupont Circle historic district, it is located just a few blocks from the Dupont Circle Metro Station. You will find it is just a 15-minute walk to the White House and many of Washington's most famous landmarks. The Swann House is available for rent by individuals and groups for business meetings and social functions. It is an ideal venue for wedding receptions, cocktail parties, and rehearsal dinners as well as board meetings, corporate retreats, small conferences and luncheons. The Swann House offers six charmingly decorated bedrooms and suites, each with a private bath and several with working fireplaces. Other amenities include oversized showers, antique pedestal sinks, and a Jacuzzi tub.

Capacity: 60 seated; 125 standing; 25 in garden.
Catering: Approved caterers list.
Rental Fee: $1,800.
Parking: Parking lot nearby. Valet parking may be arranged.
Restrictions: No amplified music.
Note: Wedding ceremonies are permitted.

The National Aquarium   202-482-2826

U.S. Department of Commerce Bldg., Room B-075
14th Street and Constitution Ave., N.W.
Washington, DC 20230

History and underwater adventures give atmosphere to the intimate spaces of the National Aquarium. This country's first public aquarium, originally founded in 1873, hides in the basement of the Department of Commerce Building. Utilizing its limited space, caterers can wonderfully transform this daytime aquarium into a setting for a memorable evening. Use the creative backdrop of 70 tanks of curious fish for your next social, literary or political gathering.

Capacity: 150 seated; 300 standing.
Catering: Approved caterers list or your own caterer. No kitchen facilities.
Rental Fee: $1,500.
Parking: On-street parking, parking lots and access to metro.
Restrictions: Available only between 5:30 p.m.-11:30 p.m.
Note: Wedding ceremonies are permitted.

White-Meyer House   202-939-5592

1624 Crescent Place, N.W. • Washington, DC 20009

This classic brick mansion was built in 1911 by American Ambassador Henry White and later purchased by *Washington Post* owner Eugene Meyer. The Georgian mansion features formal wrought iron gates and a circular driveway leading visitors up to a pillared entrance into the home's stately, grand interior. Rich walnut paneled double doors from the reception hall open into the sitting room, library and dining room. Beyond is a paved terrace overlooking the city, which provides a particularly lovely view at night. Traveling art exhibits are also regularly on display in the home.

Capacity: 175 seated with dance floor; 250 standing.
Catering: You must supply your own caterer.
Rental Fee: $5,500.

Parking: Parking on premises and in nearby lot. Valet parking
                possible.
Restrictions: No red food or beverages. No cash bars. No throwing
                confetti, etc. No smoking.
Note: Wedding ceremonies are permitted.

Woman's National Democratic Club 202-232-7363

1526 New Hampshire Avenue, N.W.
Washington, DC 20036

Built in 1892 as a private home, the Woman's National Democratic Club is one of Washington's most historic and elegant
establishments. The mansion, beautifully appointed with crystal
chandeliers, oriental rugs and period furniture, is an inviting
setting for your wedding, reception or celebration. You may hold
your ceremony in the Post/Hamlin Rooms, and then dance the
night away in the Stevenson Ballroom. For striking wedding
photos, pose in the entrance foyer with its graceful staircase, or on
the club's lovely patio. There are six additional rooms upstairs,
and a balcony that overlooks the patio. The club's professional
staff will assist you in planning your menu and will ensure your
event is truly memorable.

Capacity: 150 seated; 300 standing; 50 in garden; 100 seated in
                 Post/Hamlin Rooms.
Catering: In-house. Entrees range from $35 for lunch and $45
                 for dinner.
Rental Fee: $1,500 for members, $3,000 for non-members.
Parking: Parking garages are nearby. Valet parking may be
                 arranged.
Restrictions: No smoking. No rice, birdseed or confetti.
Note: Wedding ceremonies are permitted.

Woodrow Wilson House   202-387-4062

2340 S Street, N.W. • Washington, DC 20008

The Woodrow Wilson House, Washington's only presidential
museum, is located in the historic Embassy Row neighborhood.
The 1915 Georgian Revival townhouse offers the use of five
historically furnished rooms, a terrace and garden. Groups under
40 may dine in the presidential dining room and stroll through the
library and drawing room with their cocktails. Many of the
Wilsons' own wedding gifts and gifts of state from around the
world are on display. Larger groups may be accommodated for
wedding ceremonies in the garden or on the terrace with a tent.
The Woodrow Wilson House is a National Trust Historic Site.

Capacity: 40 seated; 200 standing; 125 in garden; 150 with tent.
Catering: Approved caterers list.
Rental Fee: $2,500.

Parking: On-street parking available for small groups. Valet parking available.

Restrictions: No red liquids. No smoking. No lit tapers or sterno in house. No amplified music or dancing in house. Music is allowed in garden, but must cease at 10:00 p.m.

Note: Wedding ceremonies are permitted.

1789 Restaurant   202-965-1789

1226 36th Street, N.W. • Washington, DC 20007

Located in a Federal-style townhouse, this fine dining establishment serves contemporary American cuisine in a formal atmosphere. The Middleburg Room, seats 56 people, has a charming bay window. The more casual F. Scott Fitzgerald next door is available for evening and daytime rentals. Decorated with original art from the 1920s and 1930s, F. Scott's has a dance floor, DJ booth and full bar.

Capacity: 60 seated; 75 standing.
Catering: In-house. Entrees range from $50 to $75 per person. Cake cutting fee if you provide your own cake.
Parking: Parking lot nearby. Complimentary valet parking is available.
Note: Wedding ceremonies are permitted.

Morrison-Clark Inn   1-800-332-7898/202-898-1200

**Massachusetts Avenue and Eleventh Street, N.W.
Washington, DC 20001**

The Morrison-Clark Historic Inn and Restaurant is a Victorian mansion located in the heart of Washington, D.C. It is the only inn to be listed on the National Register of Historic Places in the nation's capital. Built in 1864, this elegant Victorian inn offers modern comforts amidst Old-World grandeur and historic charm. Nationally ranked in *Gourmet* magazine, the restaurant features New American cuisine with southern and regional influences. The restaurant is also consistently featured in the *Washington Post's* annual "50 Favorite Restaurants." Each dining room is individually decorated and appointed with period furnishings. During pleasant weather, guests can enjoy the enclosed garden courtyard.

Capacity: 84 seated; 100 standing; 130 with tent.
Catering: In-house. Entrees range from $37 and up per person. Cake cutting fee if you provide own cake.
Parking: Parking on premises and nearby lots. Valet parking available.
Note: Wedding ceremonies are permitted.

Swann House   202-265-4414

1808 New Hampshire Avenue • Washington, DC 20009

Swann House was designed and built in 1883 in grand Richardson Romanesque style by Walter Paris, an architect in service to the British Crown and famous Washington watercolorist. Enter through an expansive arched front porch and feel the ambiance created by 12-foot ceilings outlined in 18-inch crown moldings. Fluted woodwork, inlaid wood floors, crystal chandeliers, and elaborate mantels enhance the elegance of this fine mansion. Open, airy spaces invite entertaining. Through three sets of French doors, a sunroom with a wet bar overlooks the lush private garden and pool. The mansion offers a wonderful assortment of decks, porches, patios and gardens in which to linger. Located on a prominent corner in the Dupont Circle historic district, it is located just a few blocks from the Dupont Circle Metro Station. You will find it is just a 15-minute walk to the White House and many of Washington's most famous landmarks. The Swann House is available for rent by individuals and groups for business meetings and social functions. It is an ideal venue for wedding receptions, cocktail parties, and rehearsal dinners as well as board meetings, corporate retreats, small conferences and luncheons. The Swann House offers six charmingly decorated bedrooms and suites, each with a private bath and several with working fireplaces. Other amenities include oversized showers, antique pedestal sinks, and a Jacuzzi tub.

Capacity:	60 seated; 125 standing; 25 in garden.
Catering:	Approved caterers list.
Rental Fee:	$1,800.
Parking:	Parking lot nearby. Valet parking may be arranged.
Restrictions:	No amplified music.
Note:	Wedding ceremonies are permitted.

Dumbarton House   202-337-2288

2715 Que Street, N.W. • Washington, DC 20007

Dating back to the first years of the American Republic, Dumbarton House has stood on the heights of Georgetown for almost two centuries. From the library to the dining room, through the music room to the parlor to the bedrooms upstairs, this stately brick home is filled with furniture, paintings, textiles, silver, ceramics and other period treasures. To celebrate its centennial in 1991, The National Society renovated Dumbarton House, adding a park and a large Palladian-inspired room which opens onto a terraced courtyard. Enjoy cocktails in the upper garden and dinner in the Belle Vue Room. The Belle Vue Room, with its 15-foot ceiling, hosts Society programs, educational presentations and period concerts, and is available for a variety of individual and corporate events. When docents are present, the museum is open for tour.

Capacity: 150 seated; 170 standing.
Catering: Approved caterers list.
Rental Fee: $4,000 for 4 hours.
Parking: Street parking normally available.
Restrictions: Band acceptable; no DJs. Tent mandatory.

Ella Smith House   703-739-1030

c/o Capitol Catering
3rd and Maryland Avenue, N.E. • Washington, DC 20002

Two blocks from the Capitol Building on the Senate side is this handsome Victorian mansion, built in 1889. Even as you approach the townhouse, you'll notice several distinctive features: the capacious front courtyard, its beautiful rose garden and the house's charming turret. Inside is an unusually wide center hall with a spectacular 40-foot curving staircase, complete with the original cherrywood railing. In addition to the hall, the first floor holds three rooms, each with its original fireplace, plaster cornices and woodwork. On the turret side of the house is the salon, where plush banquettes fit snugly against the bay window. Across the hall is the dining room, with paneled wainscoting and brass chandelier. Beyond the dining room is the kitchen, where a grill rests upon the century-old brick of what was once the fireplace. The second and third floor rooms are available to guests who want to view the Capitol from the turret windows.

Capacity: 40 seated; 75 standing; 25 in garden.
Catering: In-house. Entrees range from $30 to $100 per person.
Rental Fee: $500.
Restrictions: No smoking.
Note: Wedding ceremonies are permitted.

Erickson House   703-739-1030

c/o Capitol Catering
437 New Jersey Avenue, S.E. • Washington, DC 20003

Four blocks from the U.S. Capitol on the House side is this private home of a retired naval officer. Erickson House is a century-old painted brick townhouse filled with an astonishing array of oriental art and furniture acquired by the owner during his travels — Vietnamese vases, Japanese woodblock prints and Peruvian mirrors. Your event will take place in the living room, spacious hall and dining room. A large bay window, a working fireplace and sliding paneled doors that can close for privacy add to the living room's charm. Foreign art treasures rest on the oak floor of the generously sized hall. Past the staircase leading to the second floor is the dining room, which has an expandable teak table and a large harp from Paraguay. When the weather is pleasant, your party can spill out into the fenced-in front yard. From here, you can look up the street and get a tremendous view of the Capitol.

Capacity: 20 seated; 75 standing; 10 in garden.
Catering: In-house. Entree range from $30 to $100 per person.
Rental Fee: $500.
Restrictions: No smoking.
Note: Wedding ceremonies are permitted.

H.H. Leonards Mansion
on "O" Street   202-659-8787

2020 O Street, N.W. • Washington, DC 20036

Built in 1891, this elegant five-story Victorian mansion combines elegant ambience with the best of modern technology. Beautifully decorated with fine art, antiques, crystal chandeliers and fireplaces, the mansion is an enchanting and magical place. Amenities include elevator access, gorgeous bathrooms, fully equipped kitchens, and overnight accommodations. The mansion is a popular site for weddings, corporate meetings, and other events.

Capacity: 200.
Catering: In-house. Entrees range from $35 to $600 per guest.
Rental Fee: Private membership fee of $300/year.
Parking: Parking lot nearby, residential parking, and valet parking available.
Restrictions: Bus, valet and limo controls. No photographs outside.
Note: Guest rooms are available. Wedding ceremonies are permitted.

McLean Gardens Ballroom   202-966-9781

3811 Porter Street, N.W. • Washington, DC 20016

McLean Gardens Ballroom is a historic special-event facility in northwest Washington, D.C., central to Georgetown, Washington Cathedral and Embassy Row. The Ballroom boasts a 40-foot ceiling, is furnished in Williamsburg antiques, and has the appearance of a large intimate living room. It has two working fireplaces, five grand chandeliers, six 20-foot windows with a view and tremendous architectural details.

Capacity: 150 seated; 350 standing.
Catering: You must provide your own caterer.
Rental Fee: $2,250 for 8 hours, includes round tables.
Parking: Residential parking. Valet parking can be arranged.
Note: Wedding ceremonies are permitted.

Meridian House   202-939-5592

1630 Crescent Place, N.W. • Washington, DC 20009

Considered by many to be the best example of French urban architecture in the United States, Meridian House was built in 1921 as the retirement home for American Ambassador Irwin Laughlen. Meridian's entrance features an impressive limestone facade with solid oak doors, while the style of Louis XVI is reflected throughout the home's interior. Meridian House, renowned for its formal pebbled terrace shaded by linden trees, has a spacious lawn and gardens which make a perfect setting for outdoor events.

Capacity: 200 seated with dance floor; 350 standing.
Catering: You must provide your own caterer.
Rental Fee: $5,500.
Parking: Parking on premises. Valet parking can be arranged.
Restrictions: No red food or beverages. No cash bars. No throwing confetti, etc. No smoking.
Note: Wedding ceremonies are permitted indoors or outdoors.

Old Cafritz House   202-829-1388

5001 16th Street, N.W. • Washington, DC 20011

Built in the roaring 20s on Washington's "Avenue of the Presidents," the Old Cafritz House is a Mediterranean-style home of grand character. The showcase of the house is the 1,000 square-foot Grand Salon, which has been brought back to its original splendor with 14-foot beamed ceilings, wrought iron chandeliers, Mexican tile floor, and beautiful period artwork. Nineteen windows provide the room with spectacular light by day and romantic charm at night. The dining room is spacious with a beautiful beamed ceiling, a large crystal chandelier, and French doors leading to a beautifully manicured garden, landscaped with annuals and perennials ranging from hydrangeas and crepe myrtle trees, to hibiscus and palms. In addition there is a beautiful sunroom and sitting room inside.

Capacity: 100 seated; 125 standing; 120 seated or standing in garden.
Catering: Approved caterers list only.
Rental Fee: $1,600 to $2,200.
Restrictions: No smoking inside mansion.
Note: Residential parking only, but very plentiful.

Robert Todd Lincoln House   202-739-1030

1300 17th Street, N.W. • Washington, DC 20036

The Robert Todd Lincoln House, within walking distance of fashionable Connecticut Avenue and not too far from the White House itself, is the scene of gracious Pen Women receptions and executive board meetings. The twenty-room mansion was built in 1895 and gained special note when it was leased for several months in the winter of 1920 by Robert Todd Lincoln, eldest son of the former president. The spacious entrance hall, glittering chandeliers in drawing room and dining room, the sweeping staircase and the nine fireplaces each with its original mantel provide an air of dignity. The beauty of the house has been enhanced by handsome furnishings received from estates or donated by individuals from all parts of the United States.

Capacity: 50 seated; 150 standing.
Catering: In-house. Entrees range from $30 to $100 per person. Cake cutting fee if provide own cake.
Rental Fee: $500 to $1,000.
Parking: Parking lot nearby.
Restrictions: No smoking.
Note: Wedding ceremonies are permitted.

Swann House   202-265-4414

1808 New Hampshire Avenue • Washington, DC 20009

Swann House was designed and built in 1883 in grand Richardson Romanesque style by Walter Paris, an architect in service to the British Crown and famous Washington watercolorist. Enter through an expansive arched front porch and feel the ambiance created by 12-foot ceilings outlined in 18-inch crown moldings. Fluted woodwork, inlaid wood floors, crystal chandeliers, and elaborate mantels enhance the elegance of this fine mansion. Open, airy spaces invite entertaining. Through three sets of French doors, a sunroom with a wet bar overlooks the lush private garden and pool. The mansion offers a wonderful assortment of decks, porches, patios and gardens in which to linger. Located on a prominent corner in the Dupont Circle historic district, it is located just a few blocks from the Dupont Circle Metro Station. You will find it is just a 15-minute walk to the White House and many of Washington's most famous landmarks. The Swann House is available for rent by individuals and groups for business meetings and social functions. It is an ideal venue for wedding receptions, cocktail parties, and rehearsal dinners as well as board meetings, corporate retreats, small conferences and luncheons. The Swann House offers six charmingly decorated bedrooms and suites, each with a private bath and several with working fireplaces. Other amenities include oversized showers, antique pedestal sinks, and a Jacuzzi tub.

Capacity: 60 seated; 125 standing; 25 in garden.
Catering: Approved caterers list.
Rental Fee: $1,800.
Parking: Parking lot nearby. Valet parking may be arranged.
Restrictions: No amplified music.
Note: Wedding ceremonies are permitted.

White-Meyer House   202-939-5592

1624 Crescent Place, N.W. • Washington, DC 20009

This classic brick mansion was built in 1911 by American Ambassador Henry White and later purchased by *Washington Post* owner Eugene Meyer. The Georgian mansion features formal wrought iron gates and a circular driveway leading visitors up to a pillared entrance into the home's stately, grand interior. Rich walnut paneled double doors from the reception hall open into the sitting room, library and dining room. Beyond is a paved terrace overlooking the city, which provides a particularly lovely view at night. Traveling art exhibits are also regularly on display in the home.

Capacity: 175 seated with dance floor; 250 standing.
Catering: You must supply your own caterer.
Rental Fee: $5,500.
Parking: Parking on premises and in nearby lot. Valet parking possible.
Restrictions: No red food or beverages. No cash bars. No throwing confetti, etc. No smoking.
Note: Wedding ceremonies are permitted.

Woman's National Democratic Club   202-232-7363

1526 New Hampshire Avenue, N.W.
Washington, DC 20036

Built in 1892 as a private home, the Woman's National Democratic Club is one of Washington's most historic and elegant establishments. The mansion, beautifully appointed with crystal chandeliers, oriental rugs and period furniture, is an inviting setting for your wedding, reception or celebration. You may hold your ceremony in the Post/Hamlin Rooms, and then dance the night away in the Stevenson Ballroom. For striking wedding photos, pose in the entrance foyer with its graceful staircase, or on the club's lovely patio. There are six additional rooms upstairs, and a balcony that overlooks the patio. The club's professional staff will assist you in planning your menu and will ensure your event is truly memorable.

Capacity: 150 seated; 300 standing; 50 in garden; 100 seated in Post/Hamlin Rooms.

Catering: In-house. Entrees range from $35 for lunch and $45 for dinner.

Rental Fee: $1,500 for members, $3,000 for non-members.

Parking: Parking garages are nearby. Valet parking may be arranged.

Restrictions: No smoking. No rice, birdseed or confetti.

Note: Wedding ceremonies are permitted.

Woodrow Wilson House   202-387-4062

2340 S Street, N.W. • Washington, DC 20008

The Woodrow Wilson House, Washington's only presidential museum, is located in the historic Embassy Row neighborhood. The 1915 Georgian Revival townhouse offers the use of five historically furnished rooms, a terrace and garden. Groups under 40 may dine in the presidential dining room and stroll through the library and drawing room with their cocktails. Many of the Wilsons' own wedding gifts and gifts of state from around the world are on display. Larger groups may be accommodated for wedding ceremonies in the garden or on the terrace with a tent. The Woodrow Wilson House is a National Trust Historic Site.

Capacity: 40 seated; 200 standing; 125 in garden; 150 with tent.

Catering: Approved caterers list.

Rental Fee: $2,500.

Parking: On-street parking available for small groups. Valet parking available.

Restrictions: No red liquids. No smoking. No lit tapers or sterno in house. No amplified music or dancing in house. Music is allowed in garden, but must cease at 10:00 p.m.

Note: Wedding ceremonies are permitted.

Decatur House Museum   202-842-0917

748 Jackson Place, N.W. • Washington, DC 20006

Right in the heart of the District, the Decatur House Museum and Carriage House provides an elegant wedding environment. With its vaulted ceilings and floor-to-ceiling French windows opening onto a spacious courtyard, the Decatur House has carried on a 175-year tradition as a premier locale for wedding ceremonies. The first celebration was the marriage of President Monroe's daughter. This functional multi-faceted site includes a courtyard and a contemporary 2,100 square-foot Carriage House.

Capacity: Carriage House interior holds 120 seated; 250 standing; Courtyard with tent holds 220 seated; and standing combined space can accommodate 500.
Catering: Approved caterers list.
Rental Fee: $3,000 for reception. $3,500 for ceremony and reception.
Parking: Parking garages nearby.
Restrictions: No music after 11:30 p.m. Parties must end at midnight.
Note: You pay for the time guests are on site, not for caterer's set-up and take-down.

The Folger Shakespeare Library   202-675-0324

201 East Capitol Street, S.E. • Washington, DC 20003

The Folger Shakespeare Library, opened in 1932, is listed on the National Register of Historic Places. The following spaces are available for private special events. The Folger's Great Hall is styled after the royal reception rooms of Elizabethan England. Capacity is 250 for a reception, and 180 for dinner. Modeled on the royal and collegial Tudor style halls of Shakespeare's day, the Old Reading Room is used for research by scholars from around the world. Capacity is 250 for a reception, and 180 for dinner. The Board Room, decorated in an English Regency style, has a large retractable screen for slide and film presentations. Capacity is 50 for a reception or dinner. The Founder's Room evokes a Tudor-like atmosphere. Capacity is 40 for a reception or dinner. The Elizabethan Garden is also available for special events and features a garden with herbs and flowers popular in Shakespeare's time. The Office of Special Events provides liaison assistance with caterers, decorators, florists, valet parking, musicians, actors, Museum Shop services, and docents.

Capacity: 40-180 seated; 60-500 standing; 150 in garden; 150 with tent.
Catering: Approved caterers list.
Rental Fee: $2,500 to $25,000.
Parking: Valet parking available.

Restrictions: No smoking. Foods that leave stains, such as berries, are discouraged. The Library reserves the right of final approval of caterers and vendors for an event.
Note: Wedding ceremonies are permitted.

H.H. Leonards Mansion on "O" Street   202-659-8787

2020 O Street, N.W. • Washington, DC 20036

Built in 1891, this elegant five-story Victorian mansion combines elegant ambience with the best of modern technology. Beautifully decorated with fine art, antiques, crystal chandeliers and fireplaces, the mansion is an enchanting and magical place. Amenities include elevator access, gorgeous bathrooms, fully equipped kitchens, and overnight accommodations. The mansion is a popular site for weddings, corporate meetings, and other events.

Capacity: 200.
Catering: In-house. Entrees range from $35 to $600 per guest.
Rental Fee: Private membership fee of $300/year.
Restrictions: Bus, valet and limo controls. No photographs outside.
Parking: Parking lot nearby, residential parking, and valet parking available.
Note: Guest rooms are available. Wedding ceremonies are permitted.

Meridian House   202-939-5592

1630 Crescent Place, N.W. • Washington, DC 20009

Considered by many to be the best example of French urban architecture in the United States, Meridian House was built in 1921 as the retirement home for American Ambassador Irwin Laughlen. Meridian's entrance features an impressive limestone facade with solid oak doors, while the style of Louis XVI is reflected throughout the home's interior. Meridian House, renowned for its formal pebbled terrace shaded by linden trees, has a spacious lawn and gardens which make a perfect setting for outdoor events.

Capacity: 200 seated with dance floor; 350 standing.
Catering: You must provide your own caterer.
Rental Fee: $5,500.
Parking: Parking on premises. Valet parking can be arranged.
Restrictions: No red food or beverages. No cash bars. No throwing confetti, etc. No smoking.
Note: Wedding ceremonies are permitted indoors or outdoors.

The National Aquarium   202-482-2826

U.S. Department of Commerce Bldg., Room B-075
14th Street and Constitution Ave., N.W.
Washington, DC 20230

History and underwater adventures give atmosphere to the intimate spaces of the National Aquarium. This country's first public aquarium, originally founded in 1873, hides in the basement of the Department of Commerce Building. Utilizing its limited space, caterers can wonderfully transform this daytime aquarium into a setting for a memorable evening. Use the creative backdrop of 70 tanks of curious fish for your next social, literary or political gathering.

Capacity: 150 seated; 300 standing.
Catering: Approved caterers list or your own caterer. No kitchen facilities.
Rental Fee: $1,500.
Parking: On-street parking, parking lots and access to metro.
Restrictions: Available only between 5:30 p.m.-11:30 p.m.
Note: Wedding ceremonies are permitted.

National Museum
of Women in the Arts   202-783-5000

1250 New York Avenue, N.W. • Washington, DC 20005

A beautiful and well-equipped space is available for corporate and private events of all kinds. Conveniently located at New York Avenue and 13th Street, N.W., the museum is close to downtown hotels, Metro Center, the White House, Convention Center and other attractions in the heart of the nation's capital. The ground floor of the facility offers an ample reception area and exquisite ballroom. Sweeping double staircases and balustrades lead upward to a mezzanine, where guests may promenade or gaze upon the festivities below. Several galleries are also available for smaller groups, as well as the newest addition, the Reception Room in the Elisabeth A. Kasser Wing. These rooms offer the surroundings of outstanding works of art, making the event truly special. The museum's 200-seat theater/auditorium is comfortable, beautiful and functional. Outfitted with state-of-the-art Dolby sound and professional motion picture and slide capabilities, it is ideal for meetings, seminars and small performances of all kinds. Fees for the use of the museum include a donation to the museum, which is tax deductible to the extent permissible by law.

Capacity: 550 seated; 1,100 standing; 80 seated, 100 standing in Reception Room; 200 seated in Auditorium.
Catering: Approved caterers list or your own caterer. Entrees range from $18 and up.
Rental Fee: Great Hall $8,000 to $12,000. Third Floor $2,000 to $3,500. Reception Room $1,250 to $2,500.

Auditorium $800 to $1,250.
Parking: Parking lot nearby. Valet parking available.
Note: Wedding ceremonies are permitted.

Walsh-Reckord Hall of States   202-789-0031

c/o National Guard Association of the United States
One Massachusetts Avenue, N.W. • Washington, DC 20001

Located in Washington's Capitol Hill area, one block from the
magnificent Union Station, the National Guard Memorial is ideal
for meetings, fund raisers, luncheons, seminars or dinners. The
striking Walsh-Reckord Hall of States, symbolic of the National
Guard's state-federal partnership, provides a dramatic backdrop
for any function. The Memorial, home of the National Guard
Association of the United States, was designed by an award-
winning architect and maintains the true Federalist architecture
of its neighboring buildings. From the rare Tennessee pink marble
that graces the foyer and building interior to the Constitutional
green of the Hall of States, the National Guard Memorial offers
the perfect ambiance for a media function, reception, dinner or
other special event.

Capacity: 200 seated; 500 standing.
Catering: You must provide your own caterer. A fee is required
               for use of kitchen facilities, and tables and chairs.
Rental Fee: $600 to $2,100.
Parking: Paid parking on premises and nearby parking lots.
Note: Wedding ceremonies are permitted.

White-Meyer House   202-939-5592

1624 Crescent Place, N.W. • Washington, DC 20009

This classic brick mansion was built in 1911 by American Ambassador Henry White and later purchased by *Washington Post* owner
Eugene Meyer. The Georgian mansion features formal wrought
iron gates and a circular driveway leading visitors up to a pillared
entrance into the home's stately, grand interior. Rich walnut
paneled double doors from the reception hall open into the sitting
room, library and dining room. Beyond is a paved terrace overlooking the city, which provides a particularly lovely view at
night. Traveling art exhibits are also regularly on display in the
home.

Capacity: 175 seated with dance floor; 250 standing.
Catering: You must supply your own caterer.
Rental Fee: $5,500.
Parking: Parking on premises and in nearby lot. Valet parking
                possible.
Restrictions: No red food or beverages. No cash bars. No throwing
                confetti, etc. No smoking.
Note: Wedding ceremonies are permitted.

Woodrow Wilson House   202-387-4062

2340 S Street, N.W. • Washington, DC 20008

The Woodrow Wilson House, Washington's only presidential museum, is located in the historic Embassy Row neighborhood. The 1915 Georgian Revival townhouse offers the use of five historically furnished rooms, a terrace and garden. Groups under 40 may dine in the presidential dining room and stroll through the library and drawing room with their cocktails. Many of the Wilsons' own wedding gifts and gifts of state from around the world are on display. Larger groups may be accommodated for wedding ceremonies in the garden or on the terrace with a tent. The Woodrow Wilson House is a National Trust Historic Site.

Capacity: 40 seated; 200 standing; 125 in garden; 150 with tent.
Catering: Approved caterers list.
Rental Fee: $2,500.
Parking: On-street parking available for small groups. Valet parking available.
Restrictions: No red liquids. No smoking. No lit tapers or sterno in house. No amplified music or dancing in house. Music is allowed in garden, but must cease at 10:00 p.m.
Note: Wedding ceremonies are permitted.

1789 Restaurant   202-965-1789

1226 36th Street, N.W. • Washington, DC 20007

Located in a Federal-style townhouse, this fine dining establishment serves contemporary American cuisine in a formal atmosphere. The Middleburg Room, seats 56 people, has a charming bay window. The more casual F. Scott Fitzgerald next door is available for evening and daytime rentals. Decorated with original art from the 1920s and 1930s, F. Scott's has a dance floor, DJ booth and full bar.

Capacity: 60 seated; 75 standing.
Catering: In-house. Entrees range from $50 to $75 per person. Cake cutting fee if you provide your own cake.
Parking: Parking lot nearby. Complimentary valet parking is available.
Note: Wedding ceremonies are permitted.

America at Union Station   202-333-3011

c/o Ark Restaurants
3050 K Street, N.W. • Washington, DC 20007

America, situated on Capitol Hill in Union Station's Great Hall, has been featured in *Architectural Record* and many other design magazines. This multi-level eatery offers a myriad of dining options, from the station's concourse to top-tier window corners. Great views of the Capitol and surrounding areas help define the station's dramatic space. For events of 150 to 700 guests, you may reserve the entire restaurant.

Capacity: 390 seated; 700 standing.
Catering: In-house. Menus range from $15 to $40 per person.
Parking: On the premises and nearby parking lots.

B. Smith's Restaurant   202-333-3011

c/o Ark Restaurants
3050 K Street, N.W. • Washington, DC 20007

Barbara Smith brings her stylish New York restaurant concept to Union Station. This beaux arts style former presidential suite has been restored to its original turn-of-the-century decor, complete with vaulted ceilings, gold leaf accents and marble columns. Reminiscent of an era of opulence and elegance, B. Smith's will provide your guests with a unique sense of Washington. For events of 100 to 350 guests, you may reserve the entire restaurant.

Capacity: 175 seated; 350 standing.
Catering: In-house. Menus range from $15 to $40 per person.
Parking: On the premises and nearby parking lots.

Center Café   202-333-3011

3050 K Street, N.W. • Washington, DC 20007

A 2-story kiosk located in the center of historic Union Station, Center Café dominates the activity of the Main Hall. A unique and exciting party location, all of your guests will be at the center of activity in the opulence and grandeur which typifies Union Station. For events of 200 to 400 guests, you may reserve the entire restaurant. The Balcony is reached by circular brass stairways and features a marble central bar.

Capacity: 100 seated in The Terrace, 200 standing in The Terrace; 100 in The Balcony.
Catering: In-house. Menus range from $15 to $30 per person.
Parking: On the premises and nearby parking lots.

La Colline Restaurant   202-737-0400

400 N. Capitol Street, N.W. • Washington, DC 20001

Conveniently located across from Union Station, this wonderful space offers a magnificent view of the U.S. Capitol. This spectacular banquet room, with its contemporary decor, California redwood, beautiful hanging plants and floor-to-ceiling windows is a most unusual setting for your special day. The spacious terrace is perfect for wedding ceremonies and receptions during pleasant weather.

Capacity: 150 seated; 200 standing; 200 on the terrace.
Catering: In-house. Entrees range from $20 and up.
Parking: On the premises.
Note: Wedding ceremonies are permitted indoors or outdoors.

Occidental Grill   202-737-4147

1475 Pennsylvania Avenue, N.W. • Washington, DC 20004

Occidental Grill provides elegant private dining facilities for small or large wedding receptions, rehearsal dinners, brunches, and other parties. Just steps from the White House, the restaurant specializes in regional American cuisine — intriguing appetizers, grilled meats, seafood, and rich desserts. The Occidental Grill, with more than 2500 autographed photographs of this century's powerful and famous, creates an atmosphere which is quintessentially Washington, D.C. Since 1906, Occidental Grill has maintained a reputation for innovative food and friendly, attentive service.

Capacity: 150 seated; 300 standing.
Catering: In-house. Entrees vary from $20 to $35 per person. Cake cutting fee if you provide your own cake.

Rental Fee: Varies.
Parking: Parking garage nearby. Valet parking available. Complimentary after 6:00 p.m.
Note: Wedding ceremonies are permitted.

Odyssey Cruises   202-488-6010

600 Water Street, S.W. • Washington, DC 20024

Imagine exchanging vows on board the romantic *Odyssey* as it cruises the Potomac. Designed in the style of European canal ships and completely enclosed in glass, *Odyssey* provides a breathtaking view of the Capitol from the sparkling waters of the Potomac. From a ceremony against a stunning sunset to a fabulous four-course dinner, a cruise on *Odyssey* will be unforgettable. After dinner, enjoy *Odyssey's* inviting dance floors and professional entertainment. The experienced consulting and service staff will help you plan the perfect engagement party, bridal shower, rehearsal dinner, or other festivity. Party options include brunch, lunch, or dinner cruises.

Capacity: 600 seated/standing.
Catering: In-house.
Parking: Parking on premises and nearby parking lots.
Note: Wedding ceremonies are permitted.

Old Ebbitt Grill   202-347-4800

675 15th Street, N.W. • Washington, DC 20005

Old Ebbitt Grill has been a landmark gathering spot for this city's professionals, politicians, theatergoers and shoppers since 1856. Two private spaces are available. The Cabinet Room, which is fully enclosed, shares the ambience of the handsome main dining room. The Atrium is lovely, with a glass-enclosed ceiling, marble floor, and marble and gold fountain. The Atrium may be fully private or semi-private depending on group size. Old Ebbitt Grill is just around the corner from the White House, and a convenient walk to museums, monuments, cultural attractions, and shopping. Join the crowd assembled at the bar and in the high-backed booths of the handsome dining room for a fun-filled evening.

Capacity: 350 seated; 600 standing; 50 seated in Cabinet Room; 70 standing in Cabinet Room.
Catering: In-house. Entrees range from $25 to $60 per person.
Rental Fee: $50 daytime, $75 night time, $250 for entire Atrium after 6 p.m. Monday- Saturday, after 12 p.m. Sunday.
Parking: Street parking and nearby garages. Complimentary valet parking available.

Phillips Flagship   202-488-8515

900 Water Street, S.W. • Washington, DC 20024

Celebrate your wedding in the romantic splendor of Phillips Flagship. Situated on the Washington waterfront and just minutes from downtown, Phillips offers distinctive facilities for up to 2,000 guests. Choose the first-floor Marble Room with its rose-hued tones, fireplace, antique accents and adjoining Parkside Patio, an enclosed room that allows direct access to the outside patio and waterfront. Or, sweep up the grand staircase to the River Room and Upper Deck and enjoy breathtaking views of the Washington Channel, Capital Yacht Club and Hains Point Park. Choose from a wide selection of seafood, chicken, beef or vegetarian meals, or let its chefs create a delicious menu especially for your wedding or special event.

Capacity: 25 to 1,400 seated; 25 to 2,000 standing. The Marble Room seats up to 220 and an additional 100 in the enclosed Parkside Patio. The Presidential Room and Executive Room seat up to 120 people together or 60 people separately.

Catering: In-house. Entrees range from $26 to $50 per person.
Parking: On the premises, and nearby parking lot.

Sequoia Restaurant   202-333-3011

3050 K Street, N.W. • Washington, DC 20007

Located at Washington Harbour on the Potomac River, this site is the premier space for private and corporate events in the nation's capital. The atmosphere is elegant, with spacious proportions complementing the unsurpassed views of the Monuments, The Kennedy Center, Watergate and historic Virginia. The interior space is gracefully defined with walls of mahogany, floors of terrazzo & cherry, and a panoramic two-story wall of windows overlooking a terrace that descends to the water's edge.

Capacity: 500 seated; 1,500 standing; 2,500 with a tent.
Catering: In-house. Menus range from $25 to $90 per person.
Parking: On the premises and nearby parking garages.
Note: Wedding ceremonies are permitted.

Spirit Cruises   202-554-8013 ext. 626

Pier 4 • 6th & Water Streets, S.W. • Washington, DC 20024

Consider the wonder of a wedding on the water with Spirit Cruises. Celebrate your festivities on a beautiful, yacht-like ship with your choice of enclosed, climate-controlled decks banked by windows. On the outdoor promenade decks, guests can catch a fresh breeze under the open sky and enjoy a view of the Potomac's historic skyline.

Capacity: 20 to 575 seated; 120 to 600 standing.

Catering: In-house. Entrees range from $55.85 to $134 per person.

Rental Fee: Call for rates. Rates are based on a 4-hour rental.

Parking: On the premises and there is a parking lot nearby.

Note: Wedding ceremonies are permitted.

Georgetown University
Conference Center & Guest House   202-687-7642

3800 Reservoir Road, N.W. • Washington, DC 20057

This marvelous ballroom, decked with Tiffany-style lamps, exquisite English carpets, and intricate handcrafted woodwork, is just right for conferences, private parties, and wedding receptions. The Center is surrounded by the 104 dogwood-covered acres of the Georgetown University campus, and its 200-year-old Gothic architecture.

Capacity: 850 seated in grand ballroom; 1,200 standing in grand ballroom; 3,000 on terrace; 3,000 with tent.
Catering: In-house. Wedding packages range from $55 to $80 per person.
Parking: On the premises.
Note: Wedding ceremonies are permitted. Guest rooms are available. Wedding package includes bridal suite.

Mount Vernon College — Post Hall   202-625-4538

2100 Foxhall Road, N.W. • Washington, D.C. 20007

Post Hall is a gift from one of the College's most distinguished alumnae, Mrs. Marjorie Merriweather Post. The Hall is handsomely furnished with Georgian-style furniture, crystal chandeliers and a fireplace with a carved marble mantelpiece. This elegant room opens onto a stone patio overlooking the lovely campus.

Capacity: 100 seated; 150 standing; 50 on the patio.
Catering: In-house. Approved caterers list or your own caterer with prior approval from college.
Rental Fee: $700.
Parking: On the premises and nearby parking lot.
Note: Wedding ceremonies are permitted.

America at Union Station   202-333-3011

c/o Ark Restaurants
3050 K Street, N.W. • Washington, D.C. 20007

America, situated on Capitol Hill in Union Station's Great Hall, has been featured in *Architectural Record* and many other design magazines. This multi-level eatery offers a myriad of dining options, from the station's concourse to top-tier window corners. Great views of the Capitol and surrounding areas help define the station's dramatic space. For events of 150 to 700 guests, you may reserve the entire restaurant.

Capacity: 390 seated; 700 standing
Catering: In-house. Menus range from $15 to $40 per person.
Parking: On the premises and nearby parking lots.

Erickson House   703-739-1030

c/o Capitol Catering
437 New Jersey Avenue, S.E. • Washington, DC 20003

Four blocks from the U.S. Capitol on the House side is this private home of a retired naval officer. Erickson House is a century-old painted brick townhouse filled with an astonishing array of oriental art and furniture acquired by the owner during his travels — Vietnamese vases, Japanese woodblock prints and Peruvian mirrors. Your event will take place in the living room, spacious hall and dining room. A large bay window, a working fireplace and sliding paneled doors that can close for privacy add to the living room's charm. Foreign art treasures rest on the oak floor of the generously sized hall. Past the staircase leading to the second floor is the dining room, which has an expandable teak table, and a large harp from Paraguay. When the weather is pleasant, your party can spill out into the fenced-in front yard. From here, you can look up the street and get a tremendous view of the Capitol.

Capacity: 20 seated; 75 standing; 10 in garden.
Catering: In-house. Entree range from $30 to $100 per person.
Rental Fee: $500.
Restrictions: No smoking.
Note: Wedding ceremonies are permitted.

Historic Car Barn   202-333-6784

3600 M Street, N.W. • Washington, DC 20007

The Historic Car Barn is a brick structure built into a hill in Georgetown. In 1761, it was the site of a tobacco warehouse. Eventually, the barn was used to quarter horses and trolley cars, hence its name — Car Barn. Today, the penthouse offers two large rooms and a grand expanse of terrace. It features 12-foot high ceilings with grand brass chandeliers, hardwood floors, 8-foot high windows with breathtaking views of Washington and the Potomac River, working fireplace, marble foyer separating the two suites, and outside terraces with flower gardens overlooking the river.

Capacity: 250 seated; 550 standing; 400 in garden; 350 with tent.
Catering: Approved caterers list.
Rental Fee: $1,000 to $4,500.
Parking: On the premises. Valet parking. Parking garages nearby.
Note: Wedding ceremonies are permitted.

Odyssey Cruises   202-488-6010

600 Water Street, S.W. • Washington, DC 20024

Imagine exchanging vows on board the romantic *Odyssey* as it cruises the Potomac. Designed in the style of European canal ships and completely enclosed in glass, *Odyssey* provides a breathtaking view of the Capitol from the sparkling waters of the Potomac. From a ceremony against a stunning sunset to a fabulous four-course dinner, a cruise on *Odyssey* will be unforgettable. After dinner, enjoy *Odyssey's* inviting dance floors and professional entertainment. The experienced consulting and service staff will help you plan the perfect engagement party, bridal shower, rehearsal dinner, or other festivity. Party options include brunch, lunch, or dinner cruises.

Capacity: 600 seated/standing.
Catering: In-house.
Parking: Parking on premises and nearby parking lots.
Note: Wedding ceremonies are permitted.

Phillips Flagship   202-488-8515

900 Water Street, S.W. • Washington, DC 20024

Celebrate your wedding in the romantic splendor of Phillips Flagship. Situated on the Washington waterfront and just minutes from downtown, Phillips offers distinctive facilities for up to 2,000 guests. Choose the first-floor Marble Room with its rose-hued tones, fireplace, antique accents and adjoining Parkside Patio, an enclosed room that allows direct access to the outside patio and waterfront. Or, sweep up the grand staircase to the River Room and Upper Deck and enjoy breathtaking views of the Washington Channel, Capital Yacht Club and Hains Point Park. Choose from a wide selection of seafood, chicken, beef or vegetarian meals, or let its chefs create a delicious menu especially for your wedding or special event.

Capacity: 25 to 1,400 seated; 25 to 2,000 standing. The Marble Room seats up to 220 and an additional 100 in the enclosed Parkside Patio. The Presidential Room and Executive Room seat up to 120 people together or 60 people separately.

Catering: In-house. Entrees range from $26 to $50 per person.
Parking: On the premises, and parking lot nearby.

Sequoia Restaurant   **202-333-3011**

3050 K Street, N.W. • Washington, DC 20007

Located at Washington Harbour on the Potomac River, this site is the premier space for private and corporate events in the nation's capital. The atmosphere is elegant, with spacious proportions complementing the unsurpassed views of the Monuments, The Kennedy Center, Watergate and historic Virginia. The interior space is gracefully defined with walls of mahogany, floors of terrazzo & cherry, and a panoramic two-story wall of windows overlooking a terrace that descends to the water's edge.

Capacity: 500 seated; 1,500 standing; 2,500 with tent.
Catering: In-house. Menus range from $25 to $90 per person.
Parking: On the premises and nearby parking garages.
Note: Wedding ceremonies are permitted.

Spirit Cruises   **202-554-8013 ext. 626**

Pier 4 • 6th & Water Streets, S.W. • Washington, DC 20024

Consider the wonder of a wedding on the water with Spirit Cruises. Celebrate your festivities on a beautiful, yacht-like ship with your choice of enclosed, climate-controlled decks banked by windows. On the outdoor promenade decks, guests can catch a fresh breeze under the open sky and enjoy a view of the Potomac's historic skyline

Capacity: 20 to 575 seated; 120 to 600 standing.
Catering: In-house. Entrees range from $55.85 to $134 per person.
Rental Fee: Call for rates. Rates are based on a 4-hour rental.
Parking: On the premises and there is a parking lot nearby.
Note: Wedding ceremonies are permitted.

Odyssey Cruises   202-488-6010

600 Water Street, S.W. • Washington, DC 20024

Imagine exchanging vows on board the romantic *Odyssey* as it cruises the Potomac. Designed in the style of European canal ships and completely enclosed in glass, *Odyssey* provides a breathtaking view of the Capitol from the sparkling waters of the Potomac. From a ceremony against a stunning sunset to a fabulous four-course dinner, a cruise on *Odyssey* will be unforgettable. After dinner, enjoy *Odyssey's* inviting dance floors and professional entertainment. The experienced consulting and service staff will help you plan the perfect engagement party, bridal shower, rehearsal dinner, or other festivity. Party options include brunch, lunch, or dinner cruises.

Capacity: 600 seated/standing.
Catering: In-house.
Parking: Parking on premises and nearby parking lots.
Note: Wedding ceremonies are permitted.

Phillips Flagship   202-488-8515

900 Water Street, S.W. • Washington, DC 20024

Celebrate your wedding in the romantic splendor of Phillips Flagship. Situated on the Washington waterfront and just minutes from downtown, Phillips offers distinctive facilities for up to 2,000 guests. Choose the first-floor Marble Room with its rose-hued tones, fireplace, antique accents and adjoining Parkside Patio, an enclosed room that allows direct access to the outside patio and waterfront. Or, sweep up the grand staircase to the River Room and Upper Deck and enjoy breathtaking views of the Washington Channel, Capital Yacht Club and Hains Point Park. Choose from a wide selection of seafood, chicken, beef or vegetarian meals, or let its chefs create a delicious menu especially for your wedding or special event.

Capacity: 25 to 1,400 seated; 25 to 2,000 standing. The Marble Room seats up to 220 and an additional 100 in the enclosed Parkside Patio. The Presidential Room and Executive Room seat up to 120 people together or 60 people separately.
Catering: In-house. Entrees range from $26 to $50 per person.
Parking: On the premises, and parking lot nearby.

Sequoia Restaurant   202-333-3011

3050 K Street, N.W. • Washington, DC 20007

Located at Washington Harbour on the Potomac River, this site is the premier space for private and corporate events in the nation's capital. The atmosphere is elegant, with spacious proportions complementing the unsurpassed views of the Monuments, The Kennedy Center, Watergate and historic Virginia. The interior space is gracefully defined with walls of mahogany, floors of terrazzo & cherry, and a panoramic two-story wall of windows overlooking a terrace that descends to the water's edge.

Capacity: 500 seated; 1,500 standing; 2,500 with a tent.
Catering: In-house. Menus range from $25 to $90 per person.
Parking: On the premises and nearby parking garages.
Note: Wedding ceremonies are permitted.

Spirit Cruises   202-554-8013 ext. 626

Pier 4 • 6th & Water Streets, S.W. • Washington, DC 20024

Consider the wonder of a wedding on the water with Spirit Cruises. Celebrate your festivities on a beautiful, yacht-like ship with your choice of enclosed, climate-controlled decks banked by windows. On the outdoor promenade decks, guests can catch a fresh breeze under the open sky and enjoy a view of the Potomac's historic skyline

Capacity: 20 to 575 seated; 120 to 600 standing.
Catering: In-house. Entrees range from $55.85 to $134 per person.
Rental Fee: Call for rates. Rates are based on a 4-hour rental.
Parking: On the premises and there is a parking lot nearby.
Note: Wedding ceremonies are permitted.

Maryland

TABLE OF CONTENTS

The Baltimore Museum of Art   410-396-6078

10 Art Museum Drive • Baltimore, MD 21218

The impressive neo-classical style of the original building, completed in 1929, is reflected in the splendor of the Fox Court with its 16 massive Greek columns. Capped by a soaring 34-foot high painted ceiling, this stone and marble court provides an elegant setting for a wedding. The Fox Court opens into the Schaefer Court, a square atrium lined in ancient mosaics with French doors and Palladian windows that overlook a central garden. For receptions of 150 or less, you may use the Woodward Gallery or the Garden Room. The Meyerhoff Auditorium is also available for rental, and the adjourning USF&G Court can be used for cocktails and hors d'oeuvres.

Capacity: From 60 seated to 800 standing, depending upon space used.
Catering: Approved caterers list, but you may supply your own caterer provided caterer has insurance certification and can work within Museum's guidelines.
Rental Fee: Call for details.
Parking: Metered parking and nearby parking lot.
Restrictions: No eating or drinking in galleries. No ice sculptures, no frying, no decorating outdoors or decorating of art work. Museum is smoke-free.
Note: Wedding ceremonies are permitted.

Governor Calvert House   410-216-6328

58 State Circle • Annapolis, MD 21401

The 200-year-old Governor Calvert House, in the heart of historic Annapolis, is a charming setting for your wedding event. This converted former home of Lord Calvert features an atrium overlooking gardens that can accommodate up to 300 guests. It offers magnificent rooms, excellent food and unparalleled service. The staff will turn your wedding, reception or rehearsal dinner into a truly elegant affair.

Capacity: 160-260 seated; 300 standing.
Catering: In-house. Entrees range from $42.50 to $55 per person.
Parking: Parking in nearby lot.
Note: Wedding ceremonies are permitted.

National Aquarium in Baltimore   410-576-3869/3847

501 E. Pratt Street, Pier 3 • Baltimore, MD 21202

The magic and mystery of water make the National Aquarium in Baltimore ideal for couples who want a signature event. Create a mix of romance and fun, from casual to elegant, in settings appropriate for intimate parties or 800-guest galas. Secluded, tented parties on the pier are perfect for dancing under the stars. Dine near dolphins in the Marine Mammal Pavilion Underwater Viewing Area, dance in the airy Atrium, or enjoy breathtaking views in the Harbor View Room. Full-service catering is available. The Aquarium can accommodate a kosher wedding.

Capacity: 500 seated; 2,000 standing; 2,000 with tent.
Catering: In-house. Entrees begin at $20 per person and bar at $9.00 per person.
Rental Fee: $1,000 and up.
Parking: Parking in nearby lots.
Note: Wedding ceremonies are permitted.

Paul's on the South River   410-956-3410

3027 Riva Road • Annapolis, MD 21140

Paul's is decorated in soft muted tones of mauve and burgundy with recessed pink lighting, live ficus trees illuminated with tiny lights and expansive glass walls that overlook the South River.

Capacity: 250 seated; 300 standing.
Catering: In-house. Entrees range from $18.95 to $20.95 per person.
Parking: On the premises. Valet parking can be arranged.
Note: Wedding ceremonies are permitted.

Admiral Fell Inn   410-522-7377

888 South Broadway • Baltimore, MD 21231

The Admiral Fell Inn is a newly renovated inn located downtown on Baltimore's historic waterfront. Its lively and colorful historic Fell's Point neighborhood is renowned for Belgian block streets and brick sidewalks, antique shops, boutiques, art galleries, pubs, and restaurants. In its 210-year history, the inn has served as a ship chandlery, a theater, a boarding house for sailors, and, later, a seaman's YMCA. Comfortable guest rooms are furnished with custom-crafted Federal-style furnishings. The inn is just a water taxi ride away from Baltimore's Inner Harbor attractions and Little Italy, museums, theaters, and cultural institutions. Amenities include 80 guest rooms and suites (nine with Jacuzzi tubs), continental breakfast, continuous tea and coffee service in the lobby, courtesy van to nearby Inner Harbor and downtown locations, and free parking. The inn's critically acclaimed main restaurant features regional American cuisine in a romantic setting, and an exceptional wine cellar. The new rooftop ballroom and terrace boast a spectacular 360-degree view of the city.

Capacity: 120 seated; 150 standing, with dance floor; 50 in garden; 24 with tent.
Catering: In-house. Entrees range from $55 to $125 per person. Cake cutting fee if you provide your own cake.
Parking: Parking in nearby lot.
Note: Wedding ceremonies are permitted.

Argyle Country Club   301-598-5500

14600 Argyle Club Road • Silver Spring, MD 20906

A tree-lined entrance leads to the Argyle Country Club, set amid rolling hills and woods. Inside the clubhouse, experience a certain quiet charm of soft carpets, rich polished wood, and natural light. The banquet and meeting areas in the clubhouse are as functional as they are beautiful. The Ballroom, with its expansive wall of windows, is an extraordinary setting for a grand dinner, reception or meeting. The Sunset Room, with its sweeping views to the west, is a lovely location for luncheon or dinner. The President's Room is ideal for small dinners and receptions and can also be used for meetings. Fine food and beverage are part of every event at Argyle Country Club. Working out of a superb banquet kitchen, the executive chef and professional staff take pride in providing the right menu for every occasion, prepared with a special flair. Every event at Argyle Country Club, from an intimate dinner to a magnificent wedding, comes with personal, attentive service.

Capacity: 250 seated; 350 standing; 120 in garden; 250 with tent.
Catering: In-house. Entrees range from $40 to $75 per person.
Rental Fee: $750.

Parking: On the premises.
Note: Wedding ceremonies are permitted.

Armory Place   301-585-5564

925 Wayne Avenue • Silver Spring, MD 20910

Conveniently located in downtown Silver Spring, only two blocks from the metro station, Armory Place is a great location for your reception. Dominating the facility is the spacious Lee Auditorium. This bright, comfortable room is ideal when you have a sizeable guest list. Smaller rooms are available upon request.

Capacity: 300 to 350 seated; 445 standing.
Catering: Approved caterers list.
Rental Fee: $1,000 Friday and Sunday; $1,200 Saturday.
Parking: Metered and public parking.
Note: Wedding ceremonies are permitted indoors or out-
                doors.

Baltimore Museum of Art   410-396-6078

10 Art Museum Drive • Baltimore, MD 21218

The impressive neo-classical style of the original building, com-pleted in 1929, is reflected in the splendor of the Fox Court with its 16 massive Greek columns. Capped by a soaring 34-foot high painted ceiling, this stone and marble court provides an elegant setting for a wedding. The Fox Court opens into the Schaefer Court, a square atrium lined in ancient mosaics with French doors and Palladian windows that overlook a central garden. For recep-tions of 150 or less, you may use the Woodward Gallery or the Garden Room. The Meyerhoff Auditorium is also available for rental, and the adjourning USF&G Court can be used for cock-tails and hors d'oeuvres.

Capacity: From 60 seated to 800 standing, depending upon
                 space used.
Catering: Approved caterers list, but you may supply your own
                 caterer provided caterer has insurance certification
                 and can work within Museum's guidelines.
Rental Fee: Call for details.
Parking: Metered parking and nearby parking lot.
Restrictions: No eating or drinking in galleries. No ice sculptures,
                 no frying, no decorating outdoors or decorating of art
                 work. Museum is smoke-free.
Note: Wedding ceremonies are permitted.

Ceresville Mansion   301-694-5111

8529 Liberty Road • Frederick, MD 21701

Beautifully restored in the spirit of the Empire period, this elegant home boasts airy rooms, a 2,000-square-foot ballroom, intricate woodwork and fireplaces. The air-conditioned ballroom opens out to a garden terrace with a reflecting pool for an outdoor reception.

Capacity: 180 seated; 225 standing; 225 in garden; 350 with tent.
Catering: In-house. Entrees range from $45 to $75 per person.
Rental Fee: $250 to $1,750.
Parking: On the premises. Valet parking can be arranged.
Note: Wedding ceremonies are permitted indoors or outdoors.

Chase Court   410-727-1112

1112 St. Paul Street • Baltimore, MD 21202

Chase Court, in the historic neighborhood of Mt. Vernon, is an elegant and tasteful choice for your celebration. Its understated rooms are perfect for weddings, receptions and parties. The wisteria-covered gazebo is a favorite spot for wedding ceremonies, and the flower-filled garden is a beautiful site for toasts and tossing of the bouquet. However, in the meticulously restored Gothic ballroom there is a carved "Juliette" balcony which was perhaps built for that tradition. Chase Court is minutes from the Inner Harbor, a short walk from Penn Station and directly off the Jones Falls Freeway. It has abundant parking.

Capacity: 150 seated; 250 standing; 150+ in garden; 150+ with tent.
Catering: Approved caterers list. Entrees range from $20 to $30.
Rental Fee: $1,500.
Parking: Parking in nearby parking lot.
Note: Wedding ceremonies are permitted.

Clarion Hotel   410-727-7101

The George Washington Club
612 Cathedral Street • Baltimore, MD 21201

Consider having your wedding reception at this beautiful European hotel located minutes from the Harbor. Located in the heart of the arts and cultural district, this lovely hotel is a proud resident of historic Mount Vernon Square. A magnificent glass-enclosed rooftop ballroom adds a finishing note of grace and beauty to the hotel. This facility combines elegance and ambience in the grand tradition of a bygone era.

Capacity: 150.
Catering: In-house. Packages as well as customized menus.
Parking: Valet parking is available.
Note: Wedding ceremonies are permitted. Guest rooms available at preferred rates.

Columbia Inn Hotel   410-730-3900

10207 Wincopin Circle • Columbia, MD 21044

The Columbia Inn, commanding a spectacular view of Lake Kittamaqundi, is a sought-after location for receptions, anniversaries, and other joyous occasions. One ballroom leads to an outdoor terrace. The hotel is conveniently located to Merriweather Pavilion and to shopping. Wedding packages are all-inclusive. The Columbia Inn combines ambience with impeccable service.

Capacity: 250 seated; 500 standing; 80 in garden.
Catering: In-house. Entrees range from $48 to $60 per person.
Parking: On the premises.
Note: Wedding ceremonies are permitted indoors or outdoors, Sundays only. Guest rooms are available at special rates.

Conference Center at Cherry Hill Park   301-937-7116

9800 Cherry Hill Road • College Park, MD 20740-1210

This unusual complex offers a different environment for receptions — a new 3600-square-foot ballroom located in the middle of an RV resort. This wonderful site features beautiful hardwood floors, a fully functional fireplace, an 8' x 60' balcony and a commercial kitchen.

Capacity: 185 seated.
Catering: Approved caterers list or your own caterer. There is a $100 kitchen rental fee.
Rental Fee: $650 Saturday, $550 Sunday, and $450 Friday.
Parking: On the premises.
Restriction: Entire building is smoke-free.
Note: Wedding ceremonies are permitted.

Crofton Country Club   410-721-3111

1691 Crofton Parkway • Crofton, MD 21114

Crofton Country Club, now under Arnold Palmer Golf Management, has been elegantly renovated. Its new ballroom, featuring a dance floor, fireplace, natural lighting and brass chandeliers, is decorated in shades of hunter green and off-white, and is the perfect location for your wedding reception or rehearsal dinner. You are welcome to hold an indoor ceremony in the ballroom or take advantage of the picturesque grounds for a lovely outdoor wedding. The menu, offering superb regional cuisine, is prepared on site by the executive chef. The professional staff will work closely with you in planning all the details of your function. The club offers plenty of parking and is located just 10 minutes from Annapolis and 25 minutes from both Baltimore and Washington, D.C.

Capacity:	230 seated; 350 standing.
Catering:	In-house. Entrees range from $50 to $60 per person.
Parking:	On the premises.
Note:	Wedding ceremonies are permitted.

Golden Bull Grand Café   301-948-3666

7 Dalamar Street • Gaithersburg, MD 20877

One of the largest banquet facilities in the area comes with its own private entrance. Choose from one of three party areas this location has to offer and you have the makings of a great party. The main banquet room with its contemporary decor and spacious dance floor is perfect for receptions.

Capacity:	25 to 300 seated; 325 standing.
Catering:	In-house. Entrees range from $19.95 to $42.95.
Rental Fee:	There is a room fee of $25 if number of guests fall below 25.
Parking:	On the premises.
Note:	Wedding ceremonies are permitted.

Governor Calvert House   410-216-6328

58 State Circle • Annapolis, MD 21401

The 200-year-old Governor Calvert House, in the heart of historic Annapolis, is a charming setting for your wedding event. This converted former home of Lord Calvert features an atrium overlooking gardens that can accommodate up to 300 guests. It offers magnificent rooms, excellent food and unparalleled service. The staff will turn your wedding, reception or rehearsal dinner into a truly elegant affair.

Capacity:	160-260 seated; 300 standing.
Catering:	In-house. Entrees range from $42.50 to $55 per person.
Parking:	Parking in nearby lot.
Note:	Wedding ceremonies are permitted.

Grey Rock Mansion   410-484-4554

400 Grey Rock Road • Pikesville, MD 21208

This Colonial-style mansion features a stone patio and gazebo which overlook lovely landscaped formal gardens. With its breathtaking view and exquisite gardens, it serves as a beautiful setting for weddings.

Capacity: 145 seated; 200 standing; 300 in garden; 225 with tent.
Catering: In-house. Entrees range from $30 to $50 per person.
Rental Fee: $700 to $1,300.
Parking: On the premises.
Note: Wedding ceremonies are permitted.

Inn & Conference Center
University of Maryland
University College   301-985-7855

University Blvd. at Adelphi Road • College Park, MD 20742

The Chesapeake, Ft. McHenry and Founders Rooms open up to an impressive reception area. Cocktail receptions are held in the artwork-laden expansive concourse, then guests enter the banquet rooms for top-notch cuisine. The garden courtyards with fountains, lighted ivy and exquisite greenery extend from the banquet rooms for those seeking a moment outside. A portable parquet dance floor allows for a flexible room design, and the chandeliers and spot lighting add special ambience.

Capacity: 500 seated; 700 standing; 50 in garden; 200 with tent.
Catering: In-house. Complete wedding packages are available.
Parking: On the premises. Valet parking can be arranged.
Restrictions: Bride/Groom or members of the immediate family must be faculty, students or alumni of the University of Maryland system.
Note: Wedding ceremonies are permitted.

Kahler Hall   410-730-0770

5440 Old Tucker Row • Columbia, MD 21044

Situated in Columbia, Maryland, Kahler Hall is 25 minutes from Baltimore, and 45 minutes from Washington, D.C. The Ruth Keeton Ballroom with its wonderful hardwood floor is great for dancing. The beautiful lobby can be used in conjunction with the ballroom for cocktails and hors d'oeuvres. Picture a well-appointed living room—only much larger—with a freestanding woodburning fireplace. The attached patio provides an additional entertaining area when the weather is good.

Capacity: 220 seated; 300 standing.
Catering: You must supply your own caterer. Tables and chairs are provided by facility.
Rental Fee: $575 to $790.
Restrictions: No decorations may be attached to the ceiling, walls or light fixtures. No red punch or wine allowed.

La Fontaine Bleu   410-675-6090

3120 Erdman Avenue • Baltimore, MD 21213

This multi-ballroom facility features crystal chandeliers and an elegant decor. It specializes in providing excellent catering at reasonable prices.

Capacity: 500 seated; 600 standing.
Catering: In-house. Entrees begin at $20 per person.
Parking: On the premises.
Note: Wedding ceremonies are permitted.

Martin's Crosswinds   301-474-8500

7400 Greenway Center Drive • Greenbelt, MD 20770

With its beautifully decorated ballrooms, crystal chandeliers and glass murals, Martin's is well-known for its elegant receptions. Whatever you require, this location and its experienced staff can meet your needs quickly and imaginatively. Complete in-house services, including food, beverages, decorations and ample parking, are at your disposal.

Capacity: 220 seated in the Regency Ballroom; 220 seated in the Maryland Ballroom; 350 seated in The Embassy Ballroom; 350 seated in The Terrace Ballroom.
Catering: In-house and approved caterers list. Entrees range from $20 to $65 per person.
Parking: On the premises. Valet parking is available.
Note: Wedding ceremonies are permitted.

Montgomery Country Club   301-948-5393
http://Montgolf@aol.com

6550 Laytonsville Road • Laytonsville, MD 20882

Montgomery Country Club is located in a beautiful country setting in the township of Laytonsville. The newly renovated ballroom is bright and airy and has a breathtaking view of the golf course. Crystal chandeliers and beautiful draperies add a sense of richness to the room. This lovely club is fully staffed and offers full-service catering with a special touch. You don't have to be a member of this exclusive country club to enjoy its outstanding amenities and elegant facilities.

Capacity: 180 seated; 200 standing; 200 in garden; 200 with tent.
Catering: In-house.
Rental Fee: Varies. Call for more information.
Parking: On the premises.
Note: Wedding ceremonies are permitted.

Newton White Mansion   301-249-2004

2708 Enterprise Road • Mitchellville, MD 20716

Built in 1939, this house was once the home of Captain Newton H. White, who was the first commanding officer of the *USS Enterprise*. Newton White Mansion is one of the most popular settings in Prince George's County. It offers a quiet atmosphere, elegant patios, and a beautiful garden with a waterfall fountain for outdoor events.

Capacity: 125 seated; 200 standing; 200 in garden.
Catering: You must supply your own caterer. Caterer must be licensed and insured.
Rental Fee: $2,100 Saturday; $1,700 Friday and Sunday.
Parking: Free parking on the premises.
Note: Wedding ceremonies are permitted indoors or outdoors. Facility is handicap accessible.

Norbeck Country Club   301-774-7700

17200 Cashell Road • Rockville, MD 20853

Tucked away in the woods off Cashell Road between Rockville and Olney, Norbeck Country Club is a lovely setting for your wedding. The spacious ballroom has a dance floor and the adjacent room can be used for cocktails and hors d'oeuvres.

Capacity: 160 seated; 200 standing.
Catering: In-house. Entrees range from $24.95 to $45.00 per person.
Rental Fee: $325.
Parking: On the premises. Valet parking can be arranged.
Note: Wedding ceremonies are permitted. Ceremony space can accommodate 70 guests.

Historic Oakland   410-730-4801/1-800-730-4802
www.historic-oakland.com

5430 Vantage Point Road • Columbia, MD 21044

Celebrate the occasion of your marriage with family and friends at a lovely manor estate. Adding grace to the exquisite interior are crystal chandeliers, period reproductions of the original furnishings and twin fireplaces in the ballroom and foyer. The ballroom doors lead to a veranda that overlooks a beautifully landscaped lawn and an antique rose garden.

Capacity: 175 seated; 200 standing; 200 in garden.
Catering: In-house, approved caterers list, or your own caterer provided the caterer adheres to the rules and policies of the mansion.
Rental Fee: $700 to $1,500.

Parking: On the premises. Valet parking can be arranged.
Note: Wedding ceremonies are permitted indoors or outdoors.

Potomac Valley Lodge, Inc.   301-428-8283

16601 W. Willard Road • Poolesville, MD 20837

Have your celebration in an original log cabin, complete with stone fireplace! Floor-to-ceiling glass windows enclose the ballroom, which overlooks the 18-hole golf course and a perfect view. This location combines history with one of today's best loved pastimes. The ballroom, with its oak parquet flooring and brick flower beds, can accommodate rustic to elegant receptions depending on the decor chosen. Only one reception is held per day, allowing the bridal couple to have the room for their desired length of time, as well as their choice of serving times for food and beverages. The lodge provides a relaxed atmosphere and delicious food prepared "home style." Each reception is given undivided attention with a very personal touch.

Capacity: 200 seated; 200 standing.
Catering: In-house. Entrees, including full bar, range from $40 to $50 per person. Wedding packages are all-inclusive.
Parking: On the premises.

Prince George's Ballroom   301-341-7439

2411 Pinebrook Avenue • Landover, MD 20785

Surrounded by 50 acres of parkland and conveniently located, this elegant ballroom with its art-deco styling is only 30 minutes from Washington, D.C. With its beautiful hardwood floors and spacious patio, it is one of the area's most popular reception locations.

Capacity: 250 to 270 seated.
Catering: You must supply your own caterer.
Rental Fee: $900 to $1,300.
Parking: On the premises.
Note: Wedding ceremonies are permitted indoors or outdoors.

Riversdale Mansion   301-864-0420
www.smart.net/~parksrec/riversdale

4811 Riverdale Road • Riverdale, MD 20737

This recently restored early 19th-century mansion is conveniently located approximately 3 miles from I-95 and the Baltimore-Washington Parkway. Riversdale is a five-part neoclassical style house. The available rental rooms include a carpeted banquet room with wall sconces in the East Wing, and a ballroom with decorative cornice and crystal chandelier in the West Wing.

Capacity: 100.
Catering: You must supply your own caterer.
Rental Fee: $700 to $1,150.
Parking: On the premises.
Note: Wedding ceremonies are permitted indoors or out-doors.

Scarlett Place   410-561-2433

c/o Chef's Expressions
250 S. President Street • Baltimore, MD 21202

With a dramatic black and white marble foyer, two ballrooms, bridal changing area and private bath, Scarlett Place is one of the city's most elegant settings. The Scarlett Room is decorated with custom floral carpet and hand-painted columns. The Plaza Room, in grey and silver tones, features brass and crystal sconce lighting. Both rooms have large parquet dance floors and open to a terrace overlooking the Inner Harbor. From brunches to full course dinners, its award-winning catering and event team will ensure the success of your special party.

Capacity: 500 seated; 800 standing in The Scarlett Room; 180 seated; 250 standing in The Plaza Room.
Catering: In-house. Entrees range from $35 to $75 per person.
Rental Fee: $2,200 for the Scarlett Room; $1,300 for the Plaza Room.
Parking: Parking in nearby lot.
Note: Wedding ceremonies are permitted.

The Shrine of Saint Jude
Thaddeus Hall & Blue Room   301-946-0788

12701 Veirs Mill Road • Rockville, MD 20853

Accessible to I-495 and I-270, this comfortable, affordable location offers two spacious banquet rooms for receptions. It features high ceilings, chandeliers, separate stage, flexible room layout, and is handicap accessible. Amenities include a dance floor, air conditioning, tables and chairs, and ample parking.

Capacity: 125 seated in Blue Room, 250 standing in Blue Room, 300 seated with dance floor in Thaddeus Hall, 500 standing in Thaddeus Hall.
Catering: You must provide your own caterer.
Parking: On the premises.

Strong Mansion at Sugarloaf Mountain

301-869-7846 (Metro)
301-874-2024 (Frederick)

c/o Stronghold, Inc.
7901 Comus Road • Dickerson, MD 20842

Strong Mansion was built in 1912 by Chicago philanthropist Gordon Strong. The three-story Georgian home is surrounded by 3,000 woodland acres on Sugarloaf Mountain. You and your guests are welcome to roam the grounds and enjoy the beautiful antique furnishings throughout the entire home. The 22' x 60' spacious ballroom has eight large Palladian windows, two decorative fireplaces, and French doors that open on to a 15' x 34' portico. The back grounds are landscaped with formal gardens, a lily pond with a fountain, a white wooden pergola that is ideal for wedding ceremonies, and a breathtaking view of the countryside. Strong Mansion is the perfect setting for an outdoor wedding, reception, and other special events.

Capacity: 150.
Catering: You must supply your own caterer.
Rental Fee: $1,500 for 8 hours.
Parking: On the premises.
Restrictions: No smoking.
Note: Wedding ceremonies are permitted. The mansion is handicap accessible.

The Great Room at Savage Mill

301-490-1668
1-800-213-7427

8600 Foundry Street • Savage, MD 20763

This charming banquet hall in a completely restored textile mill has a 25-foot high ceiling with skylights and 14-foot high windows. In addition, it offers an 800-square-foot dance floor and a lovely outdoor deck overlooking woods and the Little Patuxent River.

Capacity: 275 seated; 375 standing; 150 on deck.
Catering: Approved caterers list or you may provide your own caterer at an additional fee. Entrees begin at $30 per person.
Rental Fee: $1,200 to $1,800.
Parking: On the premises.
Note: Wedding ceremony is permitted.

Truffles at the Belvedere

410-332-1000

1 East Chase Street • Baltimore, MD 21202

Built in 1903, this former hotel offers two magnificently restored ballrooms with Old-World charm and two smaller party rooms (including the world-famous John Eager Hower Room) with crystal chandeliers and working fireplaces for receptions. This elegant atmosphere is accentuated by modern services and amenities. Truffles "The Catering Company" is the sole provider of catering services at the historic Belvedere. The premier caterer of the Baltimore-Washington region, Truffles has earned an unsurpassed reputation for exceptional food, creativity, and presentation.

Capacity: 40 to 350 seated; 40 to 700 standing.
Catering: In-house. Entrees range from $45 to $60.
Parking: On the premises and nearby parking lot.
Note: Wedding ceremonies are permitted.

Wakefield Valley Golf
& Conference Center   410-876-8787
www.wakefield.com

1000 Fenby Farm Road • Westminster, MD 21158

Overlooking a magnificent golf course, Wakefield Valley's beautifully appointed ballroom provides a perfect setting for any occasion. Cathedral ceilings with chandeliers and skylights, luxurious carpeting, inlaid parquet dance floor, three walls of windows, indoor balcony, large deck and garden patio are just a few of the amenities that make Wakefield an excellent choice.

Capacity: 200 seated; 300 standing; 150 in garden.
Catering: In-house. Entrees with beverages are priced at $40 and above. Cake cutting, butler service, event coordinator, table linens, and centerpieces are provided at no charge.
Parking: On the premises.
Note: Wedding ceremony site available.

Westminster Catering
and Conference Center   410-857-1900

451 WMC Drive • Westminster, MD 21158

The Comfort Inn Westminster Catering and Conference Center is located in the heart of corporate, cultural and historical Westminster. The facility is within walking distance of shops, restaurants, and historical sites. Convenient to all major highways, it is located 30 minutes from Baltimore Inner Harbor, 25 minutes from Gettysburg. The hotel has 101 guest rooms, six of which are Jacuzzi suites, and five of which are efficiency units. The conference center caters weddings, rehearsal dinners, banquets, parties, and reunions, and offers a large menu selection for all occasions.

Capacity: 225 seated; 300 standing.
Catering: In-house. Entrees range from $20 to $40 per person. Cake cutting fee if you provide your own cake.

Parking: On the premises.
Note: Wedding ceremonies are permitted.

Woman's Club of Chevy Chase   301-652-8480

7931 Connecticut Avenue • Chevy Chase, MD 20815

This Club features a large room with library, stage, hardwood floors, and French doors on one side which lead to a garden and windows on the other side with art displays between them. There is a second smaller room as well as an outside area where outdoor ceremonies can be held.

Capacity: 200 seated; 300 standing.
Catering: Approved caterers list. A large equipped kitchen is available.
Rental Fee: $1,050 to $1,200 Friday evening, Saturday and Sunday.
Parking: 90 spaces on the premises. Additional spaces are nearby.
Note: Wedding ceremonies are permitted indoors or outdoors. A separate bridal party area with balcony is above the library.

Argyle Country Club   301-598-5500

14600 Argyle Club Road • Silver Spring, MD 20906

A tree-lined entrance leads to the Argyle Country Club, set amid rolling hills and woods. Inside the clubhouse, experience a certain quiet charm of soft carpets, rich polished wood, and natural light. The banquet and meeting areas in the clubhouse are as functional as they are beautiful. The Ballroom, with its expansive wall of windows, is an extraordinary setting for a grand dinner, reception or meeting. The Sunset Room, with its sweeping views to the west, is a lovely location for luncheon or dinner. The President's Room is ideal for small dinners and receptions and can also be used for meetings. Fine food and beverage are part of every event at Argyle Country Club. Working out of a superb banquet kitchen, the executive chef and professional staff take pride in providing the right menu for every occasion, prepared with a special flair. Every event at Argyle Country Club, from an intimate dinner to a magnificent wedding, comes with personal, attentive service.

Capacity: 250 seated; 350 standing; 120 in garden; 250 with tent.
Catering: In-house. Entrees range from $40 to $75 per person.
Rental Fee: $750.
Parking: On the premises.
Note: Wedding ceremonies are permitted.

Armory Place   301-585-5564

925 Wayne Avenue • Silver Spring, MD 20910

Conveniently located in downtown Silver Spring, only two blocks from the metro station, Armory Place is a great location for your reception. Dominating the facility is the spacious Lee Auditorium. This bright, comfortable room is ideal when you have a sizeable guest list. Smaller rooms are available upon request.

Capacity: 300-350 seated; 445 standing.
Catering: Approved caterers list.
Rental Fee: $1,000 Friday and Sunday; $1,200 Saturday.
Parking: Metered and public parking.
Note: Wedding ceremonies are permitted indoors or out-
               doors.

B&O Railroad Museum   410-752-2463

901 West Pratt Street • Baltimore, MD 21223-2699

At the B&O Museum, guests view an exciting array of locomotives and cars that span over a century, dating back to the earliest days of rail transportation. The rental of the facility includes full use of several 19th-century railroad buildings: the Mt. Clare Station, an 1851 depot building that guests enter through the museum; the Mt. Clare Annex, a two-story 1884 print shop building now housing the museum's archives; the Mt. Clare Theater and gift shop; and the Roundhouse, an 1884 passenger repair facility.

Capacity: 700 seated; 2,200 standing.
Catering: Approved caterers list. No kitchen facilities.
Rental Fee: $2,100 for first 200 guests, $6 each additional guest.
Parking: On the premises and nearby parking lot.
Restrictions: No helium filled balloons. No confetti. Smoking only in designated areas.
Note: Wedding ceremonies are permitted.

Baltimore Museum of Art   410-396-6078

10 Art Museum Drive • Baltimore, MD 21218

The impressive neo-classical style of the original building, completed in 1929, is reflected in the splendor of the Fox Court with its 16 massive Greek columns. Capped by a soaring 34-foot high painted ceiling, this stone and marble court provides an elegant setting for a wedding. The Fox Court opens into the Schaefer Court, a square atrium lined in ancient mosaics with French doors and Palladian windows that overlook a central garden. For receptions of 150 or less, you may use the Woodward Gallery or the Garden Room. The Meyerhoff Auditorium is also available for rental, and the adjourning USF&G Court can be used for cocktails and hors d'oeuvres.

Capacity: From 60 seated to 800 standing, depending upon space used.
Catering: Approved caterers list, but you may supply your own caterer provided caterer has insurance certification and can work within Museum's guidelines.
Rental Fee: Call for details.
Parking: Metered parking and nearby parking lot.
Restrictions: No eating or drinking in galleries. No ice sculptures, no frying, no decorating outdoors or decorating of art work. Museum is smoke-free.
Note: Wedding ceremonies are permitted.

Blair Mansion Inn   301-588-1688

7711 Eastern Avenue • Silver Spring, MD 20912

The Blair Mansion Inn was first built in 1890 by architect Stanford White, who also designed Madison Square Gardens in New York. Later renovations turned the house into an inn and a dinner theater. This graciously restored inn offers a lovely environment for a wedding reception, anniversary, or other special celebrations.

Capacity: 350 seated; 425 standing.
Catering: In-house or your own caterer with approval of facil-

ity. Entrees range from $16.95 to $25.95 per person when you use in-house caterer.

Parking: Free parking on the premises and residential parking.

Camillia Room   301-434-7314

1500 St. Camillus Drive • Silver Spring, MD 20903

Conveniently located and reasonably priced, the size of this hall and its flexibility allows it to be customized to reflect your own style. Amenities include dance floor, stage, tables and chairs, chandeliers, and ample free parking.

Capacity: 350 seated; 400 standing.
Catering: In-house. Entrees range from $18 to $22.50 per person. Only type of service offered is sit-down buffet.
Rental Fee: No fee for first four hours. $200 an hour after first four hours.
Parking: On the premises.
Note: Roman Catholic (only) wedding ceremonies are permitted.

Casey Community Center   301-258-6366

810 S. Frederick Avenue • Gaithersburg, MD 20877

The Community Center is conveniently located just east of I-270 and provides a quaint setting for a wedding reception, birthday party or special get-together. The Center has two banquet rooms, and the larger room comes with a kitchen. The rooms are decorated with elegant brass sconces with controlled lighting.

Capacity: 135 seated; 150 standing.
Catering: You must supply your own caterer. The center comes equipped with tables and chairs.
Rental Fee: $60 per hour.
Parking: On the premises.
Note: Guest rooms are available.

Chesapeake Marine Tours   410-268-7601
http://member.aol.com/boattours/cmt.html

P.O. Box 3350/Slip 20 City Dock • Annapolis, MD 21403

For a truly romantic setting, have your wedding, reception, or anniversary celebration in historic Annapolis, on the scenic Severn River, aboard one of these riverboats or corporate yacht, or at the lovely Annapolis Landing Marina waterfront facility. *Providence*, a charming 64-foot riverboat, is perfect for the wedding ceremony and reception with a DJ or band for dancing. The *Cabaret II*, a 67-foot custom motor yacht, is an elegant setting for a formal affair. Intimate weddings are graciously accommodated by smaller charter boats. The waterfront location has both lawn and banquet room facilities. Some of the finest area caterers are featured. Wedding packages are available in a variety of price ranges for groups of 20 to 200.

Capacity: 20 to 100 seated, 20 to 297 standing; 150 on the lawn.
Catering: Approved caterers list. Entrees range from $25 to $80 per person.
Rental Fee: $500 to $3,500.
Parking: On the premises, and nearby parking lot. Valet parking is required for parking at the facility.
Restrictions: Waterfront land facilities activities are limited to 10 o'clock.

Colonial Room at The Church of Christ the King   301-929-0069

2300 East-West Highway • Silver Spring, MD 20910

This location offers an elegant social hall decorated in colonial design with mirrored posts, chandeliers, wall-to-wall carpet, and lovely velvet draperies. Amenities include a large dance floor, tables and chairs, and free parking. The Colonial Room is a warm and wonderful place to entertain your family and friends at a wedding, reception, anniversary, or other special occasions.

Capacity: 300 seated; 400 standing.
Catering: In-house. Buffet entrees range from $12.50 to $16.50 per person plus gratuity and tax.
Rental Fee: $475 for 4 hours.
Parking: On the premises.

Columbia Inn Hotel   410-730-3900

10207 Wincopin Circle • Columbia, MD 21044

The Columbia Inn, commanding a spectacular view of Lake Kittamaqundi, is a sought-after location for receptions, anniversaries, and other joyous occasions. One ballroom leads to an outdoor terrace. The hotel is conveniently located to Merriweather Pavilion and to shopping. Wedding packages are all-inclusive. The Columbia Inn combines ambience with impeccable service.

Capacity: 250 seated; 500 standing; 80 in garden.
Catering: In-house. Entrees range from $48 to $60 per person.
Parking: On the premises.
Note: Wedding ceremonies are permitted indoors or outdoors, Sundays only. Guest rooms are available at special rates.

Crofton Country Club   410-721-3111

1691 Crofton Parkway • Crofton, MD 21114

Crofton Country Club, now under Arnold Palmer Golf Management, has been elegantly renovated. Its new ballroom, featuring a dance floor, fireplace, natural lighting and brass chandeliers, is decorated in shades of hunter green and off-white, and is the perfect location for your wedding reception or rehearsal dinner. You are welcome to hold an indoor ceremony in the ballroom or take advantage of the picturesque grounds for a lovely outdoor wedding. The menu, offering superb regional cuisine, is prepared on site by the executive chef. The professional staff will work closely with you in planning all the details of your function. The club offers plenty of parking and is located just 10 minutes from Annapolis and 25 minutes from both Baltimore and Washington, D.C.

Capacity: 230 seated; 350 standing.
Catering: In-house. Entrees range from $50 to $60 per person.
Parking: On the premises.
Note: Wedding ceremonies are permitted.

Fergie's Waterfront
Restaurant and Catering   1-800-292-1371

2840 Solomons Island Road • Edgewater, MD 21037

Fergie's Waterfront Restaurant & Catering will help you create the reception of your dreams. Its banquet room has an adjacent deck on the water for your cocktail hour or ceremony. The banquet room has decorated Grecian columns, large dance floor and beautiful built-in bar. Your reception could be in the main dining room with wrap-around windows overlooking the water. There is also a dance floor, and an area for cocktails and hors d'oeuvres. This facility can be used on Saturday 12:00 p.m. until 4:00 p.m. It is located one mile outside Annapolis.

Capacity: 160 seated; 200 standing.
Catering: In-house. Entrees range from $32 to $40 per person.
Parking: On the premises.
Note: Wedding ceremonies are permitted.

Golden Bull Grand Café   301-948-3666

7 Dalamar Street • Gaithersburg, MD 20877

One of the largest banquet facilities in the area comes with its own private entrance. Choose from one of three party areas this location has to offer and you have the makings of a great party. The main banquet room with its contemporary decor and spacious dance floor is perfect for receptions.

Capacity: 25 to 300 seated; 300 to 325 standing.
Catering: In-house. Entrees range from $19.95 to $42.95.
Rental Fee: There is a room fee of $25 if number of guests fall
                below 25.
Parking: On the premises.
Note: Wedding ceremonies are permitted.

Historic Baldwin Hall   410-923-3438

1358 Millersville Road • Crownsville, MD 21032

Historic Baldwin Hall is a lovely country church built in 1861.
Surrounded by landscaped gardens and mature trees, it is located
in Millersville at the intersection of Generals Highway and
Millersville Road. The spacious main hall, with its lofty ceilings,
arched windows, hardwood floors, and stage with green velvet
curtains, is a wonderful space to decorate. There's also a front
reception area, choir loft, and bride's room for changing and
privacy. The hall is available seven days a week at reasonable
rates.

Capacity: 125 seated; 299 standing.
Catering: You must supply your own caterer. A well-equipped
                kitchen with ranges, microwave, refrigerator and
                warming oven is available. Tables and chairs are
                provided. All caterers are accepted.
Rental Fee: $500.
Parking: On the premises.

The Heritage Room   301-249-1167

12010 Woodmore Road • Mitchellville, MD 20716

The Heritage Room in the Holy Family Parish Centre is situated
in a rural setting rich in history. Opened in 1992, the facility's
architecture complements the century-old Holy Family Church,
a state historical landmark. Your guests can enjoy the wooded
country setting adjacent to the exclusive Woodmore community
and the Prince George's Country Club.

Capacity: 250 seated.
Catering: In-house or approved caterers list. Package prices
                range from $21.95 to $28.95 per person (includes
                buffet meal and hall).
Parking: On the premises.
Note: Wedding ceremonies are permitted.

The Johns Hopkins University
Glass Pavilion   410-516-8209

3400 N. Charles Street • Baltimore, MD 21218

The Glass Pavilion is located in a natural wooded setting on the campus of Johns Hopkins University. It is totally encased in glass with a patio surrounding the entire room. Amenities include a permanent stage.

Capacity: 200 to 250 seated; 500 standing.
Catering: In-house or your own caterer.
Rental Fee: $975.
Parking: On the premises and nearby parking lot.
Restrictions: Available June through August 14 of each year.
Note: Wedding ceremonies are permitted indoors or outdoors.

Kahler Hall   410-730-0770

5440 Old Tucker Row • Columbia, MD 21044

Situated in Columbia, Maryland, Kahler Hall is 25 minutes from Baltimore, and 45 minutes from Washington, D.C. The Ruth Keeton Ballroom with its wonderful hardwood floor is great for dancing. The beautiful lobby can be used in conjunction with the ballroom for cocktails and hors d'oeuvres. Picture a well-appointed living room—only much larger—with a freestanding woodburning fireplace. The attached patio provides an additional entertaining area when the weather is good.

Capacity: 220 seated; 300 standing.
Catering: You must supply your own caterer. Tables and chairs are provided by facility.
Rental Fee: $575 to $790.
Restrictions: No decorations may be attached to the ceiling, walls or light fixtures. No red punch or wine allowed.

Knights of Columbus   301-530-0258

Rock Creek Council
5417 West Cedar Lane • Bethesda, MD 20814

Looking for a bargain? This comfortable and affordable location comes complete with dance floor, tables and chairs, kitchen and ample parking. The size and flexibility of this hall allows it to be customized for any type of affair. Turn it into a charming setting with your own decorating flair.

Capacity: 200 seated.
Catering: Approved caterers list or your own caterer.
Rental Fee: $650 for 4 hours.
Parking: On the premises.

La Fontaine Bleu 410-675-6090

3120 Erdman Avenue • Baltimore, MD 21213

This multi-ballroom facility features crystal chandeliers and an elegant decor. It specializes in providing excellent catering at reasonable prices.

Capacity: 500 seated; 600 standing.
Catering: In-house. Entrees begin at $20 per person.
Parking: On the premises.
Note: Wedding ceremonies are permitted.

Lodge at Little Seneca Creek 301-585-5564

14500-A Clopper Road • Boyds, MD 20841

The Lodge at Little Seneca Creek is a rustic meeting place designed as a replica of a classic log cabin. The lodge's spacious meeting hall is accented by a massive flagstone fireplace. The splendor of the oak flooring is surpassed only by the natural wood cathedral ceilings. A breathtaking view from the outdoor deck includes a pastoral scene where an outdoor wedding reception may be held.

Capacity: 120 seated; 180 standing.
Catering: Approved caterers list.
Rental Fee: $700 Friday and Sunday; $900 Saturday.
Parking: 85 parking spaces on the premises.
Note: Wedding ceremonies are permitted indoors or outdoors.

Martin's Crosswinds 301-474-8500

7400 Greenway Center Drive • Greenbelt, MD 20770

With its beautifully decorated ballrooms, crystal chandeliers and glass murals, Martin's is well-known for its elegant receptions. Whatever you require, this location and its experienced staff can meet your needs quickly and imaginatively. Complete in-house services, including food, beverages, decorations and ample parking, are at your disposal.

Capacity: 220 seated in the Regency Ballroom; 220 seated in the Maryland Ballroom; 350 seated in the Embassy Ballroom; 350 seated in the Terrace Ballroom.
Catering: In-house and approved caterers list. Entrees range from $20 to $65 per person.
Parking: On the premises. Valet parking is available.
Note: Wedding ceremonies are permitted.

Maryland Inn   410-216-6328

16 Church Circle • Annapolis, MD 21401

Located in historic Annapolis, the Maryland Inn, features a Victorian ballroom with a working fireplace and authentic chandeliers. This delightful inn has served guests with fabulous food, lovely rooms, and a staff that offers excellent service. For an elegant wedding reception or rehearsal dinner that will be remembered for years, the Maryland Inn is at your service.

Capacity: 90 seated; 200 standing.
Catering: In-house. Entrees range from $42.50 to $55 per person.
Parking: Parking in nearby lot.
Note: Wedding ceremonies are permitted.

Montgomery Country Club   301-948-5393
http://Montgolf@aol.com

6550 Laytonsville Road • Laytonsville, MD 20882

Montgomery Country Club is located in a beautiful country setting in the township of Laytonsville. The newly renovated ballroom is bright and airy and has a breathtaking view of the golf course. Crystal chandeliers and beautiful draperies add a sense of richness to the room. This lovely club is fully staffed and offers full-service catering with a special touch. You don't have to be a member of this exclusive country club to enjoy its outstanding amenities and elegant facilities.

Capacity: 180 seated; 200 standing; 200 in garden; 200 with tent.
Catering: In-house.
Rental Fee: Varies. Call for more information.
Parking: On the premises.
Note: Wedding ceremonies are permitted.

Montgomery County
Agricultural Center Inc.   301-926-3100 x202

16 Chestnut Street • Gaithersburg, MD 20877

One of the most reasonably priced locations of its kind, this marvelous party space offers a unique environment for your reception. The Center's professional staff will assist you with every aspect of your special day. Conveniently located off I-270 and MD 355 in Gaithersburg, the size of this space allows it to be customized to reflect your individual style.

Capacity: 360.
Catering: In-house or you may supply your own caterer. Entrees range from $8 to $18 per person when you use in-house caterer.

Rental Fee: $800.
Parking: On the premises.
Note: Wedding ceremonies are permitted.

Montpelier Mansion   301-953-1376

Route 197 & Muirkirk Road • Laurel, MD 20708

Located on 70 acres of rolling park land, this national historic landmark provides the perfect atmosphere for any elegant social occasion. Ceremonies and receptions can take place in a number of locations from the great entry hall to the indoor wings to the outdoor garden terraces graced by a 200-year-old summerhouse and boxwood. Guests can view furnished museum rooms during their visit. The mansion is ideal for business retreats and seminars at lower weekday rates.

Capacity: 100.
Catering: You must supply your own caterer.
Rental Fee: $800 Saturday; $700 Friday and Sunday for 7 hours. Facility requires a $400 refundable security deposit and a $50 custodial fee.
Parking: On the premises.
Restrictions: No smoking inside.
Note: Wedding ceremonies are permitted indoors or outdoors.

Norbeck Country Club   301-774-7700

17200 Cashell Road • Rockville, MD 20853

Tucked away in the woods off Cashell Road between Rockville and Olney, Norbeck Country Club is a lovely setting for your wedding. The spacious ballroom has a dance floor and the adjacent room can be used for cocktails and hors d'oeuvres.

Capacity: 160 seated; 200 standing.
Catering: In-house. Entrees range from $24.95 to $45.00 per person.
Rental Fee: $325.
Parking: On the premises. Valet parking can be arranged.
Note: Wedding ceremonies are permitted. Ceremony space can accommodate 70 guests.

Paint Branch
Unitarian Universalist Church   301-937-3666

3215 Powder Mill Road • Adelphi, MD 20783

Paint Branch Church is a beautiful location for your special event . . . an idyllic setting for weddings, receptions, concerts, birthdays, anniversaries, or other cultural and social events. This wonderful site features cathedral ceilings with wooden beams and a panoramic view of the lovely wooded area surrounding the facility, and an outdoor deck that is perfect for cocktails or dancing under the stars.

Capacity: 150-200 in Meeting Room; 100 in Kelley Room; 50 on the deck.
Catering: You must supply your own caterer.
Rental Fee: Suggested rates vary by day of week, number of guests, room selection and number of hours. Please call for schedule.
Parking: On the premises.
Restrictions: No smoking. Parties must end by 11:00 p.m. and clean-up must be finished by midnight.
Note: Wedding ceremonies are permitted indoors and out-doors.

Paul's on the South River   410-956-3410

3027 Riva Road • Annapolis, MD 21140

Paul's is decorated in soft muted tones of mauve and burgundy with recessed pink lighting, live ficus trees illuminated with tiny lights and expansive glass walls that overlook the South River.

Capacity: 250 seated; 300 standing.
Catering: In-house. Entrees range from $18.95 to $20.95 per person.
Parking: On the premises. Valet parking can be arranged.
Note: Wedding ceremonies are permitted.

Quiet Waters Park   410-222-1777

600 Quiet Waters Park Road • Annapolis, MD 21403

Located in Annapolis on the banks of the South River, this 336-acre park represents Victorian style architecture. The park design features fountains, gazebos, woodland trails and formal gardens. The park's Blue Heron Center with its formal gardens is perfect for large parties, receptions and weddings. Couples renting the Center may use the immediate lower garden area for their ceremony at no extra charge.

Capacity: 150 seated; 225 standing.
Catering: In-house.
Rental Fee: Call for more information.
Parking: On the premises.
Note: Wedding ceremonies are permitted indoors or out-doors.

Riversdale Mansion   301-864-0420
www.smart.net/~parksrec/riversdale

4811 Riverdale Road • Riverdale, MD 20737

This recently restored early 19th-century mansion is conveniently located approximately 3 miles from I-95 and the Baltimore-Washington Parkway. Riversdale is a five-part neoclassical style house. The available rental rooms include a carpeted banquet room with wall sconces in the East Wing, and a ballroom with decorative cornice and crystal chandelier in the West Wing.

Capacity: 100.
Catering: You must supply your own caterer.
Rental Fee: $700 to $1,150.
Parking: On the premises.
Note: Wedding ceremonies are permitted indoors or outdoors.

Scarlett Place   410-561-2433

c/o Chef's Expressions
250 S. President Street • Baltimore, MD 21202

With a dramatic black and white marble foyer, two ballrooms, bridal changing area and private bath, Scarlett Place is one of the city's most elegant settings. The Scarlett Room is decorated with custom floral carpet and hand-painted columns. The Plaza Room, in grey and silver tones, features brass and crystal sconce lighting. Both rooms have large parquet dance floors and open to a terrace overlooking the Inner Harbor. From brunches to full course dinners, its award-winning catering and event team will ensure the success of your special party.

Capacity: 500 seated; 800 standing in The Scarlett Room; 180 seated; 250 standing in The Plaza Room.
Catering: In-house. Entrees range from $35 to $75 per person.
Rental Fee: $2,200 for the Scarlett Room; $1,300 for the Plaza Room.
Parking: Parking in nearby lot.
Note: Wedding ceremonies are permitted.

The Great Room at Savage Mill   301-490-1668

8600 Foundry Street • Savage, MD 20763

This charming banquet hall in a completely restored textile mill has a 25-foot high ceiling with skylights and 14-foot high windows. In addition, it offers an 800-square-foot dance floor and a lovely outdoor deck overlooking woods and the Little Patuxent River.

Capacity: 275 seated; 375 standing; 150 on deck.
Catering: Approved caterers list or you may provide your own

caterer at an additional fee. Entrees begin at $30 per person.

Rental Fee: $1,200 to $1,800.
Parking: On the premises.
Note: Wedding ceremony is permitted.

The Shrine of Saint Jude
Thaddeus Hall & Blue Room   301-946-0788

12701 Veirs Mill Road • Rockville, MD 20853

Accessible to I-495 and I-270, this comfortable, affordable location offers two spacious banquet rooms for receptions. It features high ceilings, chandeliers, separate stage, flexible room layout, and is handicap accessible. Amenities include a dance floor, air conditioning, tables and chairs, and ample parking.

Capacity: 125 seated in Blue Room, 250 standing in Blue Room, 300 seated with dance floor in Thaddeus Hall, 500 standing in Thaddeus Hall.
Catering: You must provide your own caterer.
Parking: On the premises.

Truffles at the Belvedere   410-332-1000

1 East Chase Street • Baltimore, MD 21202

Built in 1903, this former hotel offers two magnificently restored ballrooms with Old-World charm and two smaller party rooms (including the world-famous John Eager Howar Room) with crystal chandeliers and working fireplaces for receptions. This elegant atmosphere is accentuated by modern services and amenities. Truffles "The Catering Company" is the sole provider of catering services at the historic Belvedere. The premier caterer of the Baltimore-Washington region, Truffles has earned an unsurpassed reputation for exceptional food, creativity, and presentation.

Capacity: 40 to 350 seated; 40 to 700 standing.
Catering: In-house. Entrees range from $45 to $60.
Parking: On the premises and nearby parking lot.
Note: Wedding ceremonies are permitted.

Westminster Catering
and Conference Center   410-857-1900

451 WMC Drive • Westminster, MD 21158

The Comfort Inn Westminster Catering and Conference Center is located in the heart of corporate, cultural and historical Westminster. The facility is within walking distance of shops, restaurants, and historical sites. Convenient to all major highways, it is located 30 minutes from Baltimore Inner Harbor, 25 minutes from Gettysburg. The hotel has 101 guest rooms, six of which are Jacuzzi suites, and five of which are efficiency units. The conference center caters weddings, rehearsal dinners, banquets, parties, and reunions, and offers a large menu selection for all occasions.

Capacity: 225 seated; 300 standing.
Catering: In-house. Entrees range from $20 to $40 per person. Cake cutting fee if you provide your own cake.
Parking: On the premises.
Note: Wedding ceremonies are permitted.

Willow Tree Inn   301-948-8832

19550 Montgomery Village Avenue • Gaithersburg, MD 20879

Overlooking the Montgomery Village Golf Course, this inn is a charming place to celebrate your wedding day. The banquet room features floor-to-ceiling windows which open onto a lovely balcony, providing spectacular indoor and outdoor views from every angle. A lovely lake adds to the tranquil scene.

Capacity: 250 seated (10 a.m. to 4 p.m.), 150 seated (6 p.m. to 10 p.m.); 300 standing (10 a.m. to 4 p.m.), 200 standing (6 p.m. to 10 p.m.)
Catering: In-house. Entrees range from $20 to $80 per person. Cake cutting fee is $50.
Parking: On the premises.
Restrictions: Wedding ceremonies, 10 a.m. to 4 p.m. only.

Woman's Club of Chevy Chase   301-652-8480

7931 Connecticut Avenue • Chevy Chase, MD 20815

This Club features a large room with library, stage, hardwood floors, and French doors on one side which lead to a garden and windows on the other side with art displays between them. There is a second smaller room as well as an outside area where outdoor ceremonies can be held.

Capacity: 200 seated; 300 standing.
Catering: Approved caterers list. A large equipped kitchen is available.
Rental Fee: $1,050 to $1,200 Friday evening, Saturday and Sunday.
Parking: 90 spaces on the premises. Additional spaces are nearby.
Note: Wedding ceremonies are permitted indoors or outdoors. A separate bridal party area with balcony is above the library.

Chesapeake Bay Adventures   1-800-394-4101

1934 Lincoln Drive, Suite B • Annapolis, MD 21401

Envision being aboard your own private yacht hosting your elegant reception, party or special event on the Chesapeake. From intimate to extravagant, these vessels will accommodate events of any size. Complete event planning and coordination is offered for weddings and receptions by land or by sea throughout the Chesapeake Bay Region and Washington, D.C.

Capacity: 2 to 500.
Catering: In-house and approved caterers list.
Rental Fee: $250 per hour.
Parking: On the premises. Nearby parking lot. Valet parking available.
Note: Wedding ceremonies are permitted indoors or outdoors.

Chesapeake Marine Tours   410-268-7601
http://member.aol.com/boattours/cmt.html

P.O. Box 3350/Slip 20 City Dock • Annapolis, MD 21403

For a truly romantic setting, have your wedding, reception, or anniversary celebration in historic Annapolis, on the scenic Severn River, aboard one of these riverboats or corporate yacht, or at the lovely Annapolis Landing Marina waterfront facility. *Providence*, a charming 64-foot riverboat, is perfect for the wedding ceremony and reception with a DJ or band for dancing. The *Cabaret II*, a 67-foot custom motor yacht, is an elegant setting for a formal affair. Intimate weddings are graciously accommodated by smaller charter boats. The waterfront location has both lawn and banquet room facilities. Some of the finest area caterers are featured. Wedding packages are available in a variety of price ranges for groups of 20 to 200.

Capacity: 20 to 100 seated, 20 to 297 standing; 150 on the lawn.
Catering: Approved caterers list. Entrees range from $25 to $80 per person.
Rental Fee: $500 to $3,500.
Parking: On the premises, and nearby parking lot.
Restrictions: Waterfront land facilities activities are limited to 10 o'clock. Valet parking is required for parking at the facility.

Patriot Cruises Inc.   410-745-3100

**Chesapeake Bay Maritime Museum Dock (Mill Street)
St. Michaels, MD 21663**

Leaving the beautiful St. Michaels Harbor you will enjoy the untouched, scenic beauty of the Wye and Miles Rivers. Built in

1990, the *Patriot* can accommodate casual to the most elegant of affairs with ease. This climate-controlled vessel is equipped with two shipboard bars and a canopied upper deck for your enjoyment. A cruise on the *Patriot* is a special mix of history, natural waterways, and culture.

Capacity:	110 seated; 170 standing.
Catering:	In-house or approved caterers list. Entrees range from $17 to $40 per person.
Rental Fee:	$1,500 for 3-hour cruise.
Parking:	On the premises and nearby lot.
Note:	Wedding ceremonies are permitted.

Cedar Lane Unitarian Church   301-493-8300

9601 Cedar Lane • Bethesda, MD 20814

Capacity: 250 in main sanctuary; 100 in chapel.
Rental Fee: $700 for main sanctuary; $400 for chapel.

Chapel at Vintage Bride   301-540-3540

23330 Federick Road • Clarksburg, MD 20871

Capacity: 125.
Rental Fee: $200.

Paint Branch Unitarian
Universalist Church   301-937-3666

3215 Powder Mill Road • Adelphi, MD 20783

Paint Branch Church is a beautiful location for your special event
. . . an idyllic setting for weddings, receptions, concerts, birthdays,
anniversaries, or other cultural and social events. This wonderful
site features cathedral ceilings with wooden beams and a panoramic view of the lovely wooded area surrounding the facility,
and an outdoor deck that is perfect for cocktails or dancing under
the stars.

Capacity: 150-200 in Meeting Room; 100 in Kelley Room; 50 on
the deck.
Rental Fee: Suggested rates vary by day of week, number of
guests, room selection and number of hours. Please
call for schedule.
Note: Wedding ceremonies are permitted indoors and outdoors.

St. Paul's Chapel   410-923-0293

**Crownsville Road & General Highway (Route 178)
Crownsville, MD 21032**

Restored Victorian chapel, built in 1861.

Capacity: 80.
Rental Fee: $300.

The Temple Hill
Baptist Church   301-897-9307/301-946-2928

9400 Rockville Pike • Bethesda, MD 20814

Capacity: 150.
Rental Fee: $300.

The Way of the Cross
Church of Christ   301-218-1183

1177 Largo Road • Upper Marlboro, MD 20774-8688
Church Hall is available for wedding receptions.

Capacity: 2,500.
Rental Fee: $1,000.

University of Maryland
Memorial Chapel at College Park   301-314-9866

1101 Memorial Chapel • College Park, MD 20742-8011

University of Maryland has two chapels for rent: the Main Chapel and the West Chapel. The chapels may be reserved more than one year in advance on a tentative basis and guaranteed a year in advance on a permanent basis.

Capacity: 422 in orchestra section; 256 in side pews; 252 in balcony in the Main Chapel; 100 in West Chapel.
Rental Fee: $300 University of Maryland affiliates; $500 general public for Main Chapel; $200 University of Maryland affiliates; $400 General public for West Chapel.

Wilde Lake Interfaith Chapel   410-730-7920

10431 Twin Rivers Road • Columbia, MD 21044

Capacity: 600 in large room; 400 in small room.
Rental Fee: $250 for 3 hours (includes rehearsal) for large room. $200 for 3 hours (includes rehearsal) for small room.

Camillia Room   301-434-7314

1500 St. Camillus Drive • Silver Spring, MD 20903

Conveniently located and reasonably priced, the size of this hall and its flexibility allows it to be customized to reflect your own style. Amenities include dance floor, stage, tables and chairs, chandeliers, and ample free parking.

Capacity: 350 seated; 400 standing.
Catering: In-house. Entrees range from $18 to $22.50 per person. Only type of service offered is sit-down buffet.
Rental Fee: No fee for first four hours. $200 an hour after first four hours.
Parking: On the premises.
Note: Roman Catholic (only) wedding ceremonies are permitted.

Colonial Room at
The Church of Christ the King   301-929-0069

2300 East-West Highway • Silver Spring, MD 20910

This location offers an elegant social hall decorated in colonial design with mirrored posts, chandeliers, wall-to-wall carpet, and lovely velvet draperies. Amenities include a large dance floor, tables and chairs, and free parking. The Colonial Room is a warm and wonderful place to entertain your family and friends at a wedding reception, anniversary, or other special occasions.

Capacity: 300 seated; 400 standing.
Catering: Buffet entrees range from $12.50 to $16.50 per person plus gratuity and tax.
Rental Fee: $475 for 4 hours.
Parking: On the premises.

The Heritage Room   301-249-1167

12010 Woodmore Road • Mitchellville, MD 20716

The Heritage Room in the Holy Family Parish Centre is situated in a rural setting rich in history. Opened in 1992, the facility's architecture complements the century-old Holy Family Church, a state historical landmark. Your guests can enjoy the wooded country setting adjacent to the exclusive Woodmore community and the Prince George's Country Club.

Capacity: 250 seated.
Catering: In-house or approved caterers list. Package prices range from $21.95 to $28.95 per person (includes buffet meal and hall).
Parking: On the premises.
Note: Wedding ceremonies are permitted.

Paint Branch
Unitarian Universalist Church   301-937-3666

3215 Powder Mill Road • Adelphi, MD 20783

Paint Branch Church is a beautiful location for your special event
. . . an idyllic setting for weddings, receptions, concerts, birthdays,
anniversaries, or other cultural and social events. This wonderful
site features cathedral ceilings with wooden beams and a panoramic
view of the lovely wooded area surrounding the facility, and an
outdoor deck that is perfect for cocktails or dancing under the stars.

Capacity: 150-200 in Meeting Room; 100 in Kelley Room; 50 on
                the deck.
Catering: You must supply your own caterer.
Rental Fee: Suggested rates vary by day of week, number of
                guests, room selection and number of hours. Please
                call for schedule.
Parking: On the premises.
Restrictions: No smoking. Parties must end by 11:00 p.m. and
                clean-up must be finished by midnight.
Note: Wedding ceremonies are permitted indoors and out-
                doors.

St. Mary's Church Hall   301-292-0527

13401 Piscataway Road • Clinton, MD 20735

Established in 1838 and located in historic Piscataway, this
church hall is a special place for weddings. Featuring an extremely
versatile layout with over 3,800 square feet, this spacious hall has
off-white walls, a 17' x 32' stage and an outdoor reception area.
Amenities include tables and chairs, kitchen facilities, dance floor
and convenient parking.

Capacity: 250 seated; 400 standing.
Catering: Approved caterers list or your own caterer.
Rental Fee: $100 per hour.
Parking: On the premises.
Note: Call for more information regarding wedding cer-
              emonies.

The Shrine of Saint Jude
Thaddeus Hall & Blue Room   301-946-0788

12701 Veirs Mill Road • Rockville, MD 20853

Accessible to I-495 and I-270, this comfortable, affordable location offers two spacious banquet rooms for receptions. It features
high ceilings, chandeliers, separate stage, flexible room layout,
and is handicap accessible. Amenities include a dance floor, air
conditioning, tables and chairs, and ample parking.

Capacity: 125 seated in Blue Room, 250 standing in Blue Room, 300 seated with dance floor in Thaddeus Hall, 500 standing in Thaddeus Hall.

Catering: You must provide your own caterer.

Parking: On the premises.

Casey Community Center   301-258-6366

810 S. Frederick Avenue • Gaithersburg, MD 20877

The Community Center is conveniently located just east of I-270 and provides a quaint setting for a wedding reception, birthday party or special get-together. The Center has two banquet rooms, and the larger room comes with a kitchen. The rooms are decorated with elegant brass sconces with controlled lighting.

Capacity: 135 seated; 150 standing.
Catering: You must supply your own caterer. The center comes equipped with tables and chairs.
Rental Fee: $60 per hour.
Parking: On the premises.
Note: Guest rooms are available.

Conference Center
at Cherry Hill Park   301-937-7116

9800 Cherry Hill Road • College Park, MD 20740-1210

This unusual complex offers a different environment for receptions—a new 3600-square-foot ballroom located in the middle of an RV resort. This wonderful site features beautiful hardwood floors, a fully functional fireplace, an 8' × 10' balcony and a commercial kitchen.

Capacity: 185 seated.
Catering: Approved caterers list or your own caterer. There is a $100 kitchen rental fee.
Rental Fee: $650 Saturday, $550 Sunday, and $450 Friday.
Parking: On the premises.
Restriction: Entire building is smoke-free.
Note: Wedding ceremonies are permitted.

Inn & Conference Center
University of Maryland
University College   301-985-7855

University Blvd. at Adelphi Road • College Park, MD 20742

The Chesapeake, Ft. McHenry and Founders Rooms open up to an impressive reception area. Cocktail receptions are held in the artwork-laden expansive concourse, then guests enter the banquet rooms for top-notch cuisine. The garden courtyards with fountains, lighted ivy and exquisite greenery extend from the banquet rooms for those seeking a moment outside. A portable parquet dance floor allows for a flexible room design, and the chandeliers and spot lighting add special ambience.

Capacity: 500 seated; 700 standing; 50 in garden; 200 with tent.
Catering: In-house. Complete wedding packages are available.
Parking: On the premises. Valet parking can be arranged.
Restrictions: Bride/Groom or members of the immediate family must be faculty, students or alumni of the University of Maryland system.
Note: Wedding ceremonies are permitted.

Montgomery County
Agricultural Center Inc.   301-926-3100 x202

16 Chestnut Street • Gaithersburg, MD 20877

One of the most reasonably priced locations of its kind, this marvelous party space offers a unique environment for your reception. The Center's professional staff will assist you with every aspect of your special day. Conveniently located off I-270 and MD 355 in Gaithersburg, the size of this space allows it to be customized to reflect your individual style.

Capacity:	360.
Catering:	In-house or you may supply your own caterer. Entrees range from $8 to $18 per person when you use in-house caterer.
Rental Fee:	$800.
Parking:	On the premises.
Note:	Wedding ceremonies are permitted.

Scarlett Place   410-561-2433

c/o Chef's Expressions
250 S. President Street • Baltimore, MD 21202

With a dramatic black and white marble foyer, two ballrooms, bridal changing area and private bath, Scarlett Place is one of the city's most elegant settings. The Scarlett Room is decorated with custom floral carpet and hand-painted columns. The Plaza Room, in grey and silver tones, features brass and crystal sconce lighting. Both rooms have large parquet dance floors and open to a terrace overlooking the Inner Harbor. From brunches to full course dinners, its award-winning catering and event team will ensure the success of your special party.

Capacity:	500 seated; 800 standing in The Scarlett Room; 180 seated; 250 standing in The Plaza Room.
Catering:	In-house. Entrees range from $35 to $75 per person.
Rental Fee:	$2,200 for the Scarlett Room; $1,300 for the Plaza Room.
Parking:	Parking in nearby lot.
Note:	Wedding ceremonies are permitted.

Wakefield Valley Golf
& Conference Center   410-876-8787
www.wakefield.com

1000 Fenby Farm Road • Westminster, MD 21158

Overlooking a magnificent golf course, Wakefield Valley's beautifully appointed ballroom provides a perfect setting for any occasion. Cathedral ceilings with chandeliers and skylights, luxurious carpeting, inlaid parquet dance floor, three walls of windows, indoor balcony, large deck and garden patio are just a few of the amenities that make Wakefield an excellent choice.

Capacity:	200 seated; 300 standing; 150 in garden.
Catering:	In-house. Entrees with beverages are priced at $40 and above. Cake cutting, butler service, event coordinator, table linens, and centerpieces are provided at no charge.

Parking: On the premises.
Note: Wedding ceremony site available.

Westminster Catering
and Conference Center   410-857-1900

451 WMC Drive • Westminster, MD 21158

The Comfort Inn Westminster Catering and Conference Center is located in the heart of corporate, cultural and historical Westminster. The facility is within walking distance of shops, restaurants, and historical sites. Convenient to all major highways, it is located 30 minutes from Baltimore Inner Harbor, 25 minutes from Gettysburg. The hotel has 101 guest rooms, six of which are Jacuzzi suites, and five of which are efficiency units. The conference center caters weddings, rehearsal dinners, banquets, parties, and reunions, and offers a large menu selection for all occasions.

Capacity: 225 seated; 300 standing.
Catering: In-house. Entrees range from $20 to $40 per person. Cake cutting fee if you provide your own cake.
Parking: On the premises.
Note: Wedding ceremonies are permitted.

Argyle Country Club   301-598-5500

14600 Argyle Club Road • Silver Spring, MD 20906

A tree-lined entrance leads to the Argyle Country Club, set amid rolling hills and woods. Inside the clubhouse, experience a certain quiet charm of soft carpets, rich polished wood, and natural light. The banquet and meeting areas in the clubhouse are as functional as they are beautiful. The Ballroom, with its expansive wall of windows, is an extraordinary setting for a grand dinner, reception or meeting. The Sunset Room, with its sweeping views to the west, is a lovely location for luncheon or dinner. The President's Room is ideal for small dinners and receptions and can also be used for meetings. Fine food and beverage are part of every event at Argyle Country Club. Working out of a superb banquet kitchen, the executive chef and professional staff take pride in providing the right menu for every occasion, prepared with a special flair. Every event at Argyle Country Club, from an intimate dinner to a magnificent wedding, comes with personal, attentive service.

Capacity: 250 seated; 350 standing; 120 in garden; 250 with tent.
Catering: In-house. Entrees range from $40 to $75 per person.
Rental Fee: $750.
Parking: On the premises.
Note: Wedding ceremonies are permitted.

Country Club of Maryland   410-823-6710

1101 Stevenson Lane • Towson, MD 21286

This private golf and country club provides the ideal setting for your perfect day. Allow the exceptional executive chef and experienced banquet staff to provide you and your guests with the finest cuisine and service. A beautiful, tented outdoor patio provides the perfect backdrop for your formal portraits. Call to arrange an appointment for a personal tour of the clubhouse.

Capacity: 250 seated; 300 standing; 100 with tent.
Catering: In-house. Entrees begin at $37 per person. You are responsible for providing your own wedding cake.
Parking: On the premises. Valet parking available for extra fee.
Note: Wedding ceremonies are permitted.

Crofton Country Club   410-721-3111

1691 Crofton Parkway • Crofton, MD 21114

Crofton Country Club, now under Arnold Palmer Golf Management, has been elegantly renovated. Its new ballroom, featuring a dance floor, fireplace, natural lighting and brass chandeliers, is decorated in shades of hunter green and off-white, and is the perfect location for your wedding reception or rehearsal dinner. You are welcome to hold an indoor ceremony in the ballroom or take advantage of the picturesque grounds for a lovely outdoor wedding.

The menu, offering superb regional cuisine, is prepared on site by the executive chef. The professional staff will work closely with you in planning all the details of your function. The club offers plenty of parking and is located just 10 minutes from Annapolis and 25 minutes from both Baltimore and Washington, D.C.

Capacity: 230 seated; 350 standing.
Catering: In-house. Entrees range from $50 to $60 per person.
Parking: On the premises.
Note: Wedding ceremonies are permitted.

Montgomery Country Club   301-948-5393
http://Montgolf@aol.com

6550 Laytonsville Road • Laytonsville, MD 20882

Montgomery Country Club is located in a beautiful country setting in the township of Laytonsville. The newly renovated ballroom is bright and airy and has a breathtaking view of the golf course. Crystal chandeliers and beautiful draperies add a sense of richness to the room. This lovely club is fully staffed and offers full-service catering with a special touch. You don't have to be a member of this exclusive country club to enjoy its outstanding amenities and elegant facilities.

Capacity: 180 seated; 200 standing; 200 in garden; 200 with tent.
Catering: In-house.
Rental Fee: Varies. Call for more information.
Parking: On the premises.
Note: Wedding ceremonies are permitted.

Norbeck Country Club   301-774-7700

17200 Cashell Road • Rockville, MD 20853

Tucked away in the woods off Cashell Road between Rockville and Olney, Norbeck Country Club is a lovely setting for your wedding. The spacious ballroom has a dance floor and the adjacent room can be used for cocktails and hors d'oeuvres.

Capacity: 160 seated; 200 standing.
Catering: In-house. Entrees range from $24.95 to $45.00 per person.
Rental Fee: $325.
Parking: On the premises. Valet parking can be arranged.
Note: Wedding ceremonies are permitted. Ceremony space can accommodate 70 guests.

Swan Point Yacht and Country Club   301-259-4411

11305 Swan Point Boulevard • Issue, MD 20645

Nestled in historic Charles County, Maryland, Swan Point Yacht and Country Club is less than an hour from the Capital Beltway.

The dining and banquet facilities in the new clubhouse are reminiscent of Maryland's gracious past. A large veranda looks out on one of the top 18-hole golf courses in the mid-Atlantic region and a spectacular view of the Potomac River. Extensive menu and bar options are available. Swan Point Yacht and Country Club can make your special day perfect from beginning to end.

Capacity: 150 seated; 200 standing.
Catering: In-house. Entrees range from $20 to $40 per person.
Rental Fee: $3.15 per person.
Parking: On the premises.
Note: Wedding ceremonies are permitted.

Willow Tree Inn   301-948-8832

**19550 Montgomery Village Avenue
Gaithersburg, MD 20879**

Overlooking the Montgomery Village Golf Course, this inn is a charming place to celebrate your wedding day. The banquet room features floor-to-ceiling windows which open onto a lovely balcony, providing spectacular indoor and outdoor views from every angle. A lovely lake adds to the tranquil scene.

Capacity: 250 seated (10 a.m. to 4 p.m.), 150 seated (6 p.m. to 10 p.m.); 300 standing (10 a.m. to 4 p.m.), 200 standing (6 p.m. to 10 p.m.)
Catering: In-house. Entrees range from $20 to $80 per person. Cake cutting fee is $50.
Parking: On the premises.
Restrictions: Wedding ceremonies, 10 a.m. to 4 p.m. only.

Woman's Club of Chevy Chase   301-652-8480

7931 Connecticut Avenue • Chevy Chase, MD 20815

This Club features a large room with library, stage, hardwood floors, and French doors on one side which lead to a garden and windows on the other side with art displays between them. There is a second smaller room as well as an outside area where outdoor ceremonies can be held.

Capacity: 200 seated; 300 standing.
Catering: Approved caterers list. A large equipped kitchen is available.
Rental Fee: $1,050 to $1,200 Friday evening, Saturday and Sunday.
Parking: 90 spaces on the premises. Additional spaces are nearby.
Note: Wedding ceremonies are permitted indoors or outdoors. A separate bridal party area with balcony is above the library.

Friendship Heights Village Center   301-656-2797

4433 South Park Avenue • Chevy Chase, MD 20815

This unique gallery is enhanced by cathedral ceilings, parquet floors, and ceiling-to-floor windows overlooking a beautifully landscaped park with fountain. It has two small classrooms, and access to a 20' x 40' patio which can be tented.

Capacity: 120 to 150 seated; 250 to 300 standing.
Catering: You must supply your own caterer. Warming kitchen and tables and chairs provided.
Rental Fee: $800 to $1,200. Available for 8-hour contract on weekends between 2:00 p.m. to 12:30 a.m. Rental time includes any deliveries, set-up and take-down of equipment and clean-up.
Parking: Limited parking on premises. Additional parking in nearby lot. Walking distance to metro, hotel, shops and restaurants.
Restrictions: No smoking in building. No set-ups in front of building or in the park.
Note: Wedding ceremonies are permitted in the main room or on the patio only.

Inn & Conference Center
University of Maryland
University College   301-985-7855

University Blvd. at Adelphi Road • College Park, MD 20742

The Chesapeake, Ft. McHenry and Founders Rooms open up to an impressive reception area. Cocktail receptions are held in the artwork-laden expansive concourse, then guests enter the banquet rooms for top-notch cuisine. The garden courtyards with fountains, lighted ivy and exquisite greenery extend from the banquet rooms for those seeking a moment outside. A portable parquet dance floor allows for a flexible room design, and the chandeliers and spot lighting add special ambience.

Capacity: 500 seated; 700 standing; 50 in garden; 200 with tent.
Catering: In-house. Complete wedding packages are available.
Parking: On the premises. Valet parking can be arranged.
Restrictions: Bride/Groom or members of the immediate family must be faculty, students or alumni of the University of Maryland system.
Note: Wedding ceremonies are permitted.

McCrillis Gardens and Gallery   301-949-8230

6910 Greentree Road • Bethesda, MD 20817

This elegant garden is another lovely outdoor setting available for wedding ceremonies, receptions, or other social affair. It is a premier five-acre shade garden with a wedding gazebo nestled among spring-flowering rhododendrons and azaleas. Seasonal interest is extended with the use of ornamental trees, shrubs, colorful bulbs, ground covers and shade-loving perennials. An added bonus is the McCrillis Gallery displaying the work of artists from around the Washington metropolitan area. A shaded lawn perfect for tented affairs is located behind McCrillis Gallery. Guests will enjoy strolling through this peaceful garden.

Capacity: 125 seated and standing.
Catering.   Approved caterers list. Licensed and insured caterers only. Kitchen facilities are available.
Rental Fee: $1,500 for 6 hours, plus a $500 security deposit.
Parking: Parking lot nearby.
Restrictions: No amplified music.

Strathmore Hall   301-530-5889

10701 Rockville Pike • North Bethesda, MD 20852

A turn-of-the-century, red-brick mansion, Strathmore Hall is surrounded by 11 acres of landscaped beauty, including a sculpture garden and pavilion. Enter through grand columns into a marble-floored foyer complete with a cherub fountain. Enjoy intimate moments with your guests as they flow through the main hall, library, music room, sun room and galleries, all filled with exhibits of local and national artists. Pose for photographs on the lovely staircase, a favorite area for wedding party pictures. All eight of the first floor rooms, a bridal room on the second floor, and the kitchen are available when you rent Strathmore.

Capacity: 225 standing; 275 tented.
Catering: Approved caterers list.
Rental Fee: $1,400 to $2,900.
Parking: On the premises.
Note: Wedding ceremonies are permitted.

TROIA at the Walters   410-752-2887

600 North Charles Street • Baltimore, MD 21201

Situated in the heart of Baltimore's historic Mount Vernon neighborhood, TROIA at the Walters offers excellence in food, service and atmosphere. Newly re-decorated by internationally famed designer Rita Saint Clair, the restaurant features a grand staircase, large columns, skylights and a large fountain that has appeared in motion picture productions.

Capacity: 135 seated, 200 standing.
Catering: In-house. Entrees range from $35 to $85 per person.
Parking: Parking lot nearby. Valet parking can be arranged.
Note: Wedding ceremonies are permitted.

Admiral Fell Inn   410-522-7377

888 South Broadway • Baltimore, MD 21231

The Admiral Fell Inn is a newly renovated inn located downtown on Baltimore's historic waterfront. Its lively and colorful historic Fell's Point neighborhood is renowned for Belgian block streets and brick sidewalks, antique shops, boutiques, art galleries, pubs, and restaurants. In its 210-year history, the inn has served as a ship chandlery, a theater, a boarding house for sailors, and, later, a seaman's YMCA. Comfortable guest rooms are furnished with custom-crafted Federal-style furnishings. The inn is just a water taxi ride away from Baltimore's Inner Harbor attractions and Little Italy, museums, theaters, and cultural institutions. Amenities include 80 guest rooms and suites (nine with Jacuzzi tubs), continental breakfast, continuous tea and coffee service in the lobby, courtesy van to nearby Inner Harbor and downtown locations, and free parking. The inn's critically acclaimed main restaurant features regional American cuisine in a romantic setting, and an exceptional wine cellar. The new rooftop ballroom and terrace boast a spectacular 360-degree view of the city.

Capacity: 120 seated; 150 standing, with dance floor; 50 in garden; 24 with tent.
Catering: In-house. Entrees range from $55 to $125 per person. Cake cutting fee if you provide your own cake.
Parking: Parking in nearby lot.
Note: Wedding ceremonies are permitted.

Antrim 1844   1-800-858-1844

30 Trevanion Road • Taneytown, MD 21787

Fall in love with the extraordinary architecture at this antebellum plantation: the verandas and balconies, and the graciously proportioned drawing rooms, all tastefully appointed with period antiques and fine art. The feeling of Old-World refinement is the hallmark of this meticulously restored mansion, situated on 25 bucolic acres, which was built in 1844 by Colonel Andrew Ege from County Antrim, Ireland, as a wedding gift to his daughter and her husband. Enjoy the best of both worlds; climb into an antique canopy featherbed with your fireplace aglow, or relax in your oversized Jacuzzi. Fourteen luxurious guest rooms are available, as are four private dining areas. Each area has a distinctive personality of its own, including a magnificent pavilion overlooking the formal gardens and croquet lawn, with seating for 200 guests. The Antrim is 70 miles from Washington, D.C., and 40 miles from Baltimore.

Capacity: 175 seated; 250 standing; 250 garden; 500 with tent.
Catering: In-house. Entrees begin at $55 per person.
Rental Fee: $1,750.

Parking: On the premises.
Note: Wedding ceremonies are permitted.

Babe Ruth Museum   410-727-1539

216 Emory Street • Baltimore, MD 21230

The sports-minded couple can celebrate their nuptials in the birthplace of George Herman "Babe" Ruth, which includes a museum, small theater and displays on Ruth, the Orioles and Maryland baseball. The museum is contained in four rowhouses, one of which is filled with 1800's furniture, with an adjoining courtyard that can be used for cocktails or an outdoor wedding.

Capacity: 50 seated; 125 standing; 25 in garden.
Catering: Approved caterers list.
Rental Fee: $400.
Parking: Residential parking and nearby parking lot.
Restrictions: No smoking inside the building.
Note: Wedding ceremonies are permitted.

Brighton Dam-Azalea Season   301-774-9124

WSSC Brighton Dam
#2 Brighton Dam Road • Brookville, MD 20833

For couples who thrive on the spur-of-the-moment excitement, what better place for a wedding than among the 22,000 azaleas at Brighton Dam. Couples wishing to be married here need only to show up with their entourage, pick a scenic site and exchange "I do's."

Capacity: Unlimited.
Rental Fee: No fee.
Parking: Limited parking nearby.
Restrictions: No chairs, food or any kind of heavy equipment such as organs, may be brought in. No rice, birdseed or confetti.
Note: No reservations are taken for weddings, and no part of the garden can be cordoned off to keep curious onlookers away. Available for six weeks each April and May from 8:00 a.m. until dusk, seven days a week.

Brookside Gardens   301-949-8230

1500 Glenallan Avenue • Wheaton, MD 20902

If you have always wanted a garden wedding — this is the place where dreams come true. Weddings, receptions and other social events can now be scheduled year-round in the conservatory, new Visitor's Center, or as a tented affair in the gardens. Whether you choose the tropical paradise offered in the colorful climate-controlled conservatory, the oriental flair of the Japanese Tea House, the carefree innocence of the Fragrance Garden or the exquisite charm of the Wedding Gazebo, your guests will appreciate the beautifully landscaped settings throughout this 50-acre garden. A new reception hall overlooks the Azalea Garden hillside and Aquatic Garden ponds.

Capacity: 125 seated; 175 standing in reception hall; 250 in garden with tent.

Catering: Approved caterers list. Licensed and insured caterers only.

Rental Fee: Ranges from $350 at the Wedding Gazebo for an hour ceremony to $2,000 for seven hours in the reception hall. $500 deposit required.

Parking: On the premises, nearby parking lot and residential parking.

Restrictions: No smoking allowed inside the building.

Note: Brides may choose one of several gazebos for wedding ceremony.

Chase Court   410-727-1112

1112 St. Paul Street • Baltimore, MD 21202

Chase Court, in the historic neighborhood of Mt. Vernon, is an elegant and tasteful choice for your celebration. Its understated rooms are perfect for weddings, receptions and parties. The wisteria-covered gazebo is a favorite spot for wedding ceremonies, and the flower-filled garden is a beautiful site for toasts and tossing of the bouquet. However, in the meticulously restored Gothic ballroom there is a carved "Juliette" balcony which was perhaps built for that tradition. Chase Court is minutes from the Inner Harbor, a short walk from Penn Station and directly off the Jones Falls Freeway. It has abundant parking.

Capacity: 150 seated; 250 standing; 150+ in garden; 150+ with tent.

Catering: Approved caterers list. Entrees range from $20 to $30.

Rental Fee: $1,500.

Parking: Parking in nearby lot.

Note: Wedding ceremonies are permitted.

The Cloisters   410-557-4494

P.O. Box 5394 • 10440 Falls Road • Baltimore, MD 21209

Many brides choose to marry their Prince Charming in this castle-like mansion, built as a private home in 1932 and incorporating parts of medieval European castles in the architecture. The stone mansion with its gables and wrought iron spiral staircase reflects a blend of Gothic and Tudor styles. Guests use the entire first floor, including the main gallery with an area for dancing and the living room which features a working fireplace. Outside ceremonies may be performed in the courtyard garden or in the amphitheater. Have your wedding in this castle . . . and live happily ever after!

Capacity: 120 seated with dance floor; 150 seated without dance floor; 200 standing.
Catering: Approved caterers list or your own caterer.
Rental Fee: $1,000 to $1,100.
Parking: On the premises.
Note: Candles are permitted with hurricanes.

Columbia Inn Hotel   410-730-3900

10207 Wincopin Circle • Columbia, MD 21044

The Columbia Inn, commanding a spectacular view of Lake Kittamaqundi, is a sought-after location for receptions, anniversaries, and other joyous occasions. One ballroom leads to an outdoor terrace. The hotel is conveniently located to Merriweather Pavilion and to shopping. Wedding packages are all-inclusive. The Columbia Inn combines ambience with impeccable service.

Capacity: 250 seated; 500 standing; 80 in garden.
Catering: In-house. Entrees range from $48 to $60 per person.
Parking: On the premises.
Note: Wedding ceremonies are permitted indoors or outdoors, Sundays only. Guest rooms are available at special rates.

Comus Inn Restaurant   301-428-8593

23900 Old Hundred Road • Comus, MD 20842

This historic inn, built in 1794, is surrounded by flowering gardens, stately trees, lovely lawns and Sugarloaf Mountain. The tastefully restored inn is the perfect country setting for weddings, rehearsal dinners, anniversaries, or any celebration. There are five private dining rooms available for meetings, banquets, and other events. The inn affords easy access to I-270 and is just 30 minutes from the Beltway.

Capacity: 150 seated; 200 in garden; 200 with tent.
Catering: In-house. Entrees range from $20 to $50 per person. Cake cutting fee is $.50 per person.
Parking: On the premises.
Note: Wedding ceremonies are permitted.

Elkridge Furnace Inn   410-379-9336
www.elkridgefurnaceinn.com

5745 Furnace Avenue • Elkridge, MD 21075

This historic manor home, built in 1810, sits on the Patapsco River in a quiet corner of Howard County, Maryland. It is just minutes from BWI Airport, Baltimore, and Washington. The Furnace Inn has been restored to its original splendor, complete with beautiful gardens containing dogwoods, magnolias, azaleas, perennials, herbs, and an assortment of annuals. The gardens overlooking the Patapsco provide a beautiful backdrop for an outdoor ceremony. In the warmer months, the tent and patio can extend your function to the beautiful outdoors. In the winter months, your guests can warm themselves by one of the working fireplaces. The Elkridge Furnace Inn features complete custom gourmet catering for the most discriminating palate. The Inn offers the charm of a bygone era coupled with outstanding food and unmatched service.

Capacity: 60 first floor; 125 house; 200 with tent.
Catering: In-house. Entrees range from $40 to $65.
Rental Fee: $1,000 for 4 hours.
Parking: On the premises.

Evergreen House of the
Johns Hopkins University   410-516-0341

4545 North Charles Street • Baltimore, MD 21210

Seated on 26 acres, Evergreen provides the Baltimore community with an elegant, gracious estate at which to hold receptions. Evergreen has three areas for wedding receptions: The Evergreen Theater Wing, which consists of the large Far East Room, Theater and Lobby, and the smaller Billiard Room. With colors and Russian folk designs chosen by a noted Russian costume and set designer and a large collection of Japanese art work, the Theater Wing provides a colorful, dramatic location for a small reception. Amenities include a catering kitchen, piano, eight round tables and attractive black lacquer chairs. The Carriage House with its mid-19th century interior, wood paneling, hardwood and carpeted floors and large sliding doors that lead to a cobblestone entrance surrounded by trees, ivy and flowers, is a quite desirable location. Dancing is permitted in the Carriage House. The Upper Garden has two areas which may be tented and a fountain with Victorian cast iron benches. It may be rented in conjunction with either the Theater or Carriage House.

Capacity: 75 in Theater; up to 400 in Carriage House.
Catering: You must supply your own caterer.
Rental Fee: Varies. Call for details.
Parking: Ample free parking on the premises.

Restrictions: No amplified music in buildings. No smoking in buildings. No dancing in theater. No open flame in any location. No wedding ceremonies.

Fantasy Island   410-729-4505

St. Helena Island, Severn River • Crownsville, MD

The Mansion, on St. Helena Island in the prestigious Severn River, is just minutes from historic downtown Annapolis. St. Helena, with its towering oak trees, beautiful flowers, ivy-covered walls and spectacular water views, is the perfect wedding site. The mansion, a gracious Federal architectural design, was built in 1931 and is a close copy of the famous John Hopkins "Homewood House." The stately residence is graced by porticos and beautiful white Doric columns. The house features magnificent mahogany and marble floors, marble fireplaces, and antique chandeliers. In the spring, the island bursts into life with pink and white dogwoods, azaleas, rhododendrons and beautiful flower gardens set against the background of the Severn River. This enchanted island is the most exciting new wedding and special event venue in the Maryland, D.C. and Virginia area. Wedding packages, for up to 150 guests, include bride and groom changing suites, transportation by pleasure boat from the Annapolis city dock, and tented reception area. Catering, photography, music and flowers can be provided. Also, you may schedule honeymoon and guest travel arrangements at discounted rates through the Fantasy Island Travel Club.

Capacity: 150 seated; unlimited standing; unlimited in garden; unlimited with tent.
Catering: Approved caterers list. Entrees range from $40 to $80 per person.
Rental Fee: $4,500.
Parking: Although there is no maximum limit on the number of guests on the island, the boat maximum is 150 on each trip; thereafter, additional cost would be incurred. Parking is required in Annapolis public areas, close to the city dock.
Note: Wedding ceremonies are permitted.

Friendship Heights Village Center   301-656-2797

4433 South Park Avenue • Chevy Chase, MD 20815

This unique gallery is enhanced by cathedral ceilings, parquet floors, and ceiling-to-floor windows overlooking a beautifully landscaped park with fountain. It has two small classrooms, and access to a 20' x 40' patio which can be tented.

Capacity: 120 to 150 seated; 250 to 300 standing; 75 to 100 seated on patio.

Catering: You must supply your own caterer. Warming kitchen and tables and chairs provided.

Rental Fee: $800 to $1,200. Available for 8-hour contract on weekends between 2:00 p.m. to 12:30 a.m. Rental time includes any deliveries, set-up and take-down of equipment and clean-up.

Parking: Limited parking on premises. Additional parking in nearby lot. Walking distance to metro, hotel, shops and restaurants.

Restrictions: No smoking in building. No set-ups in front of building or in the park.

Note: Wedding ceremonies are permitted in the main room or on the patio only.

Glenview Mansion at Rockville
Civic Center Park   301-309-3001

603 Edmonston Drive • Rockville, MD 20851

Glenview Mansion, a pillared, neo-classical home built in the style of an early 19th century plantation house, overlooks Rockville's 153-acre Civic Center Park. Surrounding grounds include beautiful boxwoods and formal gardens perfect for outside ceremonies. An indoor ceremony area is available for winter weddings. The living room, library, and Lyon room are furnished with period reproductions for casual seating. The wood-paneled dining room is available for a buffet, and marble-floored conservatory for dancing. The second floor provides picturesque porches, an art gallery, and a separate bride's room.

Capacity: 50 seated; 225 standing.
Catering: You must supply your own caterer.
Rental Fee: $1,405 to $2,021.
Parking: On the premises.
Restrictions: No smoking. No cooking (warm and serve permit only). No red wine or red dye beverages.

Governor Calvert House   410-216-6328

58 State Circle • Annapolis, MD 21401

The 200-year-old Governor Calvert House, in the heart of historic Annapolis, is a charming setting for your wedding event. This converted former home of Lord Calvert features an atrium overlooking gardens that can accommodate up to 300 guests. It offers magnificent rooms, excellent food and unparalleled service. The staff will turn your wedding, reception or rehearsal dinner into a truly elegant affair.

Capacity: 160-260 seated; 300 standing.
Catering: In-house. Entrees range from $42.50 to $55 per person.

Parking: Parking in nearby lot.
Note: Wedding ceremonies are permitted.

Gramercy Mansion Bed & Breakfast
& The Carriage House   410-486-2405

1400 Greenspring Valley Road • Stevenson, MD 21153

This historic 1902 English Tudor mansion was built by Alexander
Cassatt, brother of Mary Cassatt, the American impressionist, as
a wedding present for his daughter. Situated on 45 acres in
Baltimore's Greenspring Valley, the house and grounds were part
of the "Old Line" community and the scene of many parties and
political gatherings during its early years. Now completely restored to its former elegance, Gramercy Bed and Breakfast welcomes you for a splendid occasion.

Capacity: 150.
Catering: You must supply your own caterer. Licensed and
                insured caterers only.
Rental Fee: $1,800 for 4 hours.
Parking: On the premises.
Restrictions: Smoking outside only. No birdseed or rice. Amplified
                music inside only.

Grey Rock Mansion   410-484-4554

400 Grey Rock Road • Pikesville, MD 21208

This Colonial-style mansion features a stone patio and gazebo
which overlook lovely landscaped formal gardens. With its breathtaking view and exquisite gardens, it serves as a beautiful setting
for weddings.

Capacity: 145 seated; 200 standing; 300 in garden; 225 with tent.
Catering: In-house. Entrees range from $30 to $50 per person.
Rental Fee: $700 to $1,300.
Parking: On the premises.
Note: Wedding ceremonies are permitted.

Hammond-Harwood House   410-263-4683

19 Maryland Avenue • Annapolis, MD 21401

This facility is a national historic landmark and an outstanding
example of American colonial architecture. The building, with its
carved entrance, formal rooms and elegant scale amid a charming
garden, makes this Annapolis location a popular reception choice.

Capacity: 24 seated; 40 standing; 125 in garden.
Catering: Approved caterers list. Caterer must supply all ban-
                quet items and remove at the end of the function.
Rental Fee: $600 and up for 4 hours.

Parking: Street parking; city garage available.
Restrictions: No amplified music. Clean-up pre-approved.
Note: Wedding ceremonies are permitted indoors or outdoors.

Herrington on the Bay   410-741-5101

7149 Lake Shore Drive, Rte. 261 • Rose Haven, MD 20714

Herrington on the Bay provides a classic Caribbean-style setting overlooking the Chesapeake Bay. Located just south of Annapolis and 30 minutes east of Washington, D.C., Herrington is accessible by car or boat. Professional caterers and wedding consultants take the stress out of wedding planning. Brides and grooms relax and enjoy their ceremonies and their receptions whether they choose indoors or out on the beachfront lawns. The Herrington Inn, located on premises, offers Island-style rooms with private hot tubs. From transportation to the music to the cuisine, Herrington delivers festive, fun weddings for today's brides!

Capacity: 200 seated; 250 standing; 300 in garden; 300 with tent.
Catering: In-house. Entrees range from $18 to $32 per person.
              Cake cutting fee if you provide your own cake.
Rental Fee: $195.
Parking: On the premises.
Note: Wedding ceremonies are permitted.

Inn & Conference Center
University of Maryland
University College   301-985-7855

University Blvd. at Adelphi Road • College Park, MD 20742

The Chesapeake, Ft. McHenry and Founders Rooms open up to an impressive reception area. Cocktail receptions are held in the artwork-laden expansive concourse, then guests enter the banquet rooms for top-notch cuisine. The garden courtyards with fountains, lighted ivy and exquisite greenery extend from the banquet rooms for those seeking a moment outside. A portable parquet dance floor allows for a flexible room design, and the chandeliers and spot lighting add special ambience.

Capacity: 500 seated; 700 standing; 50 in garden; 200 with tent.
Catering: In-house. Complete wedding packages are available.
Parking: On the premises. Valet parking can be arranged.
Restrictions: Bride/Groom or members of the immediate family
                must be faculty, students or alumni of the University
                of Maryland system.
Note: Wedding ceremonies are permitted.

Inn at Mitchell House 410-778-6500

8796 Maryland Parkway • Chestertown, MD 21620

Nestled on ten rolling acres, surrounded by woods and overlooking "Stoneybrook Pond," this historic manor house, built in 1743, affords a touch of tranquility. Small wedding parties during the cooler months can enjoy its parlors, 18th-century dining room, and numerous fireplaces. Larger weddings are held outdoors on the inn's sweeping lawn with beautiful vistas. This country location invites a peaceful step back in time.

Capacity: 50 inside; 250 outside.
Catering: In-house and approved caterers list. Entrees range from $25 to $40.
Rental Fee: $400 to $700.
Parking: On the premises.
Note: Wedding ceremonies are permitted.

Kent Manor Inn 1-800-820-4511

500 Kent Manor Drive • Stevensville, MD 21666

The Kent Manor Inn, a Maryland historical site, is situated on a 226-acre plantation one hour from Washington, D.C., and Baltimore. The beautiful Victorian mansion, circa 1820, and its glass-enclosed garden house are the perfect waterfront settings for wedding ceremonies, receptions, rehearsal dinners and anniversary celebrations. The inn has fireplaces with Italian marble mantels, two conference rooms and 24 individually decorated bedrooms, some with four-poster beds. A fine dining restaurant serves lunch and dinner.

Capacity: 150 seated; 150 standing; unlimited with tent on the grounds.
Catering: In-house. Entrees range from $56 to $94 per person including bar.
Rental Fee: $300 to $1,000.
Parking: On the premises.
Note: Wedding ceremonies are permitted.

Llewelyn Fields Manor 301-570-5114

c/o Snead Enterprises
812 Lindsey Manor Lane • Silver Spring, MD 20905

Elegant, enchanting and unforgettable, this circa 1820 grand manor house is on 11 tranquil acres, only minutes from Washington, D.C. The house is beautifully furnished with period antiques, oriental rugs, dazzling chandeliers and six fireplaces. The romantic setting is suitable for both wedding ceremony and reception. Patio and gardens are perfect for tent-covered festivities with dance floor and outdoor seating.

Capacity: 50 seated inside; 200 standing; 400+ in garden; 400+
            with tent.
Catering: You must supply your own caterer.
Rental Fee: $2,000.
Parking: On the premises.
Note: Wedding ceremonies are permitted. Guest rooms are
            available.

London Town
Publik House & Garden   410-222-1919

839 Londontown Road • Edgewater, MD 21037

A national historic landmark on the banks of the South River and
minutes from Annapolis, the House at London Town shares a
dramatic waterfront setting with an eight-acre woodland garden
and glass-enclosed pavilion. Surrounded by decks and overlooking the gardens and river, the pavilion attracts numerous weddings and receptions throughout the year. Ceremonies take place
on spacious or intimate overlooks in and around the gardens. The
House was designated a national historic landmark in 1970.

Capacity: 125 indoors; 175 with tent.
Catering: Approved caterers list or your own caterer. Caterer
            must be licensed and insured.
Rental Fee: $800 and up.
Parking: On the premises.

McCrillis Gardens and Gallery   301-949-8230

6910 Greentree Road • Bethesda, MD 20817

This elegant garden is another lovely outdoor setting available for
wedding ceremonies, receptions, or other social affair. It is a
premier five-acre shade garden with a wedding gazebo nestled
among spring-flowering rhododendrons and azaleas. Seasonal
interest is extended with the use of ornamental trees, shrubs,
colorful bulbs, ground covers and shade-loving perennials. An
added bonus is the McCrillis Gallery displaying the work of artists
from around the Washington metropolitan area. A shaded lawn
perfect for tented affairs is located behind McCrillis Gallery.
Guests will enjoy strolling through this peaceful garden.

Capacity: 125 seated and standing.
Catering: Approved caterers list. Licensed and insured caterers
              only. Kitchen facilities are available.
Rental Fee: $1,500 for 6 hours, plus a $500 security deposit.
Parking: Parking lot nearby.
Restrictions: No amplified music.

Merry Sherwood Plantation   410-641-2112

8909 Worcester Highway • Berlin, MD 21811

Handsomely restored and furnished with many fine antiques, the pre-Civil War mansion is situated on 18 acres of gardens. You can descend the mahogany staircase in the magnificent entry hall and be married in the elegant grand parlor with the original marble fireplaces, or choose one of many gardens or the gazebo as a setting for your wedding and/or reception. The house is decorated inside and out for the Christmas season events. Merry Sherwood Plantation, with its roses and azaleas, flowering shrubs, 150-year-old shade trees and park-like setting, is ten minutes from Assateague National Seashore and Ocean City on the eastern shore of Maryland.

Capacity:	30 seated; 125 standing; 200+ in garden; 200+ with tent.
Catering:	Approved caterers list. Entrees range from $14 to $35 per person.
Rental Fee:	$1,500 for 75-125 guests.
Parking:	On the premises.
Restrictions:	Dancing is not allowed in the mansion but may be held under a tent.
Note:	Wedding ceremonies are permitted.

Montpelier Mansion   301-953-1376

Route 197 & Muirkirk Road • Laurel, MD 20708

Located on 70 acres of rolling park land, this national historic landmark provides the perfect atmosphere for any elegant social occasion. Ceremonies and receptions can take place in a number of locations from the great entry hall to the indoor wings to the outdoor garden terraces graced by a 200-year-old summerhouse and boxwood. Guests can view furnished museum rooms during their visit. The mansion is ideal for business retreats and seminars at lower weekday rates.

Capacity:	100.
Catering:	You must supply your own caterer.
Rental Fee:	$800 Saturday; $700 Friday and Sunday for 7 hours. Facility requires a $400 refundable security deposit and a $50 custodial fee.
Parking:	On the premises.
Restrictions:	No smoking inside.
Note:	Wedding ceremonies are permitted indoors or outdoors.

Mrs. K's Toll House   301-589-3500

9201 Colesville Road • Silver Spring, MD 20910

Mrs. K's Toll House is one of the last operating toll houses in Montgomery County. The interior of this historic building is elegantly appointed with carefully collected antiques and hand-crafted seasonal decorations. The staff will personalize your menu so that your guests may choose from more than one entree. Lush gardens provide a romantic setting for outdoor ceremonies and receptions. It is conveniently located just south of the beltway in Silver Spring, and offers plenty of well-lit parking.

Capacity: 150 seated; unlimited in garden. Can seat up to 110 with a reasonable dance floor, 150 without a dance floor.
Catering: In-house. Entrees range from $19 to $49 per person.
Parking: On the premises.
Note: Wedding ceremonies are permitted.

National Aquarium in Baltimore   410-576-3869/3847

501 E. Pratt Street, Pier 3 • Baltimore, MD 21202

The magic and mystery of water make the National Aquarium in Baltimore ideal for couples who want a signature event. Create a mix of romance and fun, from casual to elegant, in settings appropriate for intimate parties or 800-guest galas. Secluded, tented parties on the pier are perfect for dancing under the stars. Dine near dolphins in the Marine Mammal Pavilion Underwater Viewing Area, dance in the airy Atrium, or enjoy breathtaking views in the Harbor View Room. Full-service catering is available. The Aquarium can accommodate a kosher wedding.

Capacity: 500 seated; 2,000 standing; 2,000 with tent.
Catering: In-house. Entrees begin at $20 per person and bar at $9.00 per person.
Rental Fee: $1,000 and up.
Parking: Parking in nearby lots.
Note: Wedding ceremonies are permitted.

Newton White Mansion   301-249-2004

2708 Enterprise Road • Mitchellville, MD 20716

Built in 1939, this house was once the home of Captain Newton H. White, who was the first commanding officer of the *USS Enterprise*. Newton White Mansion is one of the most popular settings in Prince George's County. It offers a quiet atmosphere, elegant patios, and a beautiful garden with a waterfall fountain for outdoor events.

Capacity: 125 seated; 200 standing; 200 in garden.
Catering: You must supply your own caterer. Caterer must be licensed and insured.
Rental Fee: $2,100 Saturday; $1,700 Friday and Sunday.
Parking: Free parking on the premises.

Note: Wedding ceremonies are permitted indoors or outdoors. Facility is handicap accessible.

Historic Oakland   410-730-4801/1-800-730-4802
www.historic-oakland.com

5430 Vantage Point Road • Columbia, MD 21044

Celebrate the occasion of your marriage with family and friends at a lovely manor estate. Adding grace to the exquisite interior are crystal chandeliers, period reproductions of the original furnishings and twin fireplaces in the ballroom and foyer. The ballroom doors lead to a veranda that overlooks a beautifully landscaped lawn and an antique rose garden.

Capacity: 150 seated; 200 standing; 200 in garden.
Catering: In-house, approved caterers list or your own caterer provided the caterer adheres to the rules and policies of the mansion.
Rental Fee: $700 to $1,500.
Parking: On the premises. Valet parking can be arranged.
Note: Wedding ceremonies are permitted indoors or outdoors.

Oxon Hill Manor   301-839-7782

6901 Oxon Hill Road • Oxon Hill, MD 20745

High atop a hill overlooking the Potomac River, Oxon Hill Manor is a breathtaking historic neo-Georgian style mansion with a wrap-around terrace, reflecting pool, and formal gardens. The elegant interior consists of a drawing room, library, dining room, marbled foyer, bride's dressing room and caterer's kitchen. The main rooms all lead onto the terrace through large French doors. Ideal for wedding ceremonies and receptions, social functions, business meetings and holiday parties, Oxon Hill Manor recalls the splendor of a by-gone era and will make your event an affair to remember.

Capacity: 210 seated; 300 standing.
Catering: You must supply your own caterer.
Rental Fee: $2,400 Friday, Saturdays, Sundays and holidays. Call to inquire about weekday rates.
Parking: On the premises.
Note: Wedding ceremonies are permitted.

Quiet Waters Park   410-222-1777

600 Quiet Waters Park Road • Annapolis, MD 21403

Located in Annapolis on the banks of the South River, this 336-acre park represents Victorian style architecture. The park design features fountains, gazebos, woodland trails and formal gardens. The park's Blue Heron Center with its formal gardens is perfect for large parties, receptions and weddings. Couples renting the Center may use the immediate lower garden area for their ceremony at no extra charge.

Capacity: 150 seated; 225 standing.
Catering: In-house.
Rental Fee: Call for more information.
Parking: On the premises.
Note: Wedding ceremonies are permitted indoors or outdoors.

Reynolds Tavern   410-626-0380/1-888-626-0381

7 Church Circle, P.O. Box 748 • Annapolis, MD 21404

Located in the heart of historic Annapolis, this authentically restored building, circa 1747, provides a wonderful setting for all wedding functions including rehearsal dinners, ceremonies and receptions. The facility includes two colonial-style dining rooms, a private shady garden and terrace, a casual English pub, and four spacious lodging rooms. Whether you use one room or the entire facility, your guests will be impressed with the graceful setting, fresh and beautifully presented cuisine and attentive service. The tavern's complete wedding coordination services will make your event memorable and worry-free.

Capacity: 75 seated; 90 standing inside; 130 seated, 160 standing in garden; 100 with tent.
Catering: In-house. Entrees range from $25 to $50 per person. Cake cutting fee if you provide your own cake.
Rental Fee: Either $500 for whole facility, or a minimum food and beverage commitment.
Parking: Parking in nearby lot. Valet parking is available.
Note: Wedding ceremonies are permitted.

Rockwood Manor Park   301-299-5026

11001 MacArthur Boulevard • Potomac, MD 20854

Escape the commotion and bustle of the city and have your wedding reception in the park. Located in Potomac, Rockwood is just 20 minutes from downtown Washington and convenient to Bethesda and Rockville. You may enjoy a memorable feast in the spacious manor house, or have an elegant outdoor reception in the breathtaking gardens and patios that surround Rockwood.

Capacity: 100 seated; 150 standing; 150 in garden.
Catering: Approved caterers list.
Rental Fee: $1,400 Friday and Sunday; $1,700 Saturday.
Parking: 85 parking spaces on the premises.
Restrictions: No amplified outdoor music.

Note: Wedding ceremonies are permitted indoors or outdoors.

The Rossborough Inn   301-314-8012

Route 1 • University of Maryland • College Park, MD 20742

The Rossborough Inn is ideally suited for weddings and receptions. The dignity and grace of the charming dining rooms, English garden and courtyard create the perfect atmosphere for an elegant wedding. The inn has just added a new outdoor patio that can accommodate dancing and hors d'oeuvres.

Capacity: 145 seated; 175 standing; 300 in garden.
Catering: In-house. Entrees range from $45 to $65 per person. Cake cutting fee is $1.00 per person.
Rental Fee: $750.
Parking: On the premises, residential and nearby parking lot.
Restrictions: No smoking. No rice or birdseed.
Note: Wedding ceremonies are permitted.

Strathmore Hall   301-530-5889

10701 Rockville Pike • North Bethesda, MD 20852

A turn-of-the-century, red-brick mansion, Strathmore Hall is surrounded by 11 acres of landscaped beauty, including a sculpture garden and pavilion. Enter through grand columns into a marble-floored foyer complete with a cherub fountain. Enjoy intimate moments with your guests as they flow through the main hall, library, music room, sun room and galleries, all filled with exhibits of local and national artists. Pose for photographs on the lovely staircase, a favorite area for wedding party pictures. All eight of the first floor rooms, a bridal room on the second floor, and the kitchen are available when you rent Strathmore.

Capacity: 225 standing; 275 with tent.
Catering: Approved caterers list.
Rental Fee: $1,400 to $2,900.
Parking: On the premises.
Note: Wedding ceremonies are permitted.

Strong Mansion   301-869-7846 (Metro)
at Sugarloaf Mountain   301-874-2024 (Frederick)

c/o Stronghold, Inc.
7901 Comus Road • Dickerson, MD 20842

Strong Mansion was built in 1912 by Chicago philanthropist Gordon Strong. The three-story Georgian home is surrounded by 3,000 woodland acres on Sugarloaf Mountain. You and your guests are welcome to roam the grounds and enjoy the beautiful antique furnishings throughout the entire home. The 22' x 60' spacious ballroom has eight large Palladian windows, two decorative fireplaces, and French doors that open on to a 15' x 34' portico. The back grounds are landscaped with formal gardens, a lily pond with a fountain, a white wooden pergola that is ideal for wedding ceremonies, and a breathtaking view of the countryside. Strong Mansion is the perfect setting for an outdoor wedding, reception, and other special events.

Capacity: 150.
Catering: You must supply your own caterer.
Rental Fee: $1,500 for 8 hours.
Parking: On the premises.
Restrictions: No smoking.
Note: Wedding ceremonies are permitted. The mansion is handicap accessible.

Swan Point Yacht and Country Club   301-259-4411

11305 Swan Point Boulevard • Issue, MD 20645

Nestled in historic Charles County, Maryland, Swan Point Yacht and Country Club is less than an hour from the Capital Beltway. The dining and banquet facilities in the new clubhouse are reminiscent of Maryland's gracious past. A large veranda looks out on one of the top 18-hole golf courses in the mid-Atlantic region and a spectacular view of the Potomac River. Extensive menu and bar options are available. Swan Point Yacht and Country Club can make your special day perfect from beginning to end.

Capacity: 150 seated; 200 standing.
Catering: In-house. Entrees range from $20 to $40 per person.
Rental Fee: $3.15 per person.
Parking: On the premises.
Note: Wedding ceremonies are permitted.

The Other Barn   410-730-4610

5851 Robert Oliver Place • Columbia, MD 21045

With convenient access from Baltimore and Washington, D.C., via I-95, The Other Barn offers a memorable place for weddings. Once part of the Owings Dorsey Dairy Farm, it has been remodeled and decorated to preserve its character, providing a pleasant and relaxed atmosphere. The Loft features a large hardwood dance floor and the original wooden beam high ceilings. The Smithy-Tack Room overlooks a beautifully landscaped courtyard.

Capacity: 240 seated; 300 standing; 200 in garden.
Catering: Approved caterers list or your own caterer.
Rental Fee: $200 to $675.

Parking: On the premises. Parking lot nearby.
Note: Wedding ceremonies are permitted.

Union Mills Homestead Museum   410-848-2288

3311 Littlestown Pike • Westminster, MD 21157

If you prefer an outdoor celebration in a rural atmosphere—this is the place. Weeping willows, flower gardens and a footbridge are some of the many attractions on the land of the Homestead, a 23-room structure built in 1797.

Capacity: 250 seated in Tannery; unlimited capacity on grounds.
Catering: You must supply your own caterer.
Rental Fee: Facilities request a donation of $200 for grounds and $300 for tannery building.
Parking: On the premises.
Restrictions: Alcoholic beverages may be brought on premises, but not sold.
Note: Wedding ceremonies are permitted. Hours til dusk, April to October. One event a day.

William Paca House   410-263-5553

186 Prince George Street • Annapolis, MD 21401

This 37-room Georgian mansion, surrounded by formal English gardens complete with wooden bridge, makes this Annapolis landmark a picturesque setting and popular reception choice. Receptions take place on tented terraces overlooking the gardens of the home built by former governor William Paca for his bride.

Capacity: 150 seated; 160 standing; 150 with tent.
Catering: You must supply your own caterer. Kitchen facilities are available.
Rental Fee: $500 to $2,000 for five hours.
Parking: Parking lot nearby. Valet parking can be arranged.
Restrictions: No hard liquor, only beer and wine. Limits on decorations. Limits on music and noise levels. Licensed and insured caterers only.
Note: Wedding ceremonies are permitted outdoors only.

Woman's Club of Chevy Chase   301-652-8480

7931 Connecticut Avenue • Chevy Chase, MD 20815

This Club features a large room with library, stage, hardwood floors, and French doors on one side which lead to a garden and windows on the other side with art displays between them. There is a second smaller room as well as an outside area where outdoor ceremonies can be held.

Capacity: 200 seated; 300 standing.
Catering: Approved caterers list. A large equipped kitchen is available.
Rental Fee: $1,050 to $1,200 Friday evening, Saturday and Sunday.
Parking: 90 spaces on the premises. Additional spaces are nearby.
Note: Wedding ceremonies are permitted indoors or outdoors. A separate bridal party area with balcony is above the library.

Woodend   301-652-9188

8940 Jones Mill Road • Chevy Chase, MD 20815

Woodend is a beaux arts style mansion with classic Greek portico that overlooks sweeping lawns bordered by woods and meadows. Indoors, a Palladian window lights up a distinguished staircase and carved fireplace in the Great Hall. Step through stately French doors onto a raised terrace with a custom tent lit with chandeliers. Enjoy your romantic wedding ceremony in an enchanting grove surrounded by a canopy of trees. Woodend is a 40-acre bird sanctuary owned by the Audubon Naturalist Society and is conveniently located directly inside the beltway in Chevy Chase.

Capacity: 150 seated; 200 standing.
Catering: Approved caterers list.
Rental Fee: $1,200 to $3,100.
Parking: On the premises.
Note: Wedding ceremonies are permitted.

Woodlawn Manor   301-585-5564

16501 Norwood Road • Sandy Spring, MD 20860

Magnificent trees, rolling green landscape, garden gazebo and a unique stone barn set the stage for an elegant reception. Only minutes from busy urban centers, the Georgian-style manor house offers five spacious rooms, richly restored and tastefully furnished, to provide the charm and splendor of the 19th century. A modernized kitchen meets high-level catering requirements and ample parking is in close proximity to the manor house.

Capacity: 40 seated; 125 standing; 200 in garden.
Catering: Approved caterers list.
Rental Fee: $1,000 Friday and Sunday; $1,200 Saturday.
Parking: 48 parking spaces on the premises with overflow parking nearby.
Note: Wedding ceremonies are permitted.

Brookside Gardens   301-949-8230

1500 Glenallan Avenue • Wheaton, MD 20902

If you have always wanted a garden wedding— this is the place where dreams come true. Weddings, receptions and other social events can now be scheduled year-round in the conservatory, new Visitor's Center, or as a tented affair in the gardens. Whether you choose the tropical paradise offered in the colorful conservatory, the oriental flair of the Japanese Tea House, the carefree innocence of the Fragrance Garden or the exquisite charm of the Wedding Gazebo, your guests will appreciate the beautifully landscaped settings throughout this 50-acre garden. A new reception hall overlooks the Azalea Garden hillside and Aquatic Garden ponds.

Capacity: 125 seated; 175 standing in reception hall; 250 in garden with tent.
Catering: Approved caterers list. Licensed and insured caterers only.
Rental Fee: Ranges from $350 at the Wedding Gazebo for an hour ceremony to $2,000 for seven hours in the reception hall. $500 deposit required.
Parking: On the premises, nearby parking lot and residential parking.
Restrictions: No smoking allowed inside the building.
Note: Brides may choose one of several gazebos for wedding ceremony.

Casey Community Center   301-258-6366

810 S. Frederick Avenue • Gaithersburg, MD 20877

The Community Center is conveniently located just east of I-270 and provides a quaint setting for a wedding reception, birthday party or special get-together. The Center has two banquet rooms, and the larger room comes with a kitchen. The rooms are decorated with elegant brass sconces with controlled lighting.

Capacity: 135 seated; 150 standing.
Catering: You must supply your own caterer. The center comes equipped with tables and chairs.
Rental Fee: $60 per hour.
Parking: On the premises.
Note: Guest rooms are available.

Friendship Heights Village Center   301-656-2797

4433 South Park Avenue • Chevy Chase, MD 20815

This unique gallery is enhanced by cathedral ceilings, parquet floors, and ceiling-to-floor windows overlooking a beautifully landscaped park with fountain. It has two small classrooms, and access to a 20' x 40' patio which can be tented.

Capacity: 120 to 150 seated; 250 to 300 standing; 75 to 100 seated on patio.
Catering: You must supply your own caterer. Warming kitchen and tables and chairs provided.
Rental Fee: $800 to $1,200. Available for 8-hour contract on weekends between 2:00 p.m. to 12:30 a.m. Rental time includes any deliveries, set-up and take-down of equipment and clean-up.
Parking: Limited parking on premises. Additional parking in nearby lot. Walking distance to metro, hotel, shops and restaurants.
Restrictions: No smoking in building. No set-ups in front of building or in the park.
Note: Wedding ceremonies are permitted in the main room or on the patio only.

George Peabody Library of The Johns Hopkins University   410-659-8197
http://peabody-events.mse.jhu.edu

17 E. Mount Vernon Place • Baltimore, MD 21202

An unique architectural treasure built in 1878, The George Peabody Library is an uplifting setting for special celebrations. Located in the heart of the historic district, the superb neo-Greco building faces the open park of Mount Vernon Place and the Washington Monument. Within the large, main chamber, six book-filled tiers of gilt, cast iron balconies rise dramatically above the marble-tiled open court toward a grand skylight.

Capacity: 230 seated; 400 standing.
Catering: Approved caterers list or your own caterer with the approval of the facility.
Rental Fee: $1,675 to $2,175.
Parking: In nearby lots or garages. Valet parking can be arranged.
Restrictions: No smoking. No helium balloons. No rice, birdseed or glitter.
Note: Wedding ceremonies are permitted.

Great Blacks In Wax Museum, Inc.   410-563-6415

1601-3 East North Avenue • Baltimore, MD 21213

This unique museum showcases African-American history with 110 life-size, lifelike wax figures, including a room devoted to nine famous Marylanders. The Alberta Carson room has a gold-painted ceiling and African carved wood panels.

Capacity: 150 seated; 250 standing.
Catering: Approved caterers list.
Rental Fee: $250 plus $1.00 per person.
Parking: Residential parking. Parking lot nearby.
Note: Wedding ceremonies are permitted.

The Heritage Room   301-249-1167

12010 Woodmore Road • Mitchellville, MD 20716

The Heritage Room in the Holy Family Parish Centre is situated
in a rural setting rich in history. Opened in 1992, the facility's
architecture complements the century-old Holy Family Church,
a state historical landmark. Your guests can enjoy the wooded
country setting adjacent to the exclusive Woodmore community
and the Prince George's Country Club.

Capacity: 250 seated.
Catering: In-house or approved caterers list. Package prices
                range from $21.95 to $28.95 per person (includes
                buffet meal and hall).
Parking: On the premises.
Note: Wedding ceremonies are permitted.

Historic Baldwin Hall   410-923-3438

1358 Millersville Road • Crownsville, MD 21032

Historic Baldwin Hall is a lovely country church built in 1861.
Surrounded by landscaped gardens and mature trees, it is located
in Millersville at the intersection of Generals Highway and
Millersville Road. The spacious main hall, with its lofty ceilings,
arched windows, hardwood floors, and stage with green velvet
curtains, is a wonderful space to decorate. There's also a front
reception area, choir loft, and bride's room for changing and
privacy. The hall is available seven days a week at reasonable
rates.

Capacity: 125 seated; 299 standing.
Catering: You must must supply your own caterer. A well-
                equipped kitchen with ranges, microwave, refrigera-
                tor and warming oven is available. Tables and chairs
                are provided. All caterers are accepted.
Rental Fee: $500.
Parking: On the premises.

The Johns Hopkins University
Glass Pavilion   410-516-8209

3400 N. Charles Street • Baltimore, MD 21218

The Glass Pavilion is located in a natural wooded setting on the
campus of Johns Hopkins University. It is totally encased in glass

with a patio surrounding the entire room. Amenities include a permanent stage.

Capacity: 200 to 250 seated; 500 standing.
Catering: In-house or your own caterer.
Rental Fee: $975.
Parking: On the premises and nearby parking lot.
Restrictions: Available June through August 14 of each year.
Note: Wedding ceremonies are permitted indoors or outdoors.

Kahler Hall   410-730-0770

5440 Old Tucker Row • Columbia, MD 21044

Situated in Columbia, Maryland, Kahler Hall is 25 minutes from Baltimore, and 45 minutes from Washington, D.C. The Ruth Keeton Ballroom with its wonderful hardwood floor is great for dancing. The beautiful lobby can be used in conjunction with the ballroom for cocktails and hors d'oeuvres. Picture a well-appointed living room—only much larger—with a freestanding woodburning fireplace. The attached patio provides an additional entertaining area when the weather is good.

Capacity: 220 seated; 300 standing.
Catering: You must supply your own caterer. Tables and chairs are provided by facility.
Rental Fee: $575 to $790.
Restrictions: No decorations may be attached to the ceiling, walls or light fixtures. No red punch or wine allowed.

Knights of Columbus   301-530-0258

Rock Creek Council
5417 West Cedar Lane • Bethesda, MD 20814

Looking for a bargain? This comfortable and affordable location comes complete with dance floor, tables and chairs, kitchen and ample parking. The size and flexibility of this hall allows it to be customized for any type of affair. Turn it into a charming setting with your own decorating flair.

Capacity: 200 seated.
Catering: Approved caterers list or your own caterer.
Rental Fee: $650 for 4 hours.
Parking: On the premises.

La Fontaine Bleu   410-675-6090

3120 Erdman Avenue • Baltimore, MD 21213

This multi-ballroom facility features crystal chandeliers and an elegant decor. It specializes in providing excellent catering at reasonable prices.

Capacity: 500 seated; 600 standing.
Catering: In-house. Entrees begin at $20 per person.
Parking: On the premises.
Note: Wedding ceremonies are permitted.

Lodge at Little Seneca Creek   301-585-5564

14500-A Clopper Road • Boyds, MD 20841

The Lodge at Little Seneca Creek is a rustic meeting place designed as a replica of a classic log cabin. The lodge's spacious meeting hall is accented by a massive flagstone fireplace. The splendor of the oak flooring is surpassed only by the natural wood cathedral ceilings. A breathtaking view from the outdoor deck includes a pastoral scene where an outdoor wedding reception may be held.

Capacity: 120 seated; 180 standing.
Catering: Approved caterers list.
Rental Fee: $700 Friday and Sunday; $900 Saturday.
Parking: 85 parking spaces on the premises.
Note: Wedding ceremonies are permitted indoors or outdoors.

Montgomery County
Agricultural Center Inc.   301-926-3100 x202

16 Chestnut Street • Gaithersburg, MD 20877

One of the most reasonably priced locations of its kind, this marvelous party space offers a unique environment for your reception. The Center's professional staff will assist you with every aspect of your special day. Conveniently located off I-270 and MD 355 in Gaithersburg, the size of this space allows it to be customized to reflect your individual style.

Capacity: 360.
Catering: In-house or you may supply your own caterer. Entrees range from $8 to $18 per person when you use in-house caterer.
Rental Fee: $800.
Parking: On the premises.
Note: Wedding ceremonies are permitted.

The Other Barn   410-730-4610

5851 Robert Oliver Place • Columbia, MD 21045

With convenient access from Baltimore and Washington, D.C., via I-95, The Other Barn offers a memorable place for weddings. Once part of the Owings Dorsey Dairy Farm, it has been remodeled and decorated to preserve its character, providing a pleasant and relaxed atmosphere. The Loft features a large hardwood dance floor and the original wooden beam high ceilings. The Smithy-Tack Room overlooks a beautifully landscaped court-yard.

Capacity: 240 seated; 300 standing; 200 in garden.
Catering: Approved caterers list or your own caterer.
Rental Fee: $200 to $675.
Parking: On the premises. Parking lot nearby.
Note: Wedding ceremonies are permitted.

Admiral Fell Inn   410-522-7377

888 South Broadway • Baltimore, MD 21231

The Admiral Fell Inn is a newly renovated inn located downtown on Baltimore's historic waterfront. Its lively and colorful historic Fell's Point neighborhood is renowned for Belgian block streets and brick sidewalks, antique shops, boutiques, art galleries, pubs, and restaurants. In its 210-year history, the inn has served as a ship chandlery, a theater, a boarding house for sailors, and, later, a seaman's YMCA. Comfortable guest rooms are furnished with custom-crafted Federal-style furnishings. The inn is just a water taxi ride away from Baltimore's Inner Harbor attractions and Little Italy, museums, theaters, and cultural institutions. Amenities include 80 guest rooms and suites (nine with Jacuzzi tubs), continental breakfast, continuous tea and coffee service in the lobby, courtesy van to nearby Inner Harbor and downtown locations, and free parking. The inn's critically acclaimed main restaurant features regional American cuisine in a romantic setting, and an exceptional wine cellar. The new rooftop ballroom and terrace boast a spectacular 360-degree view of the city.

Capacity: 120 seated; 150 standing, with dance floor; 50 in garden; 24 with tent.
Catering: In-house. Entrees range from $55 to $125 per person. Cake cutting fee if you provide your own cake.
Parking: Nearby parking lot.
Note: Wedding ceremonies are permitted.

Antrim 1844   1-800-858-1844

30 Trevanion Road • Taneytown, MD 21787

Fall in love with the extraordinary architecture at this antebellum plantation: the verandas and balconies, and the graciously proportioned drawing rooms, all tastefully appointed with period antiques and fine art. The feeling of Old-World refinement is the hallmark of this meticulously restored mansion, situated on 25 bucolic acres, which was built in 1844 by Colonel Andrew Ege from County Antrim, Ireland, as a wedding gift to his daughter and her husband. Enjoy the best of both worlds; climb into an antique canopy featherbed with your fireplace aglow, or relax in your oversized Jacuzzi. Fourteen luxurious guest rooms are available, as are four private dining areas. Each area has a distinctive personality of its own, including a magnificent pavilion overlooking the formal gardens and croquet lawn, with seating for 200 guests. The Antrim is 70 miles from Washington, D.C., and 40 miles from Baltimore.

Capacity: 175 seated; 250 standing; 250 garden; 500 with tent.
Catering: In-house. Entrees begin at $55 per person.
Rental Fee: $1,750.

Parking: On the premises.
Note: Wedding ceremonies are permitted.

Armory Place   301-585-5564

925 Wayne Avenue • Silver Spring, MD 20910

Conveniently located in downtown Silver Spring, only two blocks from the metro station, Armory Place is a great location for your reception. Dominating the facility is the spacious Lee Auditorium. This bright, comfortable room is ideal when you have a sizeable guest list. Smaller rooms are available upon request.

Capacity: 300-350 seated; 445 standing.
Catering: Approved caterers list.
Rental Fee: $1,000 Friday and Sunday; $1,200 Saturday.
Parking: Metered and public parking.
Note: Wedding ceremonies are permitted indoors or outdoors.

B&O Railroad Museum   410-752-2463

901 West Pratt Street • Baltimore, MD 21223-2699

At the B&O Museum, guests view an exciting array of locomotives and cars that span over a century, dating back to the earliest days of rail transportation. The rental of the facility includes full use of several 19th-century railroad buildings: the Mt. Clare Station, an 1851 depot building that guests enter through the museum; the Mt. Clare Annex, a two-story 1884 print shop building now housing the museum's archives; the Mt. Clare Theater and gift shop; and the Roundhouse, an 1884 passenger repair facility.

Capacity: 700 seated; 2,200 standing.
Catering: Approved caterers list. No kitchen facilities.
Rental Fee: $2,100 for first 200 guests, $6 each additional guest.
Parking: On the premises and nearby parking lot.
Restrictions: No helium filled balloons. No confetti. Smoking only in designated areas.
Note: Wedding ceremonies are permitted.

Babe Ruth Museum   410-727-1539

216 Emory Street • Baltimore, MD 21230

The sports-minded couple can celebrate their nuptials in the birthplace of George Herman "Babe" Ruth, which includes a museum, small theater and displays on Ruth, the Orioles and Maryland baseball. The museum is contained in four rowhouses, one of which is filled with 1800's furniture, with an adjoining courtyard that can be used for cocktails or an outdoor wedding.

Capacity: 50 seated; 125 standing; 25 in garden.
Catering: Approved caterers list.
Rental Fee: $400.
Parking: Residential parking and nearby parking lot.
Restrictions: No smoking inside the building.
Note: Wedding ceremonies are permitted.

Blair Mansion Inn   301-588-1688

7711 Eastern Avenue • Silver Spring, MD 20912

The Blair Mansion Inn was first built in 1890 by architect Stanford White, who also designed Madison Square Gardens in New York. Later renovations turned the house into an inn and a dinner theater. This graciously restored inn offers a lovely environment for a wedding reception, anniversary, or other special celebrations.

Capacity: 350 seated; 425 standing.
Catering: In-house or your own caterer with approval of facility. Entrees range from $16.95 to $25.95 per person when you use in-house caterer.
Parking: Free parking on the premises and residential parking.

Candle Light Inn   410-788-6076

1835 Frederick Road • Catonsville, MD 21228

The Candle Light Inn has been celebrating beautiful weddings for over seventy years. Built as a private residence around 1840, the Inn gives distinction to intimate parties of 10 to 130 guests. The covered garden patio is also available either as a ceremony site or for receptions up to 70 guests. The executive chef serves a marvelous continental menu for your friends and family to enjoy in a lovely classic setting.

Capacity: 110 seated; 130 standing; 60 in garden.
Catering: In-house. Entrees range from $20 to $30 per person.
Parking: On the premises.
Note: Wedding ceremonies are permitted.

Ceresville Mansion   301-694-5111

8529 Liberty Road • Frederick, MD 21701

Beautifully restored in the spirit of the Empire period, this elegant home boasts airy rooms, a 2,000-square-foot ballroom, intricate woodwork and fireplaces. The air-conditioned ballroom opens out to a garden terrace with a reflecting pool for an outdoor reception.

Capacity: 180 seated; 225 standing; 225 in garden; 350 with tent.
Catering: In-house. Entrees range from $45 to $75 per person.

Rental Fee: $250 to $1,750.
Parking: On the premises. Valet parking can be arranged.
Note: Wedding ceremonies are permitted indoors or out-
              doors.

Chase Court   410-727-1112

1112 St. Paul Street • Baltimore, MD 21202

Chase Court, in the historic neighborhood of Mt. Vernon, is an
elegant and tasteful choice for your celebration. Its understated
rooms are perfect for weddings, receptions and parties. The
wisteria-covered gazebo is a favorite spot for wedding ceremonies, and the flower-filled garden is a beautiful site for toasts and
tossing of the bouquet. However, in the meticulously restored
Gothic ballroom there is a carved "Juliette" balcony which was
perhaps built for that tradition. Chase Court is minutes from the
Inner Harbor, a short walk from Penn Station and directly off the
Jones Falls Freeway. It has abundant parking.

Capacity: 150 seated; 250 standing; 150+ in garden; 150+ with
              tent.
Catering: Approved caterers list. Entrees range from $20 to
              $30.
Rental Fee: $1,500.
Parking: Parking in nearby lot.
Note: Wedding ceremonies are permitted.

Clarion Hotel   410-727-7101

The George Washington Club
612 Cathedral Street • Baltimore, MD 21201

Consider having your wedding reception at this beautiful European hotel located minutes from the Harbor. Located in the heart
of the arts and cultural district, this lovely hotel is a proud resident
of historic Mount Vernon Square. A magnificent glass-enclosed
rooftop ballroom adds a finishing note of grace and beauty to the
hotel. This facility combines elegance and ambience in the grand
tradition of a bygone era.

Capacity: 150.
Catering: In-house. Packages as well as customized menus.
Parking: Valet parking is available.
Note: Wedding ceremonies are permitted. Guest rooms
              available at preferred rates.

The Cloisters   410-557-4494

P.O. Box 5394 • 10440 Falls Road • Baltimore, MD 21209

Many brides choose to marry their Prince Charming in this castle-like mansion, built as a private home in 1932 and incorporating parts of medieval European castles in the architecture. The stone mansion with its gables and wrought iron spiral staircase reflects a blend of Gothic and Tudor styles. Guests use the entire first floor, including the main gallery with an area for dancing and the living room which features a working fireplace. Outside ceremonies may be performed in the courtyard garden or in the amphitheater. Have your wedding in this castle . . . and live happily ever after!

Capacity: 120 seated with dance floor; 150 seated without dance floor; 200 standing.
Catering: Approved caterers list or your own caterer.
Rental Fee: $1,000 to $1,100.
Parking: On the premises.
Note: Candles are permitted with hurricanes.

Comus Inn Restaurant   301-428-8593

23900 Old Hundred Road • Comus, MD 20842

This historic inn, built in 1794, is surrounded by flowering gardens, stately trees, lovely lawns and Sugarloaf Mountain. The tastefully restored inn is the perfect country setting for weddings, rehearsal dinners, anniversaries, or any celebration. There are five private dining rooms available for meetings, banquets, and other events. The inn affords easy access to I-270 and is just 30 minutes from the Beltway.

Capacity: 150 seated; 200 in garden; 200 with tent.
Catering: In-house. Entrees range from $20 to $50 per person. Cake cutting fee is $.50 per person.
Parking: On the premises.
Note: Wedding ceremonies are permitted.

Darnall's Chance   301-952-8010

14800 Gov. Oden Bowie Drive
Upper Marlboro, MD 20772

One of Prince George's County's and the State of Maryland's most significant historical landmarks, Darnall's Chance has been restored to its original appearance and is now open for tours and rentals. This site offers three floors, including six public rooms, exhibit area, gift shop, catering kitchen and wine cellar. Outdoor weddings and receptions may be held on the lawn.

Capacity: 100; 300 with a tent.
Catering: You must supply your own caterer. Caterer must have a valid certificate of insurance.

Rental Fee: $800 for 6 hours. The 6-hour rental includes set-up and take-down times. $100 each additional hour.
Parking: Limited parking on the premises; parking on the street.
Restrictions: No smoking. Vendors are not allowed to park on the lawn during set-up. Noise level is enforced (65 decibels up to 10 p.m., 55 decibels after 10 p.m.).
Note: Wedding ceremonies are permitted indoors or outdoors.

Elkridge Furnace Inn   410-379-9336
www.elkridgefurnaceinn.com

5745 Furnace Avenue • Elkridge, MD 21075

This historic manor home, built in 1810, sits on the Patapsco River in a quiet corner of Howard County, Maryland. It is just minutes from BWI Airport, Baltimore, and Washington. The Furnace Inn has been restored to its original splendor, complete with beautiful gardens containing dogwoods, magnolias, azaleas, perennials, herbs, and an assortment of annuals. The gardens overlooking the Patapsco provide a beautiful backdrop for an outdoor ceremony. In the warmer months, the tent and patio can extend your function to the beautiful outdoors. In the winter months, your guests can warm themselves by one of the working fireplaces. The Elkridge Furnace Inn features complete custom gourmet catering for the most discriminating palate. The Inn offers the charm of a bygone era coupled with outstanding food and unmatched service.

Capacity: 60 first floor; 125 house; 200 with tent.
Catering: In-house. Entrees range from $40 to $65.
Rental Fee: $1,000 for 4 hours.
Parking: On the premises.

Evergreen House of the Johns Hopkins University   410-516-0341

4545 North Charles Street • Baltimore, MD 21210

Seated on 26 acres, Evergreen provides the Baltimore community with an elegant, gracious estate at which to hold receptions. Evergreen has three areas for wedding receptions: The Evergreen Theater Wing, which consists of the large Far East Room, Theater and Lobby, and the smaller Billiard Room. With colors and Russian folk designs chosen by a noted Russian costume and set designer and a large collection of Japanese art work, the Theater Wing provides a colorful, dramatic location for a small reception. Amenities include a catering kitchen, piano, eight round tables and attractive black lacquer chairs. The Carriage House with its mid-19th century interior, wood paneling, hardwood and carpeted floors and large sliding doors that lead to a cobblestone entrance surrounded by trees, ivy and flowers, is a quite desirable location. Dancing is permitted in the Carriage House. The Upper

Garden has two areas which may be tented and a fountain with Victorian cast iron benches. It may be rented in conjunction with either the Theater or Carriage House.

Capacity: 75 in Theater; up to 400 in Carriage House.
Catering: You must supply your own caterer.
Rental Fee: Varies. Call for details.
Parking: Ample free parking on the premises.
Restrictions: No amplified music in buildings. No smoking in buildings. No dancing in theater. No open flame in any location. No wedding ceremonies.

George Peabody Library of The Johns Hopkins University   410-659-8197
http://peabody-events.mse.jhu.edu

17 E. Mount Vernon Place • Baltimore, MD 21202

An unique architectural treasure built in 1878, The George Peabody Library is an uplifting setting for special celebrations. Located in the heart of the historic district, the superb neo-Greco building faces the open park of Mount Vernon Place and the Washington Monument. Within the large, main chamber, six book-filled tiers of gilt, cast iron balconies rise dramatically above the marble-tiled open court toward a grand skylight.

Capacity: 230 seated; 400 standing.
Catering: Approved caterers list or your own caterer with the approval of the facility.
Rental Fee: $1,675 to $2,175.
Parking: In nearby lots or garages. Valet parking can be arranged.
Restrictions: No smoking. No helium balloons. No rice, birdseed or glitter.
Note: Wedding ceremonies are permitted.

Glenview Mansion at Rockville Civic Center Park   301-309-3001

603 Edmonston Drive • Rockville, MD 20851

Glenview Mansion, a pillared, neo-classical home built in the style of an early 19th century plantation house, overlooks Rockville's 153-acre Civic Center Park. Surrounding grounds include beautiful boxwoods and formal gardens perfect for outside ceremonies. An indoor ceremony area is available for winter weddings. The living room, library, and Lyon room are furnished with period reproductions for casual seating. The wood-paneled dining room is available for a buffet, and marble-floored conservatory for dancing. The second floor provides picturesque porches, an art gallery, and a separate bride's room.

Capacity: 50 seated; 225 standing.

Catering: You must supply your own caterer.
Rental Fee: $1,405 to $2,021.
Parking: On the premises.
Restrictions: No smoking. No cooking (warm and serve permit only). No red wine or red dye beverages.

Governor Calvert House   410-216-6328

58 State Circle • Annapolis, MD 21401

The 200-year-old Governor Calvert House, in the heart of historic Annapolis, is a charming setting for your wedding event. This converted former home of Lord Calvert features an atrium overlooking gardens that can accommodate up to 300 guests. It offers magnificent rooms, excellent food and unparalleled service. The staff will turn your wedding, reception or rehearsal dinner into a truly elegant affair.

Capacity: 160-260 seated; 300 standing.
Catering: In-house. Entrees range from $42.50 to $55 per person.
Parking: Parking in nearby lot.
Note: Wedding ceremonies are permitted.

Gramercy Mansion Bed & Breakfast
& The Carriage House   410-486-2405

1400 Greenspring Valley Road • Stevenson, MD 21153

This historic 1902 English Tudor mansion was built by Alexander Cassatt, brother of Mary Cassatt, the American impressionist, as a wedding present for his daughter. Situated on 45 acres in Baltimore's Greenspring Valley, the house and grounds were part of the "Old Line" community and the scene of many parties and political gatherings during its early years. Now completely restored to its former elegance, Gramercy Bed and Breakfast welcomes you for a splendid occasion.

Capacity: 150.
Catering: You must supply your own caterer. Licensed and insured caterers only.
Rental Fee: $1,800 for 4 hours.
Parking: On the premises.
Restrictions: Smoking outside only. No birdseed or rice. Amplified music inside only.

Grey Rock Mansion   410-484-4554

400 Grey Rock Road • Pikesville, MD 21208

This Colonial-style mansion features a stone patio and gazebo which overlook lovely landscaped formal gardens. With its breathtaking view and exquisite gardens, it serves as a beautiful setting for weddings.

Capacity: 145 seated; 200 standing; 300 in garden; 225 with tent.
Catering: In-house. Entrees range from $30 to $50 per person.
Rental Fee: $700 to $1,300.
Parking: On the premises.
Note: Wedding ceremonies are permitted.

Hammond-Harwood House   410-263-4683

19 Maryland Avenue • Annapolis, MD 21401

This facility is a national historic landmark and an outstanding example of American colonial architecture. The building, with its carved entrance, formal rooms and elegant scale amid a charming garden, makes this Annapolis location a popular reception choice.

Capacity: 24 seated; 40 standing; 125 in garden.
Catering: Approved caterers list. Caterer must supply all banquet items and remove at the end of the function.
Rental Fee: $600 and up for 4 hours.
Parking: Street parking; city garage available.
Restrictions: No amplified music. Clean-up pre-approved.
Note: Wedding ceremonies are permitted indoors or outdoors.

Historic Baldwin Hall   410-923-3438

1358 Millersville Road • Crownsville, MD 21032

Historic Baldwin Hall is a lovely country church built in 1861. Surrounded by landscaped gardens and mature trees, it is located in Millersville at the intersection of Generals Highway and Millersville Road. The spacious main hall, with its lofty ceilings, arched windows, hardwood floors, and stage with green velvet curtains, is a wonderful space to decorate. There's also a front reception area, choir loft, and bride's room for changing and privacy. The hall is available seven days a week at reasonable rates.

Capacity: 125 seated; 299 standing.
Catering: You must supply your own caterer. A well-equipped kitchen with ranges, microwave, refrigerator and warming oven is available. Tables and chairs are provided. All caterers are accepted.
Rental Fee: $500.
Parking: On the premises.

Inn at Mitchell House   410-778-6500

8796 Maryland Parkway • Chestertown, MD 21620

Nestled on ten rolling acres, surrounded by woods and overlooking "Stoneybrook Pond," this historic manor house, built in 1743, affords a touch of tranquility. Small wedding parties during the cooler months can enjoy its parlors, 18th-century dining room, and numerous fireplaces. Larger weddings are held outdoors on the inn's sweeping lawn with beautiful vistas. This country location invites a peaceful step back in time.

Capacity:	50 inside; 250 outside.
Catering:	In-house and approved caterers list. Entrees range from $25 to $40.
Rental Fee:	$400 to $700.
Parking:	On the premises.
Note:	Wedding ceremonies are permitted.

Kent Manor Inn   1-800-820-4511

500 Kent Manor Drive • Stevensville, MD 21666

The Kent Manor Inn, a Maryland historical site, is situated on a 226-acre plantation one hour from Washington, D.C., and Baltimore. The beautiful Victorian mansion, circa 1820, and its glass-enclosed garden house are the perfect waterfront settings for wedding ceremonies, receptions, rehearsal dinners and anniversary celebrations. The inn has fireplaces with Italian marble mantels, two conference rooms and 24 individually decorated bedrooms, some with four-poster beds. A fine dining restaurant serves lunch and dinner.

Capacity:	150 seated; 150 standing; unlimited with tent on the grounds.
Catering:	In-house. Entrees range from $56 to $94 per person including bar.
Rental Fee:	$300 to $1,000.
Parking:	On the premises.
Note:	Wedding ceremonies are permitted.

Liriodendron   410-879-4424

502 West Gordon Street • Bel Air, MD 21014

Liriodendron has been described as "belonging on the cliffs of Newport." The mansion's grandeur makes it one of the most sought-after wedding locations. Wisteria-draped terraces, wide porticos, boxwood garden and fountain make Liriodendron a perfect choice for a garden wedding. The beautifully detailed mantels, stairways and reception rooms inside reflect an enduring elegance.

Capacity:	Up to 200 depending on time of year and set-up required.
Catering:	Your choice of any licensed caterer.
Rental Fee:	$800 to $1,000 for 6½ hours. Four-hour party time.
Parking:	Unlimited parking on the premises.
Restrictions:	No candles, rice, birdseed, confetti or balloons.

Llewelyn Fields Manor   301-570-5114

c/o Snead Enterprises
812 Lindsey Manor Lane • Silver Spring, MD 20905

Elegant, enchanting and unforgettable, this circa 1820 grand manor house is on 11 tranquil acres, only minutes from Washington, D.C. The house is beautifully furnished with period antiques, oriental rugs, dazzling chandeliers and six fireplaces. The romantic setting is suitable for both wedding ceremony and reception. Patio and gardens are perfect for tent-covered festivities with dance floor and outdoor seating.

Capacity: 50 seated inside; 200 standing; 400+ in garden; 400+ with tent.
Catering: You must supply your own caterer.
Rental Fee: $2,000.
Parking: On the premises.
Note: Wedding ceremonies are permitted. Guest rooms are available.

London Town
Publik House & Garden   410-222-1919

839 Londontown Road • Edgewater, MD 21037

A national historic landmark on the banks of the South River and minutes from Annapolis, the House at London Town shares a dramatic waterfront setting with an eight-acre woodland garden and glass-enclosed pavilion. Surrounded by decks and overlooking the gardens and river, the pavilion attracts numerous weddings and receptions throughout the year. Ceremonies take place on spacious or intimate overlooks in and around the gardens. The House was designated a national historic landmark in 1970.

Capacity: 125 indoors; 175 with tent.
Catering: Approved caterers list or your own caterer. Caterer must be licensed and insured.
Rental Fee: $800 and up.
Parking: On the premises.

Maryland Inn   410-216-6328

16 Church Circle • Annapolis, MD 21401

Located in historic Annapolis, the Maryland Inn, features a Victorian ballroom with a working fireplace and authentic chandeliers. This delightful inn has served guests with fabulous food, lovely rooms, and a staff that offers excellent service. For an elegant wedding reception or rehearsal dinner that will be remembered for years, the Maryland Inn is at your service.

Capacity: 90 seated; 200 standing.
Catering: In-house. Entrees range from $42.50 to $55 per person.
Parking: Parking in nearby lot.
Note: Wedding ceremonies are permitted.

Merry Sherwood Plantation   410-641-2112

8909 Worcester Highway • Berlin, MD 21811

Handsomely restored and furnished with many fine antiques, the pre-Civil War mansion is situated on 18 acres of gardens. You can descend the mahogany staircase in the magnificent entry hall and be married in the elegant grand parlor with the original marble fireplaces, or choose one of many gardens or the gazebo as a setting for your wedding and/or reception. The house is decorated inside and out for the Christmas season events. Merry Sherwood Plantation, with its roses and azaleas, flowering shrubs, 150-year-old shade trees and park-like setting, is ten minutes from Assateague National Seashore and Ocean City on the eastern shore of Maryland.

Capacity: 30 seated; 125 standing; 200+ in garden; 200+ with tent.
Catering: Approved caterers list. Entrees range from $14 to $35 per person.
Rental Fee: $1,500 for 75-125 guests.
Parking: On the premises.
Restrictions: Dancing is not allowed in the mansion but may be held under a tent.
Note: Wedding ceremonies are permitted.

Montpelier Mansion   301-953-1376

Route 197 & Muirkirk Road • Laurel, MD 20708

Located on 70 acres of rolling park land, this national historic landmark provides the perfect atmosphere for any elegant social occasion. Ceremonies and receptions can take place in a number of locations from the great entry hall to the indoor wings to the outdoor garden terraces graced by a 200-year-old summerhouse and boxwood. Guests can view furnished museum rooms during their visit. The mansion is ideal for business retreats and seminars at lower weekday rates.

Capacity: 100.
Catering: You must supply your own caterer.
Rental Fee: $800 Saturday; $700 Friday and Sunday for 7 hours. Facility requires a $400 refundable security deposit and a $50 custodial fee.
Parking: On the premises.
Restrictions: No smoking inside.
Note: Wedding ceremonies are permitted indoors or outdoors.

Mrs. K's Toll House   301-589-3500

9201 Colesville Road • Silver Spring, MD 20910

Mrs. K's Toll House is one of the last operating toll houses in Montgomery County. The interior of this historic building is elegantly appointed with carefully collected antiques and hand-crafted seasonal decorations. The staff will personalize your menu so that your guests may choose from more than one entree. Lush gardens provide a romantic setting for outdoor ceremonies and receptions. It is conveniently located just south of the beltway in Silver Spring, and offers plenty of well-lit parking.

Capacity: 150 seated; unlimited in garden. Can seat up to 110 with a reasonable dance floor, 150 without a dance floor.
Catering: In-house. Entrees range from $19 to $49 per person.
Parking: On the premises.
Note: Wedding ceremonies are permitted.

Newton White Mansion   301-249-2004

2708 Enterprise Road • Mitchellville, MD 20716

Built in 1939, this house was once the home of Captain Newton H. White, who was the first commanding officer of the *USS Enterprise*. Newton White Mansion is one of the most popular settings in Prince George's County. It offers a quiet atmosphere, elegant patios, and a beautiful garden with a waterfall fountain for outdoor events.

Capacity: 125 seated; 200 standing; 200 in garden.
Catering: You must supply your own caterer. Caterer must be licensed and insured.
Rental Fee: $2,100 Saturday; $1,700 Friday and Sunday.
Parking: Free parking on the premises.
Note: Wedding ceremonies are permitted indoors or out-doors. Facility is handicap accessible.

Historic Oakland   410-730-4801/1-800-730-4802
www.historic-oakland.com

5430 Vantage Point Road • Columbia, MD 21044

Celebrate the occasion of your marriage with family and friends at a lovely manor estate. Adding grace to the exquisite interior are crystal chandeliers, period reproductions of the original furnishings and twin fireplaces in the ballroom and foyer. The ballroom doors lead to a veranda that overlooks a beautifully landscaped lawn and an antique rose garden.

Capacity: 150 seated; 200 standing; 200 in garden.
Catering: In-house, approved caterers list or your own caterer provided the caterer adheres to the rules and policies of the mansion.
Rental Fee: $700 to $1,500.
Parking: On the premises. Valet parking can be arranged.
Note: Wedding ceremonies are permitted indoors or out-doors.

Oxon Hill Manor   301-839-7782

6901 Oxon Hill Road • Oxon Hill, MD 20745

High atop a hill overlooking the Potomac River, Oxon Hill Manor is a breathtaking historic neo-Georgian style mansion with a wrap-around terrace, reflecting pool, and formal gardens. The elegant interior consists of a drawing room, library, dining room, marbled foyer, bride's dressing room and caterer's kitchen. The main rooms all lead onto the terrace through large French doors. Ideal for wedding ceremonies and receptions, social functions, business meetings and holiday parties, Oxon Hill Manor recalls the splendor of a by-gone era and will make your event an affair to remember.

Capacity: 210 seated; 300 standing.
Catering: You must supply your own caterer.
Rental Fee: $2,400 Friday, Saturdays, Sundays and holidays. Call to inquire about weekday rates.
Parking: On the premises.
Note: Wedding ceremonies are permitted.

Reynolds Tavern   410-626-0380/1-888-626-0381

7 Church Circle, P.O. Box 748 • Annapolis, MD 21404

Located in the heart of historic Annapolis, this authentically restored building, circa 1747, provides a wonderful setting for all wedding functions including rehearsal dinners, ceremonies and receptions. The facility includes two colonial-style dining rooms, a private shady garden and terrace, a casual English pub, and four spacious lodging rooms. Whether you use one room or the entire facility, your guests will be impressed with the graceful setting, fresh and beautifully presented cuisine and attentive service. The tavern's complete wedding coordination services will make your event memorable and worry-free.

Capacity: 75 seated, 90 standing inside; 130 seated, 160 seated in garden; 100 with tent.
Catering: In-house. Entrees range from $25 to $50 per person. Cake cutting fee if you provide your own cake.
Rental Fee: Either $500 for whole facility, or a minimum food and beverage commitment.
Parking: Parking in nearby lot. Valet parking is available.
Note: Wedding ceremonies are permitted.

Riversdale Mansion   301-864-0420
http://www.smart.net/net/~parksrec/riversdale

4811 Riverdale Road • Riverdale, MD 20737

This recently restored early 19th-century mansion is conveniently located approximately 3 miles from I-95 and the Baltimore-

Washington Parkway. Riversdale is a five-part neoclassical style house. The available rental rooms include a carpeted banquet room with wall sconces in the East Wing, and a ballroom with decorative cornice and crystal chandelier in the West Wing.

Capacity: 100.
Catering: You must supply your own caterer.
Rental Fee: $700 to $1,150.
Parking: On the premises.
Note: Wedding ceremonies are permitted indoors or outdoors.

Rockwood Manor Park   301-299-5026

11001 MacArthur Boulevard • Potomac, MD 20854

Escape the commotion and bustle of the city and have your wedding reception in the park. Located in Potomac, Rockwood is just 20 minutes from downtown Washington and convenient to Bethesda and Rockville. You may enjoy a memorable feast in the spacious manor house, or have an elegant outdoor reception in the breathtaking gardens and patios that surround Rockwood.

Capacity: 100 seated; 150 standing; 150 in garden.
Catering: Approved caterers list.
Rental Fee: $1,400 Friday and Sunday; $1,700 Saturday.
Parking: 85 parking spaces on the premises.
Restrictions: No amplified outdoor music.
Note: Wedding ceremonies are permitted indoors or outdoors.

The Rossborough Inn   301-314-8012

Route 1 • University of Maryland • College Park, MD 20742

The Rossborough Inn is ideally suited for weddings and receptions. The dignity and grace of the charming dining rooms, English garden and courtyard create the perfect atmosphere for an elegant wedding. The inn has just added a new outdoor patio that can accommodate dancing and hors d'oeuvres.

Capacity: 145 seated; 175 standing; 300 in garden.
Catering: In-house. Entrees range from $45 to $65 per person.
               Cake cutting fee is $1.00 per person.
Rental Fee: $750.
Parking: On the premises, residential and nearby parking lot.
Restrictions: No smoking. No rice or birdseed.
Note: Wedding ceremonies are permitted.

St. Mary's Church Hall   301-292-0527

13401 Piscataway Road • Clinton, MD 20735

Established in 1838 and located in historic Piscataway, this church hall is a special place for weddings. Featuring an extremely versatile layout with over 3,800 square feet, this spacious hall has off-white walls, a 17' x 32' stage and an outdoor reception area. Amenities include tables and chairs, kitchen facilities, dance floor and convenient parking.

Capacity: 250 seated; 400 standing.
Catering: Approved caterers list and you may supply your own caterer.
Rental Fee: $100 per hour.
Parking: On the premises.
Note: Call for more information regarding wedding ceremonies.

Strathmore Hall   301-530-5889

10701 Rockville Pike • North Bethesda, MD 20852

A turn-of-the-century, red-brick mansion, Strathmore Hall is surrounded by 11 acres of landscaped beauty, including a sculpture garden and pavilion. Enter through grand columns into a marble-floored foyer complete with a cherub fountain. Enjoy intimate moments with your guests as they flow through the main hall, library, music room, sun room and galleries, all filled with exhibits of local and national artists. Pose for photographs on the lovely staircase, a favorite area for wedding party pictures. All eight of the first floor rooms, a bridal room on the second floor, and the kitchen are available when you rent Strathmore.

Capacity: 225 standing; 275 with tent.
Catering: Approved caterers list.
Rental Fee: $1,400 to $2,900.
Parking: On the premises.
Note: Wedding ceremonies are permitted.

The Great Room at Savage Mill   301-490-1668

8600 Foundry Street • Savage, MD 20763

This charming banquet hall in a completely restored textile mill has a 25-foot high ceiling with skylights and 14-foot high windows. In addition, it offers an 800-square-foot dance floor and a lovely outdoor deck overlooking woods and the Little Patuxent River.

Capacity: 275 seated; 375 standing; 150 on deck.
Catering: Approved caterers list or you may provide your own caterer at an additional fee. Entrees begin at $30 per person.
Rental Fee: $1,200 to $1,800.
Parking: On the premises.
Note: Wedding ceremony is permitted.

Truffles at the Belvedere   410-332-1000

1 East Chase Street • Baltimore, MD 21202

Built in 1903, this former hotel offers two magnificently restored ballrooms with Old-World charm and two smaller party rooms (including the world-famous John Eager Howar Room) with crystal chandeliers and working fireplaces for receptions. This elegant atmosphere is accentuated by modern services and amenities. Truffles "The Catering Company" is the sole provider of catering services at the historic Belvedere. The premier caterer of the Baltimore-Washington region, Truffles has earned an unsurpassed reputation for exceptional food, creativity, and presentation.

Capacity: 40 to 350 seated; 40 to 700 standing.
Catering: In-house. Entrees range from $45 to $60.
Parking: On the premises and nearby parking lot.
Note: Wedding ceremonies are permitted.

Union Mills Homestead Museum   410-848-2288

3311 Littlestown Pike • Westminster, MD 21157

If you prefer an outdoor celebration in a rural atmosphere—this is the place. Weeping willows, flower gardens and a footbridge are some of the many attractions on the land of the Homestead, a 23-room structure built in 1797.

Capacity: 250 seated in Tannery; unlimited capacity on grounds.
Catering: You must supply your own caterer.
Rental Fee: Facilities request a donation of $200 for grounds and $300 for tannery building.
Parking: On the premises.
Restrictions: Alcoholic beverages may be brought on premises, but not sold.
Note: Wedding ceremonies are permitted. Hours til dusk, April to October. One event a day.

William Paca House   410-263-5553

186 Prince George Street • Annapolis, MD 21401

This 37-room Georgian mansion, surrounded by formal English gardens complete with wooden bridge, makes this Annapolis landmark a picturesque setting and popular reception choice. Receptions take place on tented terraces overlooking the gardens of the home built by former governor William Paca for his bride.

Capacity: 150 seated; 160 standing; 150 with tent.
Catering: You must supply your own caterer. Kitchen facilities are available.
Rental Fee: $500 to $2,000 for five hours.

Parking: Parking lot nearby. Valet parking can be arranged.
Restrictions: No hard liquor, only beer and wine. Limits on deco-
                rations. Limits on music and noise levels. Licensed
                and insured caterers only.
Note: Wedding ceremonies are permitted outdoors only.

Woodend   301-652-9188

8940 Jones Mill Road • Chevy Chase, MD 20815

Woodend is a beaux arts style mansion with classic Greek portico
that overlooks sweeping lawns bordered by woods and meadows.
Indoors, a Palladian window lights up a distinguished staircase
and carved fireplace in the Great Hall. Step through stately
French doors onto a raised terrace with a custom tent lit with
chandeliers. Enjoy your romantic wedding ceremony in an enchanting grove surrounded by a canopy of trees. Woodend is a 40-
acre bird sanctuary owned by the Audubon Naturalist Society
and is conveniently located directly inside the beltway in Chevy
Chase.

Capacity: 150 seated; 200 standing.
Catering: Approved caterers list.
Rental Fee: $1,200 to $3,100.
Parking: On the premises.
Note: Wedding ceremonies are permitted.

Woodlawn Manor   301-585-5564

16501 Norwood Road • Sandy Spring, MD 20860

Magnificent trees, rolling green landscape, garden gazebo and a
unique stone barn set the stage for an elegant reception. Only
minutes from busy urban centers, the Georgian-style manor
house offers five spacious rooms, richly restored and tastefully
furnished, to provide the charm and splendor of the 19th century.
A modernized kitchen meets high-level catering requirements and
ample parking is in close proximity to the manor house.

Capacity: 40 seated; 125 standing; 200 in garden.
Catering: Approved caterers list.
Rental Fee: $1,000 Friday and Sunday; $1,200 Saturday.
Parking: 48 parking spaces on the premises with overflow
               parking nearby.
Note: Wedding ceremonies are permitted.

Antrim 1844   1-800-858-1844

30 Trevanion Road • Taneytown, MD 21787

Fall in love with the extraordinary architecture at this antebellum plantation: the verandas and balconies, and the graciously proportioned drawing rooms, all tastefully appointed with period antiques and fine art. The feeling of Old-World refinement is the hallmark of this meticulously restored mansion, situated on 25 bucolic acres, which was built in 1844 by Colonel Andrew Ege from County Antrim, Ireland, as a wedding gift to his daughter and her husband. Enjoy the best of both worlds; climb into an antique canopy featherbed with your fireplace aglow, or relax in your oversized Jacuzzi. Fourteen luxurious guest rooms are available, as are four private dining areas. Each area has a distinctive personaltiy of its own, including a magnificent pavilion overlooking the formal gardens and croquet lawn, with seating for 200 guests. The Antrim is 70 miles from Washington, D.C., and 40 miles from Baltimore.

Capacity: 175 seated; 250 standing; 250 garden; 500 with tent.
Catering: In-house. Entrees begin at $55 per person.
Rental Fee: $1,750.
Parking: On the premises.
Note: Wedding ceremonies are permitted.

Comus Inn Restaurant   301-428-8593

23900 Old Hundred Road • Comus, MD 20842

This historic inn, built in 1794, is surrounded by flowering gardens, stately trees, lovely lawns and Sugarloaf Mountain. The tastefully restored inn is the perfect country setting for weddings, rehearsal dinners, anniversaries, or any celebration. There are five private dining rooms available for meetings, banquets, and other events. The inn affords easy access to I-270 and is just 30 minutes from the Beltway.

Capacity: 150 seated; 200 in garden; 200 with tent.
Catering: In-house. Entrees range from $20 to $50 per person.
               Cake cutting fee is $.50 per person.
Parking: On the premises.
Note: Wedding ceremonies are permitted.

Elkridge Furnace Inn   410-379-9336
www.elkridgefurnaceinn.com

5745 Furnace Avenue • Elkridge, MD 21075

This historic manor home, built in 1810, sits on the Patapsco River in a quiet corner of Howard County, Maryland. It is just minutes from BWI Airport, Baltimore, and Washington. The Furnace Inn has been restored to its original splendor, complete with beautiful gardens containing dogwoods, magnolias, azaleas, perennials, herbs, and an assortment of annuals. The gardens overlooking the Patapsco provide a beautiful backdrop for an outdoor ceremony. In the warmer months, the tent and patio can extend your function to the beautiful outdoors. In the winter months, your guests can warm themselves by one of the working fireplaces. The Elkridge Furnace Inn features complete custom gourmet catering for the most discriminating palate. The Inn offers the charm of a bygone era coupled with outstanding food and unmatched service.

Capacity: 60 first floor; 125 house; 200 with tent.
Catering: In-house. Entrees range from $40 to $65.
Rental Fee: $1,000 for 4 hours.
Parking: On the premises.

Gramercy Mansion Bed & Breakfast
& The Carriage House   410-486-2405

1400 Greenspring Valley Road • Stevenson, MD 21153

This historic 1902 English Tudor mansion was built by Alexander Cassatt, brother of Mary Cassatt, the American impressionist, as a wedding present for his daughter. Situated on 45 acres in Baltimore's Greenspring Valley, the house and grounds were part of the "Old Line" community and the scene of many parties and political gatherings during its early years. Now completely restored to its former elegance, Gramercy Bed and Breakfast welcomes you for a splendid occasion.

Capacity: 150.
Catering: You must supply your own caterer. Licensed and insured caterers only.
Rental Fee: $1,800 for 4 hours.
Parking: On the premises. Parking lot nearby.
Restrictions: Smoking outside only. No birdseed or rice. Amplified music inside only.

Inn at Mitchell House   410-778-6500

8796 Maryland Parkway • Chestertown, MD 21620

Nestled on ten rolling acres, surrounded by woods and overlooking "Stoneybrook Pond," this historic manor house, built in 1743, affords a touch of tranquility. Small wedding parties during the cooler months can enjoy its parlors, 18th-century dining room, and numerous fireplaces. Larger weddings are held outdoors on the inn's sweeping lawn with beautiful vistas. This country location invites a peaceful step back in time.

Capacity: 50 inside; 250 outside.
Catering: In-house and approved caterers list. Entrees range from $25 to $40.
Rental Fee: $400 to $700.

Parking: On the premises.
Note: Wedding ceremonies are permitted.

Kent Manor Inn   1-800-820-4511

500 Kent Manor Drive • Stevensville, MD 21666

The Kent Manor Inn, a Maryland historical site, is situated on a 226-acre plantation one hour from Washington, D.C., and Baltimore. The beautiful Victorian mansion, circa 1820, and its glass-enclosed garden house are the perfect waterfront settings for wedding ceremonies, receptions, rehearsal dinners and anniversary celebrations. The inn has fireplaces with Italian marble mantels, two conference rooms and 24 individually decorated bedrooms, some with four-poster beds. A fine dining restaurant serves lunch and dinner.

Capacity: 150 seated; 150 standing; unlimited with tent on the grounds.
Catering: In-house. Entrees range from $56 to $94 per person including bar.
Rental Fee: $300 to $1,000.
Parking: On the premises.
Note: Wedding ceremonies are permitted.

Maryland Inn   410-216-6328

16 Church Circle • Annapolis, MD 21401

Located in historic Annapolis, the Maryland Inn, features a Victorian ballroom with a working fireplace and authentic chandeliers. This delightful inn has served guests with fabulous food, lovely rooms, and a staff that offers excellent service. For an elegant wedding reception or rehearsal dinner that will be remembered for years, the Maryland Inn is at your service.

Capacity: 90 seated; 200 standing.
Catering: In-house. Entrees range from $42.50 to $55 per person.
Parking: Parking in nearby lot.
Note: Wedding ceremonies are permitted.

Merry Sherwood Plantation   410-641-2112

8909 Worcester Highway • Berlin, MD 21811

Handsomely restored and furnished with many fine antiques, the pre-Civil War mansion is situated on 18 acres of gardens. You can descend the mahogany staircase in the magnificent entry hall and be married in the elegant grand parlor with the original marble fireplaces, or choose one of many gardens or the gazebo as a setting for your wedding and/or reception. The house is decorated inside and out for the Christmas season events. Merry Sherwood Plantation, with its roses and azaleas, flowering shrubs, 150-year-old shade trees and park-like setting, is ten minutes from Assateague National Seashore and Ocean City on the eastern shore of Maryland.

Capacity: 30 seated; 125 standing; 200+ in garden; 200+ with tent.
Catering: Approved caterers list. Entrees range from $14 to $35 per person.
Rental Fee: $1,500 for 75-125 guests.
Parking: On the premises.
Restrictions: Dancing is not allowed in the mansion but may be held under a tent.
Note: Wedding ceremonies are permitted.

The Rossborough Inn   301-314-8012

Route 1 • University of Maryland • College Park, MD 20742

The Rossborough Inn is ideally suited for weddings and receptions. The dignity and grace of the charming dining rooms, English garden and courtyard create the perfect atmosphere for an elegant wedding. The inn has just added a new outdoor patio that can accommodate dancing and hors d'oeuvres.

Capacity: 145 seated; 175 standing; 300 in garden.
Catering: In-house. Entrees range from $45 to $65 per person. Cake cutting fee is $1.00 per person.
Rental Fee: $750.
Parking: On the premises, residential and nearby parking lot.
Restrictions: No smoking. No rice or birdseed.
Note: Wedding ceremonies are permitted.

Staub's Country Inn   301-428-8449

19800 Darnestown Road • Beallsville, MD 20839

The two best reasons for choosing Staub's Country Inn Restaurant and caterers are the food and the twelve beautiful acres on which the restaurant is located. An appealing assortment of menu options are sure to impress. Mouth-watering gourmet delights or traditional favorites are customized to fit your needs. Perfect for outdoor receptions and picnics, the open landscape provides plenty of fresh air and open space for your enjoyment. The inn's personable staff will cater to your every need.

Capacity: 30 seated inside; unlimited capacity on grounds (tent recommended).
Catering: In-house or approved caterers list. Entrees range from $12.95 to $49.95 per person.
Parking: On the premises.
Note: Wedding ceremonies are permitted.

Knights of Columbus   301-530-0258

Rock Creek Council
5417 West Cedar Lane • Bethesda, MD 20814

Looking for a bargain? This comfortable and affordable location comes complete with dance floor, tables and chairs, kitchen and ample parking. The size and flexibility of this hall allows it to be customized for any type of affair. Turn it into a charming setting with your own decorating flair.

Capacity: 200 seated.
Catering: Approved caterers list or your own caterer.
Rental Fee: $650 for 4 hours.
Parking: On the premises.

Lodge at Little Seneca Creek   301-585-5564

14500-A Clopper Road • Boyds, MD 20841

The Lodge at Little Seneca Creek is a rustic meeting place designed as a replica of a classic log cabin. The lodge's spacious meeting hall is accented by a massive flagstone fireplace. The splendor of the oak flooring is surpassed only by the natural wood cathedral ceilings. A view from the outdoor deck includes a pastoral scene where an outdoor wedding reception may be held.

Capacity: 120 seated; 180 standing.
Catering: Approved caterers list.
Rental Fee: $700 Friday and Sunday; $900 Saturday.
Parking: 85 parking spaces on the premises.
Note: Wedding ceremonies are permitted indoors or out-
               doors.

Antrim 1844   1-800-858-1844

30 Trevanion Road • Taneytown, MD 21787

Fall in love with the extraordinary architecture at this antebellum plantation: the verandas and balconies, and the graciously proportioned drawing rooms, all tastefully appointed with period antiques and fine art. The feeling of Old-World refinement is the hallmark of this meticulously restored mansion, situated on 25 bucolic acres, which was built in 1844 by Colonel Andrew Ege from County Antrim, Ireland, as a wedding gift to his daughter and her husband. Enjoy the best of both worlds; climb into an antique canopy featherbed with your fireplace aglow, or relax in your oversized Jacuzzi. Fourteen luxurious guest rooms are available, as are four private dining areas. Each area has a distinctive personality of its own, including a magnificent pavilion overlooking the formal gardens and croquet lawn, with seating for 200 guests. The Antrim is 70 miles from Washington, D.C., and 40 miles from Baltimore.

Capacity: 175 seated; 250 standing; 250 garden; 500 with tent.
Catering: In-house. Entrees begin at $55 per person.
Rental Fee: $1,750.
Parking: On the premises.
Note: Wedding ceremonies are permitted.

Blair Mansion Inn   301-588-1688

7711 Eastern Avenue • Silver Spring, MD 20912

The Blair Mansion Inn was first built in 1890 by architect Stanford White, who also designed Madison Square Gardens in New York. Later renovations turned the house into an inn and a dinner theater. This graciously restored inn offers a lovely environment for a wedding reception, anniversary, or other special celebrations.

Capacity: 350 seated; 425 standing.
Catering: In-house or your own caterer with approval of facility. Entrees range from $16.95 to $25.95 per person when you use in-house caterer.
Parking: Free parking on the premises and residential parking.

Candle Light Inn   410-788-6076

1835 Frederick Road • Catonsville, MD 21228

The Candle Light Inn has been celebrating beautiful weddings for over seventy years. Built as a private residence around 1840, the Inn gives distinction to intimate parties of 10 to 130 guests. The covered garden patio is also available either as a ceremony site or for receptions up to 70 guests. The executive chef serves a marvelous continental menu for your friends and family to enjoy in a lovely classic setting.

Capacity: 110 seated; 130 standing; 60 in garden.
Catering: In-house. Entrees range from $20 to $30 per person.
Parking: On the premises.
Note: Wedding ceremonies are permitted.

Ceresville Mansion   301-694-5111

8529 Liberty Road • Frederick, MD 21701

Beautifully restored in the spirit of the Empire period, this elegant home boasts airy rooms, a 2,000-square-foot ballroom, intricate woodwork and fireplaces. The air-conditioned ballroom opens out to a garden terrace with a reflecting pool for an outdoor reception.

Capacity: 180 seated; 225 standing; 225 in garden; 350 with tent.
Catering: In-house. Entrees range from $45 to $75 per person.
Rental Fee: $250 to $1,750.
Parking: On the premises. Valet parking can be arranged.
Note: Wedding ceremonies are permitted indoors or outdoors.

The Cloisters   410-557-4494

P.O. Box 5394 • 10440 Falls Road • Baltimore, MD 21209

Many brides choose to marry their Prince Charming in this castle-like mansion, built as a private home in 1932 and incorporating parts of medieval European castles in the architecture. The stone mansion with its gables and wrought iron spiral staircase reflects a blend of Gothic and Tudor styles. Guests use the entire first floor, including the main gallery with an area for dancing and the living room which features a working fireplace. Outside ceremonies may be performed in the courtyard garden or in the amphitheater. Have your wedding in this castle . . . and live happily ever after!

Capacity: 120 seated with dance floor; 150 seated without dance floor; 200 standing.
Catering: Approved caterers list or your own caterer.
Rental Fee: $1,000 to $1,100.
Parking: On the premises.
Note: Candles are permitted with hurricanes.

Darnall's Chance   301-952-8010

14800 Gov. Oden Bowie Drive • Upper Marlboro, MD 20772

One of Prince George's County's and the State of Maryland's most significant historical landmarks, Darnall's Chance has been restored to its original appearance and is now open for tours and rentals. This site offers three floors, including six public rooms, exhibit area, gift shop, catering kitchen and wine cellar. Outdoor weddings and receptions may be held on the lawn.

Capacity: 100; 300 with tent.
Catering: You must supply your own caterer. Caterer must have a valid certificate of insurance.
Rental Fee: $800 for 6 hours. The 6-hour rental includes set-up and take-down times. $100 each additional hour.
Parking: Limited parking on the premises; parking on the street.
Restrictions: No smoking. Vendors are not allowed to park on the lawn during set-up. Noise level is enforced (65 decibels up to 10 p.m., 55 decibels after 10 p.m.).
Note: Wedding ceremonies are permitted indoors or outdoors.

Elkridge Furnace Inn   410-379-9336
www.elkridgefurnaceinn.com

5745 Furnace Avenue • Elkridge, MD 21075

This historic manor home, built in 1810, sits on the Patapsco River in a quiet corner of Howard County, Maryland. It is just minutes from BWI Airport, Baltimore, and Washington. The Furnace Inn has been restored to its original splendor, complete with beautiful gardens containing dogwoods, magnolias, azaleas, perennials, herbs, and an assortment of annuals. The gardens overlooking the Patapsco provide a beautiful backdrop for an outdoor ceremony. In the warmer months, the tent and patio can extend your function to the beautiful outdoors. In the winter months, your guests can warm themselves by one of the working fireplaces. The Elkridge Furnace Inn features complete custom gourmet catering for the most discriminating palate. The Inn offers the charm of a bygone era coupled with outstanding food and unmatched service.

Capacity: 60 first floor; 125 house; 200 with tent.
Catering: In-house. Entrees range from $40 to $65.
Rental Fee: $1,000 for 4 hours.
Parking: On the premises.

Fantasy Island   410-729-4505

St. Helena Island, Severn River • Crownsville, MD

The Mansion, on St. Helena Island in the prestigious Severn River, is just minutes from historic downtown Annapolis. St. Helena, with its towering oak trees, beautiful flowers, ivy-covered walls and spectacular water views, is the perfect wedding site. The mansion, a gracious Federal architectural design, was built in 1931 and is a close copy of the famous John Hopkins "Homewood House." The stately residence is graced by porticos and beautiful white Doric columns. The house features magnificent mahogany and marble floors, marble fireplaces, and antique chandeliers. In the spring, the island bursts into life with pink and white dogwoods, azaleas, rhododendrons and beautiful flower gardens set against the background of the Severn River. This enchanted island is the most exciting new wedding and special-event venue in the Maryland, D.C. and Virginia area. Wedding packages, for up to 150 guests, include bride and groom changing suites, transportation by pleasure boat from the Annapolis city dock, and tented reception area. Catering, photography, music and flowers can be provided. Also, you may schedule honeymoon and guest travel arrangements at discounted rates through the Fantasy Island Travel Club.

Capacity: 150 seated; unlimited standing; unlimited in garden; unlimited with tent.
Catering: Approved caterers list. Entrees range from $40 to $80 per person.
Rental Fee: $4,500.
Parking: Although there is no maximum limit on the number of guests on the island, the boat maximum is 150 on each trip; thereafter, additional cost would be incurred. Parking is required in Annapolis public areas, close to the city dock.
Note: Wedding ceremonies are permitted.

Glenview Mansion at Rockville
Civic Center Park   301-309-3001

603 Edmonston Drive • Rockville, MD 20851

Glenview Mansion, a pillared, neo-classical home built in the style of an early 19th century plantation house, overlooks Rockville's 153-acre Civic Center Park. Surrounding grounds include beautiful boxwoods and formal gardens perfect for outside ceremonies. An indoor ceremony area is available for winter weddings. The living room, library, and Lyon room are furnished with period reproductions for casual seating. The wood-paneled dining room is available for a buffet, and marble-floored conservatory for dancing. The second floor provides picturesque porches, an art gallery, and a separate bride's room.

Capacity: 50 seated; 225 standing.
Catering: You must supply your own caterer.
Rental Fee: $1,405 to $2,021.
Parking: On the premises.
Restrictions: No smoking. No cooking (warm and serve permit only). No red wine or red dye beverages.

Gramercy Mansion Bed & Breakfast
& The Carriage House   410-486-2405

1400 Greenspring Valley Road • Stevenson, MD 21153

This historic 1902 English Tudor mansion was built by Alexander Cassatt, brother of Mary Cassatt, the American impressionist, as a wedding present for his daughter. Situated on 45 acres in Baltimore's Greenspring Valley, the house and grounds were part of the "Old Line" community and the scene of many parties and political gatherings during its early years. Now completely restored to its former elegance, Gramercy Bed and Breakfast welcomes you for a splendid occasion.

Capacity: 150.
Catering: You must supply your own caterer. Licensed and insured caterers only.
Rental Fee: $1,800 for 4 hours.
Parking: On the premises.
Restrictions: Smoking outside only. No birdseed or rice. Amplified music inside only.

Grey Rock Mansion   410-484-4554

400 Grey Rock Road • Pikesville, MD 21208

This Colonial-style mansion features a stone patio and gazebo which overlook lovely landscaped formal gardens. With its breathtaking view and exquisite gardens, it serves as a beautiful setting for weddings.

Capacity: 145 seated; 200 standing; 300 in garden; 225 with tent.
Catering: In-house. Entrees range from $30 to $50 per person.
Rental Fee: $700 to $1,300.
Parking: On the premises.
Note: Wedding ceremonies are permitted.

Hammond-Harwood House   410-263-4683

19 Maryland Avenue • Annapolis, MD 21401

This facility is a national historic landmark and an outstanding example of American colonial architecture. The building, with its carved entrance, formal rooms and elegant scale amid a charming garden, makes this Annapolis location a popular reception choice.

Capacity: 24 seated; 40 standing; 125 in garden.
Catering: Approved caterers list. Caterer must supply all banquet items and remove at the end of the function.
Rental Fee: $600 and up for 4 hours.
Parking: Street parking; city garage available.
Restrictions: No amplified music. Clean-up pre-approved.
Note: Wedding ceremonies are permitted indoors or outdoors.

Liriodendron   410-879-4424

502 West Gordon Street • Bel Air, MD 21014

Liriodendron has been described as "belonging on the cliffs of Newport." The mansion's grandeur makes it one of the most sought-after wedding locations. Wisteria-draped terraces, wide porticos, boxwood garden and fountain make Liriodendron a perfect choice for a garden wedding. The beautifully detailed mantels, stairways and reception rooms inside reflect an enduring elegance.

Capacity: Up to 200 depending on time of year and set-up required.
Catering: Your choice of any licensed caterer.
Rental Fee: $800 to $1,000 for 6$^1/_2$ hours. Four-hour party time.
Parking: Unlimited parking on the premises.
Restrictions: No candles, rice, birdseed, confetti or balloons.

Llewelyn Fields Manor   301-570-5114

c/o Snead Enterprises
812 Lindsey Manor Lane • Silver Spring, MD 20905

Elegant, enchanting and unforgettable, this circa 1820 grand manor house is on 11 tranquil acres, only minutes from Washington, D.C. The house is beautifully furnished with period antiques, oriental rugs, dazzling chandeliers and six fireplaces. The romantic setting is suitable for both wedding ceremony and reception. Patio and gardens are perfect for tent-covered festivities with dance floor and outdoor seating.

Capacity: 50 seated inside; 200 standing; 400+ in garden; 400+ with tent.
Catering: You must supply your own caterer.
Rental Fee: $2,000.
Parking: On the premises and in nearby lot.
Note: Wedding ceremonies are permitted. Guest rooms are available.

Merry Sherwood Plantation   410-641-2112

8909 Worcester Highway • Berlin, MD 21811

Handsomely restored and furnished with many fine antiques, the pre-Civil War mansion is situated on 18 acres of gardens. You can descend the mahogany staircase in the magnificent entry hall and be married in the elegant grand parlor with the original marble fireplaces, or choose one of many gardens or the gazebo as a setting for your wedding and/or reception. The house is decorated inside and out for the Christmas season events. Merry Sherwood Plantation, with its roses and azaleas, flowering shrubs, 150-year-old shade trees and park-like setting, is ten minutes from Assateague National Seashore and Ocean City on the eastern shore of Maryland.

Capacity: 30 seated; 125 standing; 200+ in garden; 200+ with tent.
Catering: Approved caterers list. Entrees range from $14 to $35 per person.

Rental Fee: $1,500 for 75-125 guests.
Parking: On the premises.
Restrictions: Dancing is not allowed in the mansion but may be
                held under a tent.
Note: Wedding ceremonies are permitted.

Montpelier Mansion   301-953-1376

Route 197 & Muirkirk Road • Laurel, MD 20708

Located on 70 acres of rolling park land, this national historic
landmark provides the perfect atmosphere for any elegant social
occasion. Ceremonies and receptions can take place in a number
of locations from the great entry hall to the indoor wings to the
outdoor garden terraces graced by a 200-year-old summerhouse
and boxwood. Guests can view furnished museum rooms during
their visit. The mansion is ideal for business retreats and seminars
at lower weekday rates.

Capacity: 100.
Catering: You must supply your own caterer.
Rental Fee: $800 Saturday; $700 Friday and Sunday for 7 hours.
                Facility requires a $400 refundable security deposit
                and a $50 custodial fee.
Parking: On the premises.
Restrictions: No smoking inside.
Note: Wedding ceremonies are permitted indoors or out-
                doors.

Newton White Mansion   301-249-2004

2708 Enterprise Road • Mitchellville, MD 20716

Built in 1939, this house was once the home of Captain Newton H.
White, who was the first commanding officer of the *USS Enterprise*. Newton White Mansion is one of the most popular settings
in Prince George's County. It offers a quiet atmosphere, elegant
patios, and a beautiful garden with a waterfall fountain for
outdoor events.

Capacity: 125 seated; 200 standing; 200 in garden.
Catering: You must supply your own caterer. Caterer must be
                licensed and insured.
Rental Fee: $2,100 Saturday; $1,700 Friday and Sunday.
Parking: Free parking on the premises.
Note: Wedding ceremonies are permitted indoors or out-
                doors. Facility is handicap accessible.

Historic Oakland　　410-730-4801/1-800-730-4802
www.historic-oakland.com

5430 Vantage Point Road • Columbia, MD 21044

Celebrate the occasion of your marriage with family and friends at a lovely manor estate. Adding grace to the exquisite interior are crystal chandeliers, period reproductions of the original furnishings and twin fireplaces in the ballroom and foyer. The ballroom doors lead to a veranda that overlooks a beautifully landscaped lawn and an antique rose garden.

Capacity:　　150 seated; 200 standing; 200 in garden.
Catering:　　In-house, approved caterers list or your own caterer provided the caterer adheres to the rules and policies of the mansion.
Rental Fee:　$700 to $1,500.
Parking:　　On the premises. Valet parking can be arranged.
Note:　　Wedding ceremonies are permitted indoors or outdoors.

Oxon Hill Manor　　　　　　　301-839-7782

6901 Oxon Hill Road • Oxon Hill, MD 20745

High atop a hill overlooking the Potomac River, Oxon Hill Manor is a breathtaking historic neo-Georgian style mansion with a wrap-around terrace, reflecting pool, and formal gardens. The elegant interior consists of a drawing room, library, dining room, marbled foyer, bride's dressing room and caterer's kitchen. The main rooms all lead onto the terrace through large French doors. Ideal for wedding ceremonies and receptions, social functions, business meetings and holiday parties, Oxon Hill Manor recalls the splendor of a by-gone era and will make your event an affair to remember.

Capacity:　　210 seated; 300 standing.
Catering:　　You must supply your own caterer.
Rental Fee:　$2,400 Friday, Saturdays, Sundays and holidays. Call to inquire about weekday rates.
Parking:　　On the premises.
Note:　　Wedding ceremonies are permitted.

Riversdale Mansion　　　　　　301-864-0420
http://www.smart.net/Çparksrec/riversdale

4811 Riverdale Road • Riverdale, MD 20737

This recently restored early 19th-century mansion is conveniently located approximately 3 miles from I-95 and the Baltimore-Washington Parkway. Riversdale is a five-part neoclassical style house. The available rental rooms include a carpeted banquet room with wall sconces in the East Wing, and a ballroom with decorative cornice and crystal chandelier in the West Wing.

Capacity:	100.
Catering:	You must supply your own caterer.
Rental Fee:	$700 to $1,150.
Parking:	On the premises.
Note:	Wedding ceremonies are permitted indoors or outdoors.

Rockwood Manor Park   301-299-5026

11001 MacArthur Boulevard • Potomac, MD 20854

Escape the commotion and bustle of the city and have your wedding reception in the park. Located in Potomac, Rockwood is just 20 minutes from downtown Washington and convenient to Bethesda and Rockville. You may enjoy a memorable feast in the spacious manor house, or have an elegant outdoor reception in the breathtaking gardens and patios that surround Rockwood.

Capacity:	100 seated; 150 standing; 150 in garden.
Catering:	Approved caterers list.
Rental Fee:	$1,400 Friday and Sunday; $1,700 Saturday.
Parking:	85 parking spaces on the premises.
Restrictions:	No amplified outdoor music.
Note:	Wedding ceremonies are permitted indoors or outdoors.

Strathmore Hall   301-530-5889

10701 Rockville Pike • North Bethesda, MD 20852

A turn-of-the-century, red-brick mansion, Strathmore Hall is surrounded by 11 acres of landscaped beauty, including a sculpture garden and pavilion. Enter through grand columns into a marble-floored foyer complete with a cherub fountain. Enjoy intimate moments with your guests as they flow through the main hall, library, music room, sun room and galleries, all filled with exhibits of local and national artists. Pose for photographs on the lovely staircase, a favorite area for wedding party pictures. All eight of the first floor rooms, a bridal room on the second floor, and the kitchen are available when you rent Strathmore.

Capacity:	225 standing; 275 with tent.
Catering:	Approved caterers list.
Rental Fee:	$1,400 to $2,900.
Parking:	On the premises.
Note:	Wedding ceremonies are permitted.

Strong Mansion at   301-869-7846 (Metro)
Sugarloaf Mountain   301-874-2024 (Frederick)

c/o Stronghold, Inc.
7901 Comus Road • Dickerson, MD 20842

Strong Mansion was built in 1912 by Chicago philanthropist Gordon Strong. The three-story Georgian home is surrounded by

3,000 woodland acres on Sugarloaf Mountain. You and your guests are welcome to roam the grounds and enjoy the beautiful antique furnishings throughout the entire home. The 22' x 60' spacious ballroom has eight large Palladian windows, two decorative fireplaces, and French doors that open on to a 15' x 34' portico. The back grounds are landscaped with formal gardens, a lily pond with a fountain, a white wooden pergola that is ideal for wedding ceremonies, and a breathtaking view of the countryside. Strong Mansion is the perfect setting for an outdoor wedding, reception, and other special events.

Capacity: 150.
Catering: You must supply your own caterer.
Rental Fee: $1,500 for 8 hours.
Parking: On the premises.
Restrictions: No smoking.
Note: Wedding ceremonies are permitted. The mansion is handicap accessible.

Swan Harbor Farm   410-939-6767

401 Oakington Road • Havre De Grace, MD 21078

Swan Harbor Farm, situated on almost five hundred acres, overlooks the Chesapeake Bay between Havre de Grace and Aberdeen, Maryland. Dating back to the 1700s, this stately home has a great hall, library, living room, dining room, kitchen and sun porch, which are perfect for weddings, receptions and rehearsal dinners. The mantels in the ground-floor rooms are among the finest Federal pieces in Harford County.

Capacity: 50+ seated; 100+ standing; 200 in garden; 200 with tent.
Catering: You must provide your own caterer. Tents, tables, chairs, and a portable dance floor for parties are available at an additional fee.
Rental Fee: $700 and up.
Parking: On the premises.
Note: Wedding ceremonies are permitted.

William Paca House   410-263-5553

186 Prince George Street • Annapolis, MD 21401

This 37-room Georgian mansion, surrounded by formal English gardens complete with wooden bridge, makes this Annapolis landmark a picturesque setting and popular reception choice. Receptions take place on tented terraces overlooking the gardens of the home built by former governor William Paca for his bride.

Capacity: 150 seated; 160 standing; 150 with tent.
Catering: You must supply your own caterer. Kitchen facilities are available.

Rental Fee: $500 to $2,000 for five hours.
Parking: Parking lot nearby. Valet parking can be arranged.
Restrictions: No hard liquor, only beer and wine. Limits on decorations. Limits on music and noise levels. Licensed and insured caterers only.
Note: Wedding ceremonies are permitted outdoors only.

Woodend   301-652-9188

8940 Jones Mill Road • Chevy Chase, MD 20815

Woodend is a beaux arts style mansion with classic Greek portico that overlooks sweeping lawns bordered by woods and meadows. Indoors, a Palladian window lights up a distinguished staircase and carved fireplace in the Great Hall. Step through stately French doors onto a raised terrace with a custom tent lit with chandeliers. Enjoy your romantic wedding ceremony in an enchanting grove surrounded by a canopy of trees. Woodend is a 40-acre bird sanctuary owned by the Audubon Naturalist Society and is conveniently located directly inside the beltway in Chevy Chase.

Capacity: 150 seated; 200 standing.
Catering: Approved caterers list.
Rental Fee: $1,200 to $3,100.
Parking: On the premises.
Note: Wedding ceremonies are permitted.

Woodlawn Manor   301-585-5564

16501 Norwood Road • Sandy Spring, MD 20860

Magnificent trees, rolling green landscape, garden gazebo and a unique stone barn set the stage for an elegant reception. Only minutes from busy urban centers, the Georgian-style manor house offers five spacious rooms, richly restored and tastefully furnished, to provide the charm and splendor of the 19th century. A modernized kitchen meets high-level catering requirements and ample parking is in close proximity to the manor house.

Capacity: 40 seated; 125 standing; 200 in garden.
Catering: Approved caterers list.
Rental Fee: $1,000 Friday and Sunday; $1,200 Saturday.
Parking: 48 parking spaces on the premises with overflow parking nearby.
Note: Wedding ceremonies are permitted.

B&O Railroad Museum　　　　　410-752-2463

901 West Pratt Street • Baltimore, MD 21223-2699

At the B&O Museum, guests view an exciting array of locomotives and cars that span over a century, dating back to the earliest
days of rail transportation. The rental of the facility includes full
use of several 19th-century railroad buildings: the Mt. Clare
Station, an 1851 depot building that guests enter through the
museum; the Mt. Clare Annex, a two-story 1884 print shop
building now housing the museum's archives; the Mt. Clare
Theater and gift shop; and the Roundhouse, an 1884 passenger
repair facility.

Capacity:　700 seated; 2,200 standing.
Catering:　Approved caterers list. No kitchen facilities.
Rental Fee:　$2,100 for first 200 guests, $6 each additional guest.
Parking:　On the premises and nearby parking lot.
Restrictions:　No helium filled balloons. No confetti. Smoking only
　　　　　in designated areas.
Note:　Wedding ceremonies are permitted.

Babe Ruth Museum　　　　　　410-727-1539

216 Emory Street • Baltimore, MD 21230

The sports-minded couple can celebrate their nuptials in the
birthplace of George Herman "Babe" Ruth, which includes a
museum, small theater and displays on Ruth, the Orioles and
Maryland baseball. The museum is contained in four rowhouses,
one of which is filled with 1800's furniture, with an adjoining
courtyard that can be used for cocktails or an outdoor wedding.

Capacity:　50 seated; 125 standing; 25 in garden.
Catering:　Approved caterers list.
Rental Fee:　$400.
Parking:　Residential parking and nearby parking lot.
Restrictions:　No smoking inside the building.
Note:　Wedding ceremonies are permitted.

The Baltimore Museum of Art　　410-396-6078

10 Art Museum Drive • Baltimore, MD 21218

The impressive neo-classical style of the original building, completed in 1929, is reflected in the splendor of the Fox Court with
its 16 massive Greek columns. Capped by a soaring 34-foot high
painted ceiling, this stone and marble court provides an elegant
setting for a wedding. The Fox Court opens into the Schaefer
Court, a square atrium lined in ancient mosaics with French doors
and Palladian windows that overlook a central garden. For receptions of 150 or less, you may use the Woodward Gallery or the
Garden Room. The Meyerhoff Auditorium is also available for

rental, and the adjourning USF&G Court can be used for cocktails and hors d'oeuvres.

Capacity: From 60 seated to 800 standing, depending upon space used.
Catering: Approved caterers list, but you may supply your own caterer provided caterer has insurance certification and can work within Museum's guidelines.
Rental Fee: Call for details.
Parking: Metered parking and nearby parking lot.
Restrictions: No eating or drinking in galleries. No ice sculptures, no frying, no decorating outdoors or decorating of art work. Museum is smoke-free.
Note: Wedding ceremonies are permitted.

The Cloisters   410-557-4494

P.O. Box 5394 • 10440 Falls Road • Baltimore, MD 21209

Many brides choose to marry their Prince Charming in this castle-like mansion, built as a private home in 1932 and incorporating parts of medieval European castles in the architecture. The stone mansion with its gables and wrought iron spiral staircase reflects a blend of Gothic and Tudor styles. Guests use the entire first floor, including the main gallery with an area for dancing and the living room which features a working fireplace. Outside ceremonies may be performed in the courtyard garden or in the amphitheater. Have your wedding in this castle . . . and live happily ever after!

Capacity: 120 seated with dance floor; 150 seated without dance floor; 200 standing.
Catering: Approved caterers list or your own caterer.
Rental Fee: $1,000 to $1,100.
Parking: On the premises.
Note: Candles are permitted with hurricanes.

Darnall's Chance   301-952-8010

14800 Gov. Oden Bowie Drive • Upper Marlboro, MD 20772

One of Prince George's County's and the State of Maryland's most significant historical landmarks, Darnall's Chance has been restored to its original appearance and is now open for tours and rentals. This site offers three floors, including six public rooms, exhibit area, gift shop, catering kitchen and wine cellar. Outdoor weddings and receptions may be held on the lawn.

Capacity: 100; 300 with tent.
Catering: You must supply your own caterer. Caterer must have a valid certificate of insurance.
Rental Fee: $800 for 6 hours. The 6-hour rental includes set-up and take-down times. $100 each additional hour.

Parking: Limited parking on the premises; parking on the street.

Restrictions: No smoking. Vendors are not allowed to park on the lawn during set-up. Noise level is enforced (65 decibels up to 10 p.m., 55 decibels after 10 p.m.).

Note: Wedding ceremonies are permitted indoors or outdoors.

Evergreen House of the Johns Hopkins University   410-516-0341

4545 North Charles Street • Baltimore, MD 21210

Seated on 26 acres, Evergreen provides the Baltimore community with an elegant, gracious estate at which to hold receptions. Evergreen has three areas for wedding receptions: The Evergreen Theater Wing, which consists of the large Far East Room, Theater and Lobby, and the smaller Billiard Room. With colors and Russian folk designs chosen by a noted Russian costume and set designer and a large collection of Japanese art work, the Theater Wing provides a colorful, dramatic location for a small reception. Amenities include a catering kitchen, piano, eight round tables and attractive black lacquer chairs. The Carriage House with its mid-19th century interior, wood paneling, hardwood and carpeted floors and large sliding doors that lead to a cobblestone entrance surrounded by trees, ivy and flowers, is a quite desirable location. Dancing is permitted in the Carriage House. The Upper Garden has two areas which may be tented and a fountain with Victorian cast iron benches. It may be rented in conjunction with either the Theater or Carriage House.

Capacity: 75 in Theater; up to 400 in Carriage House.
Catering: You must supply your own caterer.
Rental Fee: Varies. Call for details.
Parking: Ample free parking on the premises.
Restrictions: No amplified music in buildings. No smoking in buildings. No dancing in theater. No open flame in any location. No wedding ceremonies.

George Peabody Library of The Johns Hopkins University   410-659-8197
http://peabody-events.mse.jhu.edu

---

17 E. Mount Vernon Place • Baltimore, MD 21202

An unique architectural treasure built in 1878, The George Peabody Library is an uplifting setting for special celebrations. Located in the heart of the historic district, the superb neo-Greco building faces the open park of Mount Vernon Place and the Washington Monument. Within the large, main chamber, six book-filled tiers of gilt, cast iron balconies rise dramatically above the marble-tiled open court toward a grand skylight.

Capacity: 230 seated; 400 standing.
Catering: Approved caterers list or your own caterer with the approval of the facility.
Rental Fee: $1,675 to $2,175.
Parking: In nearby lots or garages. Valet parking can be arranged.
Restrictions: No smoking. No helium balloons. No rice, birdseed or glitter.
Note: Wedding ceremonies are permitted.

Great Blacks In Wax Museum, Inc.   410-563-6415

1601-3 East North Avenue • Baltimore, MD 21213

This unique museum showcases African-American history with 110 life-size, lifelike wax figures, including a room devoted to nine famous Marylanders. The Alberta Carson room has a gold-painted ceiling and African carved wood panels.

Capacity: 150 seated; 250 standing.
Catering: Approved caterers list.
Rental Fee: $250 plus $1.00 per person.
Parking: Residential parking. Parking lot nearby.
Note: Wedding ceremonies are permitted.

Hammond-Harwood House   410-263-4683

19 Maryland Avenue • Annapolis, MD 21401

This facility is a national historic landmark and an outstanding example of American colonial architecture. The building, with its carved entrance, formal rooms and elegant scale amid a charming garden, makes this Annapolis location a popular reception choice.

Capacity: 24 seated; 40 standing; 125 in garden.
Catering: Approved caterers list. Caterer must supply all banquet items and remove at the end of the function.
Rental Fee: $600 and up for 4 hours.
Parking: Street parking; city garage available.
Restrictions: No amplified music. Clean-up pre-approved.
Note: Wedding ceremonies are permitted indoors or outdoors.

Liriodendron   410-879-4424

502 West Gordon Street • Bel Air, MD 21014

Liriodendron has been described as "belonging on the cliffs of Newport." The mansion's grandeur makes it one of the most sought-after wedding locations. Wisteria-draped terraces, wide porticos, boxwood garden and fountain make Liriodendron a perfect choice for a garden wedding. The beautifully detailed mantels, stairways and reception rooms inside reflect an enduring elegance.

Capacity: Up to 200 depending on time of year and set-up required.
Catering: Your choice of any licensed caterer.
Rental Fee: $800 to $1,000 for 6¹/₂ hours. Four-hour party time.
Parking: Unlimited parking on the premises.
Restrictions: No candles, rice, birdseed, confetti or balloons.

National Aquarium in Baltimore   410-576-3869/3847

501 E. Pratt Street, Pier 3 • Baltimore, MD 21202

The magic and mystery of water make the National Aquarium in Baltimore ideal for couples who want a signature event. Create a mix of romance and fun, from casual to elegant, in settings appropriate for intimate parties or 800-guest galas. Secluded, tented parties on the pier are perfect for dancing under the stars. Dine near dolphins in the Marine Mammal Pavilion Underwater Viewing Area, dance in the airy Atrium, or enjoy breathtaking views in the Harbor View Room. Full-service catering is available. The Aquarium can accommodate a kosher wedding.

Capacity: 500 seated; 2,000 standing; 2,000 with tent.
Catering: In-house. Entrees begin at $20 per person and bar at $9.00 per person.
Rental Fee: $1,000 and up.
Parking: Parking in nearby lots.
Note: Wedding ceremonies are permitted.

TROIA at the Walters   410-752-2887

600 North Charles Street • Baltimore, MD 21201

Situated in the heart of Baltimore's historic Mount Vernon neighborhood, TROIA at the Walters offers excellence in food, service and atmosphere. Newly re-decorated by internationally famed designer Rita Saint Clair, the restaurant features a grand staircase, large columns, skylights and a large fountain that has appeared in motion picture productions.

Capacity: 135 seated, 200 standing.
Catering: In-house. Entrees range from $35 to $85 per person.
Parking: Parking lot nearby. Valet parking can be arranged.
Note: Wedding ceremonies are permitted.

Union Mills Homestead Museum   410-848-2288

3311 Littlestown Pike • Westminster, MD 21157

If you prefer an outdoor celebration in a rural atmosphere—this is the place. Weeping willows, flower gardens and a footbridge are some of the many attractions on the land of the Homestead, a 23-room structure built in 1797.

Capacity: 250 seated in Tannery; unlimited capacity on grounds.
Catering: You must supply your own caterer.
Rental Fee: Facilities request a donation of $200 for grounds and $300 for tannery building.
Parking: On the premises.
Restrictions: Alcoholic beverages may be brought on premises, but not sold.
Note: Wedding ceremonies are permitted. Hours til dusk, April to October. One event a day.

William Paca House   410-263-5553

186 Prince George Street • Annapolis, MD 21401

This 37-room Georgian mansion, surrounded by formal English gardens complete with wooden bridge, makes this Annapolis landmark a picturesque setting and popular reception choice. Receptions take place on tented terraces overlooking the gardens of the home built by former governor William Paca for his bride.

Capacity: 150 seated; 160 standing; 150 with tent.
Catering: You must supply your own caterer. Kitchen facilities are available.
Rental Fee: $500 to $2,000 for five hours.
Parking: Parking lot nearby. Valet parking can be arranged.
Restrictions: No hard liquor, only beer and wine. Limits on decorations. Limits on music and noise levels. Licensed and insured caterers only.
Note: Wedding ceremonies are permitted outdoors only.

Brookside Gardens   301-949-8230

1500 Glenallan Avenue • Wheaton, MD 20902

If you have always wanted a garden wedding— this is the place where dreams come true. Weddings, receptions and other social events can now be scheduled year-round in the conservatory, new Visitor's Center, or as a tented affair in the gardens. Whether you choose the tropical paradise offered in the colorful conservatory, the oriental flair of the Japanese Tea House, the carefree innocence of the Fragrance Garden or the exquisite charm of the Wedding Gazebo, your guests will appreciate the beautifully landscaped settings throughout this 50-acre garden. A new reception hall overlooks the Azalea Garden hillside and Aquatic Garden ponds.

Capacity: 125 seated; 175 standing in reception hall; 250 in garden with tent.
Catering: Approved caterers list. Licensed and insured caterers only.
Rental Fee: Ranges from $350 at the Wedding Gazebo for an hour ceremony to $2,000 for seven hours in the reception hall. $500 deposit required.
Parking: On the premises, nearby parking lot and residential parking.
Restrictions: No smoking allowed inside the building.
Note: Brides may choose one of several gazebos for wedding ceremony.

Friendship Heights Village Center   301-656-2797

4433 South Park Avenue • Chevy Chase, MD 20815

This unique gallery is enhanced by cathedral ceilings, parquet floors, and ceiling-to-floor windows overlooking a beautifully landscaped park with fountain. It has two small classrooms, and access to a 20' x 40' patio which can be tented.

Capacity: 120 to 150 seated; 250 to 300 standing.
Catering: You must supply your own caterer. Warming kitchen and tables and chairs provided.
Rental Fee: $800 to $1,200. Available for 8-hour contract on weekends between 2:00 p.m. to 12:30 a.m. Rental time includes any deliveries, set-up and take-down of equipment and clean-up.
Parking: Limited parking on premises. Additional parking in nearby lot. Walking distance to metro, hotel, shops and restaurants.
Restrictions: No smoking in building. No set-ups in front of building or in the park.
Note: Wedding ceremonies are permitted in the main room or on the patio only.

Glenview Mansion at Rockville
Civic Center Park   301-309-3001

603 Edmonston Drive • Rockville, MD 20851

Glenview Mansion, a pillared, neo-classical home built in the style of an early 19th century plantation house, overlooks Rockville's 153-acre Civic Center Park. Surrounding grounds include beautiful boxwoods and formal gardens perfect for outside ceremonies. An indoor ceremony area is available for winter weddings. The living room, library, and Lyon room are furnished with period reproductions for casual seating. The wood-paneled dining room is available for a buffet, and marble-floored conservatory for dancing. The second floor provides picturesque porches, an art gallery, and a separate bride's room.

Capacity: 50 seated; 225 standing.
Catering: You must supply your own caterer.
Rental Fee: $1,405 to $2,021.
Parking: On the premises.
Restrictions: No smoking. No cooking (warm and serve permit only). No red wine or red dye beverages.

Lodge at Little Seneca Creek   301-585-5564

14500-A Clopper Road • Boyds, MD 20841

The Lodge at Little Seneca Creek is a rustic meeting place designed as a replica of a classic log cabin. The lodge's spacious meeting hall is accented by a massive flagstone fireplace. The splendor of the oak flooring is surpassed only by the natural wood cathedral ceilings. A breathtaking view from the outdoor deck includes a pastoral scene where an outdoor wedding reception may be held.

Capacity: 120 seated; 180 standing.
Catering: Approved caterers list.
Rental Fee: $700 Friday and Sunday; $900 Saturday.
Parking: 85 parking spaces on the premises.
Note: Wedding ceremonies are permitted indoors or outdoors.

McCrillis Gardens and Gallery   301-949-8230

6910 Greentree Road • Bethesda, MD 20817

This elegant garden is another lovely outdoor setting available for wedding ceremonies, receptions, or other social affair. It is a premier five-acre shade garden with a wedding gazebo nestled among spring-flowering rhododendrons and azaleas. Seasonal interest is extended with the use of ornamental trees, shrubs, colorful bulbs, ground covers and shade-loving perennials. An added bonus is the McCrillis Gallery displaying the work of artists from around the Washington metropolitan area. A shaded lawn perfect for tented affairs is located behind McCrillis Gallery. Guests will enjoy strolling through this peaceful garden.

Capacity: 125 seated and standing.
Catering.   Approved caterers list. Licensed and insured caterers only. Kitchen facilities are available.
Rental Fee: $1,500 for 6 hours, plus a $500 security deposit.
Parking: Parking lot nearby.
Restrictions: No amplified music.

Prince George's Ballroom   301-341-7439

2411 Pinebrook Avenue • Landover, MD 20785

Surrounded by 50 acres of parkland and conveniently located, this elegant ballroom with its art-deco styling is only 30 minutes from Washington, D.C. With its beautiful hardwood floors and spacious patio, it is one of the area's most popular reception locations.

Capacity: 250 to 270 seated.
Catering: You must supply your own caterer.
Rental Fee: $900 to $1,300.
Parking: On the premises. Handicap parking available.
Note: Wedding ceremonies are permitted indoors or outdoors.

Quiet Waters Park   410-222-1777

600 Quiet Waters Park Road • Annapolis, MD 21403

Located in Annapolis on the banks of the South River, this 336-acre park represents Victorian style architecture. The park design features fountains, gazebos, woodland trails and formal gardens. The park's Blue Heron Center with its formal gardens is perfect for large parties, receptions and weddings. Couples renting the Center may use the immediate lower garden area for their ceremony at no extra charge.

Capacity: 150 seated; 225 standing.
Catering: In-house.
Rental Fee: Call for more information.
Parking: On the premises.
Note: Wedding ceremonies are permitted indoors or outdoors.

Rockwood Manor Park   301-299-5026

11001 MacArthur Boulevard • Potomac, MD 20854

Escape the commotion and bustle of the city and have your wedding reception in the park. Located in Potomac, Rockwood is

just 20 minutes from downtown Washington and convenient to
Bethesda and Rockville. You may enjoy a memorable feast in the
spacious manor house, or have an elegant outdoor reception in the
breathtaking gardens and patios that surround Rockwood.

Capacity: 100 seated; 150 standing; 150 in garden.
Catering: Approved caterers list.
Rental Fee: $1,400 Friday and Sunday; $1,700 Saturday.
Parking: 85 parking spaces on the premises.
Restrictions: No amplified outdoor music.
Note: Wedding ceremonies are permitted indoors or out-
               doors.

Staub's Country Inn   301-428-8449

19800 Darnestown Road • Beallsville, MD 20839

The two best reasons for choosing Staub's Country Inn Restaurant and caterers are the food and the twelve beautiful acres on
which the restaurant is located. An appealing assortment of menu
options are sure to impress. Mouth-watering gourmet delights or
traditional favorites are customized to fit your needs. Perfect for
outdoor receptions and picnics, the open landscape provides
plenty of fresh air and open space for your enjoyment. The inn's
personable staff will cater to your every need.

Capacity: 30 seated inside; unlimited capacity on grounds (tent
               recommended).
Catering: In-house or approved caterers list. Entrees range
               from $12.95 to $49.95 per person.
Parking: On the premises.
Note: Wedding ceremonies are permitted.

Union Mills Homestead Museum   410-848-2288

3311 Littlestown Pike • Westminster, MD 21157

If you prefer an outdoor celebration in a rural atmosphere—this
is the place. Weeping willows, flower gardens and a footbridge are
some of the many attractions on the land of the Homestead, a 23-
room structure built in 1797.

Capacity: 250 seated in Tannery; unlimited capacity on grounds.
Catering: You must supply your own caterer.
Rental Fee: Facilities request a donation of $200 for grounds and
               $300 for tannery building.
Parking: On the premises.
Restrictions: Alcoholic beverages may be brought on premises, but
               not sold.
Note: Wedding ceremonies are permitted. Hours til dusk,
               April to October. One event a day.

Herrington on the Bay   410-741-5101

7149 Lake Shore Drive, Rte. 261 • Rose Haven, MD 20714

Herrington on the Bay provides a classic Caribbean-style setting overlooking the Chesapeake Bay. Located just south of Annapolis and 30 minutes east of Washington, D.C., Herrington is accessible by car or boat. Professional caterers and wedding consultants take the stress out of wedding planning. Brides and grooms relax and enjoy their ceremonies and their receptions whether they choose indoors or out on the beachfront lawns. The Herrington Inn, located on premises, offers Island-style rooms with private hot tubs. From transportation to the music to the cuisine, Herrington delivers festive, fun weddings for today's brides!

Capacity: 200 seated; 250 standing; 300 in garden; 300 with tent.
Catering: In-house. Entrees range from $18 to $32 per person. Cake cutting fee if you provide your own cake.
Rental Fee: $195.
Parking: On the premises.
Note: Wedding ceremonies are permitted.

Blair Mansion Inn   301-588-1688

7711 Eastern Avenue • Silver Spring, MD 20912

The Blair Mansion Inn was first built in 1890 by architect Stanford White, who also designed Madison Square Gardens in New York. Later renovations turned the house into an inn and a dinner theater. This graciously restored inn offers a lovely environment for a wedding reception, anniversary, or other special celebrations.

Capacity: 350 seated; 425 standing.
Catering: In-house or your own caterer with approval of facility. Entrees range from $16.95 to $25.95 per person when you use in-house caterer.
Parking: Free parking on the premise and residential parking.

Candle Light Inn   410-788-6076

1835 Frederick Road • Catonsville, MD 21228

The Candle Light Inn has been celebrating beautiful weddings for over seventy years. Built as a private residence around 1840, the Inn gives distinction to intimate parties of 10 to 130 guests. The covered garden patio is also available either as a ceremony site or for receptions up to 70 guests. The executive chef serves a marvelous continental menu for your friends and family to enjoy in a lovely classic setting.

Capacity: 110 seated; 130 standing; 60 in garden.
Catering: In-house. Entrees range from $20 to $30 per person.
Parking: On the premises.
Note: Wedding ceremonies are permitted.

Carrol's Creek   410-263-8102

410 Severn Avenue • Annapolis, MD 21403

If you are looking for a reception location on the waterfront with a beautiful view of historic Annapolis and the U.S. Naval Academy, with ample free parking, professional service and creative cuisine – Carrol's Creek is the site for you! Since 1983, Carrol's Creek has been one of Annapolis' leading caterers for rehearsal dinners, weddings, corporate receptions, lunch, dinner and buffet banquets. You can reserve the entire restaurant for 100 to 260 guests.

Capacity: 160 seated inside; 25 to 100 in Starboard Room; 100 on deck.
Catering: In-house. Entrees range from $40 to $80. Cake cutting fee if client provides own cake.
Rental Fee: Varies. Call for more information.

Parking: On the premises. Valet parking may be arranged.
Note: Wedding ceremonies are permitted.

Country Club of Maryland   410-823-6710

1101 Stevenson Lane • Towson, MD 21286

This private golf and country club provides the ideal setting for your perfect day. Allow the exceptional executive chef and experienced banquet staff to provide you and your guests with the finest cuisine and service. A beautiful, tented outdoor patio provides the perfect backdrop for your formal portraits. Call to arrange an appointment for a personal tour of the clubhouse.

Capacity: 250 seated; 300 standing; 100 with tent.
Catering: In-house. Entrees begin at $37 per person. You are responsible for providing your own wedding cake.
Parking: On the premises. Valet parking available for extra fee.
Note: Wedding ceremonies are permitted.

Fergie's Waterfront
Restaurant and Catering   1-800-292-1371

2840 Solomons Island Road • Edgewater, MD 21037

Fergie's Waterfront Restaurant & Catering will help you create the reception of your dreams. Its banquet room has an adjacent deck on the water for your cocktail hour or ceremony. The banquet room has decorated Grecian columns, large dance floor and beautiful built-in bar. Your reception could be in the main dining room with wrap-around windows overlooking the water. There is also a dance floor, and an area for cocktails and hors d'oeuvres. This facility can be used on Saturday 12:00 p.m. until 4:00 p.m. It is located one mile outside Annapolis.

Capacity: 160 seated; 200 standing.
Catering: In-house. Entrees range from $32 to $40 per person.
Parking: On the premises.
Note: Wedding ceremonies are permitted.

Golden Bull Grand Café   301-948-3666

7 Dalamar Street • Gaithersburg, MD 20877

One of the largest banquet facilities in the area comes with its own private entrance. Choose from one of three party areas this location has to offer and you have the makings of a great party. The main banquet room with its contemporary decor and spacious dance floor is perfect for receptions.

Capacity: 25 to 300 seated; 325 standing.
Catering: In-house. Entrees range from $19.95 to $42.95.

Rental Fee: There is a room fee of $25 if number of guests fall
                below 25.
Parking: On the premises.
Note: Wedding ceremonies are permitted.

Mrs. K's Toll House   301-589-3500

9201 Colesville Road • Silver Spring, MD 20910

Mrs. K's Toll House is one of the last operating toll houses in
Montgomery County. The interior of this historic building is
elegantly appointed with carefully collected antiques and hand-
crafted seasonal decorations. The staff will personalize your menu
so that your guests may choose from more than one entree. Lush
gardens provide a romantic setting for outdoor ceremonies and
receptions. It is conveniently located just south of the beltway in
Silver Spring, and offers plenty of well-lit parking.

Capacity: 150 seated; unlimited in garden. Can seat up to 110
                with a reasonable dance floor, 150 without a dance
                floor.
Catering: In-house. Entrees range from $19 to $49 per person.
Parking: On the premises.
Note: Wedding ceremonies are permitted.

Reynolds Tavern   410-626-0380/1-888-626-0381

7 Church Circle, P.O. Box 748 • Annapolis, MD 21404

Located in the heart of historic Annapolis, this authentically
restored building, circa 1747, provides a wonderful setting for all
wedding functions including rehearsal dinners, ceremonies and
receptions. The facility includes two colonial-style dining rooms,
a private shady garden and terrace, a casual English pub, and four
spacious lodging rooms. Whether you use one room or the entire
facility, your guests will be impressed with the graceful setting,
fresh and beautifully presented cuisine and attentive service. The
tavern's complete wedding coordination services will make your
event memorable and worry-free.

Capacity: 75 seated; 90 standing inside; 130 seated, 160 stand-
                ing in garden; 100 with tent.
Catering: In-house. Entrees range from $25 to $50 per person.
                Cake cutting fee if you provide your own cake.
Rental Fee: Either $500 for whole facility, or a minimum food and
                beverage commitment.
Parking: Parking in nearby lot. Valet parking is available.
Note: Wedding ceremonies are permitted.

Staub's Country Inn   301-428-8449

19800 Darnestown Road • Beallsville, MD 20839

The two best reasons for choosing Staub's Country Inn Restaurant and caterers are the food and the twelve beautiful acres on which the restaurant is located. An appealing assortment of menu options are sure to impress. Mouth-watering gourmet delights or traditional favorites are customized to fit your needs. Perfect for outdoor receptions and picnics, the open landscape provides plenty of fresh air and open space for your enjoyment. The inn's personable staff will cater to your every need.

Capacity: 30 seated inside; unlimited capacity on grounds (tent recommended).
Catering: In-house or approved caterers list. Entrees range from $12.95 to $49.95 per person.
Parking: On the premises.
Note: Wedding ceremonies are permitted.

TROIA at the Walters   410-752-2887

600 North Charles Street • Baltimore, MD 21201

Situated in the heart of Baltimore's historic Mount Vernon neighborhood, TROIA at the Walters offers excellence in food, service and atmosphere. Newly re-decorated by internationally famed designer Rita Saint Clair, the restaurant features a grand staircase, large columns, skylights and a large fountain that has appeared in motion picture productions.

Capacity: 135 seated, 200 standing.
Catering: In-house. Entrees range from $35 to $85 per person.
Parking: Parking lot nearby. Valet parking can be arranged.
Note: Wedding ceremonies are permitted.

Willow Tree Inn   301-948-8832

**19550 Montgomery Village Avenue
Gaithersburg, MD 20879**

Overlooking the Montgomery Village Golf Course, this inn is a charming place to celebrate your wedding day. The banquet room features floor-to-ceiling windows which open onto a lovely balcony, providing spectacular indoor and outdoor views from every angle. A lovely lake adds to the tranquil scene.

Capacity: 250 seated (10 a.m. to 4 p.m.), 150 seated (6 p.m. to 10 p.m.); 300 standing (10 a.m. to 4 p.m.), 200 standing (6 p.m. to 10 p.m.)
Catering: In-house. Entrees range from $20 to $80 per person. Cake cutting fee is $50.

Parking: On the premises.
Restrictions: Wedding ceremonies, 10 a.m. to 4 p.m. only.

Inn & Conference Center
University of Maryland
University College   301-985-7855

University Blvd. at Adelphi Road • College Park, MD 20742

The Chesapeake, Ft. McHenry and Founders Rooms open up to
an impressive reception area. Cocktail receptions are held in the
artwork-laden expansive concourse, then guests enter the banquet rooms for top-notch cuisine. The garden courtyards with
fountains, lighted ivy and exquisite greenery extend from the
banquet rooms for those seeking a moment outside. A portable
parquet dance floor allows for a flexible room design, and the
chandeliers and spot lighting add special ambience.

Capacity: 500 seated; 700 standing; 50 in garden; 200 with tent.
Catering: In-house. Complete wedding packages are available.
Parking: On the premises. Valet parking can be arranged.
Restrictions: Bride/Groom or members of the immediate family
              must be faculty, students or alumni of the University
              of Maryland system.
Note: Wedding ceremonies are permitted.

The Johns Hopkins University
Glass Pavilion   410-516-8209

3400 N. Charles Street • Baltimore, MD 21218

The Glass Pavilion is located in a natural wooded setting on the
campus of Johns Hopkins University. It is totally encased in glass
with a patio surrounding the entire room. Amenities include a
permanent stage.

Capacity: 200 to 250 seated; 500 standing.
Catering: In-house or your own caterer.
Rental Fee: $975.
Parking: On the premises and nearby parking lot.
Restrictions: Available June through August 14 of each year.
Note: Wedding ceremonies are permitted indoors or outdoors.

The Rossborough Inn   301-314-8012

Route 1 • University of Maryland • College Park, MD 20742

The Rossborough Inn is ideally suited for weddings and receptions. The dignity and grace of the charming dining rooms,
English garden and courtyard create the perfect atmosphere for
an elegant wedding. The inn has just added a new outdoor patio
that can accommodate dancing and hors d'oeuvres.

Capacity: 145 seated; 175 standing; 300 in garden.
Catering: In-house. Entrees range from $45 to $65 per person.
              Cake cutting fee is $1.00 per person.

Rental Fee: $750.
Parking: On the premises, residential and nearby parking lot.
Restrictions: No smoking. No rice or birdseed.
Note: Wedding ceremonies are permitted.

Admiral Fell Inn 410-522-7377

888 South Broadway • Baltimore, MD 21231

The Admiral Fell Inn is a newly renovated inn located downtown on Baltimore's historic waterfront. Its lively and colorful historic Fell's Point neighborhood is renowned for Belgian block streets and brick sidewalks, antique shops, boutiques, art galleries, pubs, and restaurants. In its 210-year history, the inn has served as a ship chandlery, a theater, a boarding house for sailors, and, later, a seaman's YMCA. Comfortable guest rooms are furnished with custom-crafted Federal-style furnishings. The inn is just a water taxi ride away from Baltimore's Inner Harbor attractions and Little Italy, museums, theaters, and cultural institutions. Amenities include 80 guest rooms and suites (nine with Jacuzzi tubs), continental breakfast, continuous tea and coffee service in the lobby, courtesy van to nearby Inner Harbor and downtown locations, and free parking. The inn's critically acclaimed main restaurant features regional American cuisine in a romantic setting, and an exceptional wine cellar. The new rooftop ballroom and terrace boast a spectacular 360-degree view of the city.

Capacity: 120 seated; 150 standing, with dance floor; 50 in garden; 24 with tent.

Catering: In-house. Entrees range from $55 to $125 per person. Cake cutting fee if you provide your own cake.

Parking: Parking in nearby lot.

Note: Wedding ceremonies are permitted.

Carrol's Creek 410-263-8102

410 Severn Avenue • Annapolis, MD 21403

If you are looking for a reception location on the waterfront with a beautiful view of historic Annapolis and the U.S. Naval Academy, with ample free parking, professional service and creative cuisine – Carrol's Creek is the site for you! Since 1983, Carrol's Creek has been one of Annapolis' leading caterers for rehearsal dinners, weddings, corporate receptions, lunch, dinner and buffet banquets. You can reserve the entire restaurant for 100 to 260 guests.

Capacity: 160 seated inside; 25 to 100 in Starboard Room; 100 on deck.

Catering: In-house. Entrees range from $40 to $80. Cake cutting fee if client provides own cake.

Rental Fee: Varies. Call for more information.

Parking: On the premises. Valet parking may be arranged.

Note: Wedding ceremonies are permitted.

Chesapeake Bay Adventures   1-800-394-4101

1934 Lincoln Drive, Suite B • Annapolis, MD 21401

Envision being aboard your own private yacht hosting your elegant reception, party or special event on the Chesapeake. From intimate to extravagant, these vessels will accommodate events of any size. Complete event planning and coordination is offered for weddings and receptions by land or by sea throughout the Chesapeake Bay Region and Washington, D.C.

Capacity: 2 to 500.
Catering: In-house and approved caterers list.
Rental Fee: $250 per hour.
Parking: On the premises. Parking lot nearby. Valet parking available.
Note: Wedding ceremonies are permitted indoors or outdoors.

Chesapeake Marine Tours   410-268-7601
http://member.aol.com/boattours/cmt.html

P.O. Box 3350/Slip 20 City Dock • Annapolis, MD 21403

For a truly romantic setting, have your wedding, reception, or anniversary celebration in historic Annapolis, on the scenic Severn River, aboard one of these riverboats or corporate yacht, or at the lovely Annapolis Landing Marina waterfront facility. *Providence*, a charming 64-foot riverboat, is perfect for the wedding ceremony and reception with a DJ or band for dancing. The *Cabaret II*, a 67-foot custom motor yacht, is an elegant setting for a formal affair. Intimate weddings are graciously accommodated by smaller charter boats. The waterfront location has both lawn and banquet room facilities. Some of the finest area caterers are featured. Wedding packages are available in a variety of price ranges for groups of 20 to 200.

Capacity: 20 to 100 seated, 20 to 297 standing; 150 on the lawn.
Catering: Approved caterers list. Entrees range from $25 to $80 per person.
Rental Fee: $500 to $3,500.
Parking: On the premises, and nearby parking lot.
Restrictions: Waterfront land facilities activities are limited to 10 o'clock. Valet parking is required for parking at the facility.

Clarion Hotel   410-727-7101

The George Washington Club
612 Cathedral Street • Baltimore, MD 21201

Consider having your wedding reception at this beautiful European hotel located minutes from the Harbor. Located in the heart of the arts and cultural district, this lovely hotel is a proud resident of historic Mount Vernon Square. A magnificent glass-enclosed rooftop ballroom adds a finishing note of grace and beauty to the hotel. This facility combines elegance and ambience in the grand tradition of a bygone era.

Capacity:	150.
Catering:	In-house. Packages as well as customized menus.
Parking:	Valet parking is available.
Note:	Wedding ceremonies are permitted. Guest rooms available at preferred rates.

Columbia Inn Hotel   410-730-3900

10207 Wincopin Circle • Columbia, MD 21044

The Columbia Inn, commanding a spectacular view of Lake Kittamaqundi, is a sought-after location for receptions, anniversaries, and other joyous occasions. One ballroom leads to an outdoor terrace. The hotel is conveniently located to Merriweather Pavilion and to shopping. Wedding packages are all-inclusive. The Columbia Inn combines ambience with impeccable service.

Capacity:	250 seated; 500 standing; 80 in garden.
Catering:	In-house. Entrees range from $48 to $60 per person.
Parking:	On the premises.
Note:	Wedding ceremonies are permitted indoors or outdoors, Sundays only. Guest rooms are available at special rates.

Comus Inn Restaurant   301-428-8593

23900 Old Hundred Road • Comus, MD 20842

This historic inn, built in 1794, is surrounded by flowering gardens, stately trees, lovely lawns and Sugarloaf Mountain. The tastefully restored inn is the perfect country setting for weddings, rehearsal dinners, anniversaries, or any celebration. There are five private dining rooms available for meetings, banquets, and other events. The inn affords easy access to I-270 and is just 30 minutes from the Beltway.

Capacity:	150 seated; 200 in garden; 200 with a tent.
Catering:	In-house. Entrees range from $20 to $50 per person. Cake cutting fee is $.50 per person.
Parking:	On the premises.
Note:	Wedding ceremonies are permitted.

Fantasy Island   410-729-4505

St. Helena Island, Severn River • Crownsville, MD

The Mansion, on St. Helena Island in the prestigious Severn River, is just minutes from historic downtown Annapolis. St. Helena, with its towering oak trees, beautiful flowers, ivy-covered walls and spectacular water views, is the perfect wedding site. The mansion, a gracious Federal architectural design, was built in 1931 and is a close copy of the famous John Hopkins "Homewood House." The stately residence is graced by porticos and beautiful white Doric columns. The house features magnificent mahogany and marble floors, marble fireplaces, and antique chandeliers. In the spring, the island bursts into life with pink and white dogwoods, azaleas, rhododendrons and beautiful flower gardens set against the background of the Severn River. This enchanted island is the most exciting new wedding and special event venue in the Maryland, D.C. and Virginia area. Wedding packages, for up to 150 guests, include bride and groom changing suites, transportation by pleasure boat from the Annapolis city dock, and tented reception area. Catering, photography, music and flowers can be provided. Also, you may schedule honeymoon and guest travel arrangements at discounted rates through the Fantasy Island Travel Club.

Capacity:	150 seated; unlimited standing; unlimited in garden; unlimited with tent.
Catering:	Approved caterers list. Entrees range from $40 to $80 per person.
Rental Fee:	$4,500.
Parking:	Although there is no maximum limit on the number of guests on the island, the boat maximum is 150 on each trip; thereafter, additional cost would be incurred. Parking is required in Annapolis public areas, close to the city dock.
Note:	Wedding ceremonies are permitted.

Fergie's Waterfront
Restaurant and Catering   1-800-292-1371

2840 Solomons Island Road • Edgewater, MD 21037

Fergie's Waterfront Restaurant & Catering will help you create the reception of your dreams. Its banquet room has an adjacent deck on the water for your cocktail hour or ceremony. The banquet room has decorated Grecian columns, large dance floor and beautiful built-in bar. Your reception could be in the main dining room with wrap-around windows overlooking the water. There is also a dance floor, and an area for cocktails and hors d'oeuvres. This facility can be used on Saturday 12:00 p.m. until 4:00 p.m. It is located one mile outside Annapolis.

Capacity: 160 seated; 200 standing.
Catering: In-house. Entrees range from $32 to $40 per person.
Parking: On the premises.
Note: Wedding ceremonies are permitted.

Inn at Mitchell House 410-778-6500

8796 Maryland Parkway • Chestertown, MD 21620

Nestled on ten rolling acres, surrounded by woods and overlooking "Stoneybrook Pond," this historic manor house, built in 1743, affords a touch of tranquility. Small wedding parties during the cooler months can enjoy its parlors, 18th-century dining room, and numerous fireplaces. Larger weddings are held outdoors on the inn's sweeping lawn with beautiful vistas. This country location invites a peaceful step back in time.

Capacity: 50 inside; 250 outside.
Catering: In-house and approved caterers list. Entrees range from $25 to $40.
Rental Fee: $400 to $700.
Parking: On the premises.
Note: Wedding ceremonies are permitted.

London Town
Publik House & Garden 410-222-1919

839 Londontown Road • Edgewater, MD 21037

A national historic landmark on the banks of the South River and minutes from Annapolis, the house at London Town shares a dramatic waterfront setting with an eight-acre woodland garden and glass-enclosed pavilion. Surrounded by decks and overlooking the gardens and river, the Pavilion attracts numerous weddings and receptions throughout the year. Ceremonies take place on spacious or intimate overlooks in and around the gardens. The House was designated a national historic landmark in 1970.

Capacity: 125 indoors; 175 with tent.
Catering: Approved caterers list or your own caterer. Caterer must be licensed and insured.
Rental Fee: $800 and up.
Parking: On the premises.

National Aquarium
in Baltimore 410-576-3869/3847

501 E. Pratt Street, Pier 3 • Baltimore, MD 21202

The magic and mystery of water make the National Aquarium in Baltimore ideal for couples who want a signature event. Create a mix of romance and fun, from casual to elegant, in settings appropriate for intimate parties or 800-guest galas. Secluded, tented parties on the pier are perfect for dancing under the stars. Dine near dolphins in the Marine Mammal Pavilion Underwater Viewing Area, dance in the airy Atrium, or enjoy breathtaking views in the Harbor View Room. Full-service catering is available. The Aquarium can accommodate a kosher wedding.

Capacity: 500 seated; 2,000 standing; 2,000 with tent.
Catering: In-house. Entrees begin at $20 per person and bar at $9.00 per person.
Rental Fee: $1,000 and up.
Parking: Parking in nearby lots.
Note: Wedding ceremonies are permitted.

Oxon Hill Manor   301-839-7782

6901 Oxon Hill Road • Oxon Hill, MD 20745

High atop a hill overlooking the Potomac River, Oxon Hill Manor is a breathtaking historic neo-Georgian style mansion with a wrap-around terrace, reflecting pool, and formal gardens. The elegant interior consists of a drawing room, library, dining room, marbled foyer, bride's dressing room and caterer's kitchen. The main rooms all lead onto the terrace through large French doors. Ideal for wedding ceremonies and receptions, social functions, business meetings and holiday parties, Oxon Hill Manor recalls the splendor of a by-gone era and will make your event an affair to remember.

Capacity: 210 seated; 300 standing.
Catering: You must supply your own caterer.
Rental Fee: $2,400 Friday, Saturdays, Sundays and holidays. Call to inquire about weekday rates.
Parking: On the premises.
Note: Wedding ceremonies are permitted.

Paint Branch
Unitarian Universalist Church   301-937-3666

3215 Powder Mill Road • Adelphi, MD 20783

Paint Branch Church is a beautiful location for your special event ... an idyllic setting for weddings, receptions, concerts, birthdays, anniversaries, or other cultural and social events. This wonderful site features cathedral ceilings with wooden beams and a pan-oramic view of the lovely wooded area surrounding the facility, and an outdoor deck that is perfect for cocktails or dancing under the stars.

Capacity: 150-200 in Meeting Room; 100 in Kelley Room; 50 on the deck.
Catering: You must supply your own caterer.
Rental Fee: Suggested rates vary by day of week, number of

guests, room selection and number of hours. Please call for schedule.

Parking: On the premises.

Restrictions: No smoking. Parties must end by 11:00 p.m. and clean-up must be finished by midnight.

Note: Wedding ceremonies are permitted indoors and out-doors.

Patriot Cruises Inc.   410-745-3100

**Chesapeake Bay Maritime Museum Dock (Mill Street)
St. Michaels, MD 21663**

Leaving the beautiful St. Michaels Harbor you will enjoy the untouched, scenic beauty of the Wye and Miles Rivers. Built in 1990, the *Patriot* can accommodate casual to the most elegant of affairs with ease. This climate-controlled vessel is equipped with two shipboard bars and a canopied upper deck for your enjoyment. A cruise on the *Patriot* is a special mix of history, natural waterways, and culture.

Capacity: 110 seated; 170 standing.

Catering: In-house or approved caterers list. Entrees range from $17 to $40 per person.

Rental Fee: $1,500 for 3-hour cruise.

Parking: On the premises and in nearby lot.

Note: Wedding ceremonies are permitted.

Paul's on the South River   410-956-3410

3027 Riva Road • Annapolis, MD 21140

Paul's is decorated in soft muted tones of mauve and burgundy with recessed pink lighting, live ficus trees illuminated with tiny lights and expansive glass walls that overlook the South River.

Capacity: 250 seated; 300 standing.

Catering: In-house. Entrees range from $18.95 to $20.95 per person.

Parking: On the premises. Valet parking can be arranged.

Note: Wedding ceremonies are permitted.

Potomac Valley Lodge, Inc.   301-428-8283

16601 W. Willard Road • Poolesville, MD 20837

Have your celebration in an original log cabin, complete with stone fireplace! Floor-to-ceiling glass windows enclose the ballroom, which overlooks the 18-hole golf course and a perfect view. This location combines history with one of today's best loved pastimes. The ballroom, with its oak parquet flooring and brick flower beds, can accommodate rustic to elegant receptions depending on the decor chosen. Only one reception is held per day, allowing the bridal couple to have the room for their desired length of time, as well as their choice of serving times for food and beverages. The lodge provides a relaxed atmosphere and delicious food prepared "home style." Each reception is given undivided attention with a very personal touch.

Capacity: 200 seated; 200 standing.
Catering: In-house. Entrees, including full bar, range from $40 to $50 per person. Wedding packages are all-inclusive.
Parking: On the premises.

Prince George's Ballroom   301-341-7439

2411 Pinebrook Avenue • Landover, MD 20785

Surrounded by 50 acres of parkland and conveniently located, this elegant ballroom with its art-deco styling is only 30 minutes from Washington, D.C. With its beautiful hardwood floors and spacious patio, it is one of the area's most popular reception locations.

Capacity: 250 to 270 seated.
Catering: You must supply your own caterer.
Rental Fee: $900 to $1,300.
Parking: On the premises.
Note: Wedding ceremonies are permitted indoors or outdoors.

Strong Mansion at   301-869-7846 (Metro)
Sugarloaf Mountain   301-874-2024 (Frederick)

c/o Stronghold, Inc.
7901 Comus Road • Dickerson, MD 20842

Strong Mansion was built in 1912 by Chicago philanthropist Gordon Strong. The three-story Georgian home is surrounded by 3,000 woodland acres on Sugarloaf Mountain. You and your guests are welcome to roam the grounds and enjoy the beautiful antique furnishings throughout the entire home. The 22' x 60' spacious ballroom has eight large Palladian windows, two decorative fireplaces, and French doors that open on to a 15' x 34' portico. The back grounds are landscaped with formal gardens, a lily pond with a fountain, a white wooden pergola that is ideal for wedding ceremonies, and a breathtaking view of the countryside. Strong Mansion is the perfect setting for an outdoor wedding, reception, and other special events.

Capacity: 150.
Catering: You must supply your own caterer.
Rental Fee: $1,500 for 8 hours.
Parking: On the premises.
Restrictions: No smoking.
Note: Wedding ceremonies are permitted. The mansion is handicap accessible.

Swan Harbor Farm   410-939-6767

401 Oakington Road • Havre De Grace, MD 21078

Swan Harbor Farm, situated on almost five hundred acres, overlooks the Chesapeake Bay between Havre de Grace and Aberdeen, Maryland. Dating back to the 1700s, this stately home has a great hall, library, living room, dining room, kitchen and sun porch, which are perfect for weddings, receptions and rehearsal dinners. The mantels in the ground-floor rooms are among the finest Federal pieces in Harford County.

Capacity: 50+ seated; 100+ standing; 200 in garden; 200 with tent.
Catering: You must provide your own caterer. Tents, tables, chairs, and a portable dance floor for parties are available at an additional fee.
Rental Fee: $700 and up.
Parking: On the premises.
Note: Wedding ceremonies are permitted.

Swan Point Yacht and Country Club   301-259-4411

11305 Swan Point Boulevard • Issue, MD 20645

Nestled in historic Charles County, Maryland, Swan Point Yacht and Country Club is less than an hour from the Capital Beltway. The dining and banquet facilities in the new clubhouse are reminiscent of Maryland's gracious past. A large veranda looks out on one of the top 18-hole golf courses in the mid-Atlantic region and a spectacular view of the Potomac River. Extensive menu and bar options are available. Swan Point Yacht and Country Club can make your special day perfect from beginning to end.

Capacity: 150 seated; 200 standing.
Catering: In-house. Entrees range from $20 to $40 per person.
Rental Fee: $3.15 per person.
Parking: On the premises and in lot nearby.
Note: Wedding ceremonies are permitted.

Wakefield Valley Golf & Conference Center   410-876-8787
www.wakefield.com

1000 Fenby Farm Road • Westminster, MD 21158

Overlooking a magnificent golf course, Wakefield Valley's beautifully appointed ballroom provides a perfect setting for any occasion. Cathedral ceilings with chandeliers and skylights, luxurious carpeting, inlaid parquet dance floor, three walls of windows, indoor balcony, large deck and garden patio are just a few of the amenities that make Wakefield an excellent choice.

Capacity:	200 seated; 300 standing; 150 in garden.
Catering:	In-house. Entrees with beverages are priced at $40 and above. Cake cutting, butler service, event coordinator, table linens, and centerpieces are provided at no charge.
Parking:	On the premises.
Note:	Wedding ceremony site available.

Woodend   301-652-9188

8940 Jones Mill Road • Chevy Chase, MD 20815

Woodend is a beaux arts style mansion with classic Greek portico that overlooks sweeping lawns bordered by woods and meadows. Indoors, a Palladian window lights up a distinguished staircase and carved fireplace in the Great Hall. Step through stately French doors onto a raised terrace with a custom tent lit with chandeliers. Enjoy your romantic wedding ceremony in an enchanting grove surrounded by a canopy of trees. Woodend is a 40-acre bird sanctuary owned by the Audubon Naturalist Society and is conveniently located directly inside the beltway in Chevy Chase.

Capacity:	150 seated; 200 standing.
Catering:	Approved caterers list.
Rental Fee:	$1,200 to $3,100.
Parking:	On the premises.
Note:	Wedding ceremonies are permitted.

Woodlawn Manor   301-585-5564

16501 Norwood Road • Sandy Spring, MD 20860

Magnificent trees, rolling green landscape, garden gazebo and a unique stone barn set the stage for an elegant reception. Only minutes from busy urban centers, the Georgian-style manor house offers five spacious rooms, richly restored and tastefully furnished, to provide the charm and splendor of the 19th century. A modernized kitchen meets high-level catering requirements and ample parking is in close proximity to the manor house.

Capacity:	40 seated; 125 standing; 200 in garden.
Catering:	Approved caterers list.
Rental Fee:	$1,000 Friday and Sunday; $1,200 Saturday.
Parking:	48 parking spaces on the premises with overflow parking nearby.
Note:	Wedding ceremonies are permitted.

Carrol's Creek   410-263-8102

410 Severn Avenue • Annapolis, MD 21403

If you are looking for a reception location on the waterfront with a beautiful view of historic Annapolis and the U.S. Naval Academy, with ample free parking, professional service and creative cuisine – Carrol's Creek is the site for you! Since 1983, Carrol's Creek has been one of Annapolis' leading caterers for rehearsal dinners, weddings, corporate receptions, lunch, dinner and buffet banquets. You can reserve the entire restaurant for 100 to 260 guests.

Capacity: 160 seated inside; 25 to 100 in Starboard Room; 100 on deck.
Catering: In-house. Entrees range from $40 to $80. Cake cutting fee if client provides own cake.
Rental Fee: Varies. Call for more information.
Parking: On the premises. Valet parking may be arranged.
Note: Wedding ceremonies are permitted.

Chesapeake Bay Adventures   1-800-394-4101

1934 Lincoln Drive, Suite B • Annapolis, MD 21401

Envision being aboard your own private yacht hosting your elegant reception, party or special event on the Chesapeake. From intimate to extravagant, these vessels will accommodate events of any size. Complete event planning and coordination is offered for weddings and receptions by land or by sea throughout the Chesapeake Bay Region and Washington, D.C.

Capacity: 2 to 500.
Catering: In-house and approved caterers list.
Rental Fee: $250 per hour.
Parking: On the premises. Parking lot nearby. Valet parking available.
Note: Wedding ceremonies are permitted indoors or outdoors.

Chesapeake Marine Tours   410-268-7601
http://member.aol.com/boattours/cmt.html

P.O. Box 3350/Slip 20 City DockAnnapolis, MD 21403

For a truly romantic setting, have your wedding, reception, or anniversary celebration in historic Annapolis, on the scenic Severn River, aboard one of these riverboats or corporate yacht, or at the lovely Annapolis Landing Marina waterfront facility. *Providence*, a charming 64-foot riverboat, is perfect for the wedding ceremony and reception with a DJ or band for dancing. The *Cabaret II*, a 67-foot custom motor yacht, is an elegant setting for a formal affair.

Intimate weddings are graciously accommodated by smaller charter boats. The waterfront location has both lawn and banquet room facilities. Some of the finest area caterers are featured. Wedding packages are available in a variety of price ranges for groups of 20 to 200.

Capacity:	20 to 100 seated, 20 to 297 standing; 150 on the lawn.
Catering:	Approved caterers list. Entrees range from $25 to $80 per person.
Rental Fee:	$500 to $3,500.
Parking:	On the premises, and nearby parking lot.
Restrictions:	Waterfront land facilities activities are limited to 10 o'clock. Valet parking is required for parking at the facility.

Fantasy Island   410-729-4505

St. Helena Island, Severn River • Crownsville, MD

The Mansion, on St. Helena Island in the prestigious Severn River, is just minutes from historic downtown Annapolis. St. Helena, with its towering oak trees, beautiful flowers, ivy-covered walls and spectacular water views, is the perfect wedding site. The mansion, a gracious Federal architectural design, was built in 1931 and is a close copy of the famous John Hopkins "Homewood House." The stately residence is graced by porticos and beautiful white Doric columns. The house features magnificent mahogany and marble floors, marble fireplaces, and antique chandeliers. In the spring, the island bursts into life with pink and white dogwoods, azaleas, rhododendrons and beautiful flower gardens set against the background of the Severn River. This enchanted island is the most exciting new wedding and special event venue in the Maryland, D.C. and Virginia area. Wedding packages, for up to 150 guests, include bride and groom changing suites, transportation by pleasure boat from the Annapolis city dock, and tented reception area. Catering, photography, music and flowers can be provided. Also, you may schedule honeymoon and guest travel arrangements at discounted rates through the Fantasy Island Travel Club.

Capacity:	150 seated; unlimited standing; unlimited in garden; unlimited with tent.
Catering:	Approved caterers list. Entrees range from $40 to $80 per person.
Rental Fee:	$4,500.
Parking:	Although there is no maximum limit on the number of guests on the island, the boat maximum is 150 on each trip; thereafter, additional cost would be incurred. Parking is required in Annapolis public areas, close to the city dock.
Note:	Wedding ceremonies are permitted.

Fergie's Waterfront
Restaurant and Catering   1-800-292-1371

2840 Solomons Island Road • Edgewater, MD 21037

Fergie's Waterfront Restaurant & Catering will help you create the reception of your dreams. Its banquet room has an adjacent deck on the water for your cocktail hour or ceremony. The banquet room has decorated Grecian columns, large dance floor and beautiful built-in bar. Your reception could be in the main dining room with wrap-around windows overlooking the water. There is also a dance floor, and an area for cocktails and hors d'oeuvres. This facility can be used on Saturday 12:00 p.m. until 4:00 p.m. It is located one mile outside Annapolis.

Capacity: 160 seated; 200 standing.
Catering: In-house. Entrees range from $32 to $40 per person.
Parking: On the premises.
Note: Wedding ceremonies are permitted.

Herrington on the Bay   410-741-5101

7149 Lake Shore Drive, Rte. 261 • Rose Haven, MD 20714

Herrington on the Bay provides a classic Caribbean-style setting overlooking the Chesapeake Bay. Located just south of Annapolis and 30 minutes east of Washington, D.C., Herrington is accessible by car or boat. Professional caterers and wedding consultants take the stress out of wedding planning. Brides and grooms relax and enjoy their ceremonies and their receptions whether they choose indoors or out on the beachfront lawns. The Herrington Inn, located on premises, offers Island-style rooms with private hot tubs. From transportation to the music to the cuisine, Herrington delivers festive, fun weddings for today's brides!

Capacity: 200 seated; 250 standing; 300 in garden; 300 with tent.
Catering: In-house. Entrees range from $18 to $32 per person. Cake cutting fee if you provide your own cake.
Rental Fee: $195.
Parking: On the premises and in nearby lot.
Note: Wedding ceremonies are permitted.

Kent Manor Inn   1-800-820-4511

500 Kent Manor Drive • Stevensville, MD 21666

The Kent Manor Inn, a Maryland historical site, is situated on a 226-acre plantation one hour from Washington, D.C., and Baltimore. The beautiful Victorian mansion, circa 1820, and its glass-enclosed garden house are the perfect waterfront settings for wedding ceremonies, receptions, rehearsal dinners and anniversary celebrations. The inn has fireplaces with Italian marble mantels, two conference rooms and 24 individually decorated bedrooms, some with four-poster beds. A fine dining restaurant serves lunch and dinner.

Capacity:	150 seated; 150 standing; unlimited with tent on the grounds.
Catering:	In-house. Entrees range from $56 to $94 per person including bar.
Rental Fee:	$300 to $1,000.
Parking:	On the premises.
Note:	Wedding ceremonies are permitted.

London Town
Publik House & Garden   410-222-1919

839 Londontown Road • Edgewater, MD 21037

A national historic landmark on the banks of the South River and minutes from Annapolis, the House at London Town shares a dramatic waterfront setting with an eight-acre woodland garden and glass-enclosed pavilion. Surrounded by decks and overlooking the gardens and river, the pavilion attracts numerous weddings and receptions throughout the year. Ceremonies take place on spacious or intimate overlooks in and around the gardens. The House was designated a national historic landmark in 1970.

Capacity:	125 indoors; 175 with tent.
Catering:	Approved caterers list or your own caterer. Caterer must be licensed and insured.
Rental Fee:	$800 and up.
Parking:	On the premises.

National Aquarium
in Baltimore   410-576-3869/3847

501 E. Pratt Street, Pier 3 • Baltimore, MD 21202

The magic and mystery of water make the National Aquarium in Baltimore ideal for couples who want a signature event. Create a mix of romance and fun, from casual to elegant, in settings appropriate for intimate parties or 800-guest galas. Secluded, tented parties on the pier are perfect for dancing under the stars. Dine near dolphins in the Marine Mammal Pavilion Underwater Viewing Area, dance in the airy Atrium, or enjoy breathtaking views in the Harbor View Room. Full-service catering is available. The Aquarium can accommodate a kosher wedding.

Capacity:	500 seated; 2,000 standing; 2,000 with tent.
Catering:	In-house. Entrees begin at $20 per person and bar at $9.00 per person.
Rental Fee:	$1,000 and up.
Parking:	Parking in nearby lots.
Note:	Wedding ceremonies are permitted.

Patriot Cruises Inc.   410-745-3100

Chesapeake Bay Maritime Museum Dock (Mill Street)
St. Michaels, MD 21663

Leaving the beautiful St. Michaels Harbor you will enjoy the untouched, scenic beauty of the Wye and Miles Rivers. Built in 1990, the *Patriot* can accommodate casual to the most elegant of affairs with ease. This climate-controlled vessel is equipped with two shipboard bars and a canopied upper deck for your enjoyment. A cruise on the *Patriot* is a special mix of history, natural waterways, and culture.

Capacity: 110 seated; 170 standing.
Catering: In-house or approved caterers list. Entrees range from $17 to $40 per person.
Rental Fee: $1,500 for 3-hour cruise.
Parking: On the premises and nearby lot.
Note: Wedding ceremonies are permitted.

Paul's on the South River   410-956-3410

3027 Riva Road • Annapolis, MD 21140

Paul's is decorated in soft muted tones of mauve and burgundy with recessed pink lighting, live ficus trees illuminated with tiny lights and expansive glass walls that overlook the South River.

Capacity: 250 seated; 300 standing.
Catering: In-house. Entrees range from $18.95 to $20.95 per person.
Parking: On the premises. Valet parking can be arranged.
Note: Wedding ceremonies are permitted.

Quiet Waters Park   410-222-1777

600 Quiet Waters Park Road • Annapolis, MD 21403

Located in Annapolis on the banks of the South River, this 336-acre park represents Victorian style architecture. The park design features fountains, gazebos, woodland trails and formal gardens. The park's Blue Heron Center with its formal gardens is perfect for large parties, receptions and weddings. Couples renting the Center may use the immediate lower garden area for their ceremony at no extra charge.

Capacity: 150 seated; 225 standing.
Catering: In-house.
Rental Fee: Call for more information.
Parking: On the premises.
Note: Wedding ceremonies are permitted indoors or outdoors.

Scarlett Place   410-561-2433

c/o Chef's Expressions
250 S. President Street • Baltimore, MD 21202

With a dramatic black and white marble foyer, two ballrooms,
bridal changing area and private bath, Scarlett Place is one of the
city's most elegant settings. The Scarlett Room is decorated with
custom floral carpet and hand-painted columns. The Plaza Room,
in grey and silver tones, features brass and crystal sconce lighting.
Both rooms have large parquet dance floors and open to a terrace
overlooking the Inner Harbor. From brunches to full course
dinners, its award-winning catering and event team will ensure
the success of your special party.

Capacity: 500 seated; 800 standing in The Scarlett Room; 180
                seated; 250 standing in The Plaza Room.
Catering: In-house. Entrees range from $35 to $75 per person.
Rental Fee: $2,200 for the Scarlett Room; $1,300 for the Plaza
                Room.
Parking: Parking in nearby lot.
Note: Wedding ceremonies are permitted.

Swan Harbor Farm   410-939-6767

401 Oakington Road • Havre De Grace, MD 21078

Swan Harbor Farm, situated on almost five hundred acres,
overlooks the Chesapeake Bay between Havre de Grace and
Aberdeen, Maryland. Dating back to the 1700s, this stately home
has a great hall, library, living room, dining room, kitchen and sun
porch, which are perfect for weddings, receptions and rehearsal
dinners. The mantels in the ground-floor rooms are among the
finest Federal pieces in Harford County.

Capacity: 50+ seated; 100+ standing; 200 in garden; 200 with
               tent.
Catering: You must provide your own caterer. Tents, tables,
               chairs, and a portable dance floor for parties are
               available at an additional fee.
Rental Fee: $700 and up.
Parking: On the premises.
Note: Wedding ceremonies are permitted.

Swan Point Yacht and Country Club   301-259-4411

11305 Swan Point Boulevard • Issue, MD 20645

Nestled in historic Charles County, Maryland, Swan Point Yacht
and Country Club is less than an hour from the Capital Beltway.
The dining and banquet facilities in the new clubhouse are
reminiscent of Maryland's gracious past. A large veranda looks

out on one of the top 18-hole golf courses in the mid-Atlantic region and a spectacular view of the Potomac River. Extensive menu and bar options are available. Swan Point Yacht and Country Club can make your special day perfect from beginning to end.

Capacity: 150 seated; 200 standing.
Catering: In-house. Entrees range from $20 to $40 per person.
Rental Fee: $3.15 per person.
Parking: On the premises.
Note: Wedding ceremonies are permitted.

Virginia

TABLE OF CONTENTS

The Atrium at Meadowlark Gardens 703-255-3631

9750 Meadowlark Gardens Court • Vienna, VA 22182

Seasonal blossoms, a meandering stream and a hint of woodlands offer a bouquet of possibilities in this indoor garden at The Atrium at Meadowlark Gardens. Three walls of windows and a landscaped terrace overlook the gardens, woods and meadows of the Northern Virginia Regional Park Authority's 95-acre garden park. In the Garden Room, the cathedral ceiling rises to a dramatic, 2,000-square-foot skylight. Gazebos on a hillside, the Azalea Woods and Lake Caroline offer picturesque settings for the exchange of vows. The Atrium and the array of natural and specialty gardens are located between Routes 7 and 123, just south of the Dulles Access Road and near Tysons Corner and Wolf Trap Farm Park.

Capacity: 220 seated; 350 standing without dance floor.
Catering: You must supply your own caterer. Caterer must be approved by the Atrium's events coordinator. Pantry kitchen for warming and holding food only. No premise cooking. Caterers must have license, liquor license, and certificate of insurance.
Rental Fee: $275 to $400 per hour. Rental includes: tables, chairs, two portable bars, 15' x 18' dance floor and use of terrace and preparation kitchen. Rental period includes set-up and clean-up by the caterer.
Parking: On the premises.
Note: Wedding ceremonies are permitted indoors or outdoors. The facility hosts two weddings on Saturday: The first wedding ends at 3:00 p.m. and the second wedding starts at 5:00 p.m.

Clyde's of Tysons Corner   703-734-1907

8332 Leesburg Pike • Vienna, VA 22182

Clyde's offers a choice of its restaurant and its private dining room for weddings, receptions, rehearsal dinners and other wonderful celebrations. The elegant art deco dining room is decorated in shades of plum and has a lovely panoramic view. Clyde's provides excellent service and a catering staff which is pleased to help you plan every detail.

Capacity: 150 seated; 175 standing.
Catering: In-house.
Rental Fee: $100.
Parking: On the premises.
Note: Wedding ceremonies are permitted.

Future Homemakers of America   703-476-4900

1910 Association Drive • Reston, VA 20191-1584

Located on the terrace level of the headquarters building of
Future Homemakers of America, the conference center features
an atrium at the front entrance and a terraced, partially covered
patio at the back. Both the atrium and the patio are in full view
through the glass partitions at each end of the banquet room. The
center is carpeted and the large kitchen is a caterer's delight.

Capacity: 175 seated; 250 standing.
Catering: You must supply your own caterer.
Rental Fee: $750.
Parking: On the premises.

La Bergerie   703-683-1007

218 North Lee Street • Alexandria, VA 22314

Located in the heart of colonial Old Town Alexandria, La Bergerie
is decorated with French countryside paintings, richly appointed
leather banquettes, and crystal chandeliers. Its charming and
intimate atmosphere provides the perfect ambiance for any special
occasion. Cocktail receptions may be held in the Atrium and the
two private party rooms can be used for smaller events. French
cuisine with Basque specialties will delight your palate. Your
guests can stroll down cobblestone streets, tour quaint residences,
shop in 1700-era stores, and listen to street entertainment. La
Bergerie, located near Market Square and the famous Torpedo
Factory Arts Center, is 15 minutes from Washington, D.C., via
George Washington Parkway.

Capacity: 85 in main room; 48 in large private room; 26 in small
                 private room.
Catering: In-house. Entrees range from $13 to $25. Cake cut-
                 ting fee if you provide your own cake.
Rental Fee: None. Large room guarantee is 30 and the small room
                 guarantee is 20.
Parking: Parking lot nearby.
Note: Wedding ceremonies are permitted.

Torpedo Factory Art Center   703-838-4199

105 North Union Street • Alexandria, VA 22314

The Torpedo Factory Art Center, originally built in 1918 following World War I to manufacture torpedoes, has been transformed
into a modern art center housing 83 working artists' studios and
five cooperative galleries. The central hall, a two-story atrium, is
a unique and informal setting which can accommodate receptions
and ceremonies. It is 160 feet long and is topped with a balcony,
catwalks, large peripheral windows and a central skylight. The

hall is surrounded by glass walls displaying the artwork of the individual studios. The hall lends itself to decoration in many styles, and photographs of the site decorated for past events are available to view. The Art Center is located on the Potomac River waterfront in the heart of Old Town Alexandria, just minutes south of National Airport and inside the Beltway.

Capacity: 400 seated; 1,200 standing.
Catering: You must supply your own caterer.
Rental Fee: $1,500 for the first floor; $1,700 for first floor and balcony; $2,500 for entire building. Some additional fees for staff, security and insurance required.
Parking: Parking is available across the street and there are parking lots nearby.
Restrictions: No red wine, rice, birdseed, or glitter allowed in the Art Center. No alcohol allowed behind the Art Center on the dock/marina area.
Note: Wedding ceremonies are permitted.

Fauquier Springs Country Club   540-347-2459

9236 Tournament Drive • Warrenton, VA 20186-7848

With its breathtaking view and exquisite outdoor terraces, this location is the perfect country setting for weddings and other special occasions. The clubhouse sits on top of a hill overlooking a spectacular golf course, farm and countryside. A Victorian staircase graces the foyer, and the ballroom's many windows leads to wrap-around patios where guests can enjoy the panoramic view of the meticulously landscaped golf course. The smaller Springs Room, with its charming marble fireplace, is ideal for pictures.

Capacity: 250 seated in ballroom; 300 standing in ballroom; 50 in Springs Room.
Catering: In-house. Wedding packages range from $35 to $65 per person and are all-inclusive. Separate ala carte and custom menus are available.
Rental Fee: $100 to $1,000, depends on season and time of day.
Parking: On the premises. Handicap parking is available.
Note: Wedding ceremonies are permitted.

Hidden Creek Country Club   703-437-5222

1711 Clubhouse Road • Reston, VA 20190

Hidden Creek Country Club has a variety of function rooms suitable for receptions of any type. All rooms have a panoramic view of a beautiful 18-hole championship golf course. The Fairway Room features a spacious outdoor deck, large dance floor and an inviting fireplace. All food is created by an award-winning chef. The clubhouse is conveniently located in the heart of Reston, Virginia, minutes from Dulles Airport and thirty minutes from Washington, D.C.

Capacity: 200 seated; 300 standing; 350 with tent.
Catering: In-house. Entrees range from $50 to $65 per person.
Rental Fee: $550 for 4 hours.
Parking: On the premises.
Note: Wedding ceremonies are permitted.

✳Lansdowne Resort   703-729-8400

44050 Woodridge Parkway • Leesburg, VA 20176

At Lansdowne Resort, the staff knows how important your wedding day is to you, and are committed to making the day of your dreams a reality. It offers intimate dining areas for rehearsal dinners, exquisite menu selections from award-winning chefs, and an elegant ballroom and expansive outdoor terraces which overlook the Robert Trent Jones, Jr. golf course. A wedding specialist will be on hand to coordinate all aspects of your event, a pastry chef will work with you to design a deliciously beautiful wedding cake, and the spa staff will customize a bridal package for your party. For your guests, it offers luxurious guest rooms and spacious suites, relaxing amenities such as a championship golf course, health club, indoor and outdoor pools, and lighted tennis courts. Lansdowne Resort is also an excellent choice for corporate retreats or family reunions. Lansdowne is nestled in the scenic Potomac River Valley and is just 8 miles from Dulles Airport and less than an hour from Washington, D.C.

Capacity: 550 seated; 850 standing; 250 in pavilion.
Catering: In-house. Packages range from $70 to $85 per person. Cake cutting fee is $2.00 per person if cake is brought in.
Parking: On the premises. Valet parking is complimentary. Handicap parking is available.
Note: Wedding ceremonies are permitted indoors or outdoors. Guest rooms are available.

McLean Community Center   703-790-0123
TDD: TAPTALK

1234 Ingleside Avenue • McLean, VA 22101

Nestled in a parklike setting, the McLean Community Center is an arts and community center located just a few minutes from the Beltway and the George Washington Parkway, with plentiful free parking and professional facility staff. The Center is one of the most reasonably priced locations in the metropolitan area. The community hall wing offers several flexible choices for your reception, including a 3,000-square-foot hall with dance floor and an adjacent garden plaza. The Center's state-of-the-art commercial kitchen features pass-through and walk-through access to the community hall. The Center's fine art gallery, the Emerson Gallery, is also available for receptions. The Alden Theatre, which seats up to 424 persons, is available for private events.

Capacity: 200 seated; 350 standing in community hall.
Catering: You must supply your own caterer. A 50 percent surcharge is added for all events at which alcohol is served.
Rental Fee: $90 to $435. Resident discount available. To obtain resident rate, wedding receptions may be booked only by the couple or their immediate family.
Parking: On the premises.
Restrictions: No smoking in building.
Note: Wedding ceremonies are permitted.

Middleburg Community Center   540-687-6373

300 W. Washington Street • Middleburg, VA 20118-0265

Experience the charm of Virginia Hunt Country in Middleburg, Virginia. This wonderful site features an elegant main room, a lovely terrace room, a spacious terrace and beautifully landscaped gardens. The outdoor terrace is perfect for cocktails and hors d'oeuvres and if you've always wanted to have a garden wedding — this is the place. The newly renovated basement is available for small parties, children's parties and meetings.

Capacity: 175 seated; 250 standing; 75 in garden; 100+ with tent; 75 in basement.
Catering: You must supply your own caterer.
Rental Fee: $850, plus tax. Call for prices for basement.
Parking: On the premises.
Note: Wedding ceremonies are permitted indoors or outdoors.

The Mimslyn Inn   1-800-296-5105/540-743-5105

401 West Main Street • Luray, VA 22835

Imagine having your wedding reception at an elegant antebellum plantation that features old-fashioned southern hospitality, 14 acres of exquisite gardens and lawns, and a main lobby graced by a winding staircase and beautiful fireplace. It is sure to make you feel like Scarlett O'Hara. The Mimslyn Inn features formal gardens that are perfect for an outside ceremony and a ballroom just right to dance the night away. The chef can create a wide range of culinary fare from the simplest hor d'oeuvres to the most elegant dinner.

Capacity: 150 seated; 225 standing; 150 in garden.
Catering: In-house or your own caterer. Entrees range from $15.95 to $35.95 per person.
Rental Fee: $300 to $600.
Parking: On the premises.
Note: Wedding ceremonies are permitted indoors or outdoors. Overnight accommodations are available.

Mt. Vernon Square Ballroom   703-768-3232

2722 Arlington Drive • Alexandria, VA 22306

The Mount Vernon Square Ballroom is the perfect place for your wedding reception or any other special event. Located in the heart of the Route 1 corridor, just 3.5 miles from Route 495, the ballroom is surrounded by walls of windows offering panoramic views and an ideal setting. You and your guests can enjoy the romantic glow of the large fireplace during the winter months. The ballroom allows you the flexibility to customize your wedding and reception to meet your exact needs. It has both a service and catering kitchen and wet and dry bars, offering a broad spectrum of catering options. The ballroom's design will accommodate live bands or a disc jockey and the spacious floor plan allows lots of room for dancing.

Capacity: 200 seated; 230 standing.
Catering: Approved caterers list or your own caterer. Tables and chairs are provided by facility.

Rental Fee: $600 to $2,000. Residents receive reduced rates.
Parking: Residential parking.
Note: Wedding ceremonies are permitted.

River Farm   703-768-5700

7931 East Boulevard Drive • Alexandria, VA 22308

The elegant main house is set amid 27 acres of lawns, gardens, meadows, and woods, and commands a sweeping view of the Potomac. Over the last 20 years, the Society has established ornamental, educational and test gardens on portions of River Farm, but most of the property remains much as Washington himself would have known it when it was the northernmost tract of his farmland surrounding Mount Vernon. The house, which is registered as a "gentleman's home" by the Fairfax County Histori- cal Society, includes a 45' x 20' ballroom with a tastefully ap- pointed powder room, a large parlor overlooking the river, a dining room opening onto broad porches with garden and river views, and a charming entrance hall featuring a hand-painted floral frieze. The garden patio outside the ballroom may be tented for outdoor events. The house and gardens at River Farm may be rented for weddings, dinner parties, corporate meetings and other events. River Farm is located on the banks of the Potomac, just four miles south of Old Town Alexandria on the George Washing- ton Parkway.

Capacity: 80 to 200, depending on areas selected for event.
Catering: Approved caterers list or your own caterer. Caterer must be approved by facility. The large, state-of-the- art country kitchen is available to caterers for prepa- ration and heating of food.
Rental Fee: $2,500 to $6,400. Call for information. Comprehen- sive General Liability Insurance is required.
Parking: On the premises.
Restrictions: No amplified music. Portable toilets need to be rented for over 150 capacity.
Note: Wedding ceremonies are permitted.

Sheraton National Hotel   703-521-1900 ext. 6505

Columbia Pike at Washington Blvd. • Arlington, VA 22204

The Main Lobby has a cathedral ceiling with natural light accents. The entrance, a spacious pre-function area done in subtle shades, can be used in many creative ways. Once the stage is set, mirrors, earth tones, and soft pastels provide a canvas on which your special event is placed. Tastefully conservative chandeliers accen- tuate the 17-foot high ceilings. This site provides flexibility to create intimacy or spacious enough for a royal fanfare. Located just minutes from National Airport via complimentary shuttle, it is conveniently located for local and out-of-town guests. This beautiful hotel offers mesmerizing views of Washington, distinctive cuisine and a highly trained and experienced catering staff.

Capacity: 75 to 550 seated; 1,000 standing.
Catering: In-house. Entrees begin at $52.50 per person, inclusive.
Parking: On the premises.
Note: Wedding ceremonies are permitted. Special room rates are available for overnight guests.

Westfields Marriott   703-818-0300

14750 Conference Center Drive • Chantilly, VA 20151

Located just 30 minutes from the nation's capital, Westfields combines the architectural splendor of Virginia's finest estates with the functional excellence for which it has won numerous awards. The entry's three-and-a-half ton bronze doors exemplify the pride of craftsmanship found throughout this $70 million resort. Inside, just beyond the Lobby, a magnificent Rotunda presents a spectacular dome, classic columns and a generous portion of the center's 450 tons of Greek marble. Westfields offers a variety of indoor and outdoor settings to create an event to reflect your unique and personal tastes. The property has three elegantly furnished ballrooms and a number of intimate banquet spaces to host your special event.

Capacity: 600 seated; 900 standing; 300 in garden; 200 with tent.
Catering: In-house. Entrees begin at $85 per person. Cake cutting fee if you provide your own cake.
Rental Fee: $1,000 to $4,000.
Parking: On the premises. Valet parking is available.
Note: Wedding ceremonies are permitted indoors or outdoors.

✈ Whitehall "The Hunt Country Inn"   703-450-6666

18301 Whitehall Estate Lane • Bluemont, VA 20135

At the foothills of the Blue Ridge stands Whitehall, the treasure of majestic western Loudoun County. This country estate, rich in history and classic architecture, is the ultimate facility for your next reception, conference, or corporate retreat. It features four furnished, climate-controlled meeting rooms, picnic grounds with facilities for softball, volleyball, horseshoes, hayrides and campfires, as well as award-winning cuisine by Celebrations. You can begin your special day by saying your vows in the gracious gardens nestled among a canopy of century-old trees on 50 panoramic acres. After the ceremony, your guests can enjoy cocktails and hors d'oeuvres on the magnificent covered brick dining terrace. Then for the perfect ending to a wonderful day, entertain your guests in the ornately detailed grand ballroom, complete with musicians' balcony and marble fireplace.

Capacity: 240 seated; 380 standing; 300+ in garden; 300+ with tent.
Catering: In-house. Entrees range from $40 to $80 per person.
Rental Fee: Varies. Call for information.
Parking: On the premises.
Restrictions: No smoking inside the facility.
Note: Wedding ceremonies are permitted.

Algonkian Meeting Center
Algonkian Regional Park   703-450-4655

47001 Fairway Drive • Sterling, VA 20165

The Algonkian Meeting Center makes entertaining easy with its large reception room, portable bar and dance floor. Stone fireplaces and large windows looking onto the park and golf course add atmosphere to any reception. Delicious custom menus created by the Center's caterer are sure to please your guests. A quaint gazebo on the front lawn is a romantic setting for wedding ceremonies. Complimentary use of the gazebo is an option when renting the Loudoun Room. The Meeting Center is located in Algonkian Regional Park, which features 12 river-front vacation cottages, outdoor swimming pool, 18-hole, par-72 golf course, picnic shelters and boat ramp. The facility is excellently suited for corporate functions such as seminars, company picnics and retreats.

Capacity: 175 seated; 200 standing.
Catering: You must supply your own caterer.
Rental Fee: $875 for five hours.
Parking: On the premises.
Note: Wedding ceremonies are permitted.

American Legion Post 177   703-273-2250

3939 Oak Drive • Fairfax, VA 22030

American Legion Post 177 offers complete hall rental and catering services. The size and flexibility of this space allows it to be customized for any type of affair. The Post has two halls, both very tastefully decorated. Use your imagination and creativity to turn these rooms into a truly delightful setting. Its menu has varied and appealing selections. Post 177 is conveniently located in Fairfax City and offers substantial free parking facilities on site.

Capacity: 220 seated; 250 standing.
Catering: In-house. Entrees range from $15 to $19 per person.
Rental Fee: Varies.
Parking: On the premises.
Note: Wedding ceremonies are permitted.

The Atrium at Meadowlark Gardens 703-255-3631

9750 Meadowlark Gardens Court • Vienna, VA 22182

Seasonal blossoms, a meandering stream and a hint of woodlands offer a bouquet of possibilities in this indoor garden at The Atrium at Meadowlark Gardens. Three walls of windows and a landscaped terrace overlook the gardens, woods and meadows of the Northern Virginia Regional Park Authority's 95-acre garden park. In the Garden Room, the cathedral ceiling rises to a dramatic, 2,000-square-foot skylight. Gazebos on a hillside, the Azalea Woods and Lake Caroline offer picturesque settings for the exchange of vows. The Atrium and the array of natural and specialty gardens are located between Routes 7 and 123, just south of the Dulles Access Road and near Tysons Corner and Wolf Trap Farm Park.

Capacity: 220 seated; 350 standing without dance floor.
Catering: You must supply your own caterer. Caterer must be approved by the Atrium's events coordinator. Pantry kitchen for warming and holding food only. No premise cooking. Caterers must have license, liquor license, and certificate of insurance.
Rental Fee: $275 to $400 per hour. Rental includes: tables, chairs, two portable bars, 15' x 18' dance floor and use of terrace and preparation kitchen. Rental period includes set-up and clean-up by the caterer.
Parking: On the premises.
Note: Wedding ceremonies are permitted indoors or outdoors. The facility hosts two weddings on Saturday: The first wedding ends at 3:00 p.m. and the second wedding starts at 5:00 p.m.

Cabell's Mill   703-938-8835

c/o Historic Properties Rental Services
9601 Courthouse Road • Vienna, VA 22181

Once serving Centreville's community as a gristmill, sawmill, and a sumac mill, Cabell's Mill has been at the center of local commerce and community since its construction shortly after the Revolutionary War. It features two spacious floors and is perfect for weddings and receptions. The original chimneys and fireplaces are still in place. The building has been equipped with ceiling lighting and modernized with central air conditioning and heating. A large flagstone terrace looks out over Big Rocky Run, and is ideal for an outdoor wedding.

Capacity: 95 seated on two floors; 125 standing; 150 in garden.
Catering: You must supply your own caterer.
Rental Fee: $950.
Parking: 75 parking spaces on the premises; parking lot nearby.
Restrictions: No confetti or silly string. Birdseed may be thrown outside only. All candles must be enclosed with protection underneath. No taping, tacking, or nailing decorations to walls. No smoking indoors.
Note: Wedding ceremonies are permitted indoors or outdoors.

Clyde's of Tysons Corner   703-734-1907

8332 Leesburg Pike • Vienna, VA 22182

Clyde's offers a choice of its restaurant and its private dining room for weddings, receptions, rehearsal dinners and other wonderful celebrations. The elegant art deco dining room is decorated in shades of plum and has a lovely panoramic view. Clyde's provides excellent service and a catering staff which is pleased to help you plan every detail.

Capacity: 150 seated; 175 standing.
Catering: In-house.
Rental Fee: $100.
Parking: On the premises.
Note: Wedding ceremonies are permitted.

Dranesville Tavern   703-938-8835

c/o Historic Properties Rental Services
9601 Courthouse Road • Vienna, VA 22181

Listed on the National Register of Historic Places, Dranesville Tavern has been receiving visitors from all walks of life for nearly two centuries and is well-suited for business meetings, seminars and retreats, as well as social occasions. Dranesville is conveniently located on Leesburg Pike; Dranesville Tavern is accessible from downtown Washington, Tysons Corner, the Dulles Corridor and Leesburg. The building features a total of seven rustic rooms of varying sizes on two floors. The shady back porch overlooks a rolling meadow leading down to a rambling stream. The large kitchen is suitable for most catering needs.

Capacity: 80 seated in tavern; 99 standing in tavern; 150 in garden.
Catering: You must supply your own caterer.
Rental Fee: $700 for five hours.
Parking: On the premises. Handicap parking available.
Restrictions: No confetti or silly string. Birdseed only may be thrown outside. No open flames. No taping, tacking, or nailing decorations to the walls. Collection pieces must be properly covered with plastic and fabric protection. No smoking indoors.
Note: Wedding ceremonies are permitted indoors or outdoors.

Evans Farm Inn   703-356-8000

1696 Chain Bridge Road • McLean, VA 22101

Have you always wanted an old-fashioned country wedding? Evans Farm Inn is a charming 18th-century style building completely decorated in the old manner. You'll be carried back to the times of the Fairfaxes, the Jeffersons and the Washingtons. You may have your reception in any of the seven banquet rooms. The lovely country garden is perfect for a garden wedding or outdoor reception.

Capacity: 150 seated; 300 standing; unlimited in garden.
Catering: In-house. Entrees range from $12.95 to $31.95 per person.
Parking: On the premises.
Note: Wedding ceremonies are permitted indoors or outdoors.

Future Homemakers of America   703-476-4900

1910 Association Drive • Reston, VA 20191-1584

Located on the terrace level of the headquarters building of Future Homemakers of America, the conference center features an atrium at the front entrance and a terraced, partially covered patio at the back. Both the atrium and the patio are in full view through the glass partitions at each end of the banquet room. The center is carpeted and the large kitchen is a caterer's delight.

Capacity: 175 seated; 250 standing.
Catering: You must supply your own caterer.
Rental Fee: $750.
Parking: On the premises.

Gadsby's Tavern Restaurant   703-548-1288

138 N. Royal Street • Alexandria, VA 22314

Once the site of society balls and presidential receptions, this Williamsburg-style tavern replicates the food, furnishings, and costumes of colonial times. You may have your reception in the Tap Room or one of the more formal dining rooms. The courtyard behind the tavern can be used for cocktails and hors d'oeuvres or an outdoor wedding ceremony.

Capacity: 100 seated; 150 standing; 175 in garden; 100 seated in adjacent 19th-century ballroom.
Catering: In-house. Entrees range from $15 to $45 per person.
Rental Fee: $850.
Parking: On the premises.
Restrictions: Period music in historic part of property. Your choice of music in 19th-century ballroom.
Note: Wedding ceremonies are permitted.

The Gallery   703-502-7620

c/o Artistry Catering
14201 Sullyfield Circle • Chantilly, VA 20151

Chantilly's best kept secret, this warmly appointed facility is the perfect choice for weddings, rehearsal dinners, bridal showers, and other celebrations. Opened in 1995, The Gallery boasts picture windows, pleasant decor, carpeted main room, and hardwood reception area. All catering is done from the on-premise kitchens by Artistry Catering, recently recommended by *Washingtonian Magazine* as one of the top caterers in the area. Located one block from the new Capitol Expo Center and minutes from Dulles Airport, it is fully accessible and has ample free parking.

Capacity: 90 seated; 125 standing.
Catering: In-house. Entrees range from $25 to $60 per person. Customized menus, including kosher, begin at $18 per person.
Rental Fee: $250 to $450.
Parking: On the premises.
Restrictions: No smoking inside.
Notes: Wedding ceremonies are permitted.

Great Falls Grange   703-938-8835

c/o Historic Properties Rental Services
9601 Courthouse Road • Vienna, VA 22181

This classic public assembly hall offers two stories, high ceilings with chandeliers, large windows that allow for lots of natural light and a catering kitchen. The large upstairs hall features a full stage outfitted with theatrical lighting and curtains; side windows also provide abundant natural lighting. Ceiling fans and chandeliers hanging from the lofty ceiling complete the room's classic ambience. A spacious banquet hall downstairs adjoins the full catering kitchen. Since its completion in 1929, the Grange has been the site of town assemblies, carnivals, theatrical and musical performances and private celebrations of all kinds.

Capacity: 135 seated; 200 standing; 250 in garden.
Catering: You must supply your own caterer.
Rental Fee: $800.
Parking: On the premises.
Restrictions: Birdseed only may be thrown outside. No confetti or silly string. No open flames or candles. No smoking indoors. No taping, tacking or nailing decorations to the walls.
Note: Wedding ceremonies are permitted indoors or outdoors.

Gunston Hall   703-550-9220

10709 Gunston Road • Mason Neck • Lorton, VA 22079

Built in 1755, Gunston Hall was the plantation home of George Mason, author of the Virginia Declaration of Rights and framer of the United States Constitution. The life and times of 18th-century America are vividly evoked by the commodious house and gardens overlooking the Potomac River. Weddings and other events may be held at various locations in the beautifully restored gardens and grounds of Gunston Hall, as well as in the banquet room and adjoining fountain courtyard located in the Ann Mason Building. The elegant mansion provides the perfect backdrop for weddings and receptions. Guided tours of the historic house are included as a part of any function. Gunston Hall is a spectacular place to celebrate a special day.

Capacity: 150 seated; 225 standing; unlimited in gardens.
Catering: In-house or your own caterer. In-house entrees range from $22 to $40 per person.
Rental Fee: $1,500 to $2,300.
Parking: On the premises. Handicap parking available.
Note: Wedding ceremonies are permitted.

Hidden Creek Country Club   703-437-5222

1711 Clubhouse Road • Reston, VA 20190

Hidden Creek Country Club has a variety of function rooms suitable for receptions of any type. All rooms have a panoramic view of a beautiful 18-hole championship golf course. The Fairway Room features a spacious outdoor deck, large dance floor and an inviting fireplace. All food is created by an award-winning chef. The clubhouse is conveniently located in the heart of Reston, Virginia, minutes from Dulles Airport and thirty minutes from Washington, D.C.

Capacity: 200 seated; 300 standing; 350 with tent.
Catering: In-house. Entrees range from $50 to $65 per person.
Rental Fee: $550 for 4 hours.
Parking: On the premises.
Note: Wedding ceremonies are permitted.

La Bergerie   703-683-1007

218 North Lee Street • Alexandria, VA 22314

Located in the heart of colonial Old Town Alexandria, La Bergerie is decorated with French countryside paintings, richly appointed leather banquettes, and crystal chandeliers. Its charming and intimate atmosphere provides the perfect ambiance for any special occasion. Cocktail receptions may be held in the Atrium and the two private party rooms can be used for smaller events. French

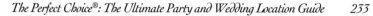

cuisine with Basque specialties will delight your palate. Your guests can stroll down cobblestone streets, tour quaint residences, shop in 1700-era stores, and listen to street entertainment. La Bergerie, located near Market Square and the famous Torpedo Factory Arts Center, is 15 minutes from Washington, D.C., via George Washington Parkway.

Capacity: 85 in main room; 48 in large private room; 26 in small private room.
Catering: In-house. Entrees range from $13 to $25. Cake cutting fee if provide own cake.
Rental Fee: None. Large room guarantee is 30 and the small room guarantee is 20.
Parking: Parking lot nearby.
Note: Wedding ceremonies are permitted.

Lansdowne Resort   703-729-8400

44050 Woodridge Parkway • Leesburg, VA 20176

At Landsdowne Resort, the staff knows how important your wedding day is to you, and are committed to making the day of your dreams a reality. It offers intimate dining areas for rehearsal dinners, exquisite menu selections from award-winning chefs, and an elegant ballroom and expansive outdoor terraces which overlook the Robert Trent Jones, Jr. golf course. A wedding specialist will be on hand to coordinate all aspects of your event, a pastry chef will work with you to design a deliciously beautiful wedding cake, and the spa staff will customize a bridal package for your party. For your guests, it offers luxurious guest rooms and spacious suites, relaxing amenities such as a championship golf course, health club, indoor and outdoor pools, and lighted tennis courts. Lansdowne Resort is also an excellent choice for corporate retreats or family reunions. Lansdowne is nestled in the scenic Potomac River Valley and is just 8 miles from Dulles Airport and less than an hour from Washington, D.C.

Capacity: 550 seated; 850 standing; 250 in pavilion.
Catering: In-house. Packages range from $70 to $85 per person. Cake cutting fee is $2.00 per person if cake is brought in.
Parking: On the premises. Valet parking is complimentary. Handicap parking is available.
Note: Wedding ceremonies are permitted indoors or outdoors. Guest rooms are available.

The Lyceum   703-838-4994

201 S. Washington Street • Alexandria, VA 22314

The Lyceum, Alexandria's History Museum, collects and interprets the history and material culture of the City of Alexandria and the surrounding northern Virginia area. This wonderful site offers one of the largest rooms available in an historic building in Old Town Alexandria. The Museum's Lecture Hall is available for weddings and receptions. The room is elegantly appointed with green wall-to-wall carpet, rose-colored draperies, and coordinating upholstered armchairs. There is a 9' x 22' platform stage, an adjoining kitchen and a concert grand piano. Arrangements can be made to have the exhibition galleries on the first floor open for viewing by your guests.

Capacity: 90 seated; 150 standing.
Catering: You must supply your own caterer. The facility provides six 8' rectangular tables, six 6' rectangular tables and 125 upholstered armchairs.
Rental Fee: $1,100 or $225 per hour.
Parking: On the premises. Handicap parking available.
Restrictions: No smoking. No rice, confetti, birdseed, etc. You must furnish dance floor, not to exceed 12' x 12'.
Note: Wedding ceremonies are permitted.

McLean Community Center   703-790-0123
TDD: TAPTALK

1234 Ingleside Avenue • McLean, VA 22101

Nestled in a parklike setting, the McLean Community Center is an arts and community center located just a few minutes from the Beltway and the George Washington Parkway, with plentiful free parking and professional facility staff. The Center is one of the most reasonably priced locations in the metropolitan area. The community hall wing offers several flexible choices for your reception, including a 3,000-square-foot hall with dance floor and an adjacent garden plaza. The Center's state-of-the-art commercial kitchen features pass-through and walk-through access to the community hall. The Center's fine art gallery, the Emerson Gallery, is also available for receptions. The Alden Theatre, which seats up to 424 persons, is available for private events.

Capacity: 200 seated; 350 standing in community center.
Catering: You must supply your own caterer. A 50 percent surcharge is added for all events at which alcohol is served.
Rental Fee: $90 to $435. Resident discount available. To obtain resident rate, wedding receptions may be booked only by the couple or their immediate family.
Parking: On the premises.
Restrictions: No smoking in building.
Note: Wedding ceremonies are permitted.

Montclair Golf, Tennis & Swim Club   703-670-3915

16500 Edgewood Drive • Dumfries, VA 22026

This country club, located just two miles from I-95, specializes in custom weddings. It offers complete packages, including food, open bar, wedding cake of bride's choice, DJ, champagne toasts, hors d'oeuvres, fresh flowers, candle centerpieces – and, most of all, peace of mind.

Capacity: 250 seated; 300+ standing.
Catering: In-house. Prices range from $50 to $75 per person.
Rental Fee: $300 to $550.
Parking: On the premises.
Note: Wedding ceremonies are permitted.

Morrison House   703-838-8000

116 South Alfred Street • Alexandria, VA 22314

Looking for a quiet, elegant, romantic escape? Look no further than Old Town Alexandria's award-winning Morrison House. The European warmth and charm of this small hotel are as welcoming as the butlers who greet you at the door. Located just minutes from National Airport and downtown Washington, D.C., the Federal style inn boasts ornate woodwork, decorative fireplaces and fanlight windows. Its 45 guest rooms, each unique, feature Federal period reproductions including mahogany four-poster beds, brass chandeliers and Italian marble baths. You may have your reception in any of the five private areas, or combine all of them for larger groups. Whatever your special occasion requires, this location with its experienced staff can meet your needs quickly and imaginatively.

Capacity: 90 seated; 130 standing; 175 with tent.
Catering: In-house. Entrees range from $60 to $125 per person.
              Cake cutting fee if you provide your own cake.
Rental Fee: $250 to $1,500.
Parking: On the premises and in lot nearby.
Note: Wedding ceremonies are permitted.

Mt. Vernon Square Ballroom   703-768-3232

2722 Arlington Drive • Alexandria, VA 22306

The Mount Vernon Square Ballroom is the perfect place for your wedding reception or any other special event. Located in the heart of the Route 1 corridor, just 3.5 miles from Route 495, the ballroom is surrounded by walls of windows offering panoramic views and an ideal setting. You and your guests can enjoy the romantic glow of the large fireplace during the winter months.

The ballroom allows you the flexibility to customize your wedding and reception to meet your exact needs. It has both a service and catering kitchen and wet and dry bars, offering a broad spectrum of catering options. The ballroom's design will accommodate live bands or a disc jockey and the spacious floor plan allows lots of room for dancing.

Capacity: 200 seated; 230 standing.
Catering: Approved caterers list or your own caterer. Tables and chairs are provided by facility.
Rental Fee: $600 to $2,000. Residents receive reduced rates.
Parking: Residential parking.
Note: Wedding ceremonies are permitted.

Seaport Inn   703-549-2341

6 King Street • Alexandria, VA 22314

This circa 1765, historic landmark previously owned by George Washington's military aide-de-camp provides a magnificent setting for wedding receptions. This location offers three elegant dining rooms. The John Fitzgerald Room, with its dark wood trim, rustic decor and complementing fireplace, is a charming asset to your party. The Potomac River Room offers a panoramic view of the Potomac River. The view, along with the room's rich brick color scheme accented with brass, creates a truly elegant atmosphere. The Williamsburg Room with its colonial decor is ideal for intimate parties.

Capacity: 130.
Catering: In-house. Entrees range from $16.95 to $20.95 per person. Cake cutting fee is $35.
Deposit: $100 to $175.
Parking: Parking garages nearby.
Note: Wedding ceremonies are permitted.

Sheraton National Hotel   703-521-1900 ext. 6505

Columbia Pike at Washington Blvd. • Arlington, VA 22204

The Main Lobby has a cathedral ceiling with natural light accents. The entrance, a spacious pre-function area done in subtle shades, can be used in many creative ways. Once the stage is set, mirrors, earth tones, and soft pastels provide a canvas on which your special event is placed. Tastefully conservative chandeliers accentuate the 17-foot high ceilings. This site provides flexibility to create intimacy or spacious enough for a royal fanfare. Located just minutes from National Airport via complimentary shuttle, it is conveniently located for local and out-of-town guests. This beautiful hotel offers mesmerizing views of Washington, distinctive cuisine and a highly trained and experienced catering staff.

Capacity: 75 to 550 seated; 1,000 standing.
Catering: In-house. Entrees begin at $52.50 per person, inclusive.
Parking: On the premises.
Note: Wedding ceremonies are permitted. Special room rates are available for overnight guests.

Wayside Inn Since 1797   540-869-1797
www.nvim.com/waysideinn

7783 Main Street • Middletown, VA 22645

This elegantly restored 18th-century inn, located one hour outside the beltway, boasts 24 lodging rooms appointed with antiques. It's an ideal location for a "dream come true" wedding and reception. Entertain on the terrace, outdoor pavilion and in the garden. At this inn, you can turn back the clock and experience the graciousness of a by-gone era.

Capacity: 150 inside; 350 with garden and patio.
Catering: In-house. Entrees begin at $25 and up.
Rental Fee: $1,000.
Parking: On the premises.
Note: Wedding ceremonies are permitted.

Williams Memorial Hall   703-385-7877 ext. 19

Fairfax Volunteer Fire Department
4081 University Drive • Fairfax, VA 22030

Located in the heart of Fairfax City, this newly renovated hall is one of the area's most affordable sites. It has a wonderful party area with a commercial kitchen, bar, and stage for raised seating. It's a true oasis — the perfect place for weddings and receptions as well as business functions. Lower fees are available for many weekday activities, such as conferences, classes, and seminars. There is ample free parking on site and more nearby.

Capacity: 250 seated; 250 standing.
Catering: You must supply your own caterer.
Rental Fee: $125 per hour plus $200 set-up fee on weekends.
Parking: On the premises.
Restrictions: Smoke-free facility.
Note: Wedding ceremonies are permitted.

Cherry Blossom Riverboat   703-684-0580

205 the Strand • Alexandria, VA 22314

Built in 1984, *The Cherry Blossom* is a re-creation of a 19th-century Victorian riverboat. Beautifully appointed with ornate iron railings, and a plush interior of brass and mahogany, it is one of the most elegant yachts cruising the Potomac. Its two interior salons are heated and air-conditioned for year-round comfort. The third deck is open air, offering a spectacular view of Old Town and the Washington, D.C., skyline.

Capacity:	250 seated; 400 standing; 75 with a tent on the third dock.
Catering:	Approved caterers list. Entrees range from $38 to $42 per person.
Parking:	Parking lot nearby. Valet parking can be arranged.
Note:	Wedding ceremonies permitted indoors or outdoors.

Hylton Memorial Chapel and Conference Center   703-590-0076

14640 Potomac Mills Road • Woodbridge, VA 22192

The chapel's entrance is marked by impressive columns and a beautiful portrayal of the Last Supper in stained glass. The two-storied chapel is a traditional Colonial Williamsburg design. Twelve-foot high stained glass windows are on each side, and at the front of the chapel is a six-foot round motif of the ascension which lights the chancel. The pipe organ is one of the few in the rows of pipes accommodating the sound for one of the few pipe organs in the area, and the pews and chancel furniture are white with mahogany trim. The main sanctuary is suitable for larger ceremonies (over 200 guests); its lower will accommodate 2,000. Both the sanctuary and the wedding chapel have a center aisle. The reception room, which will accommodate about 200, features 12-foot stained glass windows and a marble fireplace. A bridal room is available, and outside is a garden area with gazebo.

Capacity: 175 in chapel; 2,000 in main sanctuary.
Rental Fee: $600 to $800 chapel; $1,200 to $1,500 main sanctuary. Additional fees are required for other services. Call for more information.

The Longbarn   540-687-4137/540-687-3770

37129 Adams Green Lane • Middleburg, VA 20118

The quaint and charming Corn Crib Chapel is perfect for a small romantic wedding ceremony or renewal of vows.

Capacity: 60; 130 to 150 in garden; 130 to 150 with tent.
Rental Fee: Call for more information.

United Wesleyan Church   703-550-6161

520 Trin Street • Alexandria, VA 22310

Capacity: 150.
Rental Fee: $300.

Wakefield Chapel   703-938-8835

c/o Historic Properties Rental Services
9601 Courthouse Road • Vienna, VA 22181

Built in 1899, Wakefield Chapel is named for its first minister, and is the answer for anyone searching for a quaint, picturesque setting for a wedding. Guests sit on antique wooden pews, and the original pulpit is available for use. There is a large bridal dressing area on the lower level.

Capacity: 99
Rental Fee: $500 for three hours.
Parking: On the premises.
Restrictions: No confetti or silly string. Birdseed only may be thrown outside. All candles must be enclosed with something to catch the drips. No smoking indoors. No taping, tacking, or nailing decorations to the walls. No alcohol is permitted in the chapel.

St. Luke Serbian Orthodox Church   703-790-1005

6801 Georgetown Pike • McLean, VA 22101

Located on five acres of lovely countryside, this spacious hall has white walls and white linoleum. The hall overlooks a patio on one side and a grove of trees on the other side. Amenities include a huge commercial kitchen, bar, tables and chairs and convenient parking.

Capacity: 150 to 200 seated; 250 standing; 50 to 75 in garden.
Catering: You must supply your own caterer.
Rental Fee: $750 for four hours, includes use of kitchen, bar, and clean-up. Each additional hour is $125. Site provides three free hours for set-up.
Parking: On the premises.
Note: Wedding ceremonies are permitted outdoors.

McLean Community Center   703-790-0123
TDD: TAPTALK

1234 Ingleside Avenue • McLean, VA 22101

Nestled in a parklike setting, the McLean Community Center is an arts and community center located just a few minutes from the Beltway and the George Washington Parkway, with plentiful free parking and professional facility staff. The Center is one of the most reasonably priced locations in the metropolitan area. The community hall wing offers several flexible choices for your reception, including a 3,000-square-foot hall with dance floor and an adjacent garden plaza. The Center's state-of-the-art commercial kitchen features pass-through and walk-through access to the community hall. The Center's fine art gallery, the Emerson Gallery, is also available for receptions. The Alden Theatre, which seats up to 424 persons, is available for private events.

Capacity: 200 seated; 350 standing in community center.
Catering: You must supply your own caterer. A 50 percent surcharge is added for all events at which alcohol is served.
Rental Fee: $90 to $435. Resident discount available. To obtain resident rate, wedding receptions may be booked only by the couple or their immediate family.
Parking: On the premises.
Restrictions: No smoking in building.
Note: Wedding ceremonies are permitted.

Middleburg Community Center   540-687-6373

300 W. Washington Street • Middleburg, VA 20118-0265

Experience the charm of Virginia Hunt Country in Middleburg, Virginia. This wonderful site features an elegant main room, a lovely terrace room, a spacious terrace and beautifully landscaped gardens. The outdoor terrace is perfect for cocktails and hors d'oeuvres and if you've always wanted to have a garden wedding — this is the place. The newly renovated basement is available for small parties, children's parties and meetings.

Capacity: 175 seated; 250 standing; 75 in garden; 100+ with a tent; 75 in basement.
Catering: You must supply your own caterer.
Rental Fee: $850, plus tax. Call for prices for basement.
Parking: On the premises.
Note: Wedding ceremonies are permitted indoors or outdoors.

Algonkian Meeting Center
Algonkian Regional Park   703-450-4655

47001 Fairway Drive • Sterling, VA 20165

The Algonkian Meeting Center makes entertaining easy with its large reception room, portable bar and dance floor. Stone fireplaces and large windows looking onto the park and golf course add atmosphere to any reception. Delicious custom menus created by the Center's caterer are sure to please your guests. A quaint gazebo on the front lawn is a romantic setting for wedding ceremonies. Complimentary use of the gazebo is an option when renting the Loudoun Room. The Meeting Center is located in Algonkian Regional Park, which features 12 river-front vacation cottages, outdoor swimming pool, 18-hole, par-72 golf course, picnic shelters and boat ramp. The facility is excellently suited for corporate functions such as seminars, company picnics and retreats.

Capacity: 175 seated; 200 standing.
Catering: You must supply your own caterer.
Rental Fee: $875 for five hours.
Parking: On the premises.
Note: Wedding ceremonies are permitted.

Future Homemakers of America   703-476-4900

1910 Association Drive • Reston, VA 20191-1584

Located on the terrace level of the headquarters building of Future Homemakers of America, the conference center features an atrium at the front entrance and a terraced, partially covered patio at the back. Both the atrium and the patio are in full view through the glass partitions at each end of the banquet room. The center is carpeted and the large kitchen is a caterer's delight.

Capacity: 175 seated; 250 standing.
Catering: You must supply your own caterer.
Rental Fee: $750.
Parking: On the premises.

Westfields Marriott   703-818-0300

14750 Conference Center Drive • Chantilly, VA 20151

Located just 30 minutes from the nation's capital, Westfields combines the architectural splendor of Virginia's finest estates with the functional excellence for which it has won numerous awards. The entry's three-and-a-half ton bronze doors exemplify the pride of craftsmanship found throughout this $70 million resort. Inside, just beyond the Lobby, a magnificent Rotunda presents a spectacular dome, classic columns and a generous portion of the center's 450 tons of Greek marble. Westfields offers a variety of indoor and outdoor settings to create an event to reflect your unique and personal tastes. The property has three elegantly furnished ballrooms and a number of intimate banquet spaces to host your special event.

Capacity: 600 seated; 900 standing; 300 in garden; 200 with tent.
Catering: In-house. Entrees begin at $85 per person. Cake cutting fee if you provide your own cake.
Rental Fee: $1,000 to $4,000.
Parking: On the premises. Valet parking is available.
Note: Wedding ceremonies are permitted indoors or outdoors.

Williams Memorial Hall   703-385-7877 ext. 19

Fairfax Volunteer Fire Department
4081 University Drive • Fairfax, VA 22030

Located in the heart of Fairfax City, this newly renovated hall is one of the area's most affordable sites. It has a wonderful party area with a commercial kitchen, bar, and stage for raised seating. It's a true oasis — the perfect place for weddings and receptions as well as business functions. Lower fees are available for many weekday activities, such as conferences, classes, and seminars. There is ample free parking on site and more nearby.

Capacity: 250 seated; 250 standing.
Catering: You must supply your own caterer.
Rental Fee: $125 per hour plus $200 set-up fee on weekends.
Parking: On the premises.
Restrictions: Smoke-free facility.
Note: Wedding ceremonies are permitted.

Fauquier Springs Country Club 540-347-2459

9236 Tournament Drive • Warrenton, VA 20186-7848

With its breathtaking view and exquisite outdoor terraces, this location is the perfect country setting for weddings and other special occasions. The clubhouse sits on top of a hill overlooking a spectacular golf course, farm and countryside. A Victorian staircase graces the foyer, and the ballroom's many windows leads to wrap-around patios where guests can enjoy the panoramic view of the meticulously landscaped golf course. The smaller Springs Room, with its charming marble fireplace, is ideal for pictures.

Capacity: 250 seated in ballroom; 300 standing in ballroom; 50 in Springs Room.
Catering: In-house. Wedding packages range from $35 to $65 per person and are all-inclusive. Separate ala carte and custom menus are available.
Rental Fee: $100 to $1,000, depends on season and time of day.
Parking: On the premises. Handicap parking is available.
Note: Wedding ceremonies are permitted.

Hidden Creek Country Club 703-437-5222

1711 Clubhouse Road • Reston, VA 20190

Hidden Creek Country Club has a variety of function rooms suitable for receptions of any type. All rooms have a panoramic view of a beautiful 18-hole championship golf course. The Fairway Room features a spacious outdoor deck, large dance floor and an inviting fireplace. All food is created by an award-winning chef. The clubhouse is conveniently located in the heart of Reston, Virginia, minutes from Dulles Airport and thirty minutes from Washington, D.C.

Capacity: 200 seated; 300 standing; 350 with tent.
Catering: In-house. Entrees range from $50 to $65 per person.
Rental Fee: $550 for 4 hours.
Parking: On the premises.
Note: Wedding ceremonies are permitted.

Montclair Golf, Tennis & Swim Club 703-670-3915

16500 Edgewood Drive • Dumfries, VA 22026

This country club, located just two miles from I-95, specializes in custom weddings. It offers complete packages, including food, open bar, wedding cake of bride's choice, DJ, champagne toasts, hors d'oeuvres, fresh flowers, candle centerpieces – and, most of all, peace of mind.

Capacity: 250 seated; 300+ standing.
Catering: In-house. Prices range from $50 to $75 per person.
Rental Fee: $300 to $550.
Parking: On the premises.
Note: Wedding ceremonies are permitted.

Stoneleigh Tavern   703-589-1442

35279 Prestwick Court • Round Hill, VA 20175

Set in the foothills of the Blue Ridge, Stoneleigh Tavern offers a majestic site for outdoor weddings. Wedding parties and their guests will enjoy the spacious, private courtyard which is surrounded by a natural stone wall. The courtyard includes a paved tented area for dining and dancing, and an elevated grassy area provides a natural setting for ceremonies. A full-service restaurant is located on site in a pre-Civil War era mansion. Stoneleigh Tavern is located 14 miles west of Leesburg on the grounds of the Stoneleigh Golf & Country Club, and is easily accessible from the Dulles Greenway.

Capacity: 130 seated; 130 standing; 130 in garden with tent.
Catering: In-house. Entrees range from $16 to $28 per person. Cake cutting fee if you provide your own cake.
Parking: On the premises.
Restrictions: Ceremonies and receptions are held outside in the courtyard.
Note: Wedding ceremonies are permitted.

Clark House   703-938-8835

c/o Historical Properties Rental Service
9601 Courthouse Road • Vienna, VA 22181

The Clark House, a turn-of-the-century Victorian farmhouse, is an ideal site for your corporate meeting or social gathering. The formal entry hall, two large connecting rooms, and the wrap-around veranda offers your guests a glimpse back in time when entertaining was an art.

Capacity: 65 seated; 65 standing.
Catering: You must supply your own caterer. Kitchen facilities, tables and chairs are provided. Alcoholic beverages can be brought on the premises with permit.
Rental Fee: $600 for five hours.
Parking: On the premises. Additional parking nearby.
Restrictions: No confetti or silly string. Birdseed may be thrown outside only. All candles must be enclosed with protection underneath. No smoking indoors. No taping, tacking, or nailing decorations to the walls.
Note: Wedding ceremonies are permitted indoors or outdoors.

Hazel River Inn Bed and Breakfast   540-937-5854

11227 Eggborneville Road • Culpeper, VA 22701

This 18th-century inn is ideal for a romantic country wedding. The inn welcomes small receptions for any occasion, and now offers Sunday brunch and afternoon tea. You may hold your brunch or party in the sun room, or outdoors by the pool and gardens. The menu features produce and herbs grown on the premises by an in-house horticulturist.

Capacity: 30 seated; 40 standing; 100 in garden; 100 with tent.
Catering: In-house or approved caterers list. Entrees begin at $25 for lunch, $40 for dinner, and $35 for receptions.
Rental Fee: $350.
Parking: On the premises.
Note: Wedding ceremonies are permitted.

Hunter House   703-938-8835

c/o Historic Properties Rental Service
9601 Courthouse Road • Vienna, VA 22181

Built in 1890, Hunter House was home to Scottish immigrant John C. Hunter. After Prohibition ended, William Davidson operated Distillery #4 there and produced a wine which he called *Virginia Maid*. While the house maintains much of its original character, through the years it has been expanded into a spacious two-story facility. Hunter House provides an atmosphere of casual country elegance. The building features several air-conditioned rooms and a kitchen, as well as a screened-in porch. The adjacent lawn is a popular place for outdoor weddings and receptions.

Capacity: 40 seated; 75 standing; 150 in garden.
Catering: You must supply your own caterer.
Rental Fee: $800.
Parking: On the premises.
Restrictions: No confetti or silly string. Birdseed only may be thrown outside. No smoking indoors. No open flames. No taping, tacking, or nailing decorations to the walls.
Note: Wedding ceremonies permitted indoors or outdoors.

Rockland Farm Retreat   1-800-895-5098

3609 Lewiston Road • Bumpass, Virginia 23024

Built in 1839, this historic inn is a scenic 75-acre country estate. The majestic trees, quiet pastures and wildlife create a tranquil setting for your special day. Picture your wedding ceremony inside a quiet country church or in a lovely garden. The surrounding areas offer Civil War battlefields, winery tours, state parks, natural trails, horseback riding and golfing.

Capacity: 50 seated; 100 standing; 200 in garden; 300 with a tent.
Catering: In-house caterer or your own caterer. In-house entree cost is $20 per person.
Parking: On the premises.
Note: Wedding ceremonies are permitted indoors or outdoors.

Alexandria Black History
Resource Center   703-838-4356

638 N. Alfred Street • Alexandria, VA 22314

The Alexandria Black History Resource Center, Northern Virginia's only African-American history museum, offers a wedding site for couples interested in celebrating their ethnic heritage or those looking for a unique historic atmosphere. Couples have a choice of two modern exhibition galleries: the Parker-Gray Gallery and the Robert Robinson Gallery. The galleries can be combined to work as a wedding and reception site. Both galleries offer modern museum lighting which can be adjusted for dramatic effect. Used as just a reception site, the museum can accommodate 150 people. Under supervision provided by the renter, the Center's Watson Reading Room may be rented as a quiet playroom for children. The reading room, adjacent to the Center, has over 1,500 books, videos and periodicals on African-American history and culture. The Center's satellite site, the Alexandria African-American Heritage Park (located off Duke Street on Holland Lane) is a nine-acre park suitable for outdoor weddings. The Center is located in the historic Parker-Gray district of Alexandria and is an appropriate setting for intimate celebrations.

Capacity: 75 seating; 150 standing.
Catering: You must supply your own caterer. The Center has a modern catering kitchen and tables and chairs may be rented on site.
Rental Fee: $100 per hour.
Parking: The Center offers ample on-street parking, without time restrictions.
Restrictions: No smoking.
Note: Wedding ceremonies are permitted. Facility is handicapped accessible.

The Athenaeum   703-548-0035

201 Prince Street • Alexandria, VA 22314

This scaled-down copy of the Temple of Athena, built in 1852 with fluted columns across the verandah, is an historic landmark. Just one block from the Potomac River, in the heart of Old Town Alexandria, it is an intimate and romantic site for gatherings. Features include soaring ceilings, beautiful woodwork, and gleaming old floors that are fine for dancing. Tall windows offer views of cobblestoned streets and 18th-century houses. The two elegant galleries on the main level are usually hung with interesting artworks. Ceiling fans and air conditioning keep guests comfortable. A catering kitchen and the lower gallery are useful for food preparation. An enchanting garden has high brick walls draped with vines. The garden may be canopied.

Capacity: 80 seated; 175 standing; 24 seated in garden; 50 standing in garden; 225 with tent.
Catering: You must supply your own caterer.
Rental Fee: $1,100 for six hours. $185 each additional hour.
Parking: Parking lots nearby. Valet parking can be arranged.
Restrictions: Available only Saturday and Sunday. Nothing attached to walls. No DJs. All rental equipment delivered and removed on day of event. Only votive candles allowed. Art on exhibit will not be removed except by special arrangement. Caterer must be present throughout entire affair, with one worker per 30 guests. No cooking over open flame.
Note: Wedding ceremonies are permitted.

McLean Community Center   703-790-0123
TDD: TAPTALK

1234 Ingleside Avenue • McLean, VA 22101

Nestled in a parklike setting, the McLean Community Center is an arts and community center located just a few minutes from the Beltway and the George Washington Parkway, with plentiful free parking and professional facility staff. The Center is one of the most reasonably priced locations in the metropolitan area. The community hall wing offers several flexible choices for your reception, including a 3,000-square-foot hall with dance floor and an adjacent garden plaza. The Center's state-of-the-art commercial kitchen features pass-through and walk-through access to the community hall. The Center's fine art gallery, the Emerson Gallery, is also available for receptions. The Alden Theatre, which seats up to 424 persons, is available for private events.

Capacity: 200 seated; 350 standing in community center.
Catering: You must supply your own caterer. A 50 percent surcharge is added for all events at which alcohol is served.
Rental Fee: $90 to $435. Resident discount available. To obtain resident rate, wedding receptions may be booked only by the couple or their immediate family.
Parking: On the premises.
Restrictions: No smoking in building.
Note: Wedding ceremonies are permitted.

Old Town Hall   703-385-7893

3999 University Drive • Fairfax, VA 22030

Old Town Hall is the perfect place for a wedding, party, or meeting. Old Town Hall is located in the heart of the nationally recognized City of Fairfax Historic District. Built in 1900 by Joseph E. Willard, the hall was presented to the Town of Fairfax in 1902 and became the center of Fairfax social life. Although neo-

Classical in style, the hall tastefully combines Tuscan order columns with Federal-style details, such as the fanlight window over the front doors and the round-headed gabled dormers. The hall is approximately 50 feet long and 40 feet wide, with modern restroom facilities, and a new kitchen with a sink and refrigerator.

Capacity: 150 seated downstairs; 80 seated upstairs; 175 to 200 standing downstairs; 80 to 100 standing upstairs.

Catering: You must supply your own caterer.

Rental Fee: $400 to $750 for 5 hours. Additional hours are available at $75 an hour for main floor and $25 an hour upstairs. Facility requires $150 security deposit. City of Fairfax residents receive $100 discount.

Parking: Limited parking on the premises, but there are parking lots nearby.

Restrictions: No cooking allowed (warming units okay). No open flames. No taping or tacking on walls or floors. No birdseed, confetti, etc. can be thrown.

Note: Wedding ceremonies are permitted.

Torpedo Factory Art Center   703-838-4199

105 North Union Street • Alexandria, VA 22314

The Torpedo Factory Art Center, originally built in 1918 following World War I to manufacture torpedoes, has been transformed into a modern art center housing 83 working artists' studios and five cooperative galleries. The central hall, a two-story atrium, is a unique and informal setting which can accommodate receptions and ceremonies. It is 160 feet long and is topped with a balcony, catwalks, large peripheral windows and a central skylight. The hall is surrounded by glass walls displaying the artwork of the individual studios. The hall lends itself to decoration in many styles, and photographs of the site decorated for past events are available to view. The Art Center is located on the Potomac River waterfront in the heart of Old Town Alexandria, just minutes south of National Airport and inside the Beltway.

Capacity: 400 seated; 1,200 standing.

Catering: You must supply your own caterer.

Rental Fee: $1,500 for the first floor, $1,700 for first floor and balcony; $2,500 for entire building. Some additional fees for staff, security and insurance required.

Parking: Parking is available across the street and there are parking lots nearby.

Restrictions: No red wine, rice, birdseed, or glitter allowed in the Art Center. No alcohol allowed behind the Art Center on the dock/marina area.

Note: Wedding ceremonies are permitted.

The Athenaeum   703-548-0035

201 Prince Street • Alexandria, VA 22314

This scaled-down copy of the Temple of Athena, built in 1852 with fluted columns across the verandah, is an historic landmark. Just one block from the Potomac River, in the heart of Old Town Alexandria, it is an intimate and romantic site for gatherings. Features include soaring ceilings, beautiful woodwork, and gleaming old floors that are fine for dancing. Tall windows offer views of cobblestoned streets and 18th-century houses. The two elegant galleries on the main level are usually hung with interesting artworks. Ceiling fans and air conditioning keep guests comfortable. A catering kitchen and the lower gallery are useful for food preparation. An enchanting garden has high brick walls draped with vines. The garden may be canopied.

Capacity: 80 seated; 175 standing; 24 seated in garden; 50 standing in garden; 225 with tent.
Catering: You must supply your own caterer.
Rental Fee: $1,100 for six hours. $185 each additional hour.
Parking: Parking lots nearby. Valet parking can be arranged.
Restrictions: Available only Saturday and Sunday. Nothing attached to walls. No DJs. All rental equipment delivered and removed on day of event. Only votive candles allowed. Art on exhibit will not be removed except by special arrangement. Caterer must be present throughout entire affair, with one worker per 30 guests. No cooking over open flame.
Note: Wedding ceremonies are permitted.

The Atrium at Meadowlark Gardens 703-255-3631

9750 Meadowlark Gardens Court • Vienna, VA 22182

Seasonal blossoms, a meandering stream and a hint of woodlands offer a bouquet of possibilities in this indoor garden at The Atrium at Meadowlark Gardens. Three walls of windows and a landscaped terrace overlook the gardens, woods and meadows of the Northern Virginia Regional Park Authority's 95-acre garden park. In the Garden Room, the cathedral ceiling rises to a dramatic, 2,000-square-foot skylight. Gazebos on a hillside, the Azalea Woods and Lake Caroline offer picturesque settings for the exchange of vows. The Atrium and the array of natural and specialty gardens are located between Routes 7 and 123, just south of the Dulles Access Road and near Tysons Corner and Wolf Trap Farm Park.

Capacity: 220 seated; 350 standing without dance floor.
Catering: You must supply your own caterer. Caterer must be approved by the Atrium's events coordinator. Pantry kitchen for warming and holding food only. No premise

cooking. Caterers must have license, liquor license, and certificate of insurance.

Rental Fee: $275 to $400 per hour. Rental includes: tables, chairs, two portable bars, 15' x 18' dance floor and use of terrace and preparation kitchen. Rental period includes set-up and clean-up by the caterer.

Parking: On the premises.

Note: Wedding ceremonies are permitted indoors or outdoors. The facility hosts two weddings on Saturday: The first wedding ends at 3:00 p.m. and the second wedding starts at 5:00 p.m.

 ## Black Horse Inn   540-349-4242
http://www.blackhorseinn.com

8393 Meetze Road • Warrenton, VA 20187

This elegant, circa 1850, hunt-country estate complete with thoroughbred horses is located only 45 minutes from Washington, D.C. The inn – with ample enclosed porches, landscaped grounds, boxwood gardens, a gazebo and spectacular views – provides a wonderful setting for weddings, receptions, parties and anniversary celebrations. The staff's planning for such events is both talented and imaginative and its lists of menus, champagnes and wines are well chosen. The majestic bridal suite, "Great Expectations," is opulent and romantic with a magnificent bed, fireplace, private porch enclosed by French doors that overlook the front grounds, fireplace, Jacuzzi and separate dressing room. Seven additional guest rooms each have luxurious private baths. For an indoor reception, the inn can accommodate up to 100 guests for cocktails and buffet. For outdoor events, the inn can accommodate up to 150 guests. There is one distinct advantage to reserving the Black Horse Inn for your wedding. Because the rooms are included in the package price, your guests can share in the cost of the site for your wedding! The Black Horse Inn offers not only an excellent location, but also the charm and romance that make the most beautiful of wedding memories.

Capacity: 100 indoors; 150 outdoors.

Catering: In-house or approved caterers list. Entrees range from $25 to $85 per person.

Rental Fee: $1,500 for facility. Packages are available which include rooms.

Parking: On the premises.

Note: Wedding ceremonies are permitted.

Boyhood Home of Robert E. Lee   703-548-8454

607 Oronoco Street • Alexandria, VA 22314

Built in 1795 by John Potts, a friend and business associate of George Washington, this became the home of Robert E. Lee in

1812. The house is decorated in furniture and brass from the Federal Period. The house and gardens are available for weddings and receptions.

Capacity:　40 seated; 100 standing; 100 in garden.
Catering:　Approved caterers list.
Rental Fee:　$150 per hour.
Parking:　On the street and parking in nearby lot.
Restrictions:　No smoking or dance inside the home.
Note:　Wedding ceremonies are permitted indoors or outdoors.

Bristow Manor　　　　703-368-3558
11507 Valley View Drive • Bristow, VA 20136

Located near Manassas in Bristow, Virginia, just 30 minutes from the D.C. Beltway, this turn-of-the-century colonial-revival manor house with its large rooms, 14-foot high ceilings and decorative moldings, has been completely restored to its former grandeur. Today, the manor overlooks the beautiful 220-acre Bristow Manor Golf Club. This elegant manor provides the perfect atmosphere for any special occasion.

Capacity:　150 seated; 200 standing; 250 in outdoor pavilion.
Catering:　In-house. Entrees begin at $22 per person for hor d'oeuvres, $25 and up for buffet , and $32 and up for sit-down dinner.
Rental Fee:　$495 to $1,595.
Parking:　On the premises.
Restrictions:　No smoking inside home. No open flame candles.
Note:　Wedding ceremonies are permitted indoors or outdoors.

Cabell's Mill　　　　703-938-8835
c/o Historic Properties Rental Services
9601 Courthouse Road • Vienna, VA 22181

Once serving Centreville's community as a gristmill, sawmill, and a sumac mill, Cabell's Mill has been at the center of local commerce and community since its construction shortly after the Revolutionary War. It features two spacious floors and is perfect for weddings and receptions. The original chimneys and fireplaces are still in place. The building has been equipped with ceiling lighting and modernized with central air conditioning and heating. A large flagstone terrace looks out over Big Rocky Run, and is ideal for an outdoor wedding.

Capacity:　95 seated on two floors; 125 standing; 150 in garden.
Catering:　You must supply your own caterer.
Rental Fee:　$950.
Parking:　75 parking spaces on the premises; parking lot nearby.
Restrictions:　No confetti or silly string. Birdseed may be thrown outside only. All candles must be enclosed with pro-

Note: underneath. No taping, tacking, or nailing decorations to walls. No smoking indoors.
   Wedding ceremonies are permitted indoors or outdoors.

Carlyle House Historic Park 703-549-2997

121 N. Fairfax Street • Alexandria, VA 22314

Located in the heart of Old Town Alexandria, the Carlyle House provides wedding receptions and ceremonies with a touch of colonial elegance. Completed in 1753 by Scottish merchant John Carlyle, the Carlyle House with its stone construction and manor-house design is on the National Register of Historic Places. Its gardens and gazebo make a perfect backdrop when exchanging vows.

Capacity: 100 seated; 100 standing; 25 in garden.
Catering: You must supply your own caterer.
Rental Fee: $1,495.
Parking: Parking lot nearby.
Restrictions: No amplified music or sound system. No rice, flowers, birdseed or confetti may be thrown.
Note: Wedding ceremonies are permitted. Weddings and receptions may be scheduled evenings, except Monday, from 6:30 p.m. to midnight, with caterers arriving at 5:00 p.m.

Evans Farm Inn 703-356-8000

1696 Chain Bridge Road • McLean, VA 22101

Have you always wanted an old-fashioned country wedding? Evans Farm Inn is a charming 18th-century style building completely decorated in the old manner. You'll be carried back to the times of the Fairfaxes, the Jeffersons and the Washingtons. You may have your reception in any of the seven banquet rooms. The lovely country garden is perfect for a garden wedding or outdoor reception.

Capacity: 150 seated; 300 standing; unlimited in garden.
Catering: In-house. Entrees range from $12.95 to $31.95 per person.
Parking: On the premises.
Note: Wedding ceremonies are permitted indoors or outdoors.

Fauquier Springs Country Club 540-347-2459

9236 Tournament Drive • Warrenton, VA 20186-7848

With its breathtaking view and exquisite outdoor terraces, this location is the perfect country setting for weddings and other special occasions. The clubhouse sits on top of a hill overlooking a spectacular golf course, farm and countryside. A Victorian staircase graces the foyer, and the ballroom's many windows leads to wrap-around patios where guests can enjoy the panoramic view of the meticulously landscaped golf course. The smaller Springs Room, with its charming marble fireplace, is ideal for pictures.

Capacity: 250 seated in ballroom; 300 standing in ballroom; 50 in Springs Room.
Catering: In-house. Wedding packages range from $35 to $65 per person and are all-inclusive. Separate ala carte and custom menus are available.
Rental Fee: $100 to $1,000, depends on season and time of day.
Parking: On the premises. Handicap parking is available.
Note: Wedding ceremonies are permitted.

Flint Hill Public House   540-675-1700

675 Zachary Taylor Highway • Flint Hill, VA 22627

Located on five landscaped acres, this restored turn-of-the-century schoolhouse can host small or large receptions, weddings, rehearsal dinners and corporate events. You may have your ceremony in the lovely gazebo and gardens, which have a stunning view of the Blue Ridge Mountains. Inside, on the main level, is a full-service restaurant and bar with wood-burning stoves. Upstairs, two queen-sized suites, kitchen, and conference room may be used for seminars and executive retreats. This site is just moments away from antique shops, wineries, and the Skyline Drive.

Capacity: 99 seated; 250 standing; 250 in garden.
Catering: In-house. $50 cake cutting fee if you provide your own cake.
Rental Fee: $750 to $2,500 if complete facility is used.
Parking: On the premises.
Note: Wedding ceremonies are permitted indoors or outdoors.

Future Homemakers of America   703-476-4900

1910 Association Drive • Reston, VA 20191-1584

Located on the terrace level of the headquarters building of Future Homemakers of America, the conference center features an atrium at the front entrance and a terraced, partially covered patio at the back. Both the atrium and the patio are in full view through the glass partitions at each end of the banquet room. The center is carpeted and the large kitchen is a caterer's delight.

Capacity: 175 seated; 250 standing.
Catering: You must supply your own caterer.
Rental Fee: $750.
Parking: On the premises.

Gadsby's Tavern Restaurant   703-548-1288

138 N. Royal Street • Alexandria, VA 22314

Once the site of society balls and presidential receptions, this Williamsburg-style tavern replicates the food, furnishings, and costumes of colonial times. You may have your reception in the Tap Room or one of the more formal dining rooms. The courtyard behind the tavern can be used for cocktails and hors d'oeuvres or an outdoor wedding ceremony.

Capacity: 100 seated; 150 standing; 175 in garden; 100 seated in adjacent 19th-century ballroom.
Catering: In-house. Entrees range from $15 to $45 per person.
Rental Fee: $850.
Parking: On the premises.
Restrictions: Period music in historic part of property. Your choice of music in 19th-century ballroom.
Note: Wedding ceremonies are permitted.

Green Spring Manor   703-938-8835

c/o Historic Properties Rental Services
9601 Courthouse Road • Vienna, VA 22181

The Green Spring Farm Manor, circa 1760, is the centerpiece of what was once a 540-acre farm. Today, the manor house is part of Green Spring Gardens Park, and the formal grounds around the manor house are available for garden weddings. This historic manor is a great place to celebrate the occasion of your marriage.

Capacity: 100 in garden; 100 with tent.
Catering: You must supply your own caterer.
Rental Fee: $700.
Parking: On the premises.
Restrictions: Outdoors only. No confetti or silly string. Birdseed may be thrown outside only. All candles must be enclosed with something to catch the drips. No smoking indoors. No taping, tacking, or nailing decorations to the walls.
Note: Wedding ceremonies are permitted.

Gunston Hall   703-550-9220

10709 Gunston Road • Mason Neck • Lorton, VA 22079

Built in 1755, Gunston Hall was the plantation home of George Mason, author of the Virginia Declaration of Rights and framer of the United States Constitution. The life and times of 18th-century America are vividly evoked by the commodious house and gardens overlooking the Potomac River. Weddings and other events may be held at various locations in the beautifully restored gardens and grounds of Gunston Hall, as well as in the banquet room and adjoining fountain courtyard located in the Ann Mason Building. The elegant mansion provides the perfect backdrop for weddings and receptions. Guided tours of the historic house are included as a part of any function. Gunston Hall is a spectacular place to celebrate a special day.

Capacity: 150 seated; 225 standing; unlimited in gardens.
Catering: In-house or your own caterer. In-house entrees range from $22 to $40 per person.
Rental Fee: $1,500 to $2,300.
Parking: On the premises. Handicap parking available.
Note: Wedding ceremonies are permitted.

Hackwood 1-800-365-8021

534 Red Bud Road • Winchester, VA 22603

Hackwood was the center of many intriguing and historical events, including the duel between Peyton Smith and Joseph Holmes in 1809 and the 3rd Battle of Winchester during the Civil War. Originally called Hackwood Park Estate, the Georgian-style house is enhanced by a welcoming stone walk with boxwood. The grand veranda on the west side looks out over a beautifully landscaped green with a large lake in the distance. The mansion offers two large parlors on the main floor, a wide center hall, and additional space on the second level.

Capacity: 120 seated downstairs; 80 seated upstairs; 300 standing; 200 in garden; 1,000 with tent.
Catering: In-house. Entrees range from $55 to $85 per person.
Rental Fee: $1,500.
Parking: On the premises.
Note: Wedding ceremonies are permitted.

Hazel River Inn Bed and Breakfast 540-937-5854

11227 Eggborneville Road • Culpeper, VA 22701

This 18th-century inn is ideal for a romantic country wedding. The inn welcomes small receptions for any occasion, and now offers Sunday brunch and afternoon tea. You may hold your brunch or party in the sun room, or outdoors by the pool and gardens. The menu features produce and herbs grown on the premises by an in-house horticulturist.

Capacity: 30 seated; 40 standing; 100 in garden; 100 with tent.
Catering: In-house or approved caterers list. Entrees begin at $25 for lunch, $40 for dinner, and $35 for receptions.
Rental Fee: $350.
Parking: On the premises.
Note: Wedding ceremonies are permitted.

The Hermitage Inn Restaurant   703-266-1623

7134 Main Street • Clifton, VA 20124

Once a luxury retreat for the affluent, "The Clifton Hotel" was host to the likes of Ulysses S. Grant, Theodore Roosevelt and Rutherford B. Hayes. As The Hermitage Inn Restaurant, this graceful landmark has been faithfully restored to its original beauty of 1869. Charming, romantic and secluded, the restaurant is ideal for an intimate dinner for two or an elegant wedding for 200. Take a moment to enjoy the antiquity of the setting, enhanced by original hardwood floors, French doors and four fireplaces. The outdoor terrace, with a waterfall and lovely garden, is perfect for a wedding ceremony or any special event.

Capacity: 160 seated; 250 standing; 100 in garden; 160 with tent.
Catering: In-house. Entrees range from $40 to $60 per person.
Parking: On the premises.
Note: Wedding ceremonies are permitted.

Lee-Fendall House   703-548-1789

614 Oronoco Street • Alexandria, VA 22314

Built in 1785, it has been home to 37 Lees. Furnished with many of the Lee family heirlooms, it is listed on the National Register of Historic Places. The lovely white clapboard home and its garden are perfect for weddings and receptions. Guests are greeted in the garden under the massive magnolia, ancient chestnuts and ginkgo trees, or by candlelight and antiques in the historic house.

Capacity: 85 standing; 100 in garden.
Catering: Approved caterer list or your own caterer.
Rental Fee: $150 per hour.
Parking: Parking lot nearby. Residential parking.
Restrictions: No amplified musical instruments.
Note: Wedding ceremonies are permitted indoors or out-doors.

The Longbarn   540-687-4137/540-687-3770

37129 Adams Green Lane • Middleburg, VA 20118

Enjoy a picturesque European getaway in this more than 100-year-old renovated barn in historic Middleburg, Virginia. English gardens nestled under a canopy of hardwood trees surround a swimming pond and gazebo. The Longbarn features an elegant Italian country style interior with spacious bedrooms, air conditioning, fireplaces, and a large library for the pleasure and comfort of your guests. A delicious breakfast with warm breads and other specialties from the old country is served. Horseback and bicycle riding are nearby, as well as golf courses, antique shops, vineyards and fine dining. The quaint and charming Corn Crib Chapel is perfect for a small romantic wedding ceremony or renewal of vows. Treat yourself to the generous hospitality of your gracious Italian hostess and serenity of this lovely estate.

Capacity:	50 seated; 60 standing; 150 in garden; 150 with tent.
Catering:	You must supply your own caterer.
Rental Fee:	$1,550 to $2,550, includes 1 or 2 nights use of three bedrooms (double occupancy) and full breakfast.
Parking:	On the premises.
Restrictions:	No smoking indoors. No pets.
Note:	Wedding ceremonies are permitted.

Middleburg Community Center   540-687-6373

300 W. Washington Street • Middleburg, VA 20118-0265

Experience the charm of Virginia Hunt Country in Middleburg, Virginia. This wonderful site features an elegant main room, a lovely terrace room, a spacious terrace and beautifully landscaped gardens. The outdoor terrace is perfect for cocktails and hors d'oeuvres and if you've always wanted to have a garden wedding — this is the place. The newly renovated basement is available for small parties, children's parties and meetings.

Capacity:	175 seated; 250 standing; 75 in garden; 100+ with a tent; 75 in basement.
Catering:	You must supply your own caterer.
Rental Fee:	$850, plus tax. Call for prices for basement.
Parking:	On the premises.
Note:	Wedding ceremonies are permitted indoors or outdoors.

The Mimslyn Inn   1-800-296-5105/540-743-5105

401 West Main Street • Luray, VA 22835

Imagine having your wedding reception at an elegant antebellum plantation that features old-fashioned southern hospitality, 14 acres of exquisite gardens and lawns, and a main lobby graced by a winding staircase and beautiful fireplace. It is sure to make you feel like Scarlett O'Hara. The Mimslyn Inn features formal gardens that are perfect for an outside ceremony and a ballroom just right to dance the night away. The chef can create a wide range of culinary fare from the simplest hor d'oeuvres to the most elegant dinner.

Capacity:	150 seated; 225 standing; 150 in garden.
Catering:	In-house or your own caterer. Entrees range from $15.95 to $35.95 per person.
Rental Fee:	$300 to $600.
Parking:	On the premises.
Note:	Wedding ceremonies are permitted indoors or outdoors. Overnight accommodations are available.

Mt. Vernon Square Ballroom   703-768-3232

2722 Arlington Drive • Alexandria, VA 22306

The Mount Vernon Square Ballroom is the perfect place for your wedding reception or any other special event. Located in the heart of the Route 1 corridor, just 3.5 miles from Route 495, the ballroom is surrounded by walls of windows offering panoramic views and an ideal setting. You and your guests can enjoy the romantic glow of the large fireplace during the winter months. The ballroom allows you the flexibility to customize your wedding and reception to meet your exact needs. It has both a service and catering kitchen and wet and dry bars, offering a broad spectrum of catering options. The ballroom's design will accommodate live bands or a disc jockey and the spacious floor plan allows lots of room for dancing.

Capacity: 200 seated; 230 standing.
Catering: Approved caterers list or your own caterer. Tables and chairs are provided by facility.
Rental Fee: $600 to $2,000. Residents receive reduced rates.
Parking: Residential parking.
Note: Wedding ceremonies are permitted.

Norris House Inn   1-800-644-1806/703-777-1806

108 Loudoun Street, S.W. • Leesburg, VA 20175-2909

Built in 1760, the inn is located in Leesburg's Historic District and combines comfortable outdoor facilities with the charm and homey atmosphere of a bed and breakfast. The 40-foot veranda overlooks the inn's half-acre of award-winning gardens that are used for weddings and receptions. The inn's six guest rooms are provided as a part of a two-day, two-night reception package, and four other guest rooms are available in an annex. Complimentary breakfast for overnight guests is served and other meals can be arranged. The tearoom is available for bridal showers (up to 30 guests) and the patio may be used for a party on the day preceding the wedding or reception.

Capacity: 75 seated; 75 in garden; 75 with tent; 30 in tearoom.
Catering: An approved caterers list is provided, but other caterers may be used by prior arrangement.
Rental Fee: $2,950, includes six guest rooms for two nights.
Parking: Parking lot nearby.
Note: Wedding ceremonies are permitted.

Poplar Springs   540-788-4600

9245 Rogues Road • P.O. Box 275 • Casanova, VA 20139

Poplar Springs is a European-designed fieldstone manor house situated on 200 acres of rolling farmland, forests, streams and lakes.

Located in Casanova, Virginia, four miles from Historic Old Town Warrenton, it is in the heart of Fauquier County. This gorgeous 10,000 square-foot mansion has arched entrance ways, enticing fieldstone walls and dramatic timber beams. The three-story high great hall is framed by balconies, stained glass windows and double French doors. There are large flagstone terraces surrounding the house, outside both the great hall and the library. The main floor is anchored by the impressive great hall, and is adjoined by the library, dining room and sun porch. These rooms, as well as the terraces and surrounding grounds, are available for weddings, receptions, breakfasts, lunches, dinners, business meetings and cultural events. With its unique location and incredible surroundings, Poplar Springs offers the best of all worlds . . . charm, elegance, convenience and privacy.

Capacity: 200 seated; 300 standing; 300 in gardens; 1,000+ with tent.
Catering: In-house. Prices begin at $60 and up.
Rental Fee: $1,500 to $3,000.
Parking: On the premises.
Note: Wedding ceremonies are permitted indoors or outdoors.

Raspberry Plain   703-777-1888

16500 Agape Lane • Leesburg, VA 20176

Set like a jewel in the midst of 50 rolling green acres in historic Loudoun County sits the Georgian colonial estate known since 1731 as Raspberry Plain. The hall's sparkling chandeliers, detailed archway and dramatic staircase complement the elegance of the mansion's rooms: the drawing room's cherry-paneled wainscot wall with built-in bookcases, the spacious Victorian parlor, the dining room with built-in china cabinets and the light-filled conservatory with French doors leading onto the grand terrace, which has a panoramic view of the magnificent formal gardens and mountains, rolling pastures and pond. Every room in the mansion has character and charm. Period furnishings and paintings adorn the mansion. All the main rooms have glass-paneled double-pocket doors, fireplaces and original detailed ceiling moldings.

Capacity: 240 seated; 300 standing; unlimited in gardens; 200 with tent.
Catering: Approved caterers list.
Rental Fee: Starting at $1,500.
Parking: On the premises.
Restrictions: No smoking inside, but at designated outdoor areas. Dancing permitted indoor with a dance floor only.
Note: Wedding ceremonies are permitted.

River Farm 703-768-5700

7931 East Boulevard Drive • Alexandria, VA 22308

The elegant main house is set amid 27 acres of lawns, gardens, meadows, and woods and commands a sweeping view of the Potomac. Over the last 20 years, the Society has established ornamental, educational and test gardens on portions of River Farm, but most of the property remains much as Washington himself would have known it when it was the northernmost tract of his farmland surrounding Mount Vernon. The house, which is registered as a "gentleman's home" by the Fairfax County Historical Society, includes a 45' x 20' ballroom with a tastefully appointed powder room, a large parlor overlooking the river, a dining room opening onto broad porches with garden and river views, and a charming entrance hall featuring a hand-painted floral frieze. The garden patio outside the ballroom may be tented for outdoor events. The house and gardens at River Farm may be rented for weddings, dinner parties, corporate meetings and other events. River Farm is located on the banks of the Potomac, just four miles south of Old Town Alexandria on the George Washington Parkway.

Capacity: 80 to 200, depending on areas selected for event.
Catering: Approved caterers list or your own caterer. Caterer must be approved by facility. The large, state-of-the-art country kitchen is available to caterers for preparation and heating of food.
Rental Fee: $2,500 to $6,400. Call for information. Comprehensive General Liability Insurance is required.
Parking: On the premises.
Restrictions: No amplified music. Portable toilets need to be rented for over 150 capacity.
Note: Wedding ceremonies are permitted.

Rockland Farm Retreat 1-800-895-5098

3609 Lewiston Road • Bumpass, Virginia 23024

Built in 1839, this historic inn is a scenic 75-acre country estate. The majestic trees, quiet pastures and wildlife create a tranquil setting for your special day. Picture your wedding ceremony inside a quiet country church or in a lovely garden. The surrounding areas offer Civil War battlefields, winery tours, state parks, natural trails, horseback riding and golfing.

Capacity: 50 seated; 100 standing; 200 in garden; 300 with a tent.
Catering: In-house caterer or your own caterer. In-house entree cost is $20 per person.
Parking: On the premises.
Note: Wedding ceremonies are permitted indoors or outdoors.

St. Luke Serbian Orthodox Church   703-790-1005

6801 Georgetown Pike • McLean, VA 22101

Located on five acres of lovely countryside, this spacious hall has white walls and white linoleum. The hall overlooks a patio on one side and a grove of trees on the other side. Amenities include a huge commercial kitchen, bar, tables and chairs and convenient parking.

Capacity: 150 to 200 seated; 250 standing; 50 to 75 in garden.
Catering: You must supply your own caterer.
Rental Fee: $750 for four hours, includes use of kitchen, bar, and clean-up. Each additional hour is $125. Site provides three free hours for set-up.
Parking: On the premises.
Note: Wedding ceremonies are permitted outdoors.

Stoneleigh Tavern   703-589-1442

35279 Prestwick Court • Round Hill, VA 20175

Set in the foothills of the Blue Ridge, Stoneleigh Tavern offers a majestic site for outdoor weddings. Wedding parties and their guests will enjoy the spacious, private courtyard which is surrounded by a natural stone wall. The courtyard includes a paved tented area for dining and dancing, and an elevated grassy area provides a natural setting for ceremonies. A full-service restaurant is located on site in a pre-Civil War era mansion. Stoneleigh Tavern is located 14 miles west of Leesburg on the grounds of the Stoneleigh Golf & Country Club, and is easily accessible from the Dulles Greenway.

Capacity: 130 seated; 130 standing; 130 in garden with tent.
Catering: In-house. Entrees range from $16 to $28 per person. Cake cutting fee if you provide your own cake.
Parking: On the premises.
Restrictions: Ceremonies and receptions are held outside in the courtyard.
Note: Wedding ceremonies are permitted.

Valley View House and Gardens   703-321-9757

1562 Leeds Manor Road • Delaplane, VA 20144

Consider having your wedding reception in the beautiful formal gardens of this lovely historic estate. Located in the Virginia Hunt Country 12 miles west of Middleburg, the estate consists of a manor house with a formal English garden on 500 acres of meadowlands and mountains. This romantic setting of understated elegance overlooks an unspoiled valley that was the scene of numerous events in the War Between the States. Valley View is an ideal setting for garden weddings, receptions, engagement parties and rehearsal dinners.

Capacity: 50 indoor; 250 outdoor.
Catering: You must supply your own caterer.
Rental Fee: $350 to $500.
Parking: On the premises.
Note: Wedding ceremonies are permitted.

Wayside Inn Since 1797   540-869-1797
www.nvim.com/waysideinn

7783 Main Street • Middletown, VA 22645

This elegantly restored 18th-century inn, located one hour outside the beltway, boasts 24 lodging rooms appointed with antiques. It's an ideal location for a "dream come true" wedding and reception. Entertain on the terrace, outdoor pavilion and in the garden. At this inn, you can turn back the clock and experience the graciousness of a by-gone era.

Capacity: 150 inside; 350 with garden and patio.
Catering: In-house. Entrees begin at $25 and up.
Rental Fee: $1,000.
Parking: On the premises.
Note: Wedding ceremonies are permitted.

Westfields Marriott   703-818-0300

14750 Conference Center Drive • Chantilly, VA 20151

Located just 30 minutes from the nation's capital, Westfields combines the architectural splendor of Virginia's finest estates with the functional excellence for which it has won numerous awards. The entry's three-and-a-half ton bronze doors exemplify the pride of craftsmanship found throughout this $70 million resort. Inside, just beyond the Lobby, a magnificent Rotunda presents a spectacular dome, classic columns and a generous portion of the center's 450 tons of Greek marble. Westfields offers a variety of indoor and outdoor settings to create an event to reflect your personal tastes. The property has three elegantly furnished ballrooms and a number of intimate banquet spaces to host your special event.

Capacity: 600 seated; 900 standing; 300 in garden; 200 with tent.
Catering: In-house. Entrees begin at $85 per person. Cake cutting fee if you provide your own cake.
Rental Fee: $1,000 to $4,000.
Parking: On the premises. Valet parking is available.
Note: Wedding ceremonies are permitted indoors or outdoors.

Whitehall "The Hunt Country Inn" 703-450-6666

18301 Whitehall Estate Lane • Bluemont, VA 20135

At the foothills of the Blue Ridge stands Whitehall, the treasure of majestic western Loudoun County. This country estate, rich in history and classic architecture, is the ultimate facility for your next reception, conference, or corporate retreat. It features four furnished, climate-controlled meeting rooms, picnic grounds with facilities for softball, volleyball, horseshoes, hayrides and camp-fires, as well as award-winning cuisine by Celebrations. You can begin your special day by saying your vows in the gracious gardens nestled among a canopy of century-old trees on 50 panoramic acres. After the ceremony, your guests can enjoy cocktails and hors d'oeuvres on the magnificent covered brick dining terrace. Then for the perfect ending to a wonderful day, entertain your guests in the ornately detailed grand ballroom, complete with musicians' balcony and marble fireplace.

Capacity: 240 seated; 380 standing; 300+ in garden; 300+ with tent.
Catering: In-house. Entrees range from $40 to $80 per person.
Rental Fee: Varies. Call for information.
Parking: On the premises.
Restrictions: No smoking inside the facility.
Note: Wedding ceremonies are permitted.

Willow Grove Inn   540-672-5982

14079 Plantation Way • Orange, VA 22960

Willow Grove Inn, a renaissance of Southern cooking, hospital-ity, and tradition, is a magnificent 18th-century mansion steeped in history. Located on 37 acres of rolling hills and pastures, the plantation has been carefully preserved. Throughout the centu-ries, Willow Grove has retained a grace of understated elegance combined with Old-World charm. Willow Grove is the perfect setting for a garden wedding — beds of blooming peonies, flow-ering bulbs, and nodding lilies flank a grass-cushioned aisle that meets a giant willow tree. Reception tables are layered with antique damask and tea-dyed antique lace, and beautifully ap-pointed with Willow Grove's collection of antique china and silver.

Capacity: 80 seated; 150 standing; 300 in garden; 300 with tent.
Catering; In-house. Entrees $50 per person. Cake cutting fee if you provide your own cake.
Parking: On the premises.
Note: Wedding ceremonies are permitted.

Woodlawn Plantation   703-780-4000

9000 Richmond Highway • Alexandria, VA 22309

George Washington gave 2000 acres of Mount Vernon to his granddaughter and his favorite nephew as a wedding gift. In addition to the Georgian brick mansion, the site includes Frank Lloyd Wright's Pope-Leighery House, natural trails and formal gardens.

Capacity:	50 in house; 800 with a tent.
Catering:	Approved caterers list. Alcohol must be purchased through Woodlawn.
Rental Fee:	$1,850 to $2,050 for 5 hours for up to 250 persons.
Parking:	On the premises.
Note:	Wedding ceremonies are permitted.

American Legion Post 177   703-273-2250

3939 Oak Drive • Fairfax, VA 22030

American Legion Post 177 offers complete hall rental and catering services. The size and flexibility of this space allows it to be customized for any type of affair. The Post has two halls, both very tastefully decorated. Use your imagination and creativity to turn these rooms into a truly delightful setting. Its menu has varied and appealing selections. Post 177 is conveniently located in Fairfax City and offers substantial free parking facilities on site.

Capacity: 220 seated; 250 standing.
Catering: In-house. Entrees range from $15 to $19 per person.
Rental Fee: Varies.
Parking: On the premises.
Note: Wedding ceremonies are permitted.

Barns of Wolf Trap   703-938-8463

1635 Trap Road • Vienna, VA 22182

Located one-half mile south of the Wolf Trap Farm Park for the Performing Arts, The Barns are ideal for celebrated receptions and corporate and holiday parties. This historical showpiece comprises two 18th-century barns joined under one roof. The Barns offer rustic charm along with modern amenities: heating and air conditioning, fully-equipped commercial kitchen and bar, track lighting. The spacious courtyard in the center of the structure is ideal for additional seating and food stations.

Capacity: 220 seated; 350 standing and with tent.
Catering: Approved caterers list. Alcoholic beverages must be purchased from facility.
Rental Fee: $1,000 and up.
Parking: On the premises.
Restrictions: No smoking.

Great Falls Grange   703-938-8835

c/o Historic Properties Rental Services
9601 Courthouse Road • Vienna, VA 22181

This classic public assembly hall offers two stories, high ceilings with chandeliers, large windows that allow for lots of natural light and a catering kitchen. The large upstairs hall features a full stage outfitted with theatrical lighting and curtains; side windows also provide abundant natural lighting. Ceiling fans and chandeliers hanging from the lofty ceiling complete the room's classic ambience. A spacious banquet hall downstairs adjoins the full catering kitchen. Since its completion in 1929, the Grange has been the site of town assemblies, carnivals, theatrical and musical performances and private celebrations of all kinds.

Capacity: 135 seated; 200 standing; 250 in garden.
Catering: You must supply your own caterer.
Rental Fee: $800.
Parking: On the premises. Parking lot nearby.
Restrictions: Birdseed only may be thrown outside. No confetti or silly string. No open flames or candles. No smoking indoors. No taping, tacking or nailing decorations to the walls.
Note: Wedding ceremonies are permitted indoors or outdoors.

The Lyceum   703-838-4994

201 S. Washington Street • Alexandria, VA 22314

The Lyceum, Alexandria's History Museum, collects and interprets the history and material culture of the City of Alexandria and the surrounding Northern Virginia area. This wonderful site offers one of the largest rooms available in an historic building in Old Town Alexandria. The Museum's Lecture Hall is available for weddings and receptions. The room is elegantly appointed with green wall-to-wall carpet, rose-colored draperies, and coordinating upholstered armchairs. There is a 9' x 22' platform stage, an adjoining kitchen and a concert grand piano. Arrangements can be made to have the exhibition galleries on the first floor open for viewing by your guests.

Capacity: 90 seated; 150 standing.
Catering: You must supply your own caterer. The facility provides six 8' rectangular tables, six 6' rectangular tables and 125 upholstered armchairs.
Rental Fee: $1,100 or $225 per hour.
Parking: On the premises. Handicap parking available.
Restrictions: No smoking. No rice, confetti, birdseed, etc. You must furnish dance floor, not to exceed 12' x 12'.
Note: Wedding ceremonies are permitted.

Old Town Hall   703-385-7858

3999 University Drive • Fairfax, VA 22030

Old Town Hall is the perfect place for a wedding, party, or meeting. Old Town Hall is located in the heart of the nationally recognized City of Fairfax Historic District. Built in 1900 by Joseph E. Willard, the hall was presented to the Town of Fairfax in 1902 and became the center of Fairfax social life. Although neo-Classical in style, the hall tastefully combines Tuscan order columns with Federal-style details, such as the fanlight window over the front doors and the round-headed gabled dormers. The hall is approximately 50 feet long and 40 feet wide, with modern restroom facilities, and a new kitchen with a sink and refrigerator.

Capacity: 150 seated downstairs; 80 seated upstairs; 175 to 200 standing downstairs; 80 to 100 standing upstairs.

Catering: You must supply your own caterer.

Rental Fee: $400 to $750 for 5 hours. Additional hours are available at $75 an hour for main floor and $25 an hour upstairs. Facility requires $150 security deposit. City of Fairfax residents receive $100 discount.

Parking: Limited parking on the premises, but there are parking lots nearby.

Restrictions: No cooking allowed (warming units okay). No open flames. No taping or tacking on walls or floors. No birdseed, confetti, etc. can be thrown.

Note: Wedding ceremonies are permitted.

St. Luke Serbian Orthodox Church   703-790-1005

6801 Georgetown Pike • McLean, VA 22101

Located on five acres of lovely countryside, this spacious hall has white walls and white linoleum. The hall overlooks a patio on one side and a grove of trees on the other side. Amenities include a huge commercial kitchen, bar, tables and chairs and convenient parking.

Capacity: 150 to 200 seated; 250 standing; 50 to 75 in garden.

Catering: You must supply your own caterer.

Rental Fee: $750 for four hours, includes use of kitchen, bar, and clean-up. Each additional hour is $125. Site provides three free hours for set-up.

Parking: On the premises.

Note: Wedding ceremonies are permitted outdoors.

Williams Memorial Hall   703-385-7877 ext. 19

Fairfax Volunteer Fire Department
4081 University Drive • Fairfax, VA 22030

Located in the heart of Fairfax City, this newly renovated hall is one of the area's most affordable sites. It has a wonderful party area with a commercial kitchen, bar, and stage for raised seating. It's a true oasis—the perfect place for weddings and receptions as well as business functions. Lower fees are available for many weekday activities, such as conferences, classes, and seminars. There is ample free parking on site and more nearby.

Capacity: 250 seated; 250 standing.

Catering: You must supply your own caterer.

Rental Fee: $125 per hour plus $200 set-up fee on weekends.

Parking: On the premises.

Restrictions: Smoke-free facility.

Note: Wedding ceremonies are permitted.

Alexandria Black History Resource Center   703-838-4356

638 N. Alfred Street • Alexandria, VA 22314

The Alexandria Black History Resource Center, Northern Virginia's only African-American history museum, offers a wedding site for couples interested in celebrating their ethnic heritage or those looking for a unique historic atmosphere. Couples have a choice of two modern exhibition galleries: the Parker-Gray Gallery and the Robert Robinson Gallery. The galleries can be combined to work as a wedding and reception site. Both galleries offer modern museum lighting which can be adjusted for dramatic effect. Used as just a reception site, the museum can accommodate 150 people. Under supervision provided by the renter, the Center's Watson Reading Room may be rented as a quiet playroom for children. The reading room, adjacent to the Center, has over 1,500 books, videos and periodicals on African-American history and culture. The Center's satellite site, the Alexandria African-American Heritage Park (located off Duke Street on Holland Lane) is a nine-acre park suitable for outdoor weddings. The Center is located in the historic Parker-Gray district of Alexandria and is an appropriate setting for intimate celebrations.

Capacity: 75 seating; 150 standing.
Catering: You must supply your own caterer. The Center has a modern catering kitchen and tables and chairs may be rented on site.
Rental Fee: $100 per hour.
Parking: The Center offers ample on-street parking, without time restrictions.
Restrictions: No smoking.
Note: Wedding ceremonies are permitted. Facility is handicapped accessible.

The Athenaeum   703-548-0035

201 Prince Street • Alexandria, VA 22314

This scaled-down copy of the Temple of Athena, built in 1852 with fluted columns across the verandah, is an historic landmark. Just one block from the Potomac River, in the heart of Old Town Alexandria, it is an intimate and romantic site for gatherings. Features include soaring ceilings, beautiful woodwork, and gleaming old floors that are fine for dancing. Tall windows offer views of cobblestoned streets and 18th-century houses. The two elegant galleries on the main level are usually hung with interesting artworks. Ceiling fans and air conditioning keep guests comfortable. A catering kitchen and the lower gallery are useful for food preparation. An enchanting garden has high brick walls draped with vines. The garden may be canopied.

Capacity: 80 seated; 175 standing; 24 seated in garden; 50 standing in garden; 225 with tent.
Catering: You must supply your own caterer.
Rental Fee: $1,100 for six hours. $185 each additional hour.
Parking: Parking lots nearby. Valet parking can be arranged.
Restrictions: Available only Saturday and Sunday. Nothing attached to walls. No DJs. All rental equipment delivered and removed on day of event. Only votive candles allowed. Art on exhibit will not be removed except by special arrangement. Caterer must be present throughout entire affair, with one worker per 30 guests. No cooking over open flame.
Note: Wedding ceremonies are permitted.

The Bailiwick Inn   703-691-2266

4023 Chain Bridge Road • Fairfax, VA 22030

A 19th-century inn, the Bailiwick Inn is in the heart of historic Fairfax, Virginia. This meticulously restored Federal mansion has been updated to include every amenity and boasts 14 rooms, each named and styled after famous Americans. A luxuriously appointed bridal suite with king-sized bed and Jacuzzi is also available. Double parlors are the perfect location for fireside bridal teas, and elegant rehearsal dinners may be held in the charming Belvoir Room. The English garden at the back of the inn is the perfect setting for a romantic summer ceremony. Family and friends may enjoy the individually decorated lodgings after the celebration is over. Homemade breakfast and an afternoon tea are included in the room rate.

Capacity: 30 seated; 75 standing; 20 in garden; 85 with tent.
Catering: In-house. Entrees range from $35 to $45 per person.
Rental Fee: $200 parlor/function room; $2,700 full house.
Parking: On the premises.
Note: Wedding ceremonies are permitted.

Barns of Wolf Trap   703-938-8463

1635 Trap Road • Vienna, VA 22182

Located one-half mile south of the Wolf Trap Farm Park for the Performing Arts, The Barns are ideal for celebrated receptions and corporate and holiday parties. This historical showpiece comprises two 18th-century barns joined under one roof. The Barns offer rustic charm along with modern amenities: heating and air conditioning, fully-equipped commercial kitchen and bar, track lighting. The spacious courtyard in the center of the structure is ideal for additional seating and food stations.

Capacity: 220 seated; 350 standing and with tent.
Catering: Approved caterers list. Alcoholic beverages must be purchased from facility.

Rental Fee: $1,000 and up.
Parking: On the premises.
Restrictions: No smoking.

Black Horse Inn   540-349-4242

8393 Meetze Road • Warrenton, VA 20187

This elegant, circa 1850, hunt-country estate complete with thoroughbred horses is located only 45 minutes from Washington, D.C. The inn – with ample enclosed porches, landscaped grounds, boxwood gardens, a gazebo and spectacular views – provides a wonderful setting for weddings, receptions, parties and anniversary celebrations. The staff's planning for such events is both talented and imaginative and its lists of menus, champagnes and wines are well chosen. The majestic bridal suite, "Great Expectations," is opulent and romantic with a magnificent bed, fireplace, private porch enclosed by French doors that overlook the front grounds, fireplace, Jacuzzi and separate dressing room. Seven additional guest rooms each have luxurious private baths. For an indoor reception, the inn can accommodate up to 100 guests for cocktails and buffet. For outdoor events, the inn can accommodate up to 150 guests. There is one distinct advantage to reserving the Black Horse Inn for your wedding. Because the rooms are included in the package price, your guests can share in the cost of the site for your wedding! The Black Horse Inn offers not only an excellent location, but also the charm and romance that make the most beautiful of wedding memories.

Capacity: 100 indoors; 150 outdoors.
Catering: In-house or approved caterers list. Entrees range from $25 to $85 per person.
Rental Fee: $1,500 for facility. Packages are available which include rooms.
Parking: On the premises.
Note: Wedding ceremonies are permitted.

Boyhood Home of Robert E. Lee   703-548-8454

607 Oronoco Street • Alexandria, VA 22314

Built in 1795 by John Potts, a friend and business associate of George Washington, this became the home of Robert E. Lee in 1812. The house is decorated in furniture and brass from the Federal Period. The house and gardens are available for weddings and receptions.

Capacity: 40 seated; 100 standing; 100 in garden.
Catering: Approved caterers list.
Rental Fee: $150 per hour.
Parking: On the street and parking in nearby lot.
Restrictions: No smoking or dance inside the home.
Note: Wedding ceremonies are permitted indoors or outdoors.

Bristow Manor   703-368-3558

11507 Valley View Drive • Bristow, VA 20136

Located near Manassas in Bristow, Virginia, just 30 minutes from
the D.C. Beltway, this turn-of-the-century colonial-revival manor
house with its large rooms, 14-foot high ceilings and decorative
moldings, has been completely restored to its former grandeur.
Today, the manor overlooks the beautiful 220-acre Bristow Manor
Golf Club. This elegant manor provides the perfect atmosphere
for any special occasion.

Capacity: 150 seated; 200 standing; 250 in outdoor pavilion.
Catering: In-house. Entrees begin at $22 and up for hor
               d'oeuvres, $25 and up for buffet, and $32 and up for
               sit-down dinner.
Rental Fee: $495 to $1,595.
Parking: On the premises. Handicap parking is available.
Restrictions: No smoking inside home. No open flame candles.
Note: Wedding ceremonies are permitted indoors or outdoors.

Cabell's Mill   703-938-8835

c/o Historic Properties Rental Services
9601 Courthouse Road • Vienna, VA 22181

Once serving Centreville's community as a gristmill, sawmill, and
a sumac mill, Cabell's Mill has been at the center of local commerce and community since its construction shortly after the
Revolutionary War. It features two spacious floors and is perfect
for weddings and receptions. The original chimneys and fireplaces are still in place. The building has been equipped with
ceiling lighting and modernized with central air conditioning and
heating. A large flagstone terrace looks out over Big Rocky Run,
and is ideal for an outdoor wedding.

Capacity: 95 seated on two floors; 125 standing; 150 in garden.
Catering: You must supply your own caterer.
Rental Fee: $950.
Parking: 75 parking spaces on the premises; parking lot nearby.
Restrictions: No confetti or silly string. Birdseed may be thrown
               outside only. All candles must be enclosed with pro-
               tection underneath. No taping, tacking, or nailing
               decorations to walls. No smoking indoors.
Note: Wedding ceremonies are permitted indoors or outdoors.

The Campagna Center   703-549-0111

418 S. Washington Street • Alexandria, VA 22314

The Campagna Center, Inc. is an independent, non-profit social
service organization which has served women and families in
Alexandria for 50 years. Today, after a half-million dollar renova-

tion, the Center's turn-of-the-century grandeur is accentuated by modernized services and amenities. It offers rooms with lots of windows and light, hardwood floors, 14-foot ceilings with chandeliers, and a fully equipped kitchen.

Capacity: 130 seated; 175 standing.
Catering: Approved caterers list or your own caterer.
Rental Fee: Varies according to day and number of hours used. Call for details.
Parking: Limited parking on the premises, but there is a parking lot nearby.
Restrictions: No red beverages served. Amplified music up to 25 decibels. No birdseed, confetti, rice, etc.
Note: Wedding ceremonies are permitted.

Carlyle House Historic Park   703-549-2997

121 N. Fairfax Street • Alexandria, VA 22314

Located in the heart of Old Town Alexandria, the Carlyle House provides wedding receptions and ceremonies with a touch of colonial elegance. Completed in 1753 by Scottish merchant John Carlyle, the Carlyle House with its stone construction and manorhouse design is on the National Register of Historic Places. Its gardens and gazebo make a perfect backdrop when exchanging vows.

Capacity: 100 seated; 100 standing; 25 in garden.
Catering: You must supply your own caterer.
Rental Fee: $1,495.
Parking: Parking lot nearby.
Restrictions: No amplified music or sound system. No rice, flowers, birdseed or confetti may be thrown.
Note: Wedding ceremonies are permitted. Weddings and receptions may be scheduled evenings, except Monday, from 6:30 p.m. to midnight, with caterers arriving at 5:00 p.m.

Clark House   703-938-8835

c/o Historical Properties Rental Service
9601 Courthouse Road • Vienna, VA 22181

The Clark House, a turn-of-the-century Victorian farmhouse, is an ideal site for your corporate meeting or social gathering. The formal entry hall, two large connecting rooms, and the wraparound veranda offers your guests a glimpse back in time when entertaining was an art.

Capacity: 65 seated; 65 standing.
Catering: You must supply your own caterer. Kitchen facilities, tables and chairs are provided. Alcoholic beverages can be brought on the premises with permit.

Rental Fee: $600 for five hours.
Parking: On the premises. Additional parking nearby.
Restrictions: No confetti or silly string. Birdseed may be thrown
                outside only. All candles must be enclosed with pro-
                tection underneath. No smoking indoors. No taping,
                tacking, or nailing decorations to the walls.
Note: Wedding ceremonies are permitted indoors or out-
                doors.

Dranesville Tavern   703-938-8835

c/o Historic Properties Rental Services
9601 Courthouse Road • Vienna, VA 22181

Listed on the National Register of Historic Places, Dranesville
Tavern has been receiving visitors from all walks of life for nearly
two centuries and is well-suited for business meetings, seminars
and retreats, as well as social occasions. Dranesville is conveniently located on Leesburg Pike; Dranesville Tavern is accessible from downtown Washington, Tysons Corner, the Dulles
Corridor and Leesburg. The building features a total of seven
rustic rooms of varying sizes on two floors. The shady back porch
overlooks a rolling meadow leading down to a rambling stream.
The large kitchen is suitable for most catering needs.

Capacity: 80 seated in tavern; 99 standing in tavern; 150 in
                garden.
Catering: You must supply your own caterer.
Rental Fee: $700 for five hours.
Parking: On the premises. Handicap parking available.
Restrictions: No confetti or silly string. Birdseed only may be
                thrown outside. No open flames. No taping, tacking,
                or nailing decorations to the walls. Collection pieces
                must be properly covered with plastic and fabric
                protection. No smoking indoors.
Note: Wedding ceremonies are permitted indoors or out-
                doors.

Evans Farm Inn   703-356-8000

1696 Chain Bridge Road • McLean, VA 22101

Have you always wanted an old-fashioned country wedding?
Evans Farm Inn is a charming 18th-century style building completely decorated in the old manner. You'll be carried back to the
times of the Fairfaxes, the Jeffersons and the Washingtons. You
may have your reception in any of the seven banquet rooms. The
lovely country garden is perfect for a garden wedding or outdoor
reception.

Capacity: 150 seated; 300 standing; unlimited in garden.
Catering: In-house. Entrees range from $12.95 to $29.95 per
                person.

Parking: On the premises.
Note: Wedding ceremonies are permitted indoors or outdoors.

Fauquier Springs Country Club   540-347-2459

9236 Tournament Drive • Warrenton, VA 20186-7848

With its breathtaking view and exquisite outdoor terraces, this
location is the perfect country setting for weddings and other
special occasions. The clubhouse sits on top of a hill overlooking
a spectacular golf course, farm and countryside. A Victorian
staircase graces the foyer, and the ballroom's many windows leads
to wrap-around patios where guests can enjoy the panoramic view
of the meticulously landscaped golf course. The smaller Springs
Room, with its charming marble fireplace, is ideal for pictures.

Capacity: 250 seated in ballroom; 300 standing in ballroom; 50
               in Springs Room.
Catering: In-house. Wedding packages range from $35 to $65
               per person and are all-inclusive. Separate ala carte
               and custom menus are available.
Rental Fee: $100 to $1,000, depends on season and time of day.
Parking: On the premises. Handicap parking is available.
Note: Wedding ceremonies are permitted.

Flint Hill Public House   540-675-1700

675 Zachary Taylor Highway • Flint Hill, VA 22627

Located on five landscaped acres, this restored turn-of-the-century schoolhouse can host small or large receptions, weddings,
rehearsal dinners and corporate events. You may have your
ceremony in the lovely gazebo and gardens, which have a stunning
view of the Blue Ridge Mountains. Inside, on the main level, is a
full-service restaurant and bar with wood-burning stoves. Upstairs, two queen-sized suites, kitchen, and conference room may
be used for seminars and executive retreats. This site is just
moments away from antique shops, wineries, and the Skyline
Drive.

Capacity: 99 seated; 250 standing; 250 in garden.
Catering: In-house. $50 cake cutting fee if you provide your
               own cake.
Rental Fee: $750 to $2,500 (only if complete facility is used).
Parking: On the premises.
Note: Wedding ceremonies are permitted indoors or outdoors.

Gadsby's Tavern Restaurant   703-548-1288

138 N. Royal Street • Alexandria, VA 22314

Once the site of society balls and presidential receptions, this
Williamsburg-style tavern replicates the food, furnishings, and

costumes of colonial times. You may have your reception in the Tap Room or one of the more formal dining rooms. The courtyard behind the tavern can be used for cocktails and hors d'oeuvres or an outdoor wedding ceremony.

Capacity: 100 seated; 150 standing; 175 in garden; 100 seated in adjacent 19th-century ballroom.
Catering: In-house. Entrees range from $15 to $45 per person.
Rental Fee: $850.
Parking: On the premises.
Restrictions: Period music in historic part of property. Your choice of music in 19th-century ballroom.
Note: Wedding ceremonies are permitted.

Great Falls Grange   703-938-8835

c/o Historic Properties Rental Services
9601 Courthouse Road • Vienna, VA 22181

This classic public assembly hall offers two stories, high ceilings with chandeliers, large windows that allow for lots of natural light, and a catering kitchen. The large upstairs hall features a full stage outfitted with theatrical lighting and curtains; side windows also provide abundant natural lighting. Ceiling fans and chandeliers hanging from the lofty ceiling complete the room's classic ambience. A spacious banquet hall downstairs adjoins the full catering kitchen. Since its completion in 1929, the Grange has been the site of town assemblies, carnivals, theatrical and musical performances and private celebrations of all kinds.

Capacity: 135 seated; 200 standing; 250 in garden.
Catering: You must supply your own caterer.
Rental Fee: $800.
Parking: On the premises. Parking lot nearby.
Restrictions: Birdseed only may be thrown outside. No confetti or silly string. No open flames or candles. No smoking indoors. No taping, tacking or nailing decorations to the walls.
Note: Wedding ceremonies are permitted indoors or outdoors.

Green Spring Manor   703-938-8835

c/o Historic Properties Rental Services
9601 Courthouse Road • Vienna, VA 22181

The Green Spring Farm Manor, circa 1760, is the centerpiece of what was once a 540-acre farm. Today, the manor house is part of Green Spring Gardens Park, and the formal grounds around the manor house are available for garden weddings. This historic manor is a great place to celebrate the occasion of your marriage.

Capacity: 100 in garden; 100 with tent.
Catering: You must supply your own caterer.

Rental Fee: $700.
Parking: On the premises.
Restrictions: Outdoors only. No confetti or silly string. Birdseed may be thrown outside only. All candles must be enclosed with something to catch the drips. No smoking indoors. No taping, tacking, or nailing decorations to the walls.
Note: Wedding ceremonies are permitted.

Gunston Hall   703-550-9220

10709 Gunston Road • Mason Neck • Lorton, VA 22079

Built in 1755, Gunston Hall was the plantation home of George Mason, author of the Virginia Declaration of Rights and framer of the United States Constitution. The life and times of 18th-century America are vividly evoked by the commodious house and gardens overlooking the Potomac River. Weddings and other events may be held at various locations in the beautifully restored gardens and grounds of Gunston Hall, as well as in the banquet room and adjoining fountain courtyard located in the Ann Mason Building. The elegant mansion provides the perfect backdrop for weddings and receptions. Guided tours of the historic house are included as a part of any function. Gunston Hall is a spectacular place to celebrate a special day.

Capacity: 150 seated; 225 standing; unlimited in gardens.
Catering: In-house or your own caterer. In-house entrees range from $22 to $40 per person.
Rental Fee: $1,500 to $2,300.
Parking: On the premises. Handicap parking available.
Note: Wedding ceremonies are permitted.

Hackwood   800-365-8021

534 Red Bud Road • Winchester, VA 22603

Hackwood was the center of many intriguing and historical events, including the duel between Peyton Smith and Joseph Holmes in 1809 and the 3rd Battle of Winchester during the Civil War. Originally called Hackwood Park Estate, the Georgian-style house is enhanced by a welcoming stone walk with boxwood. The grand veranda on the west side looks out over a beautifully landscaped green with a large lake in the distance. The mansion offers two large parlors on the main floor, a wide center hall, and additional space on the second level.

Capacity: 120 seated downstairs; 80 seated upstairs; 300 standing; 200 in garden; 1,000 with tent.
Catering: In-house. Entrees range from $55 to $85 per person.
Rental Fee: $1,500.
Parking: On the premises.
Note: Wedding ceremonies are permitted.

Hazel River Inn Bed and Breakfast   540-937-5854

11227 Eggborneville Road • Culpeper, VA 22701

This 18th-century inn is ideal for a romantic country wedding. The inn welcomes small receptions for any occasion, and now offers Sunday brunch and afternoon tea. You may hold your brunch or party in the sun room, or outdoors by the pool and gardens. The menu features produce and herbs grown on the premises by an in-house horticulturist.

Capacity: 30 seated; 40 standing; 100 in garden; 100 with tent.
Catering: In-house or approved caterers list. Entrees begin at
                 $25 for lunch, $40 for dinner, and $35 for receptions.
Rental Fee: $350.
Parking: On the premises.
Note: Wedding ceremonies are permitted.

The Hermitage Inn Restaurant   703-266-1623

7134 Main Street • Clifton, VA 20124

Once a luxury retreat for the affluent, "The Clifton Hotel" was host to the likes of Ulysses S. Grant, Theodore Roosevelt and Rutherford B. Hayes. As The Hermitage Inn Restaurant, this graceful landmark has been faithfully restored to its original beauty of 1869. Charming, romantic and secluded, the restaurant is ideal for an intimate dinner for two or an elegant wedding for 200. Take a moment to enjoy the antiquity of the setting, enhanced by original hardwood floors, French doors and four fireplaces. The outdoor terrace, with a waterfall and lovely garden, is perfect for a wedding ceremony or any special event.

Capacity: 160 seated; 250 standing; 100 in garden; 160 with tent.
Catering: In-house. Entrees range from $40 to $60 per person.
Parking: On the premises.
Note: Wedding ceremonies are permitted.

Hunter House   703-938-8835

c/o Historic Properties Rental Service
9601 Courthouse Road • Vienna, VA 22181

Built in 1890, Hunter House was home to Scottish immigrant John C. Hunter. After Prohibition ended, William Davidson operated Distillery #4 there and produced a wine which he called *Virginia Maid*. While the house maintains much of its original character, through the years it has been expanded into a spacious two-story facility. Hunter House provides an atmosphere of casual country elegance. The building features several air-conditioned rooms and a kitchen, as well as a screened-in porch. The adjacent lawn is a popular place for outdoor weddings and receptions.

Capacity: 40 seated; 75 standing; 150 in garden.
Catering: You must supply your own caterer.
Rental Fee: $800.
Parking: On the premises.
Restrictions: No confetti or silly string. Birdseed only may be thrown outside. No smoking indoors. No open flames. No taping, tacking, or nailing decorations to the walls.
Note: Wedding ceremonies permitted indoors or outdoors.

L'Auberge Provencale   1-800-638-1702/540-837-1375

P.O. Box 119 • White Post, VA 22663

To discover the feeling of a true inn of the South of France, come to L'Auberge Provencale. Just one hour from the D.C. Beltway and two hours from Baltimore, the inn is located in Virginia Hunt Country. Have your reception, holiday celebration or retirement party at the manor house, Mt. Airy (circa 1753). Choose from one of three intimate dining rooms decorated with fine antiques, fine art, Provencale fabrics, and an eclectic menagerie of hand-crafted animals. Traveling to L'Auberge Provencale, you will take the back roads of beautiful Clark County, framed by the Shenandoah River and the gently rolling Blue Ridge Mountains. Enjoy the simple pleasures of antique shopping, horseback riding, hiking, bike riding, golfing, canoeing, fishing, or simply sitting on the spacious porch with a glass of wine.

Capacity: 75 seated; 75 standing.
Catering: In-house. Five-course dinner from $58 and up per person.
Rental Fee: $350, if number of guests exceed 25.
Parking: On the premises.
Note: Wedding ceremonies are permitted indoors or outdoors.

La Bergerie   703-683-1007

218 North Lee Street • Alexandria, VA 22314

Located in the heart of colonial Old Town Alexandria, La Bergerie is decorated with French countryside paintings, richly appointed leather banquettes, and crystal chandeliers. Its charming and intimate atmosphere provides the perfect ambiance for any special occasion. Cocktail receptions may be held in the Atrium and the two private party rooms can be used for smaller events. French cuisine with Basque specialties will delight your palate. Your guests can stroll down cobblestone streets, tour quaint residences, shop in 1700-era stores, and listen to street entertainment. La Bergerie, located near Market Square and the famous Torpedo Factory Arts Center, is 15 minutes from Washington, D.C., via George Washington Parkway.

Capacity: 85 in main room; 48 in large private room; 26 in small private room.

Catering: In-house. Entrees range from $13 to $25. Cake cut-
              ting fee if provide own cake.
Rental Fee: None. Large room guarantee is 30 and the small room
              guarantee is 20.
Parking: Parking lot nearby.
Note: Wedding ceremonies are permitted.

Lee-Fendall House   703-548-1789

614 Oronoco Street • Alexandria, VA 22314

Built in 1785, it has been home to 37 Lees. Furnished with many
of the Lee family heirlooms, it is listed on the National Register of
Historic Places. The lovely white clapboard home and its garden
are perfect for weddings and receptions. Guests are greeted in the
garden under the massive magnolia, ancient chestnuts and ginkgo
trees, or by candlelight and antiques in the historic house.

Capacity: 85 standing; 100 in garden.
Catering: Approved caterer list or your own caterer.
Rental Fee: $150 per hour.
Parking: Parking lot nearby. Residential parking.
Restrictions: No amplified musical instruments.
Note: Wedding ceremonies are permitted indoors or outdoors.

The Longbarn   540-687-4137/540-687-3770

37129 Adams Green Lane • Middleburg, VA 20118

Enjoy a picturesque European getaway in this more than 100-
year-old renovated barn in historic Middleburg, Virginia. English
gardens nestled under a canopy of hardwood trees surround a
swimming pond and gazebo. The Longbarn features an elegant
Italian country style interior with spacious bedrooms, air conditioning, fireplaces, and a large library for the pleasure and comfort
of your guests. A delicious breakfast with warm breads and other
specialties from the old country is served. Horseback and bicycle
riding are nearby, as well as golf courses, antique shops, vineyards
and fine dining. The quaint and charming Corn Crib Chapel is
perfect for a small romantic wedding ceremony or renewal of
vows. Treat yourself to the generous hospitality of your gracious
Italian hostess and serenity of this lovely estate.

Capacity: 50 seated; 60 standing; 150 in garden; 150 with tent.
Catering: You must supply your own caterer.
Rental Fee: $1,550 to $2,550, includes 1 or 2 nights use of three
              bedrooms (double occupancy) and full breakfast.
Parking: On the premises.
Restrictions: No smoking indoors. No pets.
Note: Wedding ceremonies are permitted.

The Lyceum   703-838-4994

201 S. Washington Street • Alexandria, VA 22314

The Lyceum, Alexandria's History Museum, collects and interprets the history and material culture of the City of Alexandria and
the surrounding northern Virginia area. This wonderful site offers
one of the largest rooms available in an historic building in Old
Town Alexandria. The Museum's Lecture Hall is available for
weddings and receptions. The room is elegantly appointed with
green wall-to-wall carpet, rose-colored draperies, and coordinating upholstered armchairs. There is a 9' x 22' platform stage, an
adjoining kitchen and a concert grand piano. Arrangements can
be made to have the exhibition galleries on the first floor open for
viewing by your guests.

Capacity: 90 seated; 150 standing.
Catering: You must supply your own caterer. The facility pro-
               vides six 8' rectangular tables, six 6' rectangular
               tables and 125 upholstered armchairs.
Rental Fee: $1,100 or $225 per hour.
Parking: On the premises. Handicap parking available.
Restrictions: No smoking. No rice, confetti, birdseed, etc. You
               must furnish dance floor, not to exceed 12' x 12'.
Note: Wedding ceremonies are permitted.

The Mimslyn Inn   1-800-296-5105/540-743-5105

401 West Main Street • Luray, VA 22835

Imagine having your wedding reception at an elegant antebellum old-
fashioned plantation that features old-fashioned southern hospitality, 14 acres of exquisite gardens and lawns, and a main lobby graced
by a winding staircase and beautiful fireplace. It is sure to make you
feel like Scarlett O'Hara. The Mimslyn Inn features formal gardens
that are perfect for an outside ceremony and a ballroom just right to
dance the night away. The chef can create a wide range of culinary
fare from the simplest hor d'oeuvres to the most elegant dinner.

Capacity: 150 seated; 225 standing; 150 in garden.
Catering: In-house or your own caterer. Entrees range from
               $15.95 to $35.95 per person.
Rental Fee: $300 to $600.
Parking: On the premises.
Note: Wedding ceremonies are permitted indoors or out-
               doors. Overnight accommodations are available.

Norris House Inn   1-800-644-1806/703-777-1806

108 Loudoun Street, S.W. • Leesburg, VA 20175-2909

Built in 1760, the inn is located in Leesburg's Historic District and
combines comfortable outdoor facilities with the homey atmo-

sphere and charm of a bed and breakfast. The 40-foot veranda overlooks the inn's half-acre of award-winning gardens that are used for weddings and receptions. The inn's six guest rooms are provided as a part of a two-day, two-night reception package and four other guest rooms are available in an annex. Complimentary breakfast for overnight guests is served and other meals can be arranged. The tearoom is available for bridal showers (up to 30 guests) and the patio may be used for a party on the day preceding the wedding or reception.

Capacity: 75 seated; 75 in garden; 75 with tent; 30 in tearoom.
Catering: An approved caterers list is provided, but other caterers may be used by prior arrangement.
Rental Fee: $2,950, includes six guest rooms for two nights.
Parking: Parking lot nearby.
Note: Wedding ceremonies are permitted.

The Old Schoolhouse   703-938-8835

c/o Historic Properties Rental Services
9601 Courthouse Road • Vienna, VA 22181

The Old Schoolhouse is a prime example of the traditional one-room schoolhouses which dotted the landscape in the late 1800s and early 1900s. This wonderful space offers two rooms and a small kitchen area for up to 49 people for small, intimate occasions. It can also be rented in conjunction with the Great Falls Grange for larger events.

Capacity: 49 seated and standing; 100 with tent.
Catering: You must supply your own caterer.
Rental Fee: $550.
Parking: On the premises.
Restrictions: No confetti or silly string. No open flames. Birdseed only may be thrown outside. No smoking indoors. No taping, tacking, or nailing decorations to the wall.
Note: Wedding ceremonies are permitted indoors or outdoors.

Old Town Hall   703-385-7858

3999 University Drive • Fairfax, VA 22030

Old Town Hall is the perfect place for a wedding, party, or meeting. Old Town Hall is located in the heart of the nationally recognized City of Fairfax Historic District. Built in 1900 by Joseph E. Willard, the hall was presented to the Town of Fairfax in 1902 and became the center of Fairfax social life. Although neo-Classical in style, the hall tastefully combines Tuscan order columns with Federal-style details, such as the fanlight window over the front doors and the round-headed gabled dormers. The hall is approximately 50 feet long and 40 feet wide, with modern restroom facilities, and a new kitchen with a sink and refrigerator.

Capacity: 150 seated downstairs; 80 seated upstairs; 175 to 200 standing downstairs; 80 to 100 standing upstairs.

Catering: You must supply your own caterer.

Rental Fee: $400 to $750 for 5 hours. Additional hours are available at $75 an hour for main floor and $25 an hour upstairs. Facility requires $150 security deposit. City of Fairfax residents receive $100 discount.

Parking: Limited parking on the premises, but there are parking lots nearby.

Restrictions: No cooking allowed (warming units okay). No open flames. No taping or tacking on walls or floors. No birdseed, confetti, etc. can be thrown.

Note: Wedding ceremonies are permitted.

Poplar Springs   540-788-4600

9245 Rogues Road • P.O. Box 275 • Casanova, VA 20139

Poplar Springs is a European-designed fieldstone manor house situated on 200 acres of rolling farmland, forests, streams and lakes. Located in Casanova, Virginia, four miles from Historic Old Town Warrenton, it is in the heart of Fauquier County. This gorgeous 10,000-square-foot mansion has arched entrance ways, enticing fieldstone walls and dramatic timber beams. The three-story high great hall is framed by balconies, stained glass windows and double French doors. There are large flagstone terraces surrounding the house, outside both the great hall and the library. The main floor is anchored by the impressive great hall, and is adjoined by the library, dining room and sun porch. These rooms, as well as the terraces and surrounding grounds, are available for weddings, receptions, breakfasts, lunches, dinners, business meetings and cultural events. With its unique location and incredible surroundings, Poplar Springs offers the best of all worlds . . . charm, elegance, convenience and privacy.

Capacity: 200 seated; 300 standing; 300 in gardens; 1,000+ with tent.

Catering: In-house. Prices begin at $60 and up.

Rental Fee: $1,500 to $3,000.

Parking: On the premises.

Note: Wedding ceremonies are permitted indoors or outdoors.

Raspberry Plain   703-777-1888

16500 Agape Lane • Leesburg, VA 20176

Set like a jewel in the midst of 50 rolling green acres in historic Loudoun County sits the Georgian colonial estate known since 1731 as Raspberry Plain. The hall's sparkling chandeliers, detailed archway and dramatic staircase complement the elegance of the mansion's rooms: the drawing room's cherry-paneled wainscot wall with built-in bookcases, the spacious Victorian parlor, the dining room with built-in china cabinets and the light-filled conservatory with French doors leading onto the grand terrace, which has a panoramic view of the magnificent formal gardens and mountains, rolling pastures and pond. Every room in the mansion has character and charm. Period furnishings and paintings adorn the mansion. All the main rooms have glass-paneled double-pocket doors, fireplaces and original detailed ceiling moldings.

Capacity: 240 seated; 300 standing; unlimited in gardens; 200 with tent.
Catering: Approved caterers list.
Rental Fee: Starting at $1,500.
Parking: On the premises.
Restrictions: No smoking inside, but at designated outdoor areas. Dancing permitted indoor with a dance floor only.
Note: Wedding ceremonies are permitted.

River Farm   703-768-5700

7931 East Boulevard Drive • Alexandria, VA 22308

The elegant main house is set amid 27 acres of lawns, gardens, meadows, and woods, and commands a sweeping view of the Potomac. Over the last 20 years, the Society has established ornamental, educational and test gardens on portions of River Farm, but most of the property remains much as Washington himself would have known it when it was the northernmost tract of his farmland surrounding Mount Vernon. The house, which is registered as a "gentleman's home" by the Fairfax County Historical Society, includes a 45' x 20' ballroom with a tastefully appointed powder room, a large parlor overlooking the river, a dining room opening onto broad porches with garden and river views, and a charming entrance hall featuring a hand-painted floral frieze. The garden patio outside the ballroom may be tented for outdoor events. The house and gardens at River Farm may be rented for weddings, dinner parties, corporate meetings and other events. River Farm is located on the banks of the Potomac, just four miles south of Old Town Alexandria on the George Washington Parkway.

Capacity: 80 to 200, depending on areas selected for event.
Catering: Approved caterers list or your own caterer. Caterer must be approved by facility. The large, state-of-the-art country kitchen is available to caterers for preparation and heating of food.
Rental Fee: $2,500 to $6,400. Call for information. Comprehensive General Liability Insurance is required.
Parking: On the premises.
Restrictions: No amplified music. Portable toilets need to be rented for over 150 capacity.
Note: Wedding ceremonies are permitted.

Rockland Farm Retreat   1-800-895-5098

3609 Lewiston Road • Bumpass, Virginia 23024

Built in 1839, this historic inn is a scenic 75-acre country estate.
The majestic trees, quiet pastures and wildlife create a tranquil
setting for your special day. Picture your wedding ceremony
inside a quiet country church or in a lovely garden. The surrounding areas offer Civil War battlefields, winery tours, state parks,
natural trails, horseback riding and golfing.

Capacity: 50 seated; 100 standing; 200 in garden; 300 with tent.
Catering: In-house caterer or your own caterer. In-house entree
               cost is $20 per person.
Parking: On the premises.
Note: Wedding ceremonies are permitted indoors or out-
               doors.

Seaport Inn   703-549-2341

6 King Street • Alexandria, VA 22314

This circa 1765, historic landmark previously owned by George
Washington's military aide-de-camp provides a magnificent setting for wedding receptions. This location offers three elegant
dining rooms. The John Fitzgerald Room, with its dark wood
trim, rustic decor and complementing fireplace, is a charming
asset to your party. The Potomac River Room offers a panoramic
view of the Potomac River. The view, along with the room's rich
brick color scheme accented with brass, creates a truly elegant
atmosphere. The Williamsburg Room with its colonial decor is
ideal for intimate parties.

Capacity: 130.
Catering: In-house. Entrees range from $16.95 to $20.95 per
               person. Cake cutting fee is $35.
Deposit: $100 to $175.
Parking: Parking garages nearby.
Note: Wedding ceremonies are permitted.

Stone Mansion   703-938-8835

c/o Historic Properties Rental Services
9601 Courthouse Road • Vienna, VA 22181

Commodore Walter Brooke built a small wood frame manor house
in 1777 following his service in the Virginia Naval Forces during the
Revolutionary War. Enlarged over the years, and covered in stone
in the 1940s, the mansion offers three separate banquet rooms, a
screened porch, a large formal entry with a curved staircase and a
large catering kitchen. The beautifully landscaped garden is perfect
for outdoor ceremonies or receptions.

Capacity: 50 seated; 75 standing; 150 in garden.
Catering: You must supply your own caterer.
Rental Fee: $800.
Parking: On the premises and you may park on the street.
Restrictions: No confetti or silly string. Birdseed only may be thrown outside. All candles must be enclosed and have protection underneath to catch the dripping wax. No smoking indoors. No taping, tacking, or nailing decorations to the walls.
Note: Wedding ceremonies are permitted indoors or outdoors.

Torpedo Factory Art Center   703-838-4199

105 North Union Street • Alexandria, VA 22314

The Torpedo Factory Art Center, originally built in 1918 following World War I to manufacture torpedoes, has been transformed into a modern art center housing 83 working artists' studios and five cooperative galleries. The central hall, a two-story atrium, is a unique and informal setting which can accommodate receptions and ceremonies. It is 160 feet long and is topped with a balcony, catwalks, large peripheral windows and a central skylight. The hall is surrounded by glass walls displaying the artwork of the individual studios. The hall lends itself to decoration in many styles, and photographs of the site decorated for past events are available to view. The Art Center is located on the Potomac River waterfront in the heart of Old Town Alexandria, just minutes south of National Airport and inside the Beltway.

Capacity: 400 seated; 1,200 standing.
Catering: You must supply your own caterer.
Rental Fee: $1,500 for the first floor, $1,700 for first floor and balcony; $2,500 for entire building. Some additional fees for staff, security and insurance required.
Parking: Parking is available across the street and there are parking lots nearby.
Restrictions: No red wine, rice, birdseed, or glitter allowed in the Art Center. No alcohol allowed behind the Art Center on the dock/marina area.
Note: Wedding ceremonies are permitted.

Valley View House and Gardens   703-321-9757

1562 Leeds Manor Road • Delaplane, VA 20144

Consider having your wedding reception in the beautiful formal gardens of this lovely historic estate. Located in the Virginia Hunt Country 12 miles west of Middleburg, the estate consists of a manor house with a formal English garden on 500 acres of meadowlands and mountains. This romantic setting of understated elegance overlooks an unspoiled valley that was the scene of numerous events in the War Between the States. Valley View is an ideal setting for garden weddings, receptions, engagement parties and rehearsal dinners.

Capacity: 50 indoor; 250 outdoor.
Catering: You must supply your own caterer.
Rental Fee: $350 to $500.
Parking: On the premises.
Note: Wedding ceremonies are permitted.

Wakefield Chapel   703-938-8835

c/o Historic Properties Rental Services
9601 Courthouse Road • Vienna, VA 22181

Built in 1899, Wakefield Chapel is named for its first minister, and is the answer for anyone searching for a quaint, picturesque setting for a wedding. Guests sit on antique wooden pews, and the original pulpit is available for use. There is a large bridal dressing area on the lower level.

Capacity: 99.
Rental Fee: $500 for three hours.
Parking: On the premises.
Restrictions: No confetti or silly string. Birdseed only may be thrown outside. All candles must be enclosed with something to catch the drips. No smoking indoors. No taping, tacking, or nailing decorations to the walls. No alcohol is permitted in the chapel.

Wayside Inn Since 1797   540-869-1797
www.nvim.com/waysideinn

7783 Main Street • Middletown, VA 22645

This elegantly restored 18th-century inn, located one hour outside the beltway, boasts 24 lodging rooms appointed with antiques. It's an ideal location for a "dream come true" wedding and reception. Entertain on the terrace, outdoor pavilion and in the garden. At this inn, you can turn back the clock and experience the graciousness of a by-gone era.

Capacity: 150 inside; 350 with garden and patio.
Catering: In-house. Entrees begin at $25 and up.
Rental Fee: $1,000.
Parking: On the premises.
Note: Wedding ceremonies are permitted.

Whitehall "The Hunt Country Inn"   703-450-6666

18301 Whitehall Estate Lane • Bluemont, VA 20135

At the foothills of the Blue Ridge stands Whitehall, the treasure of majestic western Loudoun County. This country estate, rich in history and classic architecture, is the ultimate facility for your next reception, conference, or corporate retreat. It features four furnished, climate-controlled meeting rooms, picnic grounds with facilities for softball, volleyball, horseshoes, hayrides and camp-fires, as well as award-winning cuisine by Celebrations. You can begin your special day by saying your vows in the gracious gardens nestled among a canopy of century-old trees on 50 panoramic acres. After the ceremony, your guests can enjoy cocktails and hors d'oeuvres on the magnificent covered brick dining terrace. Then for the perfect ending to a wonderful day, entertain your guests in the ornately detailed grand ballroom complete with musicians' balcony and marble fireplace.

Capacity:	240 seated; 380 standing; 300+ in garden; 300+ with tent.
Catering:	In-house. Entrees range from $40 to $80 per person.
Rental Fee:	Varies. Call for information.
Parking:	On the premises.
Restrictions:	No smoking inside the facility.
Note:	Wedding ceremonies are permitted.

Willow Grove Inn   540-672-5982

14079 Plantation Way • Orange, VA 22960

Willow Grove Inn, a renaissance of Southern cooking, hospital-ity, and tradition, is a magnificent 18th-century mansion steeped in history. Located on 37 acres of rolling hills and pastures, the plantation has been carefully preserved. Throughout the centu-ries, Willow Grove has retained a grace of understated elegance combined with Old-World charm. Willow Grove is the perfect setting for a garden wedding — beds of blooming peonies, flow-ering bulbs, and nodding lilies flank a grass-cushioned aisle that meets a giant willow tree. Reception tables are layered with antique damask and tea-dyed antique lace, and beautifully ap-pointed with Willow Grove's collection of antique china and silver.

Capacity:	80 seated; 150 standing; 300 in garden; 300 with tent.
Catering;	In-house. Entrees $50 per person. Cake cutting fee if you provide your own cake.
Parking:	On the premises.
Note:	Wedding ceremonies are permitted.

Woodlawn Plantation   703-780-4000

9000 Richmond Highway • Alexandria, VA 22309

George Washington gave 2000 acres of Mount Vernon to his granddaughter and his favorite nephew as a wedding gift. In addition to the Georgian brick mansion, the site includes Frank Lloyd Wright's Pope-Leighery House, natural trails and formal gardens.

Capacity: 50 in house; 800 with a tent.
Catering: Approved caterers list. Alcohol must be purchased through Woodlawn.
Rental Fee: $1,850 to $2,050 for 5 hours for up to 250 persons.
Parking: On the premises.
Note: Wedding ceremonies are permitted.

The Bailiwick Inn   703-691-2266

4023 Chain Bridge Road • Fairfax, VA 22030

A 19th-century inn, the Bailiwick Inn is in the heart of historic
Fairfax, Virginia. This meticulously restored Federal mansion has
been updated to include every amenity and boasts 14 rooms, each
named and styled after famous Americans. A luxuriously appointed bridal suite with king-sized bed and Jacuzzi is also
available. Double parlors are the perfect location for fireside
bridal teas, and elegant rehearsal dinners may be held in the
charming Belvoir Room. The English garden at the back of the inn
is the perfect setting for a romantic summer ceremony. Family and
friends may enjoy the individually decorated lodgings after the
celebration is over. Homemade breakfast and an afternoon tea are
included in the room rate.

Capacity: 30 seated; 75 standing; 20 in garden; 85 with tent.
Catering: In-house. Entrees range from $35 to $45 per person.
Rental Fee: $200 parlor/function room; $2,700 full house.
Parking: On the premises.
Note: Wedding ceremonies are permitted.

Black Horse Inn   540-349-4242

8393 Meetze Road • Warrenton, VA 20187

This elegant, circa 1850, hunt-country estate complete with thoroughbred horses is located only 45 minutes from Washington,
D.C. The inn – with ample enclosed porches, landscaped grounds,
boxwood gardens, a gazebo and spectacular views – provides a
wonderful setting for weddings, receptions, parties and anniversary celebrations. The staff's planning for such events is both
talented and imaginative and its lists of menus, champagnes and
wines are well chosen. The majestic bridal suite, "Great Expectations," is opulent and romantic with a magnificent bed, fireplace,
private porch enclosed by French doors that overlook the front
grounds, fireplace, Jacuzzi and separate dressing room. Seven
additional guest rooms each have luxurious private baths. For an
indoor reception, the inn can accommodate up to 100 guests for
cocktails and buffet. For outdoor events, the inn can accommodate up to 150 guests. There is one distinct advantage to reserving
the Black Horse Inn for your wedding. Because the rooms are
included in the package price, your guests can share in the cost of
the site for your wedding! The Black Horse Inn offers not only an
excellent location, but also the charm and romance that make the
most beautiful of wedding memories.

Capacity: 100 indoors; 150 outdoors.
Catering: In-house or approved caterers list. Entrees range
                from $25 to $85 per person.
Rental Fee: $1,500 for facility. Packages are available which in-
                clude rooms.

Parking: On the premises.
Note: Wedding ceremonies are permitted.

Hazel River Inn Bed and Breakfast   540-937-5854

11227 Eggborneville Road • Culpeper, VA 22701

This 18th-century inn is ideal for a romantic country wedding. The inn welcomes small receptions for any occasion, and now offers Sunday brunch and afternoon tea. You may hold your brunch or party in the sun room, or outdoors by the pool and gardens. The menu features produce and herbs grown on the premises by an in-house horticulturist.

Capacity: 30 seated; 40 standing; 100 in garden; 100 with tent.
Catering: In-house or approved caterers list. Entrees begin at $25 for lunch, $40 for dinner, and $35 for receptions.
Rental Fee: $350.
Parking: On the premises.
Note: Wedding ceremonies are permitted.

L'Auberge Provencale   1-800-638-1702/540-837-1375

P.O. Box 119 • White Post, VA 22663

To discover the feeling of a true inn of the South of France, come to L'Auberge Provencale. Just one hour from the D.C. Beltway and two hours from Baltimore, the inn is located in Virginia Hunt Country. Have your reception, holiday celebration or retirement party at the manor house, Mt. Airy (circa 1753). Choose from one of three intimate dining rooms decorated with fine antiques, fine art, Provencale fabrics, and an eclectic menagerie of hand-crafted animals. Traveling to L'Auberge Provencale, you will take the back roads of beautiful Clark County, framed by the Shenandoah River and the gently rolling Blue Ridge Mountains. Enjoy the simple pleasures of antique shopping, horseback riding, hiking, bike riding, golfing, canoeing, fishing, or simply sitting on the spacious porch with a glass of wine.

Capacity: 75 seated; 75 standing.
Catering: In-house. Five-course dinner begin at $58 and up per person.
Rental Fee: $350, if number of guests exceed 25.
Parking: On the premises.
Note: Wedding ceremonies are permitted indoors or outdoors.

The Longbarn   540-687-4137/540-687-3770

37129 Adams Green Lane • Middleburg, VA 20118

Enjoy a picturesque European getaway in this more than 100-year-old renovated barn in historic Middleburg, Virginia. English gardens nestled under a canopy of hardwood trees surround a swimming pond and gazebo. The Longbarn features an elegant Italian country style interior with spacious bedrooms, air conditioning, fireplaces, and a large library for the pleasure and comfort of your guests. A delicious breakfast with warm breads and other specialties from the old country is served. Horseback and bicycle riding are nearby, as well as golf courses, antique shops, vineyards and fine dining. The quaint and charming Corn Crib Chapel is perfect for a small romantic wedding ceremony or renewal of vows. Treat yourself to the generous hospitality of your gracious Italian hostess and serenity of this lovely estate.

Capacity: 50 seated; 60 standing; 150 in garden; 150 with tent.
Catering: You must supply your own caterer.
Rental Fee: $1,550 to $2,550, includes 1 or 2 nights use of three bedrooms (double occupancy) and full breakfast.
Parking: On the premises.
Restrictions: No smoking indoors. No pets.
Note: Wedding ceremonies are permitted.

The Mimslyn Inn   1-800-296-5105/540-743-5105

401 West Main Street • Luray, VA 22835

Imagine having your wedding reception at an elegant antebellum plantation that features old-fashioned southern hospitality, 14 acres of exquisite gardens and lawns, and a main lobby graced by a winding staircase and beautiful fireplace. It is sure to make you feel like Scarlett O'Hara. The Mimslyn Inn features formal gardens that are perfect for an outside ceremony and a ballroom just right to dance the night away. The chef can create a wide range of culinary fare from the simplest hor d'oeuvres to the most elegant dinner.

Capacity: 150 seated; 225 standing; 150 in garden.
Catering: In-house or your own caterer. Entrees range from $15.95 to $35.95 per person.
Rental Fee: $300 to $600.
Parking: On the premises.
Note: Wedding ceremonies are permitted indoors or outdoors. Overnight accommodations are available.

Morrison House   703-838-8000

116 South Alfred Street • Alexandria, VA 22314

Looking for a quiet, elegant, romantic escape? Look no further than Old Town Alexandria's award-winning Morrison House. The European warmth and charm of this small hotel are as welcoming as the butlers who greet you at the door. Located just minutes from National Airport and downtown Washington, D.C., the Federal style inn boasts ornate woodwork, decorative fireplaces and fanlight windows. Its 45 guest rooms, each unique, feature Federal period reproductions including mahogany four-poster beds, brass chandeliers and Italian marble baths. You may have your reception in any of the five private areas, or combine all of them for larger groups. Whatever your special occasion requires, this location with its experienced staff can meet your needs quickly and imaginatively.

Capacity: 90 seated; 130 standing; 175 with tent.
Catering: In-house. Entrees range from $60 to $125 per person. Cake cutting fee if you provide your own cake.
Rental Fee: $250 to $1,500.
Parking: On the premises and in lot nearby.
Note: Wedding ceremonies are permitted.

Norris House Inn   1-800-644-1806/703-777-1806

108 Loudoun Street, S.W. • Leesburg, VA 20175-2909

Built in 1760, the inn is located in Leesburg's Historic District and combines comfortable outdoor facilities with the charm and homey atmosphere of a bed and breakfast. The 40-foot veranda overlooks the inn's half-acre of award-winning gardens that are used for weddings and receptions. The inn's six guest rooms are provided as a part of a two-day, two-night reception package and four other guest rooms are available in an annex. Complimentary breakfast for overnight guests is served and other meals can be arranged. The tearoom is available for bridal showers (up to 30 guests) and the patio may be used for a party on the day preceding the wedding or reception.

Capacity: 75 seated; 75 in garden; 75 with tent; 30 in tearoom.
Catering: An approved caterers list is provided, but other caterers may be used by prior arrangement.
Rental Fee: $2,950, includes six guest rooms for two nights.
Parking: Parking lot nearby.
Note: Wedding ceremonies are permitted.

Rockland Farm Retreat   1-800-895-5098

3609 Lewiston Road • Bumpass, Virginia 23024

Built in 1839, this historic inn is a scenic 75-acre country estate. The majestic trees, quiet pastures and wildlife create a tranquil setting for your special day. Picture your wedding ceremony inside a quiet country church or in a lovely garden. The surrounding areas offer Civil War battlefields, winery tours, state parks, natural trails, horseback riding and golfing.

Capacity: 50 seated; 100 standing; 200 in garden; 300 with tent.
Catering: In-house caterer or your own caterer. In-house entree cost is $20 per person.
Parking: On the premises.
Note: Wedding ceremonies are permitted indoors or outdoors.

Wayside Inn Since 1797   703-869-1797
www.nvim.com/waysideinn

7783 Main Street • Middletown, VA 22645

This elegantly restored 18th-century inn, located one hour outside the beltway, boasts 24 lodging rooms appointed with antiques. It's an ideal location for a "dream come true" wedding and reception. Entertain on the terrace, outdoor pavilion and in the garden. At this inn, you can turn back the clock and experience the graciousness of a by-gone era.

Capacity: 150 inside; 350 with garden and patio.
Catering: In-house. Entrees begin at $25 and up.
Rental Fee: $1,000.
Parking: On the premises.
Note: Wedding ceremonies are permitted.

Willow Grove Inn   540-672-5982

14079 Plantation Way • Orange, VA 22960

Willow Grove Inn, a renaissance of Southern cooking, hospitality, and tradition, is a magnificent 18th-century mansion steeped in history. Located on 37 acres of rolling hills and pastures, the plantation has been carefully preserved. Throughout the centuries, Willow Grove has retained a grace of understated elegance combined with Old-World charm. Willow Grove is the perfect setting for a garden wedding—beds of blooming peonies, flowering bulbs, and nodding lilies flank a grass-cushioned aisle that meets a giant willow tree. Reception tables are layered with antique damask and tea-dyed antique lace, and beautifully appointed with Willow Grove's collection of antique china and silver.

Capacity: 80 seated; 150 standing; 300 in garden; 300 with tent.
Catering;   In-house. Entrees $50 per person. Cake cutting fee if you provide your own cake.
Parking: On the premises.
Note: Wedding ceremonies are permitted.

The Bailiwick Inn   703-691-2266

4023 Chain Bridge Road • Fairfax, VA 22030

A 19th-century inn, the Bailiwick Inn is in the heart of historic Fairfax, Virginia. This meticulously restored Federal mansion has been updated to include every amenity and boasts 14 rooms, each named and styled after famous Americans. A luxuriously appointed bridal suite with king-sized bed and Jacuzzi is also available. Double parlors are the perfect location for fireside bridal teas, and elegant rehearsal dinners may be held in the charming Belvoir Room. The English garden at the back of the inn is the perfect setting for a romantic summer ceremony. Family and friends may enjoy the individually decorated lodgings after the celebration is over. Homemade breakfast and an afternoon tea are included in the room rate.

Capacity: 30 seated; 75 standing; 20 in garden; 85 with tent.
Catering: In-house. Entrees range from $35 to $45 per person.
Rental Fee: $200 parlor/function room; $2,700 full house.
Parking: On the premises.
Note: Wedding ceremonies are permitted.

Black Horse Inn   540-349-4242

8393 Meetze Road • Warrenton, VA 20187

This elegant, circa 1850, hunt-country estate complete with thoroughbred horses is located only 45 minutes from Washington, D.C. The inn – with ample enclosed porches, landscaped grounds, boxwood gardens, a gazebo and spectacular views – provides a wonderful setting for weddings, receptions, parties and anniversary celebrations. The staff's planning for such events is both talented and imaginative and its lists of menus, champagnes and wines are well chosen. The majestic bridal suite, "Great Expectations," is opulent and romantic with a magnificent bed, fireplace, private porch enclosed by French doors that overlook the front grounds, fireplace, Jacuzzi and separate dressing room. Seven additional guest rooms each have luxurious private baths. For an indoor reception, the inn can accommodate up to 100 guests for cocktails and buffet. For outdoor events, the inn can accommodate up to 150 guests. There is one distinct advantage to reserving the Black Horse Inn for your wedding. Because the rooms are included in the package price, your guests can share in the cost of the site for your wedding! The Black Horse Inn offers not only an excellent location, but also the charm and romance that make the most beautiful of wedding memories.

Capacity: 100 indoors; 150 outdoors.
Catering: In-house or approved caterers list. Entrees range from $25 to $85 per person.
Rental Fee: $1,500 for facility. Packages are available which include rooms.

Parking: On the premises.
Note: Wedding ceremonies are permitted.

Bristow Manor   703-368-3558

11507 Valley View Drive • Bristow, VA 20136

Located near Manassas in Bristow, Virginia, just 30 minutes from
the D.C. Beltway, this turn-of-the-century colonial-revival manor
house with its large rooms, 14-foot high ceilings and decorative
moldings, has been completely restored to its former grandeur.
Today, the manor overlooks the beautiful 220-acre Bristow Manor
Golf Club. This elegant manor provides the perfect atmosphere
for any special occasion.

Capacity: 150 seated; 200 standing; 250 in outdoor pavilion.
Catering: In-house. Entrees begin at $22 and up for hor
                  d'oeuvres, $25 and up for buffet, and $32 and up for
                  sit-down dinner.
Rental Fee: $495 to $1,595.
Parking: On the premises.
Restrictions: No smoking inside home. No open flame candles.
Note: Wedding ceremonies are permitted indoors or out-
                  doors.

The Campagna Center   703-549-0111

418 S. Washington Street • Alexandria, VA 22314

The Campagna Center, Inc. is an independent, non-profit social
service organization which has served women and families in
Alexandria for 50 years. Today, after a half-million dollar renovation, the Center's turn-of-the-century grandeur is accentuated by
modernized services and amenities. It offers rooms with lots of
windows and light, hardwood floors, 14-foot ceilings with chandeliers, and a fully equipped kitchen.

Capacity: 130 seated; 175 standing.
Catering: Approved caterers list or your own caterer.
Rental Fee: Varies according to day and number of hours used.
                  Call for details.
Parking: Limited parking on the premises, but there is a park-
                  ing lot nearby.
Restrictions: No red beverages served. Amplified music up to 25
                  decibels. No birdseed, confetti, rice, etc.
Note: Wedding ceremonies are permitted.

Carlyle House Historic Park   703-549-2997

121 N. Fairfax Street • Alexandria, VA 22314

Located in the heart of Old Town Alexandria, the Carlyle House
provides wedding receptions and ceremonies with a touch of colonial

elegance. Completed in 1753 by Scottish merchant John Carlyle, the Carlyle House with its stone construction and manor-house design is on the National Register of Historic Places. Its gardens and gazebo make a perfect backdrop when exchanging vows.

Capacity: 100 seated; 100 standing; 25 in garden.
Catering: You must supply your own caterer.
Rental Fee: $1,495.
Parking: Parking lot nearby.
Restrictions: No amplified music or sound system. No rice, flowers, birdseed or confetti may be thrown.
Note: Wedding ceremonies are permitted. Weddings and receptions may be scheduled evenings, except Monday, from 6:30 p.m. to midnight, with caterers arriving at 5:00 p.m.

Gunston Hall   703-550-9220

10709 Gunston Road • Mason Neck • Lorton, VA 22079

Built in 1755, Gunston Hall was the plantation home of George Mason, author of the Virginia Declaration of Rights and framer of the United States Constitution. The life and times of 18th-century America are vividly evoked by the commodious house and gardens overlooking the Potomac River. Weddings and other events may be held at various locations in the beautifully restored gardens and grounds of Gunston Hall, as well as in the banquet room and adjoining fountain courtyard located in the Ann Mason Building. The elegant mansion provides the perfect backdrop for weddings and receptions. Guided tours of the historic house are included as a part of any function. Gunston Hall is a spectacular place to celebrate a special day.

Capacity: 150 seated; 225 standing; unlimited in gardens.
Catering: In-house or your own caterer. In-house entrees range from $22 to $40 per person.
Rental Fee: $1,500 to $2,300.
Parking: On the premises. Handicap parking available.
Note: Wedding ceremonies are permitted.

Hackwood   800-365-8021

534 Red Bud Road • Winchester, VA 22603

Hackwood was the center of many intriguing and historical events, including the duel between Peyton Smith and Joseph Holmes in 1809 and the 3rd Battle of Winchester during the Civil War. Originally called Hackwood Park Estate, the Georgian-style house is enhanced by a welcoming stone walk with boxwood. The grand veranda on the west side looks out over a beautifully landscaped green with a large lake in the distance. The mansion offers two large parlors on the main floor, a wide center hall, and additional space on the second level.

Capacity: 120 seated downstairs; 80 seated upstairs; 300 standing; 200 in garden; 1,000 with tent.
Catering: In-house. Entrees range from $55 to $85 per person.
Rental Fee: $1,500.
Parking: On the premises.
Note: Wedding ceremonies are permitted.

L'Auberge Provencale   1-800-638-1702/540-837-1375

P.O. Box 119 • White Post, VA 22663

To discover the feeling of a true inn of the South of France, come to L'Auberge Provencale. Just one hour from the D.C. Beltway and two hours from Baltimore, the inn is located in Virginia Hunt Country. Have your reception, holiday celebration or retirement party at the manor house, Mt. Airy (circa 1753). Choose from one of three intimate dining rooms decorated with fine antiques, fine art, Provencale fabrics, and an eclectic menagerie of hand-crafted animals. Traveling to L'Auberge Provencale, you will take the back roads of beautiful Clark County, framed by the Shenandoah River and the gently rolling Blue Ridge Mountains. Enjoy the simple pleasures of antique shopping, horseback riding, hiking, bike riding, golfing, canoeing, fishing, or simply sitting on the spacious porch with a glass of wine.

Capacity: 75 seated; 75 standing.
Catering: In-house. Five-course dinner begin at $58 and up per person.
Rental Fee: $350, if number of guests exceed 25.
Parking: On the premises.
Note: Wedding ceremonies are permitted indoors or outdoors.

Lee-Fendall House   703-548-1789

614 Oronoco Street • Alexandria, VA 22314

Built in 1785, it has been home to 37 Lees. Furnished with many of the Lee family heirlooms, it is listed on the National Register of Historic Places. The lovely white clapboard home and its garden are perfect for weddings and receptions. Guests are greeted in the garden under the massive magnolia, ancient chestnuts and ginkgo trees, or by candlelight and antiques in the historic house.

Capacity: 85 standing; 100 in garden.
Catering: Approved caterer list or your own caterer.
Rental Fee: $150 per hour.
Parking: Parking lot nearby. Residential parking.
Restrictions: No amplified musical instruments.
Note: Wedding ceremonies are permitted indoors or outdoors.

Morrison House   703-838-8000

116 South Alfred Street • Alexandria, VA 22314

Looking for a quiet, elegant, romantic escape? Look no further than Old Town Alexandria's award-winning Morrison House. The European warmth and charm of this small hotel are as welcoming as the butlers who greet you at the door. Located just minutes from National Airport and downtown Washington, D.C., the Federal style inn boasts ornate woodwork, decorative fireplaces and fanlight windows. Its 45 guest rooms, each unique, feature Federal period reproductions including mahogany four-poster beds, brass chandeliers and Italian marble baths. You may have your reception in any of the five private areas, or combine all of them for larger groups. Whatever your special occasion requires, this location with its experienced staff can meet your needs quickly and imaginatively.

Capacity: 90 seated; 130 standing; 175 with tent.
Catering: In-house. Entrees range from $60 to $125 per person. Cake cutting fee if you provide your own cake.
Rental Fee: $250 to $1,500.
Parking: On the premises and in lot nearby.
Note: Wedding ceremonies are permitted.

Poplar Springs   540-788-4600

9245 Rogues Road • P.O. Box 275 • Casanova, VA 20139

Poplar Springs is a European-designed fieldstone manor house situated on 200 acres of rolling farmland, forests, streams and lakes. Located in Casanova, Virginia, four miles from Historic Old Town Warrenton, it is in the heart of Fauquier County. This gorgeous 10,000-square-foot mansion has arched entrance ways, enticing fieldstone walls and dramatic timber beams. The three-story high great hall is framed by balconies, stained glass windows and double French doors. There are large flagstone terraces surrounding the house, outside both the great hall and the library. The main floor is anchored by the impressive great hall, and is adjoined by the library, dining room and sun porch. These rooms, as well as the terraces and surrounding grounds, are available for weddings, receptions, breakfasts, lunches, dinners, business meetings and cultural events. With its unique location and incredible surroundings, Poplar Springs offers the best of all worlds . . . charm, elegance, convenience and privacy.

Capacity: 200 seated; 300 standing; 300 in gardens; 1,000+ with tent.
Catering: In-house. Prices begin at $60 and up.
Rental Fee: $1,500 to $3,000.
Parking: On the premises.
Note: Wedding ceremonies are permitted indoors or outdoors.

Raspberry Plain   703-777-1888

16500 Agape Lane • Leesburg, VA 20176

Set like a jewel in the midst of 50 rolling green acres in historic
Loudoun County sits the Georgian colonial estate known since
1731 as Raspberry Plain. The hall's sparkling chandeliers, detailed archway and dramatic staircase complement the elegance of
the mansion's rooms: the drawing room's cherry-paneled wainscot wall with built-in bookcases, the spacious Victorian parlor,
the dining room with built-in china cabinets and the light-filled
conservatory with French doors leading onto the grand terrace,
which has a panoramic view of the magnificent formal gardens
and mountains, rolling pastures and pond. Every room in the
mansion has character and charm. Period furnishings and paintings adorn the mansion. All the main rooms have glass-paneled
double-pocket doors, fireplaces and original detailed ceiling moldings.

Capacity: 240 seated; 300 standing; unlimited in gardens; 200
                 with tent.
Catering: Approved caterers list.
Rental Fee: Starting at $1,500.
Parking: On the premises.
Restrictions: No smoking inside, but at designated outdoor areas.
                 Dancing permitted indoor with a dance floor only.
Note: Wedding ceremonies are permitted.

River Farm   703-768-5700

7931 East Boulevard Drive • Alexandria, VA 22308

The elegant main house is set amid 27 acres of lawns, gardens,
meadows, and woods, and commands a sweeping view of the
Potomac. Over the last 20 years, the Society has established
ornamental, educational and test gardens on portions of River
Farm, but most of the property remains much as Washington
himself would have known it when it was the northernmost tract of
his farmland surrounding Mount Vernon. The house, which is
registered as a "gentleman's home" by the Fairfax County Historical Society, includes a 45' x 20' ballroom with a tastefully appointed
powder room, a large parlor overlooking the river, a dining room
opening onto broad porches with garden and river views, and a
charming entrance hall featuring a hand-painted floral frieze. The
garden patio outside the ballroom may be tented for outdoor events.
The house and gardens at River Farm may be rented for weddings,
dinner parties, corporate meetings and other events. River Farm is
located on the banks of the Potomac, just four miles south of Old
Town Alexandria on the George Washington Parkway.

Capacity: 80 to 200, depending on areas selected for event.
Catering: Approved caterers list or your own caterer. Caterer
                 must be approved by facility. The large, state-of-the-

art country kitchen is available to caterers for preparation and heating of food.

Rental Fee: $2,500 to $6,400. Call for information. Comprehensive General Liability Insurance is required.

Parking: On the premises.

Restrictions: No amplified music. Portable toilets need to be rented for over 150 capacity.

Note: Wedding ceremonies are permitted.

Stone Mansion   703-938-8835

c/o Historic Properties Rental Services
9601 Courthouse Road • Vienna, VA 22181

Commodore Walter Brooke built a small wood frame manor house in 1777 following his service in the Virginia Naval Forces during the Revolutionary War. Enlarged over the years, and covered in stone in the 1940s, the mansion offers three separate banquet rooms, a screened porch, a large formal entry with a curved staircase and a large catering kitchen. The beautifully landscaped garden is perfect for outdoor ceremonies or receptions.

Capacity: 50 seated; 75 standing; 150 in garden.

Catering: You must supply your own caterer.

Rental Fee: $800.

Parking: On the premises and you may park on the street.

Restrictions: No confetti or silly string. Birdseed only may be thrown outside. All candles must be enclosed and have protection underneath to catch the dripping wax. No smoking indoors. No taping, tacking, or nailing decorations to the walls.

Note: Wedding ceremonies are permitted indoors or outdoors.

Valley View House and Gardens   703-321-9757

1562 Leeds Manor Road • Delaplane, VA 20144

Consider having your wedding reception in the beautiful formal gardens of this lovely historic estate. Located in the Virginia Hunt Country 12 miles west of Middleburg, the estate consists of a manor house with a formal English garden on 500 acres of meadowlands and mountains. This romantic setting of understated elegance overlooks an unspoiled valley that was the scene of numerous events in the War Between the States. Valley View is an ideal setting for garden weddings, receptions, engagement parties and rehearsal dinners.

Capacity: 50 indoor; 250 outdoor.

Catering: You must supply your own caterer.

Rental Fee: $350 to $500.

Parking: On the premises.
Note: Wedding ceremonies are permitted.

Whitehall "The Hunt Country Inn"   703-450-6666

18301 Whitehall Estate Lane • Bluemont, VA 20135

At the foothills of the Blue Ridge stands Whitehall, the treasure of majestic western Loudoun County. This country estate, rich in history and classic architecture, is the ultimate facility for your next reception, conference, or corporate retreat. It features four furnished, climate-controlled meeting rooms, picnic grounds with facilities for softball, volleyball, horseshoes, hayrides and camp-fires, as well as award-winning cuisine by Celebrations. You can begin your special day by saying your vows in the gracious gardens nestled among a canopy of century-old trees on 50 panoramic acres. After the ceremony, your guests can enjoy cocktails and hors d'oeuvres on the magnificent covered brick dining terrace. Then for the perfect ending to a wonderful day, entertain your guests in the ornately detailed grand ballroom, complete with musicians' balcony and marble fireplace.

Capacity: 240 seated; 380 standing; 300+ in garden; 300+ with tent.
Catering: In-house. Entrees range from $40 to $80 per person.
Rental Fee: Varies. Call for information.
Parking: On the premises.
Restrictions: No smoking inside the facility.
Note: Wedding ceremonies are permitted.

Willow Grove Inn   540-672-5982

14079 Plantation Way • Orange, VA 22960

Willow Grove Inn, a renaissance of Southern cooking, hospital-ity, and tradition, is a magnificent 18th-century mansion steeped in history. Located on 37 acres of rolling hills and pastures, the plantation has been carefully preserved. Throughout the centu-ries, Willow Grove has retained a grace of understated elegance combined with Old-World charm. Willow Grove is the perfect setting for a garden wedding — beds of blooming peonies, flow-ering bulbs, and nodding lilies flank a grass-cushioned aisle that meets a giant willow tree. Reception tables are layered with antique damask and tea-dyed antique lace, and beautifully ap-pointed with Willow Grove's collection of antique china and silver.

Capacity: 80 seated; 150 standing; 300 in garden; 300 with tent.
Catering;   In-house. Entrees $50 per person. Cake cutting fee if you provide your own cake.
Parking: On the premises.
Note: Wedding ceremonies are permitted.

Woodlawn Plantation   703-780-4000

9000 Richmond Highway • Alexandria, VA 22309

George Washington gave 2000 acres of Mount Vernon to his granddaughter and his favorite nephew as a wedding gift. In addition to the Georgian brick mansion, the site includes Frank Lloyd Wright's Pope-Leighery House, natural trails and formal gardens.

Capacity: 50 in house; 800 with a tent.
Catering: Approved caterers list. Alcohol must be purchased through Woodlawn.
Rental Fee: $1,850 to $2,050 for 5 hours for up to 250 persons.
Parking: On the premises.
Note: Wedding ceremonies are permitted.

Alexandria Black History Resource Center   703-838-4356

638 N. Alfred Street • Alexandria, VA 22314

The Alexandria Black History Resource Center, Northern Virginia's only African-American history museum, offers a wedding site for couples interested in celebrating their ethnic heritage or those looking for a unique historic atmosphere. Couples have a choice of two modern exhibition galleries: the Parker-Gray Gallery and the Robert Robinson Gallery. The galleries can be combined to work as a wedding and reception site. Both galleries offer modern museum lighting which can be adjusted for dramatic effect. Used as just a reception site, the museum can accommodate 150 people. Under supervision provided by the renter, the Center's Watson Reading Room may be rented as a quiet playroom for children. The reading room, adjacent to the Center, has over 1,500 books, videos and periodicals on African-American history and culture. The Center's satellite site, the Alexandria African-American Heritage Park (located off Duke Street on Holland Lane) is a nine-acre park suitable for outdoor weddings. The Center is located in the historic Parker-Gray district of Alexandria and is an appropriate setting for intimate celebrations.

Capacity: 75 seating; 150 standing.
Catering: You must supply your own caterer. The Center has a modern catering kitchen and tables and chairs may be rented on site.
Rental Fee: $100 per hour.
Parking: The Center offers ample on-street parking, without time restrictions.
Restrictions: No smoking.
Note: Wedding ceremonies are permitted. Facility is handicapped accessible.

The Athenaeum   703-548-0035

201 Prince Street • Alexandria, VA 22314

This scaled-down copy of the Temple of Athena, built in 1852 with fluted columns across the verandah, is an historic landmark. Just one block from the Potomac River, in the heart of Old Town Alexandria, it is an intimate and romantic site for gatherings. Features include soaring ceilings, beautiful woodwork, and gleaming old floors that are fine for dancing. Tall windows offer views of cobblestoned streets and 18th-century houses. The two elegant galleries on the main level are usually hung with interesting artworks. Ceiling fans and air conditioning keep guests comfortable. A catering kitchen and the lower gallery are useful for food preparation. An enchanting garden has high brick walls draped with vines. The garden may be canopied.

Capacity: 80 seated; 175 standing; 24 seated in garden; 50 standing in garden; 225 with tent.
Catering: You must supply your own caterer.
Rental Fee: $1,100 for six hours. $185 each additional hour.
Parking: Parking lots nearby. Valet parking can be arranged.
Restrictions: Available only Saturday and Sunday. Nothing attached to walls. No DJs. All rental equipment delivered and removed on day of event. Only votive candles allowed. Art on exhibit will not be removed except by special arrangement. Caterer must be present throughout entire affair, with one worker per 30 guests. No cooking over open flame.
Note: Wedding ceremonies are permitted.

Boyhood Home of Robert E. Lee   703-548-8454

607 Oronoco Street • Alexandria, VA 22314

Built in 1795 by John Potts, a friend and business associate of George Washington, this became the home of Robert E. Lee in 1812. The house is decorated in furniture and brass from the Federal Period. The house and gardens are available for weddings and receptions.

Capacity: 40 seated; 100 standing; 100 in garden.
Catering: Approved caterers list.
Rental Fee: $150 per hour.
Parking: On the street and parking lot nearby.
Restrictions: No smoking or dance inside the home.
Note: Wedding ceremonies are permitted indoors or outdoors.

Gadsby's Tavern Restaurant   703-548-1288

138 N. Royal Street • Alexandria, VA 22314

Once the site of society balls and presidential receptions, this Williamsburg-style tavern replicates the food, furnishings, and costumes of colonial times. You may have your reception in the Tap Room or one of the more formal dining rooms. The courtyard behind the tavern can be used for cocktails and hors d'oeuvres or an outdoor wedding ceremony.

Capacity: 100 seated; 150 standing; 175 in garden; 100 seated in adjacent 19th-century ballroom.
Catering: In-house. Entrees range from $15 to $45 per person.
Rental Fee: $850.
Parking: On the premises.
Restrictions: Period music in historic part of property. Your choice of music in 19th-century ballroom.
Note: Wedding ceremonies permitted outside only.

The Lyceum   703-838-4994

201 S. Washington Street • Alexandria, VA 22314

The Lyceum, Alexandria's History Museum, collects and interprets the history and material culture of the City of Alexandria and the surrounding northern Virginia area. This wonderful site offers one of the largest rooms available in an historic building in Old Town Alexandria. The Museum's Lecture Hall is available for weddings and receptions. The room is elegantly appointed with green wall-to-wall carpet, rose-colored draperies, and coordinating upholstered armchairs. There is a 9' x 22' platform stage, an adjoining kitchen and a concert grand piano. Arrangements can be made to have the exhibition galleries on the first floor open for viewing by your guests.

Capacity: 90 seated; 150 standing.
Catering: You must supply your own caterer. The facility provides six 8' rectangular tables, six 6' rectangular tables and 125 upholstered armchairs.
Rental Fee: $1,100 or $225 per hour.
Parking: On the premises. Handicap parking available.
Restrictions: No smoking. No rice, confetti, birdseed, etc. You must furnish dance floor, not to exceed 12' x 12'.
Note: Wedding ceremonies are permitted.

Woodlawn Plantation   703-780-4000

9000 Richmond Highway • Alexandria, VA 22309

George Washington gave 2000 acres of Mount Vernon to his granddaughter and his favorite nephew as a wedding gift. In addition to the Georgian brick mansion, the site includes Frank Lloyd Wright's Pope-Leighery House, natural trails and formal gardens.

Capacity: 50 in house; 800 with a tent.
Catering: Approved caterers list. Alcohol must be purchased through Woodlawn.
Rental Fee: $1,850 to $2,050 for 5 hours for up to 250 persons.
Parking: On the premises.
Note: Wedding ceremonies are permitted.

Algonkian Meeting Center
Algonkian Regional Park   703-450-4655

47001 Fairway Drive • Sterling, VA 20165

The Algonkian Meeting Center makes entertaining easy with its large reception room, portable bar and dance floor. Stone fireplaces and large windows looking onto the park and golf course add atmosphere to any reception. Delicious custom menus created by the Center's caterer are sure to please your guests. A quaint gazebo on the front lawn is a romantic setting for wedding ceremonies. Complimentary use of the gazebo is an option when renting the Loudoun Room. The Meeting Center is located in Algonkian Regional Park, which features 12 river-front vacation cottages, outdoor swimming pool, 18-hole, par-72 golf course, picnic shelters and boat ramp. The facility is excellently suited for corporate functions such as seminars, company picnics and retreats.

Capacity: 175 seated; 200 standing.
Catering: You must supply your own caterer.
Rental Fee: $875 for five hours.
Parking: On the premises.
Note: Wedding ceremonies are permitted.

The Atrium at Meadowlark Gardens 703-255-3631

9750 Meadowlark Gardens Court • Vienna, VA 22182

Seasonal blossoms, a meandering stream and a hint of woodlands offer a bouquet of possibilities in this indoor garden at The Atrium at Meadowlark Gardens. Three walls of windows and a landscaped terrace overlook the gardens, woods and meadows of the Northern Virginia Regional Park Authority's 95-acre garden park. In the Garden Room, the cathedral ceiling rises to a dramatic, 2,000-square-foot skylight. Gazebos on a hillside, the Azalea Woods and Lake Caroline offer picturesque settings for the exchange of vows. The Atrium and the array of natural and specialty gardens are located between Routes 7 and 123, just south of the Dulles Access Road and near Tysons Corner and Wolf Trap Farm Park.

Capacity: 220 seated; 350 standing without dance floor.
Catering: You must supply your own caterer. Caterer must be approved by the Atrium's events coordinator. Pantry kitchen for warming and holding food only. No premise cooking. Caterers must have license, liquor license, and certificate of insurance.
Rental Fee: $275 to $400 per hour. Rental includes: tables, chairs, two portable bars, 15' x 18' dance floor and use of

terrace and preparation kitchen. Rental period includes set-up and clean-up by the caterer.

Parking: On the premises.

Note: Wedding ceremonies are permitted indoors or outdoors. The facility hosts two weddings on Saturday: The first wedding ends at 3:00 p.m. and the second wedding starts at 5:00 p.m.

Barns of Wolf Trap   703-938-8463

1635 Trap Road • Vienna, VA 22182

Located one-half mile south of the Wolf Trap Farm Park for the Performing Arts, The Barns are ideal for celebrated receptions and corporate and holiday parties. This historical showpiece comprises two 18th-century barns joined under one roof. The Barns offer rustic charm along with modern amenities: heating and air conditioning, fully-equipped commercial kitchen and bar, track lighting. The spacious courtyard in the center of the structure is ideal for additional seating and food stations.

Capacity: 220 seated; 350 standing and with tent.

Catering: Approved caterers list. Alcoholic beverages must be purchased from facility.

Rental Fee: $1,000 and up.

Parking: On the premises.

Restrictions: No smoking.

Green Spring Manor   703-938-8835

c/o Historic Properties Rental Service
9601 Courthouse Road • Vienna, VA 22181

The Green Spring Farm Manor, circa 1760, is the centerpiece of what was once a 540-acre farm. Today, the manor house is part of Green Spring Gardens Park, and the formal grounds around the manor house are available for garden weddings. This historic manor is a great place to celebrate the occasion of your marriage.

Capacity: 100 in garden; 100 with tent.

Catering: You must supply your own caterer.

Rental Fee: $700.

Parking: On the premises and nearby lot.

Restrictions: Outdoors only. No confetti or silly string. Birdseed may be thrown outside only. All candles must be enclosed with something to catch the drips. No smoking indoors. No taping, tacking, or nailing decorations to the walls.

Note: Wedding ceremonies are permitted.

Hunter House   703-938-8835

c/o Historic Properties Rental Service
9601 Courthouse Road • Vienna, VA 22181

Built in 1890, Hunter House was home to Scottish immigrant John C. Hunter. After Prohibition ended, William Davidson operated Distillery #4 there and produced a wine which he called *Virginia Maid*. While the house maintains much of its original character, through the years it has been expanded into a spacious two-story facility. Hunter House provides an atmosphere of casual country elegance. The building features several air-conditioned rooms and a kitchen, as well as a screened-in porch. The adjacent lawn is a popular place for outdoor weddings and receptions.

Capacity: 40 seated; 75 standing; 150 in garden.
Catering: You must supply your own caterer.
Rental Fee: $800.
Parking: On the premises.
Restrictions: No confetti or silly string. Birdseed only may be thrown outside. No smoking indoors. No open flames. No taping, tacking, or nailing decorations to the walls.
Note: Wedding ceremonies permitted indoors or outdoors.

The Old Schoolhouse   703-938-8835

c/o Historic Properties Rental Services
9601 Courthouse Road • Vienna, VA 22181

The Old Schoolhouse is a prime example of the traditional one-room schoolhouses which dotted the landscape in the late 1800s and early 1900s. This wonderful space offers two rooms and a small kitchen area for up to 49 people for small, intimate occasions. It can also be rented in conjunction with the Great Falls Grange for larger events.

Capacity: 49 seated and standing; 100 with tent.
Catering: You must supply your own caterer.
Rental Fee: $550.
Parking: On the premises.
Restrictions: No confetti or silly string. No open flames. Birdseed only may be thrown outside. No smoking indoors. No taping, tacking, or nailing decorations to the wall.
Note: Wedding ceremonies are permitted indoors or outdoors.

Stone Mansion   703-938-8835

c/o Historic Properties Rental Services
9601 Courthouse Road • Vienna, VA 22181

Commodore Walter Brooke built a small wood frame manor house
in 1777 following his service in the Virginia Naval Forces during the
Revolutionary War. Enlarged over the years, and covered in stone
in the 1940s, the mansion offers three separate banquet rooms, a
screened porch, a large formal entry with a curved staircase and a
large catering kitchen. The beautifully landscaped garden is perfect
for outdoor ceremonies or receptions.

Capacity: 50 seated; 75 standing; 150 in garden.
Catering: You must supply your own caterer.
Rental Fee: $800.
Parking: On the premises and you may park on the street.
Restrictions: No confetti or silly string. Birdseed only may be
               thrown outside. All candles must be enclosed and
               have protection underneath to catch the dripping
               wax. No smoking indoors. No taping, tacking, or
               nailing decorations to the walls.
Note: Wedding ceremonies are permitted indoors or out-
               doors.

Lansdowne Resort   703-729-8400

44050 Woodridge Parkway • Leesburg, VA 20176

At Landsdowne Resort, the staff knows how important your wedding day is to you, and are committed to making the day of your dreams a reality. It offers intimate dining areas for rehearsal dinners, exquisite menu selections from award-winning chefs, and an elegant ballroom and expansive outdoor terraces which overlook the Robert Trent Jones, Jr. golf course. A wedding specialist will be on hand to coordinate all aspects of your event, a pastry chef will work with you to design a deliciously beautiful wedding cake, and the spa staff will customize a bridal package for your party. For your guests, it offers luxurious guest rooms and spacious suites, relaxing amenities such as a championship golf course, health club, indoor and outdoor pools, and lighted tennis courts. Lansdowne Resort is also an excellent choice for corporate retreats or family reunions. Lansdowne is nestled in the scenic Potomac River Valley and is just 8 miles from Dulles Airport and less than an hour from Washington, D.C.

Capacity: 550 seated; 850 standing; 250 in pavilion.
Catering: In-house. Packages range from $70 to $85 per person. Cake cutting fee is $2.00 per person if cake is brought in.
Parking: On the premises. Valet parking is complimentary. Handicap parking is available.
Note: Wedding ceremonies are permitted indoors or outdoors. Guest rooms are available.

Westfields Marriott   703-818-0300

14750 Conference Center Drive • Chantilly, VA 20151

Located just 30 minutes from the nation's capital, Westfields combines the architectural splendor of Virginia's finest estates with the functional excellence for which it has won numerous awards. The entry's three-and-a-half ton bronze doors exemplify the pride of craftsmanship found throughout this $70 million resort. Inside, just beyond the Lobby, a magnificent Rotunda presents a spectacular dome, classic columns and a generous portion of the center's 450 tons of Greek marble. Westfields offers a variety of indoor and outdoor settings to create an event to reflect your personal tastes. The property has three elegantly furnished ballrooms and a number of intimate banquet spaces to host your special event.

Capacity: 600 seated; 900 standing; 300 in garden; 200 with tent.
Catering: In-house. Entrees begin at $85 per person. Cake cutting fee if you provide your own cake.
Rental Fee: $1,000 to $4,000.
Parking: On the premises. Valet parking is available.
Note: Wedding ceremonies are permitted indoors or outdoors.

America at Tysons Corner   202-333-3011

c/o Ark Restaurants
3050 K Street, N.W. • Washington, D.C. 20007

America, located in the upscale Tysons Corner Center, is Northern Virginia's ideal location for group events and memorable occasions. The restaurant provides four unique events spaces that may be used separately or in various combinations. Like its sister restaurant at Union Station, America's decor represents the diversity of our culture and regions. You may reserve the entire restaurant for events of 150 to 500 guests.

Capacity: 335 seated; 500 standing.
Catering: In-house. Menus range from $15 to $40 per person.
Parking: On the premises and nearby parking lot.

The Bailiwick Inn   703-691-2266

4023 Chain Bridge Road • Fairfax, VA 22030

A 19th-century inn, the Bailiwick Inn is in the heart of historic Fairfax, Virginia. This meticulously restored Federal mansion has been updated to include every amenity and boasts 14 rooms, each named and styled after famous Americans. A luxuriously appointed bridal suite with king-sized bed and Jacuzzi is also available. Double parlors are the perfect location for fireside bridal teas, and elegant rehearsal dinners may be held in the charming Belvoir Room. The English garden at the back of the inn is the perfect setting for a romantic summer ceremony. Family and friends may enjoy the individually decorated lodgings after the celebration is over. Homemade breakfast and an afternoon tea are included in the room rate.

Capacity: 30 seated; 75 standing; 20 in garden; 85 with tent.
Catering: In-house. Entrees range from $35 to $45 per person.
Rental Fee: $200 parlor/function room; $2,700 full house.
Parking: On the premises.
Note: Wedding ceremonies are permitted.

Charlie Brown's Lakeside   703-497-0333

2233 Tacketts Mill Drive • Lakeridge, VA 22192

From waterside dining to a warm fireplace setting, the staff at Charlie Brown's Lakeside will help you create your special event with optimum service and superb food.

Capacity: 250 seated; 250 standing.
Catering: In-house. Entrees begin at $15.95 per person.
Parking: On the premises.
Note: Wedding ceremonies are permitted.

Clyde's of Tysons Corner   703-734-1907

8332 Leesburg Pike • Vienna, VA 22182

Clyde's offers a choice of its restaurant and its private dining room for weddings, receptions, rehearsal dinners and other wonderful celebrations. The elegant art deco dining room is decorated in shades of plum and has a lovely panoramic view. Clyde's provides excellent service and a catering staff which is pleased to help you plan every detail.

Capacity: 150 seated; 175 standing.
Catering: In-house.
Rental Fee: $100.
Parking: On the premises.
Note: Wedding ceremonies are permitted.

Flint Hill Public House   540-675-1700

675 Zachary Taylor Highway • Flint Hill, VA 22627

Located on five landscaped acres, this restored turn-of-the-century schoolhouse can host small or large receptions, weddings, rehearsal dinners and corporate events. You may have your ceremony in the lovely gazebo and gardens which have a stunning view of the Blue Ridge Mountains. Inside, on the main level, is a full-service restaurant and bar with wood-burning stoves. Upstairs, two queen-sized suites, kitchen, and conference room may be used for seminars and executive retreats. This site is just moments away from antique shops, wineries, and the Skyline Drive.

Capacity: 99 seated; 250 standing; 250 in garden.
Catering: In-house. $50 cake cutting fee if you provide your own cake.
Rental Fee: $750 to $2,500 (only if complete facility is used).
Parking: On the premises.
Note: Wedding ceremonies are permitted indoors or outdoors.

The Hermitage Inn Restaurant   703-266-1623

7134 Main Street • Clifton, VA 20124

Once a luxury retreat for the affluent, "The Clifton Hotel" was host to the likes of Ulysses S. Grant, Theodore Roosevelt and Rutherford B. Hayes. As The Hermitage Inn Restaurant, this graceful landmark has been faithfully restored to its original beauty of 1869. Charming, romantic and secluded, the restaurant is ideal for an intimate dinner for two or an elegant wedding for 200. Take a moment to enjoy the antiquity of the setting, enhanced by original hardwood floors, French doors and four fireplaces. The outdoor terrace, with a waterfall and lovely garden, is perfect for a wedding ceremony or any special event.

Capacity:	160 seated; 250 standing; 100 in garden; 160 with tent.
Catering:	In-house. Entrees range from $40 to $60 per person.
Parking:	On the premises.
Note:	Wedding ceremonies are permitted.

L'Auberge Provencale   1-800-638-1702/540-837-1375

P.O. Box 119 • White Post, VA 22663

To discover the feeling of a true inn of the South of France, come to L'Auberge Provencale. Just one hour from the D.C. Beltway and two hours from Baltimore, the inn is located in Virginia Hunt Country. Have your reception, holiday celebration or retirement party at the manor house, Mt. Airy (circa 1753). Choose from one of three intimate dining rooms decorated with fine antiques, fine art, Provencale fabrics, and an eclectic menagerie of hand-crafted animals. Traveling to L'Auberge Provencale, you will take the back roads of beautiful Clark County, framed by the Shenandoah River and the gently rolling Blue Ridge Mountains. Enjoy the simple pleasures of antique shopping, horseback riding, hiking, bike riding, golfing, canoeing, fishing, or simply sitting on the spacious porch with a glass of wine.

Capacity:	75 seated; 75 standing.
Catering:	In-house. Five-course dinner begin at $58 and up per person.
Rental Fee:	$350, if number of guests exceed 25.
Parking:	On the premises.
Note:	Wedding ceremonies are permitted indoors or outdoors.

La Bergerie   703-683-1007

218 North Lee Street • Alexandria, VA 22314

Located in the heart of colonial Old Town, Alexandria, La Bergerie is decorated with French countryside paintings, richly appointed leather banquettes, and crystal chandeliers. Its charming and intimate atmosphere provides the perfect ambiance for any special occasion. Cocktail receptions may be held in the Atrium and the two private party rooms can be used for smaller events. French cuisine with Basque specialties will delight your palate. Your guests can stroll down cobblestone streets, tour quaint residences, shop in 1700-era stores, and listen to street entertainment. La Bergerie, located near Market Square and the famous Torpedo Factory Arts Center, is 15 minutes from Washington, D.C., via George Washington Parkway.

Capacity:	85 in main room; 48 in large private room; 26 in small private room.
Catering:	In-house. Entrees range from $13 to $25. Cake cutting fee if you provide your own cake.

Rental Fee: None. Large room guarantee is 30 and the small room
                guarantee is 20.
Parking: Parking lot nearby.
Note: Wedding ceremonies are permitted.

Seaport Inn   703-549-2341

6 King Street • Alexandria, VA 22314

This circa 1765, historic landmark previously owned by George
Washington's military aide-de-camp provides a magnificent setting for wedding receptions. This location offers three elegant
dining rooms. The John Fitzgerald Room, with its dark wood
trim, rustic decor and complementing fireplace, is a charming
asset to your party. The Potomac River Room offers a panoramic
view of the Potomac River. The view, along with the room's rich
brick color scheme accented with brass, creates a truly elegant
atmosphere. The Williamsburg Room with its Colonial decor is
ideal for intimate parties.

Capacity: 130.
Catering: In-house. Entrees range from $16.95 to $20.95 per
                person. Cake cutting fee is $35.
Deposits: $100 to $175.
Parking: Parking garages nearby.
Note: Wedding ceremonies are permitted.

Stoneleigh Tavern   703-589-1442

35279 Prestwick Court • Round Hill, VA 20175

Set in the foothills of the Blue Ridge, Stoneleigh Tavern offers a
majestic site for outdoor weddings. Wedding parties and their
guests will enjoy the spacious, private courtyard which is surrounded by a natural stone wall. The courtyard includes a paved
tented area for dining and dancing, and an elevated grassy area
provides a natural setting for ceremonies. A full-service restaurant is located on site in a pre-Civil War era mansion. Stoneleigh
Tavern is located 14 miles west of Leesburg on the grounds of the
Stoneleigh Golf & Country Club, and is easily accessible from the
Dulles Greenway.

Capacity: 130 seated; 130 standing; 130 in garden with tent.
Catering: In-house. Entrees range from $16 to $28 per person.
                Cake cutting fee if you provide your own cake.
Parking: On the premises.
Restrictions: Ceremonies and receptions are held outside in the
                courtyard.
Note: Wedding ceremonies are permitted.

The Campagna Center   703-549-0111

418 S. Washington Street • Alexandria, VA 22314

The Campagna Center, Inc. is an independent, non-profit social service organization which has served women and families in Alexandria for 50 years. Today, after a half-million dollar renovation, the Center's turn-of-the-century grandeur is accentuated by modernized services and amenities. It offers rooms with lots of windows and light, hardwood floors, 14-foot ceilings with chandeliers, and a fully equipped kitchen.

Capacity: 130 seated; 175 standing.
Catering: Approved caterers list or your own caterer.
Rental Fee: Varies according to day and number of hours used. Call for details.
Parking: Limited parking on the premises, but there is a parking lot nearby.
Restrictions: No red beverages served. Amplified music up to 25 decibels. No birdseed, confetti, rice, etc.
Note: Wedding ceremonies are permitted.

America at Tysons Corner 202-333-3011

c/o Ark Restaurants
3050 K Street, N.W. • Washington, D.C. 20007

America, located in the upscale Tysons Corner Center, is Northern Virginia's ideal location for group events and memorable occasions. The restaurant provides four unique events spaces that may be used separately or in various combinations. Like its sister restaurant at Union Station, America's decor represents the diversity of our culture and regions. You may reserve the entire restaurant for events of 150 to 500 guests.

Capacity: 335 seated; 500 standing.
Catering: In-house. Menus range from $15 to $40 per person.
Parking: On the premises and nearby parking lot.

Charlie Brown's Lakeside 703-497-0333

2233 Tacketts Mill Drive • Lakeridge, VA 22192

From waterside dining to a warm fireplace setting, the staff will help you create your special event with optimum service and superb food.

Capacity: 250 seated; 250 standing.
Catering: In-house. Entrees begin at $15.95 per person.
Parking: On the premises.
Note: Wedding ceremonies are permitted.

Cherry Blossom Riverboat 703-684-0580

205 the Strand • Alexandria, VA 22314

Built in 1984, *The Cherry Blossom* is a re-creation of a 19th-century Victorian riverboat. Beautifully appointed with ornate iron railings and a plush interior of brass and mahogany, it is one of the most elegant yachts cruising the Potomac. Its two interior salons are heated and air-conditioned for year-round comfort. The third deck is open air, offering a spectacular view of Old Town and the Washington, D.C., skyline.

Capacity: 250 seated; 400 standing; 75 with a tent on the third dock.
Catering: Approved caterers list. Entrees range from $38 to $42 per person.
Parking: Parking lot nearby. Valet parking can be arranged.
Note: Wedding ceremonies permitted indoors or outdoors.

Evans Farm Inn   703-356-8000

1696 Chain Bridge Road • McLean, VA 22101

Have you always wanted an old-fashioned country wedding?
Evans Farm Inn is a charming 18th-century style building completely decorated in the old manner. You'll be carried back to the
times of the Fairfaxes, the Jeffersons and the Washingtons. You
may have your reception in any of the seven banquet rooms. The
lovely country garden is perfect for a garden wedding or outdoor
reception.

Capacity: 150 seated; 300 standing; unlimited in garden.
Catering: In-house. Entrees range from $12.95 to $31.95 per
               person.
Parking: On the premises.
Note: Wedding ceremonies are permitted indoors or out-
               doors.

Hidden Creek Country Club   703-437-5222

1711 Clubhouse Road • Reston, VA 20190

Hidden Creek Country Club has a variety of function rooms
suitable for receptions of any type. All rooms have a panoramic
view of a beautiful 18-hole championship golf course. The Fairway Room features a spacious outdoor deck, large dance floor and
an inviting fireplace. All food is created by an award-winning chef.
The clubhouse is conveniently located in the heart of Reston,
Virginia, minutes from Dulles Airport and thirty minutes from
Washington, DC.

Capacity: 200 seated; 300 standing; 350 with tent.
Catering: In-house. Entrees range from $50 to $65 per person.
Rental Fee: $550 for 4 hours.
Parking: On the premises.
Note: Wedding ceremonies are permitted.

The Longbarn   540-687-4137/540-687-3770

37129 Adams Green Lane • Middleburg, VA 20118

Enjoy a picturesque European getaway in this more than 100-
year-old renovated barn in historic Middleburg, Virginia. English
gardens nestled under a canopy of hardwood trees surround a
swimming pond and gazebo. The Longbarn features an elegant
Italian country style interior with spacious bedrooms, air conditioning, fireplaces, and a large library for the pleasure and comfort
of your guests. A delicious breakfast with warm breads and other
specialties from the old country is served. Horseback and bicycle
riding are nearby, as well as golf courses, antique shops, vineyards
and fine dining. The quaint and charming Corn Crib Chapel is
perfect for a small romantic wedding ceremony or renewal of

vows. Treat yourself to the generous hospitality of your gracious Italian hostess and serenity of this lovely estate.

Capacity: 50 seated; 60 standing; 150 in garden; 150 with tent.
Catering: You must supply your own caterer.
Rental Fee: $1,550 to $2,550, includes 1 or 2 nights use of three bedrooms (double occupancy) and full breakfast.
Parking: On the premises.
Restrictions: No smoking indoors. No pets.
Note: Wedding ceremonies are permitted.

Montclair Golf, Tennis & Swim Club   703-670-3915

16500 Edgewood Drive • Dumfries, VA 22026

This country club, located just two miles from I-95, specializes in custom weddings. It offers complete packages, including food, open bar, wedding cake of bride's choice, DJ, champagne toasts, hors d'oeuvres, fresh flowers, candle centerpieces – and, most of all, peace of mind.

Capacity: 250 seated; 300+ standing.
Catering: In-house. Prices range from $50 to $75 per person.
Rental Fee: $300 to $550.
Parking: On the premises.
Note: Wedding ceremonies are permitted.

Poplar Springs   540-788-4600

9245 Rogues Road • P.O. Box 275 • Casanova, VA 20139

Poplar Springs is a European-designed fieldstone manor house situated on 200 acres of rolling farmland, forests, streams and lakes. Located in Casanova, Virginia, four miles from Historic Old Town Warrenton, it is in the heart of Fauquier County. This gorgeous 10,000-square-foot mansion has arched entrance ways, enticing fieldstone walls and dramatic timber beams. The three-story high great hall is framed by balconies, stained glass windows and double French doors. There are large flagstone terraces surrounding the house, outside both the great hall and the library. The main floor is anchored by the impressive great hall, and is adjoined by the library, dining room and sun porch. These rooms, as well as the terraces and surrounding grounds, are available for weddings, receptions, breakfasts, lunches, dinners, business meetings and cultural events. With its unique location and incredible surroundings, Poplar Springs offers the best of all worlds . . . charm, elegance, convenience and privacy.

Capacity: 200 seated; 300 standing; 300 in gardens; 1,000+ with tent.
Catering: In-house. Prices begin at $60 and up.
Rental Fee: $1,500 to $3,000.

Parking: On the premises.
Note: Wedding ceremonies are permitted indoors or out-
               doors.

Raspberry Plain   703-777-1888

16500 Agape Lane • Leesburg, VA 20176

Set like a jewel in the midst of 50 rolling green acres in historic
Loudoun County sits the Georgian colonial estate known since
1731 as Raspberry Plain. The hall's sparkling chandeliers, detailed archway and dramatic staircase complement the elegance of
the mansion's rooms: the drawing room's cherry-paneled wainscot wall with built-in bookcases, the spacious Victorian parlor,
the dining room with built-in china cabinets and the light-filled
conservatory with French doors leading onto the grand terrace,
which has a panoramic view of the magnificent formal gardens
and mountains, rolling pastures and pond. Every room in the
mansion has character and charm. Period furnishings and paintings adorn the mansion. All the main rooms have glass-paneled
double-pocket doors, fireplaces and original detailed ceiling moldings.

Capacity: 240 seated; 300 standing; unlimited in gardens; 200
               with tent.
Catering: Approved caterers list.
Rental Fee: Starting at $1,500.
Parking: On the premises.
Restrictions: No smoking inside, but at designated outdoor areas.
               Dancing permitted indoor with a dance floor only.
Note: Wedding ceremonies are permitted.

River Farm   703-768-5700

7931 East Boulevard Drive • Alexandria, VA 22308

The elegant main house is set amid 27 acres of lawns, gardens,
meadows, and woods and commands a sweeping view of the
Potomac. Over the last 20 years, the Society has established
ornamental, educational and test gardens on portions of River
Farm, but most of the property remains much as Washington
himself would have known it when it was the northernmost tract of
his farmland surrounding Mount Vernon. The house, which is
registered as a "gentleman's home" by the Fairfax County Historical Society, includes a 45' x 20' ballroom with a tastefully appointed
powder room, a large parlor overlooking the river, a dining room
opening onto broad porches with garden and river views, and a
charming entrance hall featuring a hand-painted floral frieze. The
garden patio outside the ballroom may be tented for outdoor events.
The house and gardens at River Farm may be rented for weddings,
dinner parties, corporate meetings and other events. River Farm is
located on the banks of the Potomac, just four miles south of Old
Town Alexandria on the George Washington Parkway.

Capacity: 80 to 200, depending on areas selected for event.

Catering: Approved caterers list or your own caterer. Caterer must be approved by facility. The large, state-of-the-art country kitchen is available to caterers for preparation and heating of food.

Rental Fee: $2,500 to $6,400. Call for information. Comprehensive General Liability Insurance is required.

Parking: On the premises.

Restrictions: No amplified music. Portable toilets need to be rented for over 150 capacity.

Note: Wedding ceremonies are permitted.

Sheraton National Hotel   703-521-1900 ext. 6505

Columbia Pike at Washington Blvd. • Arlington, VA 22204

High above Washington's monumental skyline is the ultimate room with a view — The Sheraton National's Galaxy Ballroom — the perfect setting for weddings and receptions. Located just minutes from National Airport via complimentary shuttle, it is conveniently located for local and out-of-town guests. This beautiful hotel offers mesmerizing views of Washington, D.C., distinctive cuisine and a highly trained and experienced catering staff.

Capacity: 75 to 170 seated; 200 standing.

Catering: In-house. Entrees begin at $52.50 per person, inclusive.

Parking: On the premises.

Note: Wedding ceremonies are permitted. Special rates available for overnight guests.

Stoneleigh Tavern   703-589-1442

35279 Prestwick Court • Round Hill, VA 20175

Set in the foothills of the Blue Ridge, Stoneleigh Tavern offers a majestic site for outdoor weddings. Wedding parties and their guests will enjoy the spacious, private courtyard which is surrounded by a natural stone wall. The courtyard includes a paved tented area for dining and dancing, and an elevated grassy area provides a natural setting for ceremonies. A full-service restaurant is located on site in a pre-Civil War era mansion. Stoneleigh Tavern is located 14 miles west of Leesburg on the grounds of the Stoneleigh Golf & Country Club, and is easily accessible from the Dulles Greenway.

Capacity: 130 seated; 130 standing; 130 in garden with tent.

Catering: In-house. Entrees range from $16 to $28 per person. Cake cutting fee if provide own cake.

Parking: On the premises.

Restrictions: Ceremonies and receptions are held outside in the courtyard.

Note: Wedding ceremonies are permitted.

Valley View House and Gardens   703-321-9757

1562 Leeds Manor Road • Delaplane, VA 20144

Consider having your wedding reception in the beautiful formal gardens of this lovely historic estate. Located in the Virginia Hunt Country 12 miles west of Middleburg, the estate consists of a manor house with a formal English garden on 500 acres of meadowlands and mountains. This romantic setting of under-stated elegance overlooks an unspoiled valley that was the scene of numerous events in the War Between the States. Valley View is an ideal setting for garden weddings, receptions, engagement parties and rehearsal dinners.

Capacity: 50 indoor; 250 outdoor.
Catering: You must supply your own caterer.
Rental Fee: $350 to $500.
Parking: On the premises.
Note: Wedding ceremonies are permitted.

Charlie Brown's Lakeside   703-497-0333

2233 Tacketts Mill Drive • Lakeridge, VA 22192

From waterside dining to a warm fireplace setting, the staff will help you create your special event with optimum service and superb food.

Capacity: 250 seated; 250 standing.
Catering: In-house. Entrees begin at $15.95 per person.
Parking: On the premises.
Note: Wedding ceremonies are permitted.

Cherry Blossom Riverboat   703-684-0580

205 the Strand • Alexandria, VA 22314

Built in 1984, *The Cherry Blossom* is a re-creation of a 19th-century Victorian riverboat. Beautifully appointed with ornate iron railings and a plush interior of brass and mahogany, it is one of the most elegant yachts cruising the Potomac. Its two interior salons are heated and air-conditioned for year-round comfort. The third deck is open air, offering a spectacular view of Old Town and the Washington, D.C., skyline.

Capacity: 250 seated; 400 standing; 75 with a tent on the third dock.
Catering: Approved caterers list. Entrees range from $38 to $42 per person.
Parking: Parking lot nearby. Valet parking can be arranged.
Note: Wedding ceremonies permitted indoors or outdoors.

Seaport Inn   703-549-2341

6 King Street • Alexandria, VA 22314

This circa 1765, historic landmark previously owned by George Washington's military aide-de-camp provides a magnificent setting for wedding receptions. This location offers three elegant dining rooms. The John Fitzgerald Room, with its dark wood trim, rustic decor and complementing fireplace, is a charming asset to your party. The Potomac River Room offers a panoramic view of the Potomac River. The view, along with the room's rich brick color scheme accented with brass, creates a truly elegant atmosphere. The Williamsburg Room with its colonial decor is ideal for intimate parties.

Capacity: 130.
Catering: In-house. Entrees range from $16.95 to $20.95 per person. Cake cutting fee is $35.
Deposits: $100 to $175.
Parking: Parking garages nearby.
Note: Wedding ceremonies are permitted.

Torpedo Factory Art Center   703-838-4199

105 North Union Street • Alexandria, VA 22314

The Torpedo Factory Art Center, originally built in 1918 following World War I to manufacture torpedoes, has been transformed
into a modern art center housing 83 working artists' studios and
five cooperative galleries. The central hall, a two-story atrium, is
a unique and informal setting which can accommodate receptions
and ceremonies. It is 160 feet long and is topped with a balcony,
catwalks, large peripheral windows and a central skylight. The
hall is surrounded by glass walls displaying the artwork of the
individual studios. The hall lends itself to decoration in many
styles, and photographs of the site decorated for past events are
available to view. The Art Center is located on the Potomac River
waterfront in the heart of Old Town Alexandria, just minutes
south of National Airport and inside the Beltway.

Capacity: 400 seated; 1,200 standing.
Catering: You must supply your own caterer.
Rental Fee: $1,500 for the first floor, $1,700 for first floor and
balcony; $2,500 for entire building. Some additional
fees for staff, security and insurance required.
Parking: Parking is available across the street and there are
parking lots nearby.
Restrictions: No red wine, rice, birdseed, or glitter allowed in the
Art Center. No alcohol allowed behind the Art Center
on the dock/marina area.
Note: Wedding ceremonies are permitted.

Woodlawn Plantation   703-780-4000

9000 Richmond Highway • Alexandria, VA 22309

George Washington gave 2000 acres of Mount Vernon to his
granddaughter and his favorite nephew as a wedding gift. In
addition to the Georgian brick mansion, the site includes Frank
Lloyd Wright's Pope-Leighery House, natural trails and formal
gardens.

Capacity: 50 in house; 800 with a tent.
Catering: Approved caterers list. Alcohol must be purchased
through Woodlawn.
Rental Fee: $1,850 to $2,050 for 5 hours for up to 250 persons.
Parking: On the premises.
Note: Wedding ceremonies are permitted.

Surrounding States

TABLE OF CONTENTS

Crystal Ballroom   302-764-9240

728 Philadelphia Pike • Wilmington, DE 19809

The Crystal Ballroom is one of Delaware's most attractive reception facilities, with a spacious dance floor that can accommodate up to 75 people. In addition, the Ballroom has a hospitality suite that offers a private and secluded area where the bridal party may enjoy complimentary beverages and hor d'oeuvres. Whatever your special occasion requires, the Ballroom's experienced catering staff can meet your needs quickly and imaginatively.

Capacity: 300 seated; 500 standing.
Catering: In-house. Entrees range from $15.68 to $30 per person.
Rental Fee: $400 to $750.
Parking: On the premises.
Note: Wedding ceremonies are permitted.

The Terrace at Greenhill   302-575-1990

800 North DuPont Rd. • Wilmington, DE 19807

Located in Westover Hills, The Terrace at Greenhill features spectacular views of the golf course and the skyline of Wilmington. It has two banquet rooms, both decorated in pink and hunter green. The larger room holds 170, while the smaller room, with fireplace and chandeliers, holds 60. This picturesque location sets the stage for a memorable event.

Capacity: 170 seated; 250 standing.
Catering: In-house. Entrees range from $39.95 to $49.95 per person.
Parking: On the premises.
Note: Wedding ceremonies are permitted.

Highland House Bed & Breakfast   717-258-3744

108 Bucher Hill • Boiling Springs, PA 17007

Built around 1780, the historic Ironmaster's Mansion at Boiling Springs is set on a slope and overlooks graduated terraces that lead down to Children's Lake. The mansion, which now operates as a premier bed and breakfast known as the Highland House, is a lovely location for weddings and small, elegant receptions. The main parlor room has a 12-foot ceiling, fireplace, and a splendid view of the lake. Halfway up the circular staircase is a landing with a beautiful stained glass window. Wedding ceremonies may take place either inside Highland House or on its delightful front porch.

Capacity: 40 seated in house; 50 standing in house; 150 in garden; 150 with tent.
Catering: You must supply your own caterer.
Rental Fee: $1,000.
Parking: On the premises.
Restrictions: Music must stop at 9:00 p.m. and reception must end at 10:00 p.m.
Note: Wedding ceremonies are permitted.

The Mercersburg Inn   717-328-5231

405 South Main Street • Mercersburg, PA 17236

Located just 90 minutes west of Washington and Baltimore, and just a picnic basket away from Gettysburg and Antietam Battlefields, Harper's Ferry, and Berkeley Springs, Mercersburg is surrounded by the rolling green farmlands of the picturesque Cumberland Valley, which is just 10 minutes from the Whitetail Ski Resort and the renowned championship golf club, Greencastle Greens. Nestled at the foot of the Tuscarora range of the Blue Ridge Mountains, Mercersburg has played a role in every aspect of American history for over 250 years. The Mercersburg Inn is available for rental for any special occasion – from a romantic wedding to a grand reception; a small dinner party to an elegant rehearsal dinner. The Inn provides the perfect blend of casual charm and elegant amenities to make any event a memorable occasion.

Capacity: 125 seated, 150 standing in summer months; 80 seated, 100 standing in winter months.

Catering: In-house. Entrees begin at $19.50 and up. Cake cutting fee if you provide your own cake.

Rental Fee: $500 to $650. Additional hours are available at a cost of $75 to $100 per hour.

Parking: On the premises.

Restrictions: Requires rental of all guest rooms for two nights in peak season and one night in off-season.

Note: Wedding ceremonies are permitted.

Boydville The Inn at Martinsburg   304-263-1448

601 South Queen Street • Martinsburg, WV 25401

Boydville, a stone mansion which once hosted Henry Clay, Stonewall Jackson and other historical figures, is now an inn retreat for weddings, parties and business events. The inn and several outbuildings are on 10 parklike acres, with churches nearby. Guests enjoy the delightful touches of true craftsmanship: original mantel and doorway woodwork, fanlights and window glass. Matching chandeliers in the front parlors were brought from France prior to the Civil War, as was a hand-painted mural which graces a bedroom wall. Original rocking chairs on the long porch, complete with a view of stately old trees, give guests another treat. The ivy-covered, brick-walled courtyard and gardens add charm to this delightful inn.

Capacity: 75 seated; 150 standing; 500 in garden; 300 with tent.
Catering: Approved caterers list or you may provide your own caterer.
Rental Fee: $550 up to 40 people. Additional $10 per person over 40.
Parking: On the premises.
Note: Wedding ceremonies are permitted at an additional fee.

Hillbrook Inn 304-725-4223

Summit Point Road • Charles Town, WV 25414

Hillbrook is a wonderful European-style country house hotel atop a limestone ridge on seventeen acres of rolling countryside near Charles Town, West Virginia, an hour from Washington, D.C. Sweeping lawns, unspoiled woodlands, meandering streams, tranquil ponds and magnificent perennial gardens embrace the Tudor manor house. Hillbrook Inn is filled with intriguing antiques, richly colored oriental carpets, and dramatic art from around the world. Extraordinary seven-course dinners are served fireside in the intimate dining room. Cozy guest rooms promise a good night's sleep. Hillbrook is particularly suitable for smaller weddings. The wide bridge spanning Bullskin Run is a superb setting for a summer ceremony. Lush lawns provide ample space for seated events and ancient boxwoods lend a shady spot for a champagne toast. Crackling fires in the high vaulted living room provide an enticing winter setting. Hillbrook has been named one of the ten best inns in the United States and was featured gourmet getaway in both *Washingtonian* and *Baltimore Magazine*.

Capacity: 60 seated; 150 standing; 200 in garden; 100 with tent.
Catering: In-house. Entrees begin at $22 per person.
Rental Fee: Varies.
Parking: On the premises.
Note: Wedding ceremonies are permitted.

The Perfect Choice

☐ Is the site available for your date?

☐ Is it large enough for the number of guests invited?

☐ Does it have adequate parking? Handicapped parking?

☐ Is the facility handicap accessible?

☐ What type of deposit is required? When is it due?
When is the balance due? What is the refund policy in
case of cancellation?

☐ How soon must the site be reserved?

☐ Does the room have separate heating/air conditioning
controls? Can you adjust them, or will someone be
available to adjust them?

☐ Will the site provide catering? What is the cost?

☐ Are you required to use their caterers or can you provide
your own caterer?

☐ Are there enough tables and chairs available?
Who will set them up?

☐ Is there a dance floor? Or do you have to rent one?

☐ Will the site provide a microphone? public address system?

☐ Are there enough electrical outlets for the entertainment? Are they operable?

☐ Will the site provide bartenders or can you provide your own? What is the cost per bartender?

☐ What is the liquor policy? Can you supply the liquor?

☐ Does the site provide valet parking? Is there a fee?

☐ Who is responsible for clean-up?

☐ Will someone be on hand to let the vendors in? (e.g., caterer, florist, baker)

☐ What time must the facility be vacated? Is there a penalty if it hasn't been vacated in time?

☐ Will yours be the only event scheduled or will events be held before and after?

☐ Can the site be used for both the ceremony and reception?

☐ Are there rooms available for the bride, groom and attendants to change into their wedding attire or going-away clothes?

☐ Is there a piano, or other musical instruments, at the site? Is there a charge to use them? Can they be removed if not needed?

☐ Is the location accessible to all major interstates and what is the proximity to the ceremony location?

Washington, D.C.

Maryland

Virginia

Delaware

Pennsylvania

West Virginia

The Perfect Choice®

ALPHABETICAL INDEX

John Hopkins University Glass Pavilion 98, 144, 198

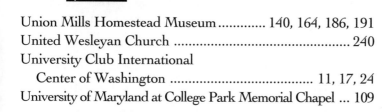

Betty Dunkins

is the owner of Tying The Knot Wedding Service and has been an independent wedding consultant for 10 years. Her achievements have led to her being one of only 30 Accredited Bridal Consultants™ certified by the Association of Bridal Consultants. Her articles have appeared in *Bride's Day* magazine, *The Washington Post*, *The Recorder*, *Free Press*, and *The Gazette*. A noted authority, Betty has been interviewed by a number of wedding publications, has appeared on national and local television programs, and is a requested speaker for wedding associations and seminars. She and her husband live in Silver Spring, Maryland.

Joy Gray

is the owner of "Joyous Occasions", a special events consulting service. Formerly a member of the Association of Bridal Consultants, she was an independent wedding consultant for 10 years. Ms. Gray has been featured in the *Washington Post*, various local newspapers, and on BET. She is one of three resource people for the northeast region identified in *Jumping The Broom* by Harriet Coles. She currently resides in Arlington, Virginia.

N O T E S

The Perfect Choice®

The Ultimate Party and Wedding Location Guide

NEW EDITION Completely Revised and Updated

Washington, DC · Maryland · Virginia

This wonderful resource contains descriptions of over 200 wedding, party and reception locations.

- Area listings include locations in Washington, DC, Maryland, and Virginia.

- Surrounding States listings include locations in Delaware, Pennsylvania, and West Virginia.

- Site capacities range from as few as 25 to 1,000 or more.

- A description of each facility is provided.

- Sites are listed geographically, categorically, and alphabetically.

- Costs, catering information, parking availability, restrictions and phone numbers are included.

This book is an invaluable resource for anyone planning a wedding or special event.

O R D E R   F O R M

☐ YES, please send _____ copies of *The Perfect Choice*® at $19.95 each.

$19.95 × _____copies = $_____

Maryland residents add 5% Sales Tax = $_____

Add $3.00 S/H 1st book, = $_____
$1.00 each additional book

Check/Money Order Enclosed   Total = $_____
☐ or bill my Visa/MasterCard/NOVUS

Name _____

Address _____

City _____ State____ Zip_____

Credit card Information: ☐ VISA   ☐ MasterCard   ☐ DISCOVER NOVUS

Acct # _____ Exp. Date____/___

Signature_____Daytime Phone_____

Orders shipped within 2-4 weeks. Volume discounts available. Price subject to change.

Mail to: Gray McPherson Publishing Co. • P.O. Box 6080 • Dept WP-98 • Silver Spring, MD 20916

Fax this form to 301-384-7365 or call toll-free 1-800-350-2028 to place your order.